MEMOIRS OF THE CONFEDERATE WAR FOR INDEPENDENCE

D1471030

SOUTHERN CLASSICS SERIES

HEROS VON BORCKE

Memoirs
of the
Confederate War
for Independence

J.S. SANDERS & COMPANY

NASHVILLE

1999

First published in book form by
W. Blackwood & Sons, Edinburgh, 1866.

J.S. Sanders & Company edition published 1999.

LIBRARY OF CONGRESS CATALOGING-IN-PUBLICATION DATA

Borcke, Heros von, 1835-1895.
    Memoirs of the Confederate War for Independence /
by Heros von Borcke. – 1st J.S. Sanders ed.
            p.   cm. – (Southern classics series)
    Originally published: Edinburgh: W. Blackwood and
    Sons, 1866.
    ISBN 1-879941-31-7 (pbk. : alk. paper)
    1. Borcke, Heros von, 1835-1895. 2. United States – History
    – Civil War, 1861-1865 – Personal narratives, Confederate.
    3. United States – History – Civil War, 1861-1865 –
    Campaigns. 4. Confederate States of America. Army of
    Northern Virginia – Biography. 5. Soldiers of fortune –
    Confederate States of America – Biography. 6. Prussians –
    Confederate States of America – Biography. 7. Stuart, Jeb,
    1833-1864.   I. Title.   II. Series: Southern classics series
    (Nashville, Tenn.)
    E605.B73 1999
    973.7'82—dc21   99-17640
                                                          CIP

J.S. Sanders & Company
Post Office Box 50331
Nashville, Tennessee 37205

Printed in the United States of America

1 3 5 7 9 10 8 6 4 2

CONTENTS

CHAPTER IX

CHAPTER X

CHAPTER XI

CHAPTER XII

CHAPTER XIII

CONTENTS

CHAPTER XX

CHAPTER XXI

CHAPTER XXII

CHAPTER XXIII

CHAPTER XXIV

PREFACE

THE kind interest with which the public received the Memoirs as they appeared in 'Blackwood's Magazine' induced me to think of republishing them. When they were on the point of republication, the news reached me that my King had called his people to arms against Austria and her allies. I offered at once my sword to my native country, and had the proud satisfaction of fighting, in the army of Prince Frederick Charles, in the great battle of Königsgräetz, and of taking part in the victorious advance through Bohemia, Moravia, and the Duchy of Austria. A new great war has turned the interest of the public to new matters,—many months have passed away since the termination of the great American struggle,—and many may have forgotten that the splendid Army of Virginia was ever in existence; but I do not hesitate to publish my account of battles lost and won, trusting that there are many still left who will read with some interest the simple narrative of a soldier who is proud to have shared the sufferings and the glory of the unfortunate people of the late Confederacy.

HEROS VON BORCKE,
OF THE 3D PRUSSIAN DRAGOONS.

PRUSSIA, *October* 25, 1866.

CHAPTER I

VOYAGE, AND ARRIVAL IN THE STATES

ON the 29th day of April 1862, I embarked at Queenstown on board the fine new steamer Hero, a vessel which had been built for running the blockade into the ports of the Confederate States of America, and was soon upon the bright waters of the Channel, bound for the theatre of war in the New World. Several most agreeable companions shared with me the accommodations of the steamer, and with smooth seas and pleasant skies we made a delightful voyage of twenty days to Nassau, unattended by any other than the ordinary incidents of the ocean transit. Off the Spanish coast we skirted a heavy gale; but as we proceeded from high to low latitudes the weather became every day more and more charming, until we ran upon an even keel into the blue phosphorescent seas that lave the coral reefs of the Bahamas. Here we met with an interruption which seemed likely for a time to terminate my American adventures, if I may be allowed the Hibernicism, before they had begun. As we were nearing the island of New Providence, within sight of the island of Abaco, a steamer appeared on our quarter bearing towards us under English colours. The captain of the Hero, apprehending no trouble from a vessel which he mistook for the regular English mail-packet, kept on his course, though it would have been an easy matter to escape the pursuit of the stranger had he supposed her intentions were unfriendly. As we came within range, a light puff of smoke from the stranger's side, and the whiz of a shell through the air a little astern of us, made it clear enough that the purpose was to board the Hero; and accordingly our engines were immediately stopped, and there speedily danced alongside a small boat, from which three Federal officers ascended to our decks. The steamer proved to be the U.S. gunboat Mercedita, and her commander, not doubting for a moment that he had made a valuable capture, had sent off a boat's crew to take possession of his prize. Whether the officers who represented him were annoyed at discovering that the Hero was not as yet liable to capture, or whether incivility was habitual to them, it is certain that they behaved towards us with a degree of rudeness such as I have rarely witnessed. After a detention of five hours, however, we were permitted to continue our course; the Federal officers rowed back to the Mercedita, and we had the satisfaction of seeing that vigilant cruiser soon become a mere speck on the evening horizon.

I was the more disturbed by this most unwelcome visitation, because it deprived me of many valuable papers and MSS., letters of introduction, and the like, which, fearing they might be seized and read by our visitors, I burned upon their approach.

A few hours later the island of Abaco appeared plainly in view, and with the rich sunset we ran past the islets of coral, each tufted with tropical vegetation, which mark the entrance of the harbour of Nassau. The cargo of the Hero consisting in great part of powder, we were compelled, in accordance with the regulations of the port, to lie-to five miles off shore; but the vessel having been signalled, a boat was soon sent to us, from which stepped aboard a young English midshipman who could not have been more than fourteen years of age, but who seemed fully conscious of the importance wherewith he was clothed by her Majesty's uniform. This beardless officer, having taken a look at the ship's papers and a glass of grog with becoming dignity, returned to Nassau, leaving us ill content to remain all night in the steamer, from which we saw the sparkling lights of the city and caught the delicious perfume wafted seaward from the island. At six o'clock next morning we found the ship surrounded by barges filled with negroes, who clamoured loudly for the privilege of taking us ashore. We had some difficulty in conducting negotiations from the ship's side amid the horrible din that assailed our ears, but we at last succeeded in securing a boat with six dusky oarsmen, two or three of them Africans by birth, who pulled us to the landing in two and a half hours. The sun poured down upon the sea with almost intolerable fervour, but there was refreshment in looking into the cool blue water, which was so marvellously clear that we could easily distinguish the pebbles strewn upon the bottom at the depth of forty feet.

New Providence is the smallest of the Bahamas, belonging to the West Indian Archipelago, and contains about 13,000 inhabitants, of whom two-thirds are free negroes, under the colonial government of Great Britain. Nassau, its only port, was a gay enough little place at the time of my visit, though, doubtless, with the discontinuance of its trade with the Southern ports, through the Federal blockade, it has subsided into its normal quietude; the busy population that was then seen upon its wharves has most probably disappeared, and the buzz of animated conversation is heard no more on summer evenings along the verandahs of the Royal Victoria Hotel. This large and comfortable establishment occupies the highest point of the island, and looks down upon the town, which stretches away to the right and left, terraced from the sea in regular gradations of ascent. What strikes one most forcibly in the external appearance of Nassau are the violent contrasts it presents to the eye. Nothing is subdued. The white Spanish houses absolutely glister in the overpowering glare of the sun. The roofs are as white as if they were covered with snow, being constructed, like the walls, of the coral formation of the island. The streets and roadways are dazzlingly white, and an impalpable dust rises in white clouds from every passing vehicle. The men are dressed in white from top to toe—white muslin turbans around their straw hats, and their feet encased in white canvass shoes, like those worn by the boating crews of the Thames rowing-clubs. Such are the lights of the picture. The shadows are supplied by the dark foliage of the orange and banana trees, the dense shade of the laurel thickets, and the intense black of the faces of the negroes. Black waiters at the hotel, black shopkeepers in the town, black soldiers on guard, black *belles* on the promenade—the effect was striking against the whiteness of the buildings and the thoroughfares. The "irrepressible negro" asserts himself immensely at Nassau. He seeks, and not altogether in vain, to unite the greatest possible amount of consequence with the least possible amount of work. But the negro women amused me most of any. In all their native hideousness of form and feature, they bedizen their persons with European costumes, of every fashion, fabric, and colour, and walk the streets with a solemn dignity that even a Spanish hidalgo might envy.

I had not supposed that I should be so much impressed with the variety and beauty of the vegetable and insect life of the tropics; but even the broiling sun did not deter me from making daily little excursions around the island, armed with a white cotton umbrella, and wearing, after the manner of the foreign residents, the broad-brimmed Panama hat with its encircling muslin turban. I must have afforded some amusement to the natives, and others familiar with tropical scenery, as I stalked abroad thus defended, stopping every now and then to examine some strange and beautiful flower, or to admire the innumerable humming-birds and gorgeous butterflies that fluttered above it, or to purchase, at the stalls of the incessantly chattering negresses, luscious fruits which they offered me, and of which I did not even know the name. The heat of the day was tempered, up to the hour of 10 A.M., by a mild sea-breeze, but the air then became perfectly calm and slumberous, and about mid-day the sun was burning with such power that one felt oppressed as by a leaden weight upon the chest. I rose generally at five in the morning and strolled down to the negro cottages, some of which were very pleasant little dwellings, and all were surrounded by small gardens filled with a profusion of fruit and flowers. Here I first saw the pine-apple growing in the open air, the orange-tree, heavy with its golden globes and fragrant blossoms, the palmetto, and the cocoa-palm with its ripening nuts, the cactus of every size, from the small creeper, winding along the rocks and walls, to the large tree-like specimen that lifts its head high above the ground, and flings out its scarlet bloom like a banner in the air. Near to the hotel was a magnificent cotton-tree of tremendous size, the trunk being fifteen feet in diameter, and the branches covering nearly an acre of ground, which was justly esteemed the pride of the island. Here, as indeed everywhere else, were hundreds of lizards darting over the rocky surface, of which the most interesting was the chameleon, so strangely and rapidly changing its colours.

Among the guests in the Royal Victoria Hotel at this time were many gentlemen of the Confederate States, who, as soon as my intentions were made known to them, manifested the liveliest interest in my behalf; and a number of captains of steamers destined for Southern parts, with like unanimity, offered me a free passage to the "sunny South." It was our custom to assemble on the highest verandah of the building to witness the setting of the sun, which seemed to dive into the blue ocean, reddening and gilding with transient splendours the distant reefs of coral. No lingering, pensive twilight, such as belongs to the latitude of England in the long days of summer, marks the approach of night in the Bahamas. For a brief period sky and wave are tinged with crimson, and then "at one stride came the dark." The decline of the sun was the signal for all the flowers, shrivelled and half-killed by the day's heat, to open their long-closed petals, lading the air with voluptuous perfumes, which were borne to us by every passing breeze. Myriads of fire-flies glittered around us; the temperature was delightful; the stars shone with a brilliancy unknown to me; and I enjoyed the strange, mysterious beauty of those tropical nights more deeply than I can express.

I had linked my fortunes upon the Atlantic with those of the Hero, but it very soon appeared that she would be obliged to unload a portion of her cargo at Nassau, and thus be detained at that port for several weeks. The news from America by every arrival became more and more exciting. It appeared inevitable that heavy battles would very soon be fought before Richmond, and I earnestly desired to take an active part in them. My position, besides, was embarrassing. My letters of introduction and recommendation had been destroyed. I did not know a human being in the foreign country whither I was going, nor did I even speak the English language. I was at a loss, therefore, to conjecture how I should carry out my objects. At this juncture, one of my travelling companions, Mr W., readily apprehending my difficulty, gave me the best proof of his friendship by offering to run the blockade with me in the next steamer to Charleston, and accompany me, without loss of time, to Richmond, where he would present me to the authorities. Accordingly we found ourselves, five days after our arrival at Nassau, early on the morning of the 22d May, on board the steamer

Kate, and soon Nassau, with its white houses and white streets, and dark laurel thickets, and harbour crowded with steamers, among which I regarded with peculiar interest the well-known Nashville, was far behind us.

The first two days of our voyage to Charleston passed without incident, but on the morning of the third we ran in sight of the coast of Florida, and the greatest excitement prevailed in our small community, the Federal blockading squadron being, as we knew, not far distant. Our furnaces were fed with the anthracite coal of America, which emits but little smoke to arrest the notice of blockaders; yet we proceeded very cautiously at half-speed, until we arrived within fifty miles by chart of Charleston harbour, when we stopped to await the protecting darkness of the coming night. At that time running the blockade was not thought so easy a matter as it afterwards proved to be, and the anxiety of many of our passengers began to be gravely and, in some cases, ludicrously exhibited. The vigilant captain did not leave the mast-head; and whoever could procure a marine glass swept the line of sea and sky for hours together, looking out in every direction with the greatest solicitude for the dreaded sails of the Federal cruisers. I had myself got my arms ready, and gathered together such of my effects as I supposed I should need most in future campaigning, so that in case we should be chased and obliged to abandon the vessel I might be able to carry them with me in the small boat. But no cruiser appeared, all remained quiet, and about dusk the sky began to be darkened with heavy clouds, which were greeted by us with extreme satisfaction. There was a large quantity of powder on board the Kate, and this powder for some reason had been stored immediately beneath the decks: we had therefore an uncomfortably reasonable prospect of being blown into eternity by the first shell from the Federal fleet that should be only too well directed. The captain had informed us of this circumstance before he consented to receive us as passengers, but we willingly accepted the risk, "trusting to luck" as to the steamer and ourselves. At nightfall our engines were again set in motion; the clouds had overspread the whole firmament; only here and there a star twinkled through the black canopy; and the sombre silence was unbroken save by the sound of the paddles striking against the water, and the whispers of our ship's company, who were all on deck peering most anxiously into the surrounding darkness.

It was about an hour past midnight when, reaching the entrance of the harbour of Charleston, we discovered a red light on our right hand, a green light on our left hand, and seven or eight others of various colours at a little distance all around us. These were the Federal blockaders awaiting their prey, and right between them had we to pass. The excitement now mounted to its highest point. The reflection of the red light upon the water ran out towards us like the coil of a fiery serpent, seeming to touch the wheelhouse, and to sport with the reflection of the green light from the opposite quarter, and we expected every moment to hear the booming of the blockaders' guns; but good fortune favoured us—the dreaded lights were soon glimmering in our wake—and from the frowning fortress of Sumter there thundered forth, as we interpreted it, a friendly salute that gladdened every heart. With no complimentary intentions, however, was this gun fired. We had been mistaken for an enemy, and had a narrow escape of being sent to the bottom by Confederate cannoneers, after having safely passed the perils of the blockade. But the good fortune of the Kate did not forsake her in this critical moment. Our engines were immediately stopped, a boat came off from the fort, explanations and congratulations were interchanged, after which we moved in perfect security up the harbour. Nature demanded rest after so much fatigue, sleeplessness, and excitement, and I was fast asleep when the Kate ran slowly into the dock.

The early morning found me awake and looking with great interest upon the strange land where I knew not what the immediate future had in store for me. Charleston lay before me in the full splendour of the newly-risen sun, and pre-sented—with its harbour full of vessels, its commodious villa-like private dwellings, its luxuriant gardens, its straight streets lined on either side by noble trees, its sparkling sea-front, against which the blue wave broke gently—a magnificent appearance. As I walked into the town I could not fail to remark the absence of that bustle one usually finds in a large city. This was explained by the fact that an attack by the Federal fleet was daily expected, in consequence of which many places of business were closed, and many families had gone into the interior. But if the traffic of the town was suspended, the streets gave evidence everywhere of great military activity. Companies of infantry in every variety of dress and armed with all sorts of weapons were marching about, and cavalrymen in the most picturesque costumes were galloping up and down on fine-looking horses. Accus-tomed as I was to European discipline and uniform, I must confess that on me the first impression of these Confederate soldiers was not favourable, and far was I from any idea how soon these same men would excite my highest admiration on the battle-field. But I had little opportunity for extended observation at Charleston. The train for Richmond left the station about noon, and I was of its passengers, wondering at the odd-shaped, long lumbering railway carriage or "car," rolling, rapidly and dangerously, with more than fifty other occupants, towards the scene of military operations in Vir-ginia. I need say nothing of the wretched railway system, or want of system, of America; the single line of rails, the loosely-built road-bed, the frightful trestle-work over deep gorges, the frail wooden bridges thrown across rushing rivers, and the headlong speed at which the train is often urged on its perilous way. With every month of the war the railroads of the Southern States became worse and worse, until a long journey by rail—say from Montgomery to Richmond—was as hazardous as picket duty on the Potomac. But our journey to Richmond was safely and comfortably accomplished. Whizzing through the rice and cotton fields, the oozy swamps and dark pine-woods of the two Carolinas, we came at last to forests of oak and hickory, alternating with peaceful-looking farms and fertile estates in the fair land of the "Old Dominion;" and, crossing the James river upon a bridge of giddy elevation, we entered within the walls of the Confederate capital.

Richmond, the seat of government of Virginia, and, for four years, of the Confederate States, had at that time about 70,000 inhabitants. Unrivalled in America for the picturesque beauty of its situation on the north bank of the James river, it impressed the stranger most agreeably by its general air of comfort, cleanliness, and thrift. Opposite the upper portion of the city the river flows between lofty hills over a rocky bed, which breaks it into innumerable cascades, murmuring in the stillness of the night a perpetual lullaby to the inhabitants. In the immediate centre of the town is a pretty little park, with several fine statues, some trumpery fountains, and a grove of umbrageous lindens, surrounding the Capitol, a large building of brick and stucco, erected in 1785, which looks noble in the distant view, but is mean and paltry upon near approach. The streets are long and straight, intersecting each other, with few exceptions, at right angles, and shaded throughout the larger part of the city's limits by native trees, the maple and tulip-poplar predominating. Pleasant dwellings, with porticoes and trellised verandahs, embowered in gardens, crowned the hills—dwellings that still remain to render more painful by contrast the ruin caused by the great conflagration which, three years later, laid the whole business quarter of the town in ashes. The external aspect of Richmond, at the period of my first acquaintance with it, was indeed very striking. It was the season of roses, and Nature, unconscious of war, had arrayed herself in all her pomp to welcome the ardent and prodigal Southern summer. Nothing could seem more peaceful than Franklin Street at evening, with groups of ladies and officers in the porticoes enjoying the cool hours that succeeded to the fierce heats of the day. Nothing could more plainly denote the condition of war than the appearance of the principal thoroughfares and the highways leading into the country. The din of active preparation struck continuously upon the ear in the roar of the forge, and the clatter of the army-waggon, and the heavy tramp of armed men. Large bodies of troops were marching and countermarching through the streets, orderlies and couriers were galloping about in every direction, and the notes of the fife and drum had hardly died away in the distance before the echoes were waked by the stormier music of a full military band. The vast army of M'Clellan hovered upon the northern and eastern skirts of the city, and over the line of the Chickahominy, which might be faintly traced from the tops of the highest buildings, his camp-fires could even be seen by night, and his balloons of observation, hanging like oranges in the sky, were clearly discernible in the afternoon. It was plain enough that an attack of the enemy in heavy force was expected at any moment. Under such exciting circumstances it was no less remarkable than gratifying to see how calmly and with what perfect confidence the people awaited the momentous events which were so near at hand.

In the uncertain state of affairs at Richmond, the prices of all articles in the shops augmented daily, but I converted my gold into Confederate money at a broker's at the liberal rate of two for one, and thought it a very clever financial operation. The difficulties I met with, however, in securing a position in the army were far greater than I had expected. The ashes of my letters of introduction were suspended in the restless waters of the Atlantic. The Government, I found, was disinclined to give commissions to foreigners, all the officers of the Confederate army at that time, except the general and staff officers, being elected by the men; and although Mr W., by repeated applications to the different authorities, had done all in his power to further my interests, he had met with no success whatever. At length, on the evening of his departure from the city, he informed me that he had seen the Secretary of War, General Randolph, who had manifested much interest in my situation, and would grant me an interview at one o'clock the next day. At the appointed hour I repaired to the War Department, and was received with great kindness by General Randolph, a most intelligent and amiable gentleman, who, after I had endeavoured to explain to him my plans and wishes in execrable English, gave me a letter to General J. E. B. Stuart, then commanding the cavalry of the army defending Richmond, and, at the same time, an order to procure a horse at the Government stables, with the advice to lose not a moment if I desired to see something of the impending battles. The Government stables were full of good horses, and I had no difficulty in finding an excellent chestnut mare, which afterwards carried me nobly on many a hard ride. At the earliest dawn of morning, on the 30th, an orderly reported to me with the mare in front of my hotel, and I jumped into the saddle, well equipped from head to foot, full of strength and buoyant in spirits, to ride forward to the field.

We trotted out of the city, and across the wooded plain through which runs the Brooke turnpike, passing the extensive fortifications and the long lines of the Confederate army.

With the liveliest interest I looked upon these masses of warrior-like men, in their ill-assorted costumes, who had come with alacrity from the Carolinas, from distant Mississippi and yet more distant Texas, from sunny Florida, from fertile Georgia, from Alabama, land of mountain and cane-brake, from the regions of Louisiana, to imperil their lives in the defence of their much-loved South, and for the expulsion of the invader from its borders. Brigade after brigade we saw awaiting the summons to the battle which was so soon to come. It was no easy matter to find General Stuart, who, as commanding officer of the outposts, was anywhere along the extended lines, and the sun was near its setting when we reached the camp of the 1st Virginia Cavalry. Here I presented myself for information to the officer in command, Colonel Fitzhugh Lee, who assured me that it would be next to impossible to find General Stuart that night, and kindly offered me the hospitality of his tent. As threatening thunder-clouds were driving up the western horizon, and I was much fatigued by my day's ride, I gladly accepted the invitation. The camp was a novelty to me in the art of castrametation. The horses were not picketed in regular lines as in European armies, but were scattered about anywhere in the neighbour-ing wood, some tethered to swinging limbs, some tied to small trees, others again left to browse at will upon the undergrowth. In a very short time I was perfectly at home in the Colonel's tent, where the officers of his regiment had assembled, and where the lively strains of the banjo alter-nated with patriotic songs and animated discourse. During the evening a supper was served which, under existing cir-cumstances, was really luxurious, and one of the chief dishes of which consisted of the eggs of the terrapin found in a creek near the camp by Colonel Lee's faithful negro servant, who was at once head-cook, valet, and steward. I am sure that no work of art from the kitchen of the Café Riche could have been more gratifying to my hungry appetite than these terrapin's eggs taken out of a Virginia swamp and cooked upon the instant in a cavalry encampment. Soon after supper we retired to rest, but little sleep came to my weary eyelids; for a terrible hurricane, accompanied by thunder and lightning, raged throughout the night, the peals of thunder shaking the earth, and the flashes of lightning almost blinding me with their incessant vivid glare. I was awake and fully dressed the next morning when, with the first glimpse of the sun breaking through the battered clouds, the trumpet sounded to saddle, and Colonel Lee informed me that he had just received marching orders. He added that he should start in fifteen minutes, and my best chance of meeting General Stuart was to ride with the regiment. It was marvellous to see how recently these unmilitary-looking troopers obeyed the orders of their colonel, and with what discipline and rapidity the breaking up of the camp was managed. I suffered the whole regiment, 800 strong, to pass me, that I might observe more narrowly its composition. The scrutiny called forth my admiration. The men were all Virginians, whose easy and graceful seat betrayed the constant habit of horseback exercise, and they were mounted mostly on blooded animals, some of which the most ambitious Guardsman or the most particular "swell" in London would have been glad to show off in Hyde Park. Looking back across three eventful years to that morning's march, I realise how little it was in my thought that my lot should be knit so closely with that of these brave fellows in fatigue and in fight, and that I should have to mourn the loss of, alas! so many who afterwards fell around me in battle. After a ride of three hours, passing directly through Richmond to the opposite side of the city, we reached our destination, and Colonel Lee pointed out to me a man, galloping rapidly along on an active, handsome horse. This was Stuart, the man whose arrival I awaited so anxiously, and who subsequently became one of the truest and best friends I have had in this world.

General Stuart was a stoutly-built man, rather above the middle height, of a most frank and winning expression, the lower part of his fine face covered with a thick brown beard, which flowed over his breast. His eye was quick and piercing, of a light blue in repose, but changing to a darker tinge under high excitement. His whole person seemed instinct with vitality, his movements were alert, his observation keen and rapid, and altogether he was to me the model of a dashing cavalry leader. Before the breaking out of hostilities between the North and South, he had served in the 1st United States Cavalry, of which regiment General Joseph E. Johnston was the Lieut.-Colonel, against the Indians of the Far West, and was severely wounded in an encounter with the Cheyennes on the Solomon's Fork of the Kansas river, in July 1857. In that wild life of the prairie, now chasing the buffalo, now pursuing the treacherous savage, Stuart had passed nearly all his waking hours in the saddle, and thus became one of the most fearless and dexterous horsemen in America, and he had acquired a love of adventure which made activity a necessity of his being. He delighted in the neighing of the charger and the clangour of the bugle, and he had something of Murat's weakness for the vanities of military parade. He betrayed this latter quality in his jaunty uniform, which consisted of a small grey jacket, trousers of the same stuff, and over them high military boots, a yellow silk sash, and a grey slouch hat, surmounted by a sweeping black ostrich plume. Thus attired, sitting gracefully on his fine horse, he did not fail to attract the notice and admiration of all who saw him ride along. This is not the place to expatiate on the military character of General Stuart. His deeds will form the most considerable portion of this narrative, and out of them an estimate of his soldierly qualities will naturally grow up in the reader's mind.

At the moment of our first meeting we could exchange but a few words. The battle was just about to commence, and my presentation to him was necessarily hurried and informal. After reading General Randolph's letter, he said he should be glad to have me at his side during the day's fight, and then presented me to a number of well-mounted young officers, members of his Staff, and to General Longstreet and his suite. At this instant the roar of the artillery gave the signal that the "ball had opened," and the whole cavalcade, the generals leading, proceeded in rapid gallop to the front.

CHAPTER II

31st May 1862

THIS sanguinary fight owes its strange name to seven solitary pine-trees, standing just at the place where death raged most terribly, and where the battle was decided in favour of our arms. About 30,000 men were engaged on our side, whilst the enemy brought about 45,000 into the field. The ground was very unfavourable for operations on either side—a broad wooded flat, intersected with morasses and open spaces; and the roads were bad and marshy beyond description, owing to the late violent rains.

I do not propose giving a general description of the engagement, but shall confine myself to my personal experiences and impressions, for having no military position as yet, and only taking part in it as a deeply interested spectator, I had no insight into the plan of the commanding general.

As General Stuart's cavalry could be of little service in the fight, he had been ordered to place it in reserve at the centre, and on the right and left flanks; but he himself was as usual in the thickest of the fray, giving assistance, counsel, and encouragement to the rest, and letting nothing escape his observation.

General Longstreet commanded the right wing, and had taken up position on a hill commanding an extended view.

The battle was beginning: along the whole line rang the sharp irregular fire of the skirmishers, only now and then broken by the thunder of one of the numerous batteries; soon, however, the cannonade became general, and the rattle of small arms preceding the boom of the heavy guns sounded like the sharp explosive crackle one hears before the deeper rumbling of the thunder.

It was at this moment that General Stuart sent me with the first order to Colonel Lee. To reach him I had to ride more to the front, and to cross a morass, where some horses belonging to the ambulances were standing. Just as I rode past I heard a loud whiz in the air, and saw one of the horses struck down, and at the same moment was almost deafened by an explosion, which covered me with mud and water. This was the first shell that had burst so close to me, and a strange feeling came over me at the thought of having been so near death. It was not fear, but a vivid realisation of the pitiless power of destruction which is let loose in war. I discharged my commission without farther adventure, and returned to the Generals.

The battle had meanwhile been turning in our favour; our troops were slowly pressing back the whole Federal line; only in the centre of our right wing a North Carolina brigade had begun to give way a little before the superior strength of the enemy. Instantly General Stuart was at the spot, encouraging the troops to hold the position until our reinforcements could arrive. I followed him into the hail of bullets, of whizzing grape and bursting bombs, one of which rolled between my horse's legs.

Our men had now expended almost all their ammunition,

and were falling back, when General Stuart, here with threats, there with eloquent entreaties, rallied them, and brought them forward again into the battle to check the enemy as they pressed hard upon us.

A Virginia brigade soon came up as reinforcement. With banners flying, and loud war-cries, they threw themselves unhesitatingly on the foe, driving them before them, and taking their earthworks, which bristled with cannon.

The setting sun lighted up with crimson splendour a broad and bloody battle-field, strewn with the dead and wounded of the enemy, and as many brave Confederate soldiers. Numerous prisoners were being brought up from all sides, whom every man and officer not absolutely required to fill the thinning ranks was employed to convey away. Thus I was commissioned by the General to conduct eight soldiers, and a Lieutenant-Colonel who had been wounded in the neck, to join the other prisoners already on their way, by hundreds, to Richmond. These men had been captured by General Stuart and myself in the *mêlée* that succeeded the impetuous onset of the Virginians. Terrible was it to see on every side the wounded returning from the battle: here a man with his head bleeding, there another with shattered arm or leg, reddening the path with his blood; then the more severely wounded in the ambulances, groaning and wailing in a manner that made my heart shrink. I was then little accustomed to scenes like this.

In this battle, though it could not be called a general one, and though its consequences were of no great importance, the victory, though costly, was complete. Thousands of our brave soldiers were killed or wounded, and amongst them several generals, one being Johnston the General-in-chief who, just at the close of the fight, was wounded in the shoulder by a ball.

General Stuart remained on the battle-field till late at night, and we galloped off together after the last cannon-shots had died away. The ride to headquarters was a dreadful one: hundreds of conveyances, some taking the wounded to Richmond, some coming out from the city with provisions for the troops, were crossing each other in the almost impassable turnpike, and the groans and cries of the wounded were mingled with the curses and shouts of drivers, whose vehicles obstructed the way with broken wheels or exhausted horses.

Many of the inhabitants of Richmond had sent their carriages, and the hotels their omnibuses, to bring off the wounded: the greater number of these slightly-built equipages lay broken in the road, and would never again be available for any purpose whatever.

General Stuart's headquarters were at a farmhouse named Montebello, which was situated on a hill near Richmond, and from which we had a splendid view of the town, the river, and the environs. To this house we galloped for a short night's rest. Here General Stuart thanked me with only too much warmth for the small services I had rendered during the battle, and said that he would have much pleasure in placing me on his Staff as a volunteer aide-de-camp.

Sunday, 1st June

We returned very early the next morning to the battle-field, where there seemed to be a renewal of the fight; faint musketry fire was audible, and the thunder of cannon roared through the morning air.

Not without risk did we reach the field, so rotten was the way and so full of holes, often from four to five feet in depth, and filled with water, so that one could not ride a hundred yards without one's horse slipping and falling. Hundreds of waggons were stuck fast in the road, many of them upset, with the horses lying drowned in front of them, and several still filled with wounded men groaning piteously.

After a considerable time we reached the scene of the previous day's victory. Never shall I forget the impression made upon me by this first sight of death and devastation to which I afterwards became so well accustomed.

The most horrible spectacle was that presented near the bastions and earthworks which the day before had been stormed by our men. Friend and foe were lying here indiscriminately side by side, mown down in multitudes by musketry and by the guns which we had afterwards taken. The enemy's artillery had here lost all their horses, which lay by dozens, piled one upon another, and all around the ground was strewn with weapons, haversacks, cartridge-boxes, ammunition, &c. These articles, abandoned by the enemy, were used by us most profitably for the better equipment of our own troops.

A South Carolina brigade had taken up its position in the intrenchments near us, and the men lay behind the breastwork full of confidence and good-humour, quite unmindful of the heaps of slain, and breakfasting on the enemy's provisions, which had been left behind in great quantities.

General Stuart had scarcely ridden with us into the intrenchments, when a cannon-ball hissed over our heads and tore up the earth about fifty yards behind us. Other shots followed in rapid succession, and each time the balls came nearer and nearer to our little group. General Stuart, paying no attention to the cannonade, remained until he had completed his observations of this portion of the field, and then desired me to ride with him to our extreme right. We had to cross an open field, and as soon as we had reached it the firing began anew. Nearer and nearer to us fell the shells, exploding with a deafening report and covering us with earth. We were evidently a mark for the fire of a whole battery, and even

General Stuart, who till now had tranquilly pursued his way, turned round in surprise when the fragments of an exploded grenade flew hissing between us, and said, "Lieutenant, they are firing at us here; let us ride a little faster!"

We had still about three hundred paces to go before a friendly grove would hide us from the enemy, but this short distance seemed to me like so many miles, and was one of the hottest rides I ever had in my life. The Federals divined our intention only two well, and overwhelmed us with the fire of a whole battery, so that it is almost a miracle that the General and I escaped uninjured.

As we afterwards learned, the Yankees had stationed a scout at the top of a lofty pine-tree, who, when he saw the General, gave the artillery the first direction: he paid for it with his life, for one of our sharp-shooters detected him, and by a well-directed bullet brought him down.

The battle was not renewed; the firing grew fainter and fainter, until towards one o'clock it ceased almost entirely. About this time we returned to the spot where General Longstreet had taken his position the day before, and where several of our generals were assembled, to whom I was presented by General Stuart. President Davis soon came up, congratulating the Generals, and expressing his great satisfaction at the issue of the day.

I had now the opportunity of closely observing General Longstreet for the first time. He was a stout man, of middle height, and most agreeable countenance; his long brown beard gave something leonine to his appearance; an engaging simplicity was his prevailing characteristic, manifested not less in his manners than in his dress. It consisted, like that of most of the leading generals of the Confederate army, of a small black felt hat, a tunic-like grey coat, much faded, on the collar and sleeves of which the devices indicating his rank were scarcely distinguishable, a pair of grey trousers, and military boots with Mexican spurs; a small sword was his only weapon. His steady courage—displayed rather by perfect composure under fire, and serene indifference to the extremest peril, than, like that of Stuart, in fiery charges and daring enterprise—his constant energy in the campaign and obstinacy in the fight, and his strict obedience to orders, made him one of the most useful, as he was always among the most conspicuous, officers in the Confederate service. By these he gained the full confidence of the army and its commanding general, Robert E. Lee, who used to call him his war-horse. Longstreet's soldiers were perfectly devoted to him, and I have frequently heard friendly contentions between officers and men of his corps, and those of Stonewall Jackson's, as to which of the two was the most meritorious and valuable officer.

President Jefferson Davis is a tall thin man, with sharply-defined features, an air of easy command, and frank, unaffected, gentlemanlike manners. I had the honour of being presented to him, and was struck with the simple friendly tone in which he conversed with me. He examined with great interest an excellent Damascus blade, an old and tried friend of mine, and said he was very glad to know that he had so good a sword and so strong an arm to wield it in his army.

The next day did not pass without excitement. A renewed attack from the enemy was expected, and our troops were kept for the greater part of the day under arms. From time to time a single report of cannon was heard, generally fired from our side at the air-balloon which the Yankees had sent up for reconnoitring. General Stuart, who commanded our outposts, was constantly in motion, and we were seldom out of the saddle. Our rendezvous and momentary halting-place was near a small farmhouse standing peacefully among hickory and oak trees. Turned into an hospital, the ghastly features and mutilated limbs of the wounded men stretched upon their beds of pain within the building, formed a dreadful contrast to the cheerful exterior.

On the 5th everything was quiet again. On the 6th General Stuart changed his headquarters, and we removed with bag and baggage to a farmhouse about four miles distant, inhabited only by an old man named Waddle. This place, standing at some distance from the highroad, was surrounded by copses and thickets, and afforded us a capital opportunity of recovering from our fatigues. We had to provide our own food, which, in consequence of the prevailing scarcity, was scanty and bad; a little bacon and maize-bread composed our breakfast, dinner, and supper, and we thought it an extraordinary luxury when we could gather wild strawberries enough in the wood to make a dish to add to our repast.

General Stuart, though he sometimes employed me to carry reports to the different generals, usually took me with him on his short reconnoitring rides, in order to make me acquainted with the surrounding country, the position of the army, and the commanders of the divisions and brigades.

Towards dusk on the 8th we set out on one of these expeditions, escorted by half-a-dozen of our couriers, and I soon perceived that our ride was to be extended to a greater distance than usual. It was late in the evening when we reached the last of our outposts, and I was not a little surprised when the General here dismissed his escort, and desired me alone to accompany him farther. Silently we rode through the lonely wood, whilst the darkness grew deeper and deeper around us, and the stillness of the forest was only broken by the strange tones of the tree-frog and the melancholy cry of the whip-poor-will.

We soon found ourselves within the enemy's lines; at any moment we might stumble upon one of their patrols; and General Stuart smiled significantly when he saw me examining the loads of my revolver, and observed that we would not employ firearms except in the last resort, and that in case of an encounter we must make use of our sabres. This ride was strangely exciting to me; now that I have become so accustomed to such expeditions, I could go through it with the most perfect composure, but then I was feverishly agitated, and every rustling bough, every bird flying past, increased the strain.

After a ride of about five miles we reached a small house, and on General Stuart's knocking at the door in a peculiar manner it was opened to us. The house was inhabited by an Irishman and his family; and here General Stuart had appointed a rendezvous with one of the spies, in order to obtain an authentic report of the enemy's position. This man had not arrived, so we fastened our horses to the fence and went into the house. Hour after hour went by, but still no one came, and it was past midnight when General Stuart became convinced that some unlooked-for hindrance must be detaining him. No persuasion nor promises of money, not even my offer to accompany him, could induce the old Irishman or his son, a lad of seventeen, to walk over to the spy's abode, which was about two miles distant, and near one of the enemy's camps. So the General and I were obliged ourselves to undertake this dangerous expedition, and with the first glimmer of daylight we mounted our horses and cautiously set off. The peculiar repugnance of the Yankees to patrolling at night and the heavy rain favouring our enterprise, we arrived without misadventure at the man's dwelling just as the reveillé was sounding in the camp only 400 paces distant. The spy being very ill in bed, General Stuart had to dismount and go to his bedside; and when the General, extremely well satisfied with the information he had obtained, swung himself into the saddle, and we galloped back, it was with a great sense of relief we approached our lines, where we were greeted with delight by our men, who had begun to entertain considerable anxiety on our account.

Such rides and expeditions were habitual with this bold General, and we often escaped as by a miracle from the dangers which surrounded us. It was only by this exposure of himself that he could insure the extraordinary success which invariably crowned his expeditions and military operations.

The object of this excursion soon appeared. Our cavalry force received orders to provide themselves with rations for three days, and on the 12th we commenced that ride round the army of General M'Clellan which attracted so much attention even in Europe.

June 12, 1862

It was two o'clock in the morning, and we were all fast asleep, when General Stuart's clear voice awoke us with the words, "Gentlemen, in ten minutes every man must be in his saddle!"

In half the time all the members of the Staff were dressed, and the horses had been fed; and the ten minutes were scarcely up when we galloped off to overtake the main body, which we reached by about five o'clock. Our command was composed of parts of the different regiments of the brigade, and consisted of about 2500 cavalry, with two pieces of horse-artillery. None of us knew where we were going; General Stuart only communicated the object of the expedition to the colonels commanding; nevertheless every one followed our honoured leader with perfect confidence. We marched the whole day long without halting, and towards evening bivouacked near the little town of Taylorsville in Hanover County, where we were already within the enemy's lines. At daybreak we again mounted our horses, and our vanguard was soon reported to have met with a party of the enemy's dragoons, who on their approach had hurried off in hasty flight. Without waiting to pursue them, we continued our march, greeted everywhere with enthusiasm by the inhabitants, especially by the ladies, who for a long time had seen none other than Federal troops. I was in company with Stuart the whole time, constantly near the vanguard, and could note that every operation was initiated and superintended by the General himself. A few miles from Hanover Court-house we surprised a picket of the enemy's cavalry, every man of which fell into our hands from the suddenness of our attack. Whilst we were occupied with sending the prisoners to the rear, our advance-guard came back at a run, hotly pursued by a large body of the enemy's dragoons. Our leading squadron spurred immediately forward to meet the attack, and, having obtained General Stuart's permission, I joined them as with loud war-cries they hurled themselves against the blue masses of the enemy. The Yankees were not able to withstand the impetuous onset of the Virginia horsemen, and, after a *mêlée* of a very few minutes, there commenced a most exciting chase, which was continued for nearly three miles. Friend and foe were soon enveloped in blinding clouds of dust, through which pistol and carbine shots were seen darting to and fro like flashes of lightning. The larger number of the enemy escaped, thanks to their fresher animals, but we took many of them prisoners, and their dead and wounded men and horses encumbered the road as we pushed along. Half an hour later our advance-guard again came in collision with the enemy, who had rallied, and, with strong reinforcements, were awaiting us. Two squadrons of the 9th Virginia Cavalry were immediately sent forward to the attack, and I received orders from General Stuart to hasten with our main column to the scene of action. I rode at once to bring on the main column; but though I used the utmost speed to get back in time to take part in the charge, when I arrived at the scene of the sharp conflict the work had already been done. The enemy's lines were broken and in full flight, leaving many of their dead and wounded, and a large number of prisoners, among whom were several officers, in our hands. We had to lament the loss of the gallant Captain Latané, who, while boldly leading his men, fell pierced by five bullets. In a few seconds the 1st Virginia Cavalry had arrived, and we instantly dashed forward in pursuit.

The enemy made one more attempt to rally, but their lines were broken by our furious attack; they fled in confusion, and we chased them in wild pursuit across an open field, through their camp, and far into the woods. When we had returned to their camp the work of destruction began. Every one tried to rescue for himself as much as possible of the articles of luxury with which the Yankees had overloaded themselves, but few succeeded in the end; for, in accordance with the well-laid plan of our leader, flames flashed up, now in one place, now in another, and in a few minutes the whole camp was enveloped in one blaze, hundreds of tents burning together presenting a wonderfully beautiful spectacle. Many horses and mules, and two captured standards, were all that we carried off with us. After half an hour's halt our destroying cavalry again set forth; our track of blood and fire pointing out to the enemy the path which we had taken.

We now found ourselves in the heart of the enemy's position, and their encampment lay around us on all sides. At one point of our journey, the house occupied by the Federal Commander-in-Chief, General M'Clellan, as his headquarters, surrounded by the white tents of a very large camp, was plainly visible at the distance of about two and a half miles. Our situation would have been one of extraordinary peril, had not the boldness and rapidity of our movements disabled and paralysed our adversaries.

On either side of the road we constantly seized upon unsuspecting Federal soldiers, who had no idea of the close proximity of the dreaded Stuart until collared by his horsemen. A considerable number of waggons laden with provisions and goods fell into our hands, among them one containing the personal stores of General M'Clellan, with his cigars, wines, and other dainties. But we could not be burdened with booty, so the entire train was committed to the flames, the champagne popped bootlessly, and the cabanas wasted their fragrance on the air. Three transport-ships which lay in the river Pamunkey near at hand, laden with wheat, corn, and provisions from all quarters, were seized by us, together with the guard and the agents stationed there, and ere long the flames mounting towards heaven proclaimed how complete was our work of destruction. A brigade of the enemy's cavalry here sought to intercept our way and to detain us till the troops, which were marching upon us from all sides, could arrive; but it was broken by our first attack, and crossed our path no more.

Thus towards evening we reached the railroad which was so useful to the enemy in giving them communication with the north; and just as the demolition of the road-bed was about to begin, the train was seen coming up. Without delay General Stuart posted a portion of his men on either side of the embankment, with orders to fire if the train refused to stop at the station. The train moved slowly nearer and nearer, puffing off the steam, and we could soon perceive that it was laden with soldiers, most of them being in open carriages. As the command to stop was disregarded, but on the contrary the movement of the train was accelerated, firing began along our whole line. The engine-driver was shot down by Captain Farley, to whom I had lent my blunderbuss; but before the deadly bullet reached him he had put the train in somewhat quicker motion, so that we could not make ourselves masters of it.

A battle of the strangest description now arose. Some of the soldiers in the train returned our fire, others sprang out to save themselves by flight, or lay down flat at the bottom of the carriages. The train, though its motion had been quickened, was not going at so rapid a pace that we could not keep up with it by galloping hard. Meantime, having had my hat almost knocked off my head by one of the enemy's bullets, I became so wildly excited that, without heeding our own fire, I spurred my horse over the embankment, and very soon had discharged all the five charges of my revolver at the foe. We heard later that few of the occupants of the train had escaped unhurt; the greater part were either killed or severely wounded. I reproached myself afterwards with having so given the reins to my passion; but after all I only acted in obedience to orders and the requirements of war. After having done as much injury as we could to the railroad, we proceeded on our march, whilst the last beams of the sun lighted up the scene of destruction.

It had been a hard ride and a hard day's work, and my parched tongue was cleaving to the roof of my mouth, when one of our men galloped up to me, and held out a bottle of champagne, saying, "Captain, you did pretty hot work to-day. I got this bottle of champagne for you out of M'Clellan's waggon. It will do you good." Never in my life have I enjoyed a bottle of wine so much. Late in the evening a baggage-train and two sutler's waggons fell into our hands, and we took possession of a large quantity of luxuries, such as pickles, oysters, preserved fruits, oranges, lemons, and cigars.

About ten o'clock we had an hour's rest to feed our horses, and then rode on all the night through towards the Chickahominy River, which we reached at five o'clock in the morning. From the reports we had received we expected to find little difficulty in fording the stream, but who can describe our astonishment at finding it so swollen by the rain which had fallen in the mountains during the past twenty-four hours that the water was more than fifteen feet deep! At the same time our rear-guard announced that a whole division of the enemy was on our track. Every one felt the weight of the danger that threatened us, every one looked with anxiety towards our leader, who, with the greatest possible calmness and coolness, gave his orders and made his arrangements. Two regiments and two pieces of horse-artillery were ordered, in case of an attack, to cover our retreat; whilst all the other available men were dismounted, some of them being employed to build bridges, the others to swim the river with the horses. A bridge for foot-passengers was hastily constructed across the stream, which was about ninety feet in breadth, and the saddles, &c., were carried over it. All the swimmers took the unsaddled horses through the river, some riding them, others swimming by their side, with one hand holding the mane and the other directing the horse. This last expedient I thought the best, and in this manner I took sixty-five horses myself through the angry torrent. After about four hours' work a second bridge for the artillery was completed, and more than half the horses had reached the other side of the river; also the prisoners, about five hundred in number, and hundreds of captured horses and mules. The first cannon was drawn by the soldiers across the bridge, which, standing the test well, the second soon followed, and then the reserve regiments. Towards noon all were in safety on the other bank, General Stuart being the last man to cross the bridge, which we then destroyed. Hitherto I had had no sensation of fatigue, but after this hard work in the water I felt it severely in all my limbs, and we had still to march the remainder of the day and all the night before we could rest in security. Both horses and men performed wonders during this expedition. We were in the saddle almost uninterruptedly for two days and two nights, fighting for a considerable part of the time, and for ten miles working our way through the swamps of the Chickahominy, which had been hitherto considered impassable.

On the morning of the 15th we arrived safely within our lines, and bivouacked about six miles from Richmond. As soon as I had attended to my horse, who had carried me nobly through the severe fatigue, I fell fast asleep, and so continued during the whole day and night. We had been wonderfully successful in our expedition, having made a wide circuit through the enemy's immense army, and thoroughly acquainted ourselves with its position, which had been our chief object. At the same time, we had destroyed the enemy's communication, burned property to the amount of millions, captured hundreds of prisoners, horses, and mules, and put the whole Federal army in fear and consternation. We were warmly greeted everywhere on our return, and every sort of honour was paid to General Stuart's name. This ovation was extended to officers and men, and wherever any one who had taken part in this famous expedition was seen, he was besieged with questions, gazed at as a hero, and entreated to relate his own adventures and the story of the ride.

The Richmond press teemed with praises of General Stuart and his followers, and even the journals of New York did not fail to render homage to the conception and execution of this bold enterprise.

I had been very fortunate during the expedition in rendering services of various kinds to General Stuart, which obtained his cordial recognition in the Official Report, and in this manner secured for me at once a position in the Confederate army.*

A quiet time now followed at headquarters. Both horses and men needed rest after exertions so long continued and fatiguing. The weather was glorious, and all nature had put on the full beauty of spring. Around the house which we inhabited white and red roses bloomed in sweet profusion, covering and climbing over the walls, and the wild honeysuckle added its fragrance to that of hundreds of magnolias blossoming in the neighbouring swamp. In the fierce heats of June no refreshment could be more delicious than that afforded by the shade and perfume that dwelt along the cool densely-wooded morass, as, in our rides about the camp, we frequently crossed the small tributary rivulets, and let our horses drink of the dark, clear water flowing over the pebbly bottom.

My relations with General Stuart had now become of a most friendly and intimate character. The greater part of my time was spent in his company. In this manner I became acquainted with his amiable and accomplished young wife, and his two bright-eyed little children, Flora and Jemmy, five and three years of age respectively, whose tender affections I was not long in securing. Mrs Stuart, during a considerable period of the war, lived from time to time at her husband's headquarters, as they might be established at a point more or less safe and accessible; and I do not remember that I have ever seen a more interesting family circle than they presented, when, after a long ride or hazardous reconnaissance, General

---

*I trust I may be pardoned for introducing here that passage in the Report which refers to the part I took in the expedition. General Stuart says:—

"Amongst those who rendered efficient services in this expedition I cannot forget to mention Heros Von Borcke, formerly of the Prussian Brandenburg Dragoons, who distinguished himself by his gallantry, and won the admiration

Stuart would seem to forget, for a brief interval, the dangers and duties of his exciting life in the enjoyment of his domestic happiness. The bold rider and dashing swordsman playing with his children, or listening to his wife as she sang him a ballad, was a picture the soft lights of which were in effective and pleasing contrast with the Rembrandt shadows of the dark wood and the rude warriors that lay there. General Stuart had married a daughter to Colonel Philip St George Cooke, of the U.S. Dragoons, a Virginian by birth, and West-Pointer by military education, who had remained in the Federal service, and was now making war upon his native State as a brigadier-general of President Lincoln's appointment. On several occasions, during the campaigns in Virginia, General Stuart came very near making a prisoner of his father-in-law; and I believe it would have given him greater satisfaction to send General Cooke under escort to Richmond than to capture the mighty M'Clellan himself.

The military family of General Stuart consisted of fourteen or fifteen high-spirited young fellows, boon companions in the bivouac, and excellent soldiers in the fight, of whom, alas! seven were afterwards killed in battle, three received honourable and dangerous wounds, the effects of which will follow them through life, and two were carried off by the enemy to languish in loathsome Northern prisons. It was, indeed, a hazardous service upon which we had entered; but little disturbed were we by a thought of the peril, or if such a thought ever intruded upon us, it was only to unite together in closer friendship the sharers of a common destiny.

On the morning of the 20th June, General Stuart, with a significant smile, gave me his official report of the Pamunkey expedition to carry to the Secretary of War, General Ran-

---

of all who witnessed his bravery and his military conduct during the expedition. He highly deserves promotion."

dolph. I soon perceived the meaning of this smile when the commission of captain in the Confederate Cavalry was delivered to me by the Secretary, with the most flattering expressions respecting my conduct. Full of gratitude, I returned to headquarters with a sense of hearty satisfaction such as I had not known for a long time. We were not, however, to rest many days at headquarters on the laurels of the Pamunkey expedition. During the night of the 25th there came again to us marching orders: before midnight all were in readiness; but as there was no moon, the darkness detained us till the morning, when the rising sun found us in the saddle, fresh and eager for the performance of whatever duties the day might impose. Events of the greatest military significance were on the wing—events on which the eyes of the world were to be fixed, and by which the genius of more than one commander was to be determined—events whose place in history will for ever remain undisturbed by the unhappy issue of the American War.

CHAPTER III

THE real importance of the Pamunkey expedition, in giving General Lee a perfect insight into the position of the army of M'Clellan, now manifested itself in the most brilliant light. As the Federal Commander-in-Chief had fortified himself most strongly on his right wing, which rested on the small village of Mechanicsville, five miles north-east of Richmond, General Jackson had been ordered with his army from the valley of the Shenandoah, numbering between 25,000 and 30,000 men, to fall upon the enemy's right flank, and, turning it, to give Lee the opportunity for a general attack. General Thomas Jonathan Jackson, known alike to friends and foes as "Stonewall," from the steadiness and rock-like firmness of front which his command always presented to the enemy, had come up by rapid marches, without the enemy's knowledge, to execute this order. General Stuart's cavalry command and one division of infantry were sent to strengthen him, and this was the beginning of the sanguinary and to us successful seven days' fighting before Richmond.

During the night of the 26th we arrived at the camps of

Jackson's famous soldiers, which had been pitched near Ashland, a station on the Richmond and Fredericksburg Railroad, and were greeted by them with loud cheers. After a short period of repose we were again in the saddle. General Stuart had received directions from General Jackson to cover his left flank, so we marched with great caution, sending out numerous patrols and reconnoitring detachments. Our march was directed towards Mechanicsville, where the enemy's right wing rested, as I have said, on strong fortifications. With the exception of encounters with small patrols, we saw little of the enemy until five o'clock in the afternoon, when Jackson's vanguard attacked them, and was soon engaged in a sharp skirmish. At the same time the distant thunder of cannon was sounding over from Mechanicsville, where Longstreet had attacked the enemy in their strong position. Jackson at once brought up his troops with his usual celerity of movement, and towards six o'clock the battle was at its height.

Our cavalry was in reserve, and as we had reason to fear an attack on the left flank, General Stuart despatched me with a small body of men on a reconnoitring expedition, which was so far successful that, after about half an hour's ride, we came upon a strong detachment of the enemy's cavalry, who instantly set to work to chase us. We returned at a hard gallop, the enemy behind us in hot pursuit. General Stuart, perceiving this, placed two pieces of horse-artillery in the road, which, as soon as we had passed them, greeted the enemy with grape-shot. This created extreme confusion among our pursuers; they left their dead and wounded behind them, and took to immediate flight, followed by one of our regiments. Meanwhile the battle was going in our favour; the enemy were driven from one position to another, and by ten o'clock at night were retreating. We encamped for the remainder of the night upon the battle-field, and rose with the earliest beams of the sun.

27th June 1862

In the immediate neighbourhood of Coal Harbour, a small collection of houses some fifteen miles distant from Richmond and ten or twelve miles east of Mechanicsville, the enemy, to the number of 60,000 men, had taken a new position, strengthened by natural as well as artificial fortifications. Jackson had with him in all, including his reinforcements, about 40,000 men, every one of whom followed with enthusiasm and entire confidence their beloved, admired leader. Our cavalry force occupied its old position on the left flank of our army, and during the forenoon of the 27th had several encounters with the enemy's horse, all which, as was usual at that time, terminated in our favour.

One of these encounters, an affair of a few minutes, was with a newly-organised regiment of Federal Lancers. They stood 300 yards from us in line of battle, and presented, with their glittering lances, from the point of each of which fluttered a red-and-white pennon, and their fresh, well-fitting blue uniforms turned up with yellow, a fine martial appearance. One of our regiments was immediately ordered to attack them; but before our Virginia horsemen got within fifty yards of their line, this magnificent regiment, which had doubtless excited the liveliest admiration in the Northern cities on its way to the seat of war, turned tail and fled in disorder, strewing the whole line of their retreat with their picturesque but inconvenient arms. The entire skirmish, if such it may be called, was over in less time than is required to record it; and I do not believe that out of the whole body of 700 men more than twenty retained their lances. Their sudden and total discomfiture furnished a striking proof of the fact that this weapon, formidable enough in the hand of one accustomed to wield it, is a downright absurdity and encumbrance to the inexperienced.

About two o'clock in the afternoon the battle became general along the lines, and at three o'clock raged in its full fury. The fire of musketry rolled continuously, and more than 150 howitzers and Napoleon and Parrot guns opened all around us, and united in one incessant roar. The ground being not favourable for cavalry operations, we occupied a place on the left wing of the line of battle, but were nearly all day under fire of the enemy's cannon. General Stuart, accompanied by his Staff and personal escort, pressed forward with his two batteries of horse-artillery, which, under the command of my gallant friend John Pelham, soon did most admirable execution. The enemy at once concentrated the fire of five batteries on this point, and every kind of missile hurtled heavily through the smoky air, spreading death and destruction on all sides. I had many a hot ride during the afternoon through this tempest of shot and shell, and it appears now almost incomprehensible that I escaped uninjured.

It was about five o'clock when General Stuart returned with us to his cavalry, which had been, and were still, suffering severely from the fire of a battery that had been boldly pressed forward to a favourable position, and kept thundering down on our much-exposed horsemen with rapid and terrible discharges. Just as we were galloping along the line, the enemy opened upon us with grape and canister, and our men began to waver a little, the ranks getting into some confusion. At this moment General Stuart, who had to ride a few hundred yards farther to meet Colonel Fitz Lee, turned round to me, saying, "Captain, I wish you to remain here with my Staff and escort until I come back, to give a good example to the men." So we had to stand for many minutes in this diabolical fire of canister, which came rattling along the hard dry ground, or howled over us right and left—a pretty severe trial. It requires but little courage to attack the enemy, or even to ride about composedly under fire, in comparison with what is demanded to sit quietly in face of several batteries, from which, with every momentary puff of smoke from the mouths of the guns, one may reasonably expect the messenger of death. A shell which exploded directly over our heads tore nearly to pieces the captain of the squadron nearest to me, with whom I had just been talking, and killed or wounded several of the men. But our example had a telling effect; the ranks closed up and remained in good order until the command was given, and the long line of horsemen, soon in rapid trot, disappeared behind a range of friendly hills.

General Stuart and Staff now galloped forward again to our artillery, which in the mean time had lost many men and horses, but was still answering with the greatest energy the galling fire of the numerous batteries of the enemy. Just at this time a little incident occurred, which, in the very carnival of death, provoked our hearty laughter. One of our Staff-officers, Captain——, whom we had often joked about the nimble and successful manner in which he dodged the shells of the enemy, and who had this day again made the politest obeisance to their missiles, annoyed at our raillery, had declared that he would never again bow at their approach, and was sitting with the utmost gravity bolt-upright in the saddle, when a 12-pounder solid shot screamed through the air only a few feet over his head. Down went the head not merely to the saddle, but, with the body to which it was still securely attached, to the earth, amidst the convulsive shouts of his comrades and the cannoneers. Another incident which we witnessed about the same time, produced no less merriment amid the fury of the battle. A wounded man was borne along by two of his comrades, his limbs hanging motionless and his head dangling bout as if life was nearly extinct. The fire of the enemy was still murderous, and one of the carriers, struck by a musket-ball, fell to the ground, dropping his charge, who, seeing himself in great danger, suddenly revived, and, jumping up, took to his heels with the most surprising agility. The explosive laughter which followed him in his rapid flight all along our lines absolutely drowned for a few moments the tumult and hurly-burly of the engagement.

About six o'clock in the evening I was sent by General Stuart to order to the front two squadrons of our Georgia regiment to attack one of the Federal batteries which, without proper support, had been making a very bold advance. The enemy had brought up to the distant heights twenty pieces of rifled ordnance, which, by undue elevation, firing too high for the effect they desired, were playing upon an open space of ground over which I had to ride. The fire was so terrific that I found one of our reserve batteries, not actively engaged at the moment, entirely deserted by its gunners, who had sought protection with the horses in a deep ravine, and who cried out to me to dismount and join them, or certain death must be my fate. I pushed on, and reached my destination in safety; but galloping back I felt a stunning blow across the spine, and at the same moment my horse rolled over with me. I was confident the animal had been struck by cannon-ball; but, to my great surprise, I was not able to discover any wound. As I was myself unhurt, I remounted my brave animal, and continued my way. A solid shot had passed close to my horse's back, and the current of air set in motion by its passage had knocked over both horse and rider. Afterwards, during the war, I witnessed many similar cases of prostration of men and animals by "windage."

At seven o'clock in the evening the battle had taken the most favourable turn for our arms. At this time the enemy, who had offered throughout the day the most obstinate resistance, intrenched in very strong positions, and attacking us in the centre with 25,000 regular troops, the *élite* of M'Clellan's army, began slowly to give way before the impetuous valour of our men, who drove these veterans from one intrenchment to another, until, at eight P.M., they were in full retreat, and the victory was ours.

Thousands of prisoners, among whom were two generals, several colonels, and many inferior officers, a large number of field-pieces, and many flags, fell into our hands. General Stuart, with his cavalry, was immediately sent in pursuit of the enemy's flying columns, which we chased for nearly five miles, until the darkness of the night stopped our further progress. Returning, we were compelled to ride with great caution, for the field was strewn with wounded men, many of whom had crept to the edge of the highroad to get within reach of the ambulances. There is no sadder sight than that of a battle-field after the conflict is over. Happily, night at this moment veiled from us its full horrors; but there was an overwhelming sense of utter hopelessness in riding among so many poor fellows, whom one would have so much liked to assist, even with the "cup of cold water,"—brave fellows, groaning in their agony, and calling upon every passer-by for help—with an entire consciousness on our part of the fearful aggregate of the misery, and, alas! of the little we could do for its alleviation.

We encamped upon the field of battle. About midnight I felt myself touched on the shoulder; and when, grasping the hilt of my sword, I abruptly demanded who was there, a mild voice answered me, "General Jackson." The great Confederate leader was in search of General Stuart. Stuart, who slept on my right, was immediately aroused; and Jackson, accepting my invitation so to do, sat down on my blankets by his side. I left them alone, those grand warriors, in their midnight council, and wandered about, meditating on the stirring events of the day. I was deeply impressed by the blackness of the night and the profound stillness of the slumbering camp. Here and there a camp-fire shed a red glow around, and the stillness was only too mournfully interrupted by the groans of wounded and dying men, who, not many hours before, had been full of health and hope.

At the early dawn of morning, on the 28th of June, all was in motion again, as General Stuart had received orders to proceed at once with his cavalry to the White House on the Pamunkey river, where immense supplies for M'Clellan's army had been collected. I was exceedingly disappointed, when, ordering my horse to be saddled, my mulatto servant reported that my brave chestnut was unable to rise, in consequence of the injuries sustained by the heavy contusion of the previous day—injuries from which it never recovered. I had no choice, therefore, but to remain behind until I could procure another animal. But I was not idle. Acting in concert with Captain Fitzhugh, of General Stuart's Staff, and assisted by a dozen couriers, I employed myself in collecting and placing under guard the prisoners that were still coming in by fifties and hundreds from every part of the extensive battle-field. Among these prisoners was a major of artillery, who had served with General Stuart in the old regular army of the United States, and who had been acquainted with Captain Fitzhugh before the war. He was a most intelligent and agreeable man, but seemed greatly annoyed by his capture. After some hesitation, however, he accepted the rude hospitality of our little camp, and shared our meagre breakfast, consisting of soup and hard bread. He talked very sensibly of the war and of the recent battle, and expressed his great admiration for Lee, Jackson, and Stuart.

About 10 A.M. I was able to turn the prisoners over to one of Jackson's officers; and then, mounting a horse which was kindly offered me by one of our couriers, I set out for a ride over the field of the fight. It was, indeed, a sad and cruel spectacle. Death had raged fearfully in many places, especially where our troops had been compelled to storm the strong intrenchments of the enemy. On some of these perilous slopes the dead bodies might be seen piled three or four deep. I was struck here by the piteous contrast presented by the bodies of two of our dead which were lying side by side. I can never forget the sight; I can see them now—one a man of more than fifty, who had been shot through the head, and whose silvery white hair was dabbled in his blood; the other, next to him, a lad of sixteen, whose frank face was lighted up by clustering fair hair, and whose small hands were crossed over his heart, where the enemy's bullet had struck him.

Among Jackson's men on the previous day I had looked with astonishment at a soldier from Mississippi—a perfect giant, whose appearance had attracted the more attention from a vest of bear-skin that he wore. Here among the dead I found him again, with a small hole in the breast, which had been sufficient to make an end at once of all his strength and vigour.

Many stories had been recited in camp about a tremendous bayonet-fight, hand to hand, during the battle, between our Texans and the New York Zouaves, and it was said that two of these determined antagonists had pierced each other through and through with their formidable and fatal weapons, and that their dead bodies had been found standing erect in the very attitude in which each had received his death-wound. Curiosity carried me to the spot. An obstinate struggle had indeed taken place there between the troops named, which had ended in the utter annihilation of the much-vaunted Zouaves, whose bodies, dressed in flashy red uniforms, were scattered about all over the ground like the scarlet poppies in a corn-field; but the never-erring bullet of the famous Texan marksmen had brought them down, not the bayonet. I carefully examined many of the corpses, and found only three or four with bayonet-wounds, and these had been received evidently after the bullets. These accounts of bayonet-fights are current after every general engagement, and are frequently embodied in subsequent "histories," so called; but as far as my experience goes, recalling all the battles in which I have borne a part, bayonet-fights rarely if ever occur, and exist only in the imagination.

About mid-day I returned to our encampment, where I found, to my great delight, a fresh horse that Captain Fitzhugh had procured for me, and a company of our cavalry which was just starting to join our comrades at the White House. As the officer in command pretended to know the way very well, I made up my mind at once to join them; and after a march of more than six hours, discovered, to my intense disgust, that the captain had missed his road completely. As night was now approaching, and squads of the enemy's cavalry were reported in every direction, nothing was left to us but to return to our starting-point, which we reached again about midnight. Our return not a little surprised and annoyed Captain Fitzhugh, who, in the mean time, had received intelligence from General Stuart, and orders for me to join him on the following morning.

During our march back to camp, passing one of our picket-posts, we found our men there in great excitement, and were informed by them that the enemy had poisoned all the wells and springs in the neighbourhood, in consequence of which several of their number were in a dying condition. Three or four, indeed, were very bad; but although I do not love the Yankees, I am quite sure they were entirely innocent of this. The sufferers had been made ill by the too abundant use of bad apple-brandy, which will kill anybody.

The first streak of day of the 29th found us once more in the saddle, marching gaily along through the dense green forests of oak and hickory. We had a long ride before us, and as we had information from Stuart that active work was to be done, we hastened forward as rapidly as possible. The distant thunder of cannon soon announced to us that the fight had opened; but eagerly as we pushed our horses, it was nearly twelve o'clock when we reached a plateau about two miles from the White House, only to learn that the battle was over. At the foot of this plateau extended, about two miles in breadth, and in length as far as the eye could reach, the green fertile valley of the Pamunkey, whose yellow waters flowed directly past the "plantation," or estate, of the White House, the property of our Colonel, William H. F. Lee. This wide verdant flat was covered with thousands of tents and store-houses, and formed the main depot of the Federal army, numbering, before the late battles, at least 150,000 men. The enemy's cavalry, forced to fly by the celerity of Stuart's attack, had, in their rapid retreat, set fire to all the principal buildings; and from more than a hundred different points vast volumes of smoke were rising in the air, while the stately mansion of Colonel Lee was wreathed in flames. All over the field our horsemen were busy as ants, here rescuing from destruction quantities of valuable provisions, there enjoying luxuries of which they had long been deprived, that were scattered in the greatest profusion on every hand. I found General Stuart on the very brink of the Pamunkey, where he had established his headquarters in a delightfully cool spot, beneath the boughs of a gigantic plantain, regaling himself with iced lemonade, which he shared with me, and which fell upon my tongue like nectar. Ice, lemons, crushed sugar, and many other dainties and delicacies, which we knew only by recollection, were heaped around us in large piles, for the benefit of any one who would reach out his hand to take them. The General was in excellent spirits, and received me most cordially, losing no time in recounting to me the splendid results of his expedition. He had broken the enemy's cavalry by his first attack, taken many prisoners, captured untold wealth of spoil, and, what amused and delighted him most of all, disabled and driven off a Federal gunboat by the fire of his dismounted sharpshooters and two pieces of horse-artillery. After a few minutes' rest, my curiosity led me through the burning encampment. Never in my life had I seen such enormous quantities of commissary stores—never had I supposed that an army of invasion would voluntarily encumber itself with such an incalculable amount of useless luxuries. Hundreds of boxes of oranges and lemons were piled up together, many of which, broken, sent the golden fruit rolling all over the ground. Great pyramids of barrels of white and brown sugar, and of salt fish, and eggs packed in salt, were blazing on all sides. One of the burning barrels of eggs we knocked open, and found its contents roasted *à merveille,* which gave us, with other edibles within easy reach, such a repast as we had not enjoyed for many months. Not far from us, as we thus feasted, were little mountains of hams of bacon, and boxes of arms, uniforms, and equipments for more than 10,000 men. An equal number of the latter we discovered in the river, as well as two transports, laden with whisky and other liquors, which had been sunk by the enemy on our approach, but which we raised and secured with little difficulty. A large number of railway carriages and new locomotive engines, and a pontoon train, also fell into our hands. In strolling through the more distant camps, I had the good fortune to secure a fine horse which had been left behind by his Federal owner in the hurry of his departure; but I lost my prize very soon afterwards.

In one of the houses near by I discovered the body of a handsome young man, an officer, who had been killed in one of the late battles. The body had been so skilfully embalmed that one could almost believe the poor fellow only slept. I set a guard over the corpse to protect it from casual injury, and it was soon afterwards delivered to the relatives of the deceased. The report was circulated in camp, and obtained some credence, that it was one of the French princes of the Orleans family, who were then serving on the Staff of General M'Clellan, and had taken part in the recent engagements; but this story was never believed by General Stuart or myself.

Late at night I returned exceedingly weary to camp, to find such rest as the myriads of musquitoes would allow me.

The following day the work of saving, and destroying what could not be saved, out of the spoils at the White House, was continued, and then we moved off to join the army of General Lee, at that moment pursuing the enemy on his retreat to Harrison's Landing, on James river. We left behind one regiment as a guard over the property, estimated at millions of dollars in value, which we had collected to be transported to Richmond and the military depots of our army. While the operations I have just detailed had been going on under Stuart at the White House, General Lee had been very active—engaging the enemy and driving him further back every day. That we might regain the main body as speedily as possible, we marched for the remainder of the day without stopping in the hot sun, and encamped at nightfall upon the exact spot on the Chickahominy where, a few weeks before, we had made so narrow an escape. At daybreak next morning we received orders to move as rapidly as we might eight miles higher up the river, to ford it in the neighbourhood of Bottom's Bridge, and, falling upon the flank of the Federal army, to intercept its hasty retreat; but upon reaching this point we received counter orders, as the

Federal army had already passed, and we rode back in full gallop to Forge Bridge, our starting-point. Here we found that the enemy, anticipating our movement, had posted artillery and sharpshooters in advantageous position on the river-bank, and we were accordingly received with a very determined resistance. Soon, however, Pelham came up with his horse-artillery, and, by a well-directed fire, opened a passage for us. The enemy retreated in precipitation, leaving their dead and wounded all along the course of their flight, and we were able to take but a very few prisoners. The sun was now pouring down with intense fervour, and as our horses were wellnigh exhausted with our rapid marching and counter-marching, we were compelled to take a few hours' rest on the roadside. We lay down in a corner of the fence beneath the shade of some cherry-trees hanging full of their delicious fruit, the bunches unfortunately just a little too high to serve our parched mouths with grateful refreshment. Stuart and I were standing on the highest rail of the fence, trying with difficulty to pluck some of the cherries, when he laughingly said to me, "Captain, you charge the Yankees so well, why do you not attack this cherry-tree and bring it down?" Without hesitation I jumped from my elevated position, grasping the higher part of the trunk, and breaking down the tree, amid the loud cheers and laughter of the Staff and the soldiers around, who finished the spoil, now so easily to be gathered, in an incredibly short time.

In the midst of our mirth over the fallen cherry-tree, we were interrupted by the heavy boom of artillery brought to us from the heights of Malvern Hill, where a sanguinary battle had just begun, and we were again ordered into the saddle. From the weary condition of our horses, however, our march in the direction of the cannonade was but a slow one; and it was not until late in the evening that we arrived upon the field of action, where the fate of the day had already been decided, the enemy having retreated under cover of his gunboats on James river. For the first time at Malvern Hill, in the progress of the American war, was it satisfactorily shown how important in a battle is the concentration of a large number of pieces of artillery upon one point; and the army of General M'Clellan was only saved from their utter destruction by sixty guns, which, being very favourably posted in his centre, poured dismay and death into our attacking columns. The effect was more disastrous than had been before produced by artillery. In this battle our losses were very heavy, and I may say that the victory was ours only from the ignorance of our position on the part of the enemy, who retreated exactly at the moment when he had gained the most important success.

As this battle was the last of the famous seven days' fighting before Richmond, I may be allowed to submit a very few remarks in review of the memorable struggle and its brilliant results. The fight began on the 26th June at Mechanicsville, and ended on the 2d July after Malvern Hill. M'Clellan, whose lines extended across the Chickahominy in a semicircle around Richmond, from the James river to the strong position of Mechanicsville, had in the first two days of the contest been completely whipped by Jackson on the right, and that portion of his army north of the Chickahominy had been driven to the south side, where the subsequent engagements of Fraser's Farm on the 29th, Willis's Church on the 30th, and, last of all, Malvern Hill, drove him in rapid retreat to his unassailable place of refuge at Westover, on the James river. At this point a large flotilla of gunboats protected him from any further attack on our part, and numerous transports supplied him with abundant provisions, ammunition, and reinforcements. M'Clellan's retreat was indeed masterly, and too much credit cannot be paid him for the skill with which he managed to hold his own, and check the advance of our victorious troops at Malvern Hill. His final success, however, in saving his army, was due to the inexcusable tardiness and disobedience of orders displayed by some of our Confederate generals. The fault was certainly not in General Lee's dispositions.

Our whole loss in killed and wounded was about 9000 men—that of the enemy amounted to 16,500, besides several thousand prisoners. The amount of artillery and ammunition, and more especially of small-arms, equipments, and commissary stores, that fell into our hands, was enormous.

CHAPTER IV

RIDE TO RICHMOND — EXPEDITION ON THE JAMES RIVER —
A PRISONER OF THE NINTH VIRGINIA CAVALRY — FISHING
AND SHOOTING — SUNDAY IN CAMP — HEADQUARTERS AT
HANOVER COURT-HOUSE — CAMP SCENES — FIGHTS AND
RECONNAISSANCES — RATTLESNAKE AND BULL-FROG —
DEPARTURE FROM DUNDEE.

DURING the night which followed the battle of Malvern
Hill, we encamped in the orchard of a small farmhouse
near the field, but our repose was made exceedingly uncomfortable by heavy showers of rain following one another in
rapid succession until the dawn. Profiting by the darkness of
the night and the disturbance created by the storm, a spy,
who had been captured by some of our men, and who had
been condemned to be hanged the next morning, contrived to
make his escape. I was rather glad of it. He was an old man
of more than sixty, and I had seen him riding along with us all
the day on a miserable mule, his hands tied behind him, with
such a terrified expression upon his ashy features, that I
regarded the poor sinner as sufficiently punished by the
agony he had already undergone. The morning opened
heavily with rain, and I rose shivering from the damp ground
to attend on General Stuart, from whom I received orders to
ride at once into Richmond for the purpose of executing

some important duties there. As my old grey was very nearly broken down by hard riding, and I might hope to exchange him in Richmond, my captured horse having been lost in the rapidity of our recent movements—and as, in all probability, fighting was not to be renewed—I started gladly upon this expedition. My ride took me over the battle-field and along a portion of the line of the enemy's former retreat. I looked with astonishment at the effect of the heavy artillery-fire of the enemy upon some portions of the forest. Hundreds of the largest trees were riven and shattered, and lay in fragments around, as if all the thunderbolts of heaven had been hurled against them; and in many places the fallen trunks and branches barricaded the road so that it was difficult to get along at all. For miles the ground was thickly strewn with muskets, knapsacks, blankets, and other equipments that had been thrown away in their flight by the soldiers of the retreating Federal army. It was nearly night when I reached Richmond. Wet, cold, and weary, I rode immediately to the hotel and sought my bed—a luxury which no one can thoroughly appreciate until he has long been deprived of it, and compelled as I had been for several nights to sleep in his clothes on the hard ground.

The Spotswood Hotel at this time was crowded with guests, among whom, a neighbour of my own, was no less distinguished a person than a Federal General, M'Call, who had been taken prisoner in one of the recent battles. As might naturally have been expected, the joy of the people of Richmond was very great at the deliverance of their city from the hands of the enemy; but they took their good fortune with a very becoming composure, and spoke and acted just as if, in their judgment, with such an army as that of General Lee, under such commanders, between them and the invading force, the struggle for the Confederate capital could have had no other result. No powder was wasted in salutes over the victory, no bonfires blazed, no windows were illuminated, and the general appearance of Richmond was in all respects unchanged from what it had been a month before.

My business in Richmond was speedily transacted, and the following day, having procured an excellent horse, I set out with fresh courage and spirits to rejoin my General. Our army in the mean time had been pushed forward towards the James river, being close upon the enemy's formidable positions at Westover; and as I rode along, I heard from time to time the heavy ordnance of the gunboats, which threw their tremendous projectiles wherever the grey uniforms came in sight. Generals R. E. Lee, Longstreet, and Stuart had established their headquarters together in the extensive farmyard of a Mr Phillips, which spot I reached late in the evening, after a long and dusty ride. Here for a few days we enjoyed rest and comparative quiet. Our generals were often in council of war, undecided whether or not to attack the enemy. On the morning of the 6th, General Stuart removed his headquarters about two miles lower down the river to the plantation of a Mr C., old friends of ours, where we were received, especially by the ladies, with great kindness and enthusiasm.

About dusk on the 6th the General started with two of our regiments, the 4th and the 9th, and six pieces of our horse-artillery, to lay an ambush for the Federal gunboats, which every night came steaming up the river with fresh troops and supplies for their army. Having been detained by some duty at headquarters, I left about an hour later than the column, quite alone, and had on my ride a little adventure which gave rise to a great deal of merriment at my expense. I had been informed by one of our patrols that detachments of the enemy's cavalry had been seen in the neighbourhood, and I had therefore moved on with no little vigilance and circumspection. It was a beautiful night, the air was full of the fragrance of the wild-flowers and forest-blossoms, and myriads of fire-flies glittered in the surrounding darkness. Suddenly, through the profound stillness of the night, there struck upon my quick ear the sound of hoofs upon my right hand, and out of a small dark bridle-path on the side of the road there emerged a horseman, who wore, as well as I could distinguish, the Federal uniform. "Halt!" said I. The stranger halted. "What is your regiment?" "Eighth Illinois" (hostile cavalry). The answer had no sooner been given than, putting spurs to my horse, I rushed upon my antagonist, who, seeing my revolver levelled with uncomfortably accurate aim at his breast, surrendered himself without the least hesitation as my prisoner. As I was conducting my capture to the spot where the 9th Virginia Cavalry was stationed, I perceived that he was riding an admirable horse, which I regarded with infinite satisfaction as already my property. He entertained me on the way with many stories about the Yankee army, how long he had served in it, &c. &c. When we had reached our regiment, however, he came out suddenly in the new character of a member of the corps, a private in the ranks, who had replaced his own tattered Confederate uniform with the uniform and cap of a captured Federal soldier, and who had taken me, from my foreign accent, for a Federal officer. As he made this recital, not without a certain latent satire at my prowess in making a prisoner of a private of the 9th Virginia Cavalry, I confess that, recalling his extreme terror at the moment of his surrender, I lost all patience with him, and again levelling my pistol at him, I gave him to understand that I would make short work of him at any future repetition of his jests. But I did not get my fine horse; for upon turning over my prisoner, whom I still supposed to be a Yankee, to Colonel Fitzhugh Lee, he recognised in him at once a man of his own command, who had most imprudently assumed one of the captured Federal uniforms. This substitution of dress was unfortunately very often done by our men, and many a poor fellow has been killed by his own friends because he could not resist the temptation of discarding his duty rags for a new blue coat and trousers. In addition to the loss of my captured horse, I was very much teased for my mistake, and General Stuart often laughingly asked me, "How many prisoners of the 9th Virginia have you taken lately?"

Pursuing my ride, after having disposed of the Confederate prisoner, I found General Stuart at a point upon the river-bank where Captain Stephen D. Lee, who later distinguished himself as a general at Vicksburg and in the Western campaigns, had placed the six pieces of artillery in a very favourable position. We had not long to wait before opening fire. The expected Yankee transports, five in number, soon came in sight, and passed us slowly not more than one hundred yards distant from our battery. Our pieces thundered all together, and kept up an incessant discharge. The effect on the transports, which were densely crowded with Federal troops, cannot be described. We could distinctly hear our balls and shells crashing through the sides of the vessels, the cries of the wounded on board, and the confused random commands of the officers. One of the smaller transports sank in a few minutes, the others escaped more or less injured. In a very short time, hearing the approach of a whole flotilla of gunboats, under very heavy pressure of steam, for the protection of the transports, we quickly limbered up, and were already a mile nearer to our encampment, when, to our amusement, the enemy, with his ponderous 100-pounder guns, concentrated an appalling fire upon the point we had just left.

During the next few days nothing disturbed the quiet of our camp, and on the 8th I had the pleasure of receiving from the Post-Quartermaster at Richmond a noble black horse to replace the chestnut disabled in the battle of Coal Har-

bour—an animal which, by its speed and magnificent jumping, saved my life several times during my later campaigns.

It would be impossible to give an idea of the impoverish-
ment and utter destitution of the country, which the presence
of two immense armies had deprived of everything, and
which the recent battles had devastated with fire. The sad and
sickening evidences of the shock of arms were only too
plainly visible on every side. Upon the numberless festering
carcasses of horses and mules the sun poured down with a
tropical blaze, while the air was also poisoned with the stench
from human bodies that had been hastily buried but a few
inches below the surface. For many miles around nothing
could be procured to support life. I well recollect that
Captain Stuart of our Staff and myself were digging for a
whole day in the garden of a little farmhouse for a few
miserable onions and diseased potatoes to appease our
hunger. Such is the condition of a region of country, no
matter how fertile and productive it may have been in former
days, over which war has expended its fury.

On the evening of the 9th we were suddenly brought to
horse again by a fierce demonstration of the enemy, who
drove in our pickets, but was repulsed without much difficulty. On the 10th we received information that General
M'Clellan had determined to embark his army on his transports at Harrison's Landing, and at the same time orders to
march to Hanover county, on the opposite side of Richmond,
to recruit our horses, and organise some better system of
procuring forage and provisions.

Leaving the regiments behind us, General Stuart and I
galloped off together along the road to Richmond. On our
way we stopped at the house of the Irish family, where, more
than a month before, we had spent some anxious hours, on
the occasion of our midnight ride to hold a rendezvous with
the spy just previous to the Pamunkey expedition, and where

we were now received with abundant chit-chat by the loquacious landlady, who supplied us with fresh milk and blackberries. It was late in the evening when we reached the city, where the General pressed me to accompany him in a visit to the President—a pleasure which I was compelled to deny myself in consequence of the shabby condition of my garments. As we remained in town the whole of the next day, I took advantage of the opportunity to fit myself out with a full uniform of the newest gloss, consisting of a light grey frock-coat with buff facings, dark blue trousers, and a little black cocked-hat with sweeping ostrich plume, the regulation dress for staff-officers, which is as picturesque as it is suitable for active service.

On the morning of the 12th we set out for Hanover county, where our headquarters had been established upon the farm of a Mr Timberlake, near Atlee's Station, on the line of the Virginia Central Railway. Mr Timberlake's house was situated in the midst of a forest of lofty oak and hickory trees, around which stretched fertile fields. The proprietor himself was a pleasant, jovial old gentleman, who had two sons in our cavalry; and as he remitted no exertions to make us comfortable, we had really nothing to desire. On the 14th Mrs Stuart arrived at a neighbouring mansion, and as she had accepted the General's invitation to share our camp dinner, I galloped over—the faithful mulatto "Bob" following with a led horse—to escort her to our headquarters. It was always a pleasure to me to ride with the Virginia ladies, who, with rare exceptions, are admirable horsewomen, to whom no fence is too high and no ditch too wide. Mrs Stuart was often with us, coming whenever we could look forward to a few days of inactivity. Her children were the pets of the whole camp; and during those brief but frequent interludes of domesticity, we were all united together as members of one family.

On the 17th we had a brigade drill and a review of our

entire cavalry force, which demonstration was attended by a large number of spectators, principally the ladies of the neighbourhood, among whom General Stuart had many acquaintances and admirers, for he was always the hero and idol of the gentle sex. When the military performance was over, he galloped around from carriage to carriage, presenting us in turn to the fair inmates, and inviting them to drive over and take a look at our camp, which was not more than a mile distant. As several families accepted the invitation, Captain Fitzhugh and myself were sent in advance to make suitable preparations for their reception. With Mr Timberlake's kind permission, assisted by a little army of negro servants, we plundered his house of its chairs and sofas, which were disposed in a semicircle beneath an immense tent-fly that had been among the spoils taken from the enemy at the White House; and our hastily improvised *al fresco* drawing-room was quite complete and effective in its arrangements when the carriages arrived upon the ground. For refreshment we had cool fresh milk and ginger-cakes for the ladies, and the Virginia mint-julep for the gentlemen; animated talk alternated with patriotic songs on all sides, and our guests took away with them the impression that camp-life was not so bad after all.

We occupied ourselves now chiefly with fishing and shooting, as had the red Indians of those woods and streams two hundred years ago. The Chickahominy afforded us abundance of perch and cat-fish, which were welcome additions to the supplies of our mess-table; but taking the fish was attended with many discomforts and difficulties. From the peculiar formation of the river-banks, high and densely skirted with trees, we were forced to wade about in the shallow stream, where we are vigorously attacked by the most voracious horse-leeches, which fastened themselves on our exposed legs in such numbers as to make it necessary to go ashore every five minutes to shake them off. The small hare of Virginia darted about in every direction in the fields and thickets; but shooting the grey squirrel, which was quite new to me, afforded me the best sport; and from the great agility of the animal, it was by no means so easy a matter as one might suppose. The foliage of the hickory, in which the grey squirrel has his favourite abode, is very dense, and the active little creature knows so well how to run along the opposite side of the limb from the gentleman with the gun, that one must be as much on the alert as his game to fire exactly at the moment when it is in sight and unprotected. The grey squirrel is smaller than the red or fox squirrel, and as it subsists principally on chestnuts and hickory-nuts, its meat is very delicate. I had some repugnance to eating them at first, as disagreeably suggestive, in their appearance, of rats; but I soon learned to appreciate the game, and it became one of my most highly valued dishes.

On the 18th, about noon, as I had just returned from one of my little shooting expeditions, General Stuart having gone off to Richmond on duty, I found Captain Fitzhugh engaged in entertaining an Englishman, Lord Edward St Maur, who had given us the pleasure of being our guest for the day. As our mess supplies were limited, I was not a little concerned as to the materials for a dinner; but William, our negro cook, hearing that I had two squirrels in my game-bag, undertook to make a pie of them, and did this so successfully that I had the satisfaction to find the *pâté* highly relished by my lord, who said he had never tested anything better in his life.

On Sunday the 19th we had divine service in the camp. The officiating clergyman was the Rev. Mr Landstreet, chaplain of the 1st Virginia Cavalry, and the spot was an open place in the midst of the primitive forest. I was deeply impressed by the peculiar solemnity of the scene. It was indeed a striking picture,—hundreds of bearded warriors lying about on the grass, and listening with the utmost attention to the eloquent words of the preacher, beneath the green dome formed by the interlacing branches of the gigantic trees over their heads.

On the 21st July we received orders again to remove our encampment, and the spot chosen for it was in the immediate neighbourhood of the Court-house of the county of Hanover, which we reached the evening of that day. The Court-house building was erected in the year 1730, and any structure dating from this period is regarded in America as a very ancient and venerable edifice. Within its walls, in the palmy day of his imperial declamation, the great orator Patrick Henry, "the forest-born Demosthenes," had pleaded the celebrated "Parsons' Cause" in a speech the traditions of which yet live freshly in Virginia. It is a small building of red brick, pleasantly situated on a hill commanding a pretty view, several miles in extent, of fertile fields and dark-green woods, and a clear stream, which winds like a silvery thread through the distant valley. The Court-house and several offices belonging to it are surrounded by a shady enclosed grove of locust and plantain trees, about five acres in area. Here we established our headquarters. The cavalry regiments and horse-artillery were encamped in full view all around us— nearly 8000 men, with their grazing horses, white tents, and waving battle-flags—an animated panorama of active military life. Here our position was one of great comfort and enjoyment. Our tents were all put up with some regard to regularity; our mess arrangements were better ordered; we made frequent visits to the houses of the neighbouring planters, and we might have dismissed the war and its hardships from our minds, had not the enemy, who already occupied Fredericksburg in heavy force, made it necessary for us, as a matter of proper precaution, to maintain an extended line of pickets.

The occurrence of my birthday on the 23d was the

occasion to me of a pleasant little surprise in the presentation
of a beautiful bouquet and the congratulations of my comrades on the Staff, and I had hoped to spend the day in social
delights and *dolce far niente*; but about ten A.M. we received
intelligence that the enemy, advancing in strength from
Fredericksburg, had fallen, about fifteen miles distant, upon
one of our squadrons on picket, dispersed it, and taken off
with them a number of prisoners and horses. At twelve
o'clock we started in pursuit with three regiments, amounting
to about 2000 men, and two pieces of artillery. We reached
the scene about dusk, and found, to our great disappointment, that the enemy had taken the back track about
mid-day, and that there was now no chance of overtaking
them. But General Stuart, having proceeded so far, determined to extend his expedition to a more thorough reconnaissance, and accordingly encamped for the night upon the
farm of a Mr Anderson, whence we made an early departure
on the following morning. When I came to mount my horse
for the march, I found with infinite annoyance that my
saddle-bags, containing articles of great value to me, had
been stolen by one of the negro camp-followers, who were
always lounging in large numbers about our encampments.
But one soon becomes accustomed to these little personal
losses in war. To-day you lose something of utility, to-morrow
you take it back from the enemy with usury; indeed, the
whole of my equipments consisted of spoils taken from the
Yankees.

Our march was continued throughout the day on the 24th,
and we arrived about dusk at a point ten miles from
Fredericksburg, where we halted and fed our horses in a large
clover-field. General Stuart threw forward his pickets with
great caution, so that we might not be observed by the enemy,
intending during the night to make a sudden attack on
Fredericksburg, in the hope of driving the Yankees out of the

town, or at least of alarming the garrison. This enterprise, however, was not favoured by the elements. About eleven P.M. there burst upon us a tremendous thunderstorm, with such a deluging downpour of rain, that the Mataponi, with its four tributaries, the Ma, Ta, Po, and Ni, in our rear, which we had forded easily, must soon have become so much swollen as to make recrossing impossible. It was therefore necessary to start on a rapid retreat. The Indian name *Mataponi* is made up of four separate names of one syllable, as the river which bears this name is made up of the four several rivulets which become confluent at one point, and it furnishes us with a proof how practical the aboriginal inhabitants of America were in their nomenclature. We managed to ford the last of these streams with difficulty, and arrived only in the afternoon of the following day at our latest point of departure, Mr Anderson's. Here we left our command to rest the fatigued men and horses, and Captain Blackford of our Staff and myself accompanied General Stuart upon a hand-car, propelled by two negroes, along the railroad directly to Hanover Court-house, which place we reached at sunset.

A few days now passed in perfect tranquillity, and we had the pleasure of paying occasional visits to our friends in the neighbourhood, most frequently of all at the hospitable mansion of Dr P., known as Dundee, which was one of the most charming places in the fair land of the Old Dominion. The house is situated on an elevated point in the midst of a beautiful oak grove which opens on the garden side, affording a lovely vista over richly-cultivated fields, with a blue range of hills for background in the far distance. Around the house there was a profusion of flowers, and the entire *locale* was so sweet a paradise, that it was the highest of satisfactions to us soldiers, accustomed to the roar of cannon and images of death and carnage, to enjoy the serene quiet that reigned in its grounds and apartments, and the charming society of the family circle that dwelt there.

On Sunday evening the 26th we were assembled as usual on the verandah, enjoying the coolness of the twilight hours, delicious after the fierce heats of the summer day, when suddenly our attention was attracted by flames issuing from the roof of one of the farm stables, about 500 yards distant. As most of the negroes were absent, paying their Sunday visits, or otherwise spending their weekly holiday, the lightly-built stables and the cattle in them were in imminent danger of destruction. Of course we eagerly hastened to the spot to render what aid we could in extinguishing the fire or saving the property. After half an hour's hard work we succeeded in getting the fire under; and though all of us, and myself especially, were more or less burned in the face and hands, we felt highly gratified to have rendered some service to people who had shown us the most marked and constant kindness. General Stuart, who always had his joke, gave the ladies a most absurd and extravagant account of my individual exertions, declaring that he had seen me running out of the burning building with a mule under one arm and two little pigs under the other.

On the 29th we had another brigade drill, which drew together a considerable number of spectators. The place was an extended level plain, very favourable for manœuvres, and the whole drill was executed with as much precision as would have been exhibited by regular troops, and afforded indeed a most brilliant spectacle. The fine day ended with the most terrible hurricane I ever witnessed. Thousands of trees were torn up by their roots and hurled in the air. Houses were everywhere unroofed. It may well be supposed that every tent of our encampment was prostrated, and that general confusion and disorder marked the spot.

The next day General Stuart surprised and gladdened me inexpressibly by placing in my hands my commission as major and adjutant-general of cavalry, which he had brought with him from Richmond. The General himself had been created a Major-General. Our cavalry, strongly reinforced by regiments from North and South Carolina, had been formed into a division consisting of three brigades, commanded by Brigadier-Generals Hampton, Fitz Lee, and Robertson, with three batteries of horse-artillery, amounting in all to about 15,000 well-mounted men.

On the 4th of August the trumpet sounded again for the march, as a reconnaissance in force was to be undertaken in the direction of Port Royal and Fredericksburg. With four regiments and one battery we pushed on all day until we reached the village of Bowling Green, about twenty miles distant, where we made a bivouac for the night. On the 5th, the hottest day of the whole summer, we continued our march, and arrived at Port Royal at eleven o'clock in the morning, just after a squadron of the enemy's cavalry, already apprised of our approach, had retreated lower down the Rappahannock. The joy of the inhabitants at our coming was touching to witness. The ladies, many of them with their cheeks wet with tears, carried refreshments around among our soldiers, and manifested, with the deepest emotion, their delight in seeing the grey uniforms, and their gratitude at their deliverance from the oppressor. At one P.M. we resumed our march, halting only for a few minutes at the charming cottage of a lady, where, at a later period, I was to spend some pleasant days, which had just then been left by a band of Yankee marauders, one of whom had robbed an old negro servant of the family of his silver watch. The negro, who recognised Captain Blackford as an old friend of the household, complained to him most piteously of this treatment, and implored him to enforce restitution of his property. About three o'clock we overtook these marauders, whom our advance-guard had made prisoners, and upon one of the skulking fellows we at once discovered the watch, which, to the satisfaction of us all, and to the grinning delight of its rightful owner, Captain Blackford restored to him.

At sunset we reached Round Oak Church, only twelve miles distant from Fredericksburg, where we bivouacked, taking the precaution to form a long cordon of pickets and vedettes, who took care that the enemy should not be informed of our movements from any of our followers, by allowing no one to pass outside their line. At the same time we sent forward some of our Texan scouts, who, soon returning, reported the enemy encamped in large numbers about five miles from Fredericksburg. One of the scouts, a man famous in his profession, had been shot by one of the Yankee sentinels, and brought back with him an arm badly shattered.

In our bivouac I met with a little adventure that turned out fortunately enough, but might have cost me my life. Fatigued by the long ride, and exhausted by the intense heat of the day, I had spread my blanket, soon after my arrival, near an old log, which in former days had been used as a step by the ladies in mounting and dismounting on their rides to church, but which I now proposed, in its decay, should serve me as a pillow. Resting my head upon it I fell at once into a deep sleep, from which I was presently awakened by something crawling over my hand. I quickly shook off the object, which gave out a sharp, clear, rattling sound, and which I perceived in the bright light of the moon to be a snake more than four feet in length that raised itself at me in an attitude that meant mischief. Sleeping, as I always did, with my arms by my side, it was the work of a moment to draw my keen Damascus blade* and sever the reptile in twain. Excited, however, by this unfamiliar hostile attack, and finding that the dissevered parts of the body continued to manifest vitality in wriggling about on the grass, I dealt yet several heavy blows at my enemy, and the noise of the encounter aroused the General with the whole of his Staff. Arms in their hands, they hastened to the scene of action, believing that not fewer than a hundred Yankees had fallen upon me. A roar of laughter burst from them at the nature of my mid-night combat; but the affair seemed less ridiculous when they discovered that I had killed one of the largest specimens of the American rattlesnake, a reptile as venomous as the East Indian cobra, whose bite is certain and speedy death—a fate which I had very narrowly escaped. I could obtain little sleep during the remainder of the night; and was ready to move before sunrise when the command was given to mount.

Our march lay in the direction of Massaponax Church, about eight miles distant from Fredericksburg, on the Telegraph Road—a wide plank turnpike leading directly to Richmond. We had been informed by our spies and patrols that a Federal force of 8000 men, with the usual complement of artillery, under the command of Generals Hatch and Gibbon, was on an expedition to destroy the most important line of railway communication with our army, and burn the depots of supplies at Hanover Junction. Riding as usual with the advance-guard, I was the first to discover the hostile column when we had reached a point within half a mile of the Telegraph Road. I immediately gave the order to halt, and

---

*This Damascus blade, which will be frequently mentioned hereafter in my narrative, was a straight double-edged sword of tremendous size and excellent temper, which I had worn from the commencement of my military career in the Prussian Cuirassiers of the Guards. It was even better known in the Confederate army than myself; and many who were unable to pronounce my foreign name correctly used to speak of me as "the Prussian with the big sword." Stuart

rode back to give information of the enemy's presence to
General Stuart, who made his dispositions with his accustomed celerity. The main body of the enemy had already
passed the spot where the road along which we were moving
intersected the Telegraph Road, and only their long waggon-
train with its escort remained behind. Two regiments, with
two pieces of artillery, were ordered to turn to the left in
pursuit of the column; one regiment, the 3d Virginia, was
ordered to attack the waggon-train; and one regiment, with
the rest of the artillery, was kept in reserve. I joined in the
attack on the waggon-train, and the surprise and confusion
of the escort cannot be described, when with a yell the
horsemen in grey dashed out of the dark wood, and the
Yankees knew at once that the so-much-dreaded Stuart
was again upon them. Many of the drivers endeavoured to
turn back with their waggons and seek safety in the speed
of their teams, while for a time the escort maintained a
feeble defence; but the waggons were rapidly overtaken, the
escort cut down, captured, or dispersed; and the whole of
the heavily-loaded train, with ninety prisoners, fell into
our hands—our own loss having been two men mortally
wounded.

General Stuart now collected his whole force, except a
single squadron left on picket at Massaponax Church, and
pressed with all possible haste upon the main body of the
enemy, who in the outset were totally surprised, and fled in
disorderly rout before us for several miles. As soon as they
discovered, however, that they had only cavalry and a few
pieces of artillery against them, they made a stand, and

---

wrote to me after the battle of Gettysburg, in which, being prostrated by
wounds, I did not participate, referring to the operations of his cavalry, "My
dear Von, I cannot tell you how much I missed you and your broad blade at
Gettysburg."

became in turn the assailants. Numerous batteries opened fire upon us; and their long lines of tirailleurs advanced in beautiful order. On this occasion I had a good laugh at General Stuart. Among other novelties in offensive warfare, the enemy employed against us in the fight one-pounder cannons, the balls of which being curiously shaped made a peculiar sound in their passage through the air. Just as the General and I had been placing two of our pieces in favourable position, and were riding nearer to the front, one of these exasperating little balls passed directly between us; and my brave General, whom many a time I had seen, amid the heaviest artillery-fire, perfectly indifferent to shot and shell hissing around him, now, as the new projectile whizzed past us with its unfamiliar music, made it the politest bow imaginable.

In this combat I also saw for the first time exploding rifle-balls used in action. They fell on all sides, bursting with a crackling noise in the trees and on the ground, without doing much execution. After a short but sharp contest, General Stuart gave orders for the retreat, which was conducted with his usual skill along by-paths through the woods; and our disappearance from the field was so sudden and complete, that the enemy could not possibly imagine what had become of their recent antagonists. I was myself sent to give the necessary advice to the squadron left on picket, with orders then to follow the command in the direction it had taken. Returning to join my companions, I was compelled to cross an open field over which the enemy were advancing, and saw at once that their first line of tirailleurs had been pushed forward so far, that for the length of 300 yards I must pass in front of them at a distance of not more than 150 paces. I immediately set my horse in rapid gallop; and though the bullets whistled around my head with every stride of the animal, I escaped unhurt, and soon overtook the General.

The success of our expedition had indeed been brilliant. Besides the damage done to the enemy in killing and wounding many of their men, and in capturing 200 prisoners and a valuable waggon-train, we had defeated their plans, saved the railway and our supply depots from destruction, and so demoralised them, by making them feel that the vigilant and indefatigable Stuart was always in their rear, that they never organised another such raid from Fredericksburg. Late at night we again arrived at Bowling Green, where we encamped, and the next day returned to Hanover Court-house. The General, Captain Blackford, and myself, galloping ahead of the troops, reached headquarters late in the afternoon, but in time to pay a visit in the evening to the family at Dundee. Here we found Mrs Stuart and her children, and Mrs Blackford, who had arrived during our absence, and who remained as guests at the hospitable mansion for several weeks.

During the past week our army, principally Jackson's corps, had been moving along the Central Railway towards Gordonsville and Orange Court-house, as the new Federal commander, General Pope, had been concentrating a large army in the neighbourhood of Culpepper to try a new route in the Federal "On to Richmond." The next day, after our arrival at headquarters, Stuart received a dispatch summoning him to meet Jackson at Gordonsville, to which place he went off alone by rail, leaving us to the enjoyment of an interval of repose.

It was a delightful period, filled up with visits at camp from the gentlemen of the region around, long evening rides with our lady friends, and pleasant reunions. In the mornings I amused myself with my revolver shooting the tremendous bull-frog of the swamps, nearly as large as a rabbit, the legs of which were esteemed a great delicacy by my American friends, and appeared every day upon our breakfast-table. I ate them twice, and found the meat in flavour and appearance very similar to young chicken, but I could never overcome my early prejudice against them,—a little weakness for which I was often derided by my comrades.

An incident now happened to me annoyingly illustrative of the treachery and ingratitude of the negro character. My servant Scott came to me with an affecting story of the serious illness of his wife, which so excited my sympathy that I not only obtained permission for him to visit his suffering spouse, but supplied him liberally with money, the contributions of myself and companions, to pay the expenses of his journey. The rascal disappeared, carrying off with him the greater part of my wardrobe, and we never saw him again.

Our days of inaction were now drawing rapidly to an end. General Stuart, having taken a distinguished part in the battle of Cedar Run, where Jackson had utterly routed the advanced corps of Pope's army, came back with marching orders on the 15th. Our regiments were to be in motion early next morning, and the General and Staff were to overtake him in the afternoon by rail. We dined for the last time at Dundee, and with grateful hearts took leave of our kind friends. I need not describe the parting scene between General Stuart and his family. I will only say that his dear lady did not suffer me to quit the house until I had promised to watch over her husband in the hour of battle, and do all in my power to prevent him from rashly exposing himself to danger.

CHAPTER V

WHEN the train which we were to take for Gordonsville reached the Hanover Court-house Station on the afternoon of the 16th August, our horses having been already safely placed in a stock-car awaiting its arrival, it was so densely crowded with troops, many of them lying stretched out on the tops of the carriages, that the General and Staff, not wishing to deprive any of these brave fellows of their seats, determined to ride on the tender of the locomotive, where, in the best possible spirits, we made ourselves as comfortable as the circumstances of the case would allow. There is a feeling of great buoyancy in the breast of the soldier when, after a period of unusual inactivity, he goes forward again to the field—one seems to one's self so strong, and looks so gaily forward to the coming campaign. Too much occupied with the future to indulge in reveries of the past, or regrets for happy hours "departed never to return," we filled up the time with talk and song as we rolled rapidly through the beautiful country, of which, by reason of the thick clouds of smoke that enveloped us, we could catch only occasional glimpses. We arrived at Gordonsville just at daybreak. When the morning light grew strong enough to enable us to see each other, we broke out at the same moment into a hearty roar of laughter, for it revealed faces as black as Ethiopia. The engine had been covering us with soot from the time we left Hanover Court-house, and it required many ablutions to restore the natural colour of our skins. After an hour's delay thus employed, and partaking of a light break-fast, we proceeded by special train to Orange Court-house, where we brought up at eleven o'clock in the morning.

We now mounted our horses and rode through the numer-ous encampments of our army to the headquarters of General Robert E. Lee, where we tarried an hour, and then proceeded to the camp of Jackson, a few miles off, which we reached about three P.M., just in time for dinner. The great Stonewall gave but little thought to the comforts of life, but he was so much the pet of the people that all the planters and farmers in whose neighbourhood he erected his simple tent, vied with each other in supplying him abundantly with the delicacies of the table; and accordingly we found an excellent dinner set out, to which we did full justice. Immediately after rising from the repast, General Stuart despatched Captain Fitzhugh and Lieutenant Dabney of his Staff to the little village of Verdiersville, where he expected the arrival of Fitz Lee's brigade, and desired me to accompany himself on a little reconnaissance to Clark's Mountain, where we had erected a signal-station, from which, it was said, there was a wide view of the plains of Culpepper, dotted over with the encampments of the Federal army. On our way we met one of our scouts, Mosby, who had acted as courier to General Stuart, and who subsequently so greatly distinguished himself in the guerilla warfare he conducted. Knowing him well acquainted with the position of the enemy, the General ordered him to ride with us. The view from the summit of Clark's Mountain is indeed magnificent. On the right the eye ranges over the dark green of the immense forests which line the borders of the Rappahannock and Rapidan rivers for many miles, while in front stretches the vast fertile valley of Culpepper, engirdled in the remote landscape by the Blue Ridge, whose mountain-tops, thickly wooded, afforded, in their dark-blue tint as we saw them, a lovely contrast with the splendour of the evening sky. There were abundant signs of active military life in this valley. Many thousands of tents were to be seen, the thin blue smoke of their camp-fires rising straight up in the still air; regiments of infantry were marching and counter-marching in various directions, and long waggon-trains were moving along the distant roads, escorted by cavalry detachments with gay pennons and guidons. From every indication we were convinced, as we set out on our return, that the enemy was preparing a general movement, probably a retrograde one; and this proved to be the fact.

18th August

It was late in the night when we reached the little village of Verdiersville, finding there Fitzhugh and Dabney, who reported, to General Stuart's great surprise, that our cavalry had not as yet arrived. Captain Fitzhugh was sent immediately in search of it, while the rest of us bivouacked in the little garden of the first farmhouse on the right of the village. Being so far outside of our lines we did not unsaddle, taking off only our blankets; and, for myself, I observed the precaution of lying down with my weapons, which made Lieutenant Dabney ask my why I would persist in making myself so uncomfortable; but he had reason to regret that he had not the prudence to profit by my example. We slept little during the night, and were awake with the dawn. About four A.M. we heard the heavy trampling of a long column of cavalry and the rumbling of artillery, and saw through the mist of the morning a strong body of horsemen crossing the road which led through the village, about 400 yards distant from us. General Stuart, confidently believing that this was Fitz Lee's brigade, sent Mosby and the only other courier we had with us to order the command to halt, and inform the commanding officer that he wished to see him immediately. A few seconds later we heard pistol-shots in rapid succession, and saw our two men coming towards us at a full run, a whole squadron of the enemy in close pursuit. I stood close to the General, handing him his blankets, as the Yankees, not more than a hundred and fifty yards from us, came rattling along. Stuart, without hat or haversack, jumped into the saddle, and, lifting his animal lightly and cleverly over the garden enclosure, gained the open field; after him Dabney, leaving behind him his sword and pistols. I had to run about fifteen steps to the place where my horse was tied to the fence, and reaching it, I unfastened the bridle, but had no time to throw the reins over his head. The animal became excited, and reared and plunged fearfully, and I was obliged to vault upon his back without the rein—a feat which I safely accomplished, and afterwards succeeded in forcing him through the garden gate, which was opportunely held open for me by the old lady of the house. Here I came directly upon the major who commanded the detachment, who placed his revolver at my breast and demanded my surrender; but before he or his men could divine my intentions, by a smart slap on my horse's head I turned it in the right direction, and, putting the spurs deep into his flanks, I extricated myself by a tremendous flying leap from the hostile circle which was rapidly drawing closer and closer around me. A shower of carbine and pistol bullets followed my retreating figure, and the Yankees, enraged by the trick I had played them, dashed after me in hot and furious pursuit. The greater number of my pursuers I soon left far behind me, thanks to the speed of my noble black charger; but a few, and the major foremost among them, were still close upon me. The latter discharged at me three barrels of his revolver, one of the bullets passing through my uniform without scratching the skin. After a race of nearly a mile the Yankees gave up the game, and I was able to get hold of my bridle, having been until then, so far as all management of my horse was concerned, in a perfectly helpless condition. Captain Fitzhugh, who had been taken prisoner by the same troops the previous night while on his way to look after Fitz Lee's brigade, and who, having given his parole, had been allowed to witness the whole affair, told me afterwards that he could not understand how I ever made my escape, and that at every shot fired by the major he had shut his eyes so that he might not see me fall.

Soon after getting clear of my pursuers I was joined by Mosby, and we rode back some distance to see what had become of our companions. We soon found the General bareheaded, looking at the disappearing column of the enemy, who were carrying off in triumph his beautiful hat, the present of a lady in Baltimore, and his haversack, containing some important maps and documents. Dabney made a sorry appearance as he came up without his arms, and I could not help maliciously asking him if he felt quite comfortable now. Stuart covered his head with his handkerchief as a protection against the sun, and we could not look at each other, despite our heat and indignation, without laughing heartily at the figures we respectively cut. The driver of a sutler's waggon belonging to a Georgia regiment whom we fell in with on our return, happily supplied General Stuart with a new hat; but the tidings of our mishap and adventure had spread like lightning through the whole army, and excited a great sensation. Wherever we passed an encampment on our way, the troops cheered us, and vociferously inquired of General Stuart what had become of his hat?

Fitz Lee's brigade, which had been detained by bad roads and a misconception of orders, did not join us until late that night, when Robertson's brigade also arrived on the Rapidan. Hampton's command had been left behind on the lines of the Chickahominy on picket duty. It was a great satisfaction to be with our troops again, and to be assured that an opportunity would soon be afforded us of paying off the Yankees for their recent attentions to us. On the morning of the 19th we marched with General Fitz Lee's brigade towards the Rapidan, where Robertson's command had encamped. There we bivouacked, and made our preparations for the fight which would in all probability take place on the following day. The army of General Pope had retreated, in accordance with our expectations, for a considerable distance, and taken a new position on the north side of the Rappahannock, leaving a large body of cavalry on our side of the river, in the neighbourhood of Brandy Station, on the Orange and Alexandria Railroad. This force we had orders to drive off.

20th August

At daybreak, with two brigades, we crossed the Rapidan. The passage was attended with difficulty, especially with the artillery, on account of the depth of the water. Lee's brigade was sent to the right, in the direction of Kelly's Ford; General Stuart and Staff marched with Robertson's brigade in the direction of Stevensburg, about one mile from Brandy Station, and both commands were to unite near the latter place. Our advance-guard came first in contact with the enemy, who, broken by the attack, fled in great confusion, and were pursued through the little village and more than a mile beyond it. The joy of the inhabitants, who for a long time had seen none but Federal soldiers, and who had been very badly treated by them, cannot be described. Men, women, and children came running out of all the houses towards us with loud exclamations of delight, many thanking God on their knees for their deliverance from the enemy. A venerable old lady asked permission to kiss our battle-flag, which had been borne throughout so many victorious fights, and blessed it with tears. The enthusiasm was so great that old men and boys, all that were able to carry a gun, in spite of our earnest remonstrances, followed our column to join in the fight with the detested Yankees.

The enemy, strongly reinforced, had now taken position about two miles from Stevensburg, on the outskirts of an extensive wood. Several small detachments had been pushed nearer towards us, and were patrolling on our flanks. One of these, in strength about half a squadron, mounted on grey horses, operated with great dash; but, advancing imprudently, was cut off by a body of our men, who fell upon them like a thunderbolt, killing and taking prisoners all but six, who saved themselves by the fleetness of their horses. The Federals dismounted many of their cavalrymen; and their line of sharpshooters, about a mile in length, poured upon us from the dense undergrowth a heavy fire, wounding several of our men and horses. This checked for a time our onward movement; but a large number of our troops, having been also dismounted, engaged the Federal tirailleurs with great gallantry, and we then charged with the main body upon the enemy's centre, and quickly drove them from their position. In the *mêlée* I captured a very good horse, which was unfortunately wounded very soon afterwards; but I took from it an excellent saddle and bridle that had belonged to an officer.

The enemy's retreat was now so rapid it was difficult to keep up with them, so that General Stuart, in order not to exhaust all our horses, took only one regiment, the 7th, in the pursuit with him, giving orders to the rest to follow at an easy trot. We were not long in reaching the heights near Brandy Station, from which we saw the Federal cavalry in line of battle in the large open plain before it. They were about 3500 strong, and, being drawn up in beautiful order, presented, with their arms glittering in the sun and their waving battle-flags, a splendid spectacle. Our brave fellows of the 7th were immediately placed to confront them, and the sharp-shooters of both parties were soon engaged in a brisk skirmish. With great impatience and anxiety we now waited the arrival of our reserves, and courier after courier was sent to hurry them to the spot. As even our colour-sergeant had to perform orderly duty, I took the battle-flag from his hands. This act attracted the attention of the enemy's sharpshooters at a distance of 800 yards, and they kept up, from that remote point, for some time, a surprisingly well-directed fire at me, one of their bullets cutting a new rent in the glorious old ensign.

The enemy now commenced his serious attack, and as our position, by reason of his vastly superior numbers, was a precarious one, General Stuart, taking the standard himself, ordered me to gallop in haste to our reserves, assume myself the command, and bring them up as fast as the horses could run. After a short, sharp ride, I reached the regiments, and with a loud voice commanded them, in the name of their

General, to move forward at a gallop. As I was well known to every man in the division, the order was at once obeyed, and in a few minutes I arrived with the column at the spot where General Stuart awaited us with the greatest solicitude, just in time to form hurriedly our lines and dash onward with the wild Virginia yell to the rescue of the 7th. Occupying the place of honour in front of the regiments, I shared to the full extent the excitement of the onset. The enemy, as usual, received us with a rattling volley, which emptied several saddles; but a few seconds more and we were in the midst of them, and their beautiful lines, which we had so much admired, had broken into flight. I had the satisfaction here of saving my life by a magnificent blow upon one of my antagonists, who, at the very moment of firing at me, received my full right-cut on the lower part of the neck, severing his head nearly from his body.

During the confusion of the *mêlée*, I discovered suddenly that a fresh squadron of the enemy was attacking us on the right flank, a manœuvre which, in the disorder inevitable after a charge, might have turned out disastrously for us; and, collecting about eighty of our men around me, I threw myself with this comparatively small force upon them. They at once slackened their pace, and when we had got within forty yards of them, halted, and received us with a volley which had very little effect. Upon this they fled precipitately, and were chased by us into the woods, where many of them were cut down and made prisoners. The main body of the enemy meanwhile had rallied several times, but again and again they had to yield before our impetuous advance, until the last of them were driven through the waves of the Rappahannock, where their infantry and artillery, strongly posted on the farther bank, offered them protection, leaving behind many of their dead and wounded and several hundred prisoners.

I had a happy feeling when riding out of the battle and

wiping the blood from my sword on my horse's mane. I was complimented by General Stuart most warmly for my behaviour, and to this day it is to me one of the most exciting recollections of the war. The whole had been a genuine cavalry-fight, with sabres crossing and single combat—incidents that very rarely occur in modern warfare—reminding me very much of the battle-pieces of the Dutch painter Wouvermans. The Yankees gave a most amusing description of me in their newspapers. In their accounts of the fight it was stated that the rebels in their charge had been led on by a giant, mounted on a tremendous horse, and brandishing wildly over his head a sword as long and big as a fence-rail, who had made a terrible impression on their troops. Fitz Lee did not arrive with his brigade on the battle-field until five o'clock in the afternoon, having himself had a hard encounter with a strong force of the enemy, which he had succeeded in driving back, taking many prisoners. The rest of the day we were busy in burying the dead and taking care of the wounded. I occupied myself chiefly with nursing Captain Redmond Burke of our Staff, who, while charging gallantly by my side, had received a bullet in the leg. We bivouacked on the battle-field, which is now a desert where the bones of men and animals are bleaching on every hand. Many fights afterwards took place on the same ground, and the place is historic. Future generations of Virginians, as they pick up rusted bits of shell, and bullets, and fragments of broken weapons, with which the whole field has been so often strewn, will recall with pride the noble deeds done by their fathers in the battles at Brandy Station.

21st August

During the night and early in the morning a large party of our army had arrived in the vicinity of Brandy Station, and soon after day-light the boom of artillery from Jackson's corps, which was in advance, announced to us that Old Stonewall was already at work. General Robert E. Lee had established his headquarters in a grove quite near us, and as we could get nothing for breakfast, we gladly accepted his invitation to share his own frugal meal, which consisted of rye coffee, bread, and wild honey. Orders were now given us to proceed immediately to the front and co-operate with Jackson in the event of any further extensive operations being attempted. The firing of the morning we soon found to have been nothing more than an artillery duel between some of Jackson's guns and the Federal batteries, from which the latter withdrew after one of their caissons had been exploded. Some infantry and cavalry, which had been posted on the opposite bank of the river, having also disappeared, we received orders to cross the Rappahannock, with two regiments of horse and a section of rifle pieces, and reconnoitre the enemy's position. As the road we had to take was tortuous, leading through several ravines up the hilly country on the other side of Cunningham's Ford, and thus affording the enemy a good opportunity for ambush, I was sent ahead with sixty of our men, to gain the heights as quickly as possible, and select without delay a favourable position for our guns. This we found readily enough, on a commanding hill in the midst of a corn-field, as we met with no resistance, and saw only a few squads of cavalry afar off. Riding over the ground where the enemy's batteries had recently been placed, I was surprised at the evidences it presented of the tremendous effects of Jackson's artillery. The spot where the caisson had been blown up was covered with dead and wounded men, and muskets and all sorts of equipments lay around, which had been thrown away by the supporting force. As this had consisted of new levies, the men had been demoralised by our well-directed fire, and fled in utter stampede upon the explosion of an ammunition-chest in the very midst of them. Among other things, I captured here one of the enemy's large regimental drums, which I presented to one of Jackson's regiments, to the delight of every man in it.

Scarcely had our rifle pieces been put in position, when there came in sight a considerable force of the enemy's cavalry, which was held in check only by the accurate aim and rapid service of our gunners, and the bold advance of the 5th Virginia Cavalry under Colonel Rosser on our left. We very soon discovered, however, that just now the enemy was disinclined to allow any further proceedings on our part. Several batteries from different points opened upon us, and a large body of infantry made its appearance, throwing forward at double-quick two lines of skirmishers in excellent order. The command was at once given for us to retire; and as Colonel Rosser's regiment, by reason of the enemy's rapid advance, had been placed in great danger of being cut off, I was sent to warn him of the peril of his position, leaving him to get out of it as best he could. I reached Rosser in safety, but, to rejoin General Stuart without loss of time, I was compelled to ride back along the same line, upon which the enemy's skirmishers had been pushing closer and closer, and where again shot after shot was fired at me. It is not a pleasant experience to serve, for so long a distance, as a target for practised marksmen, and to count the chances, with every lope of one's horse, of getting safely past them. The last eight or ten of these tirailleurs were not more than eighty or a hundred yards distant from my path, and I could distinctly hear the officer calling out to his men to take a quiet aim and bring that impudent rebel officer down. But they missed me, and the tall stalks of a neighbouring corn-field soon concealed me for a time from their view. My troubles, however, were not yet over. On getting in sight of the ford, I discovered it to be already occupied by the Yankee cavalry, who imme-

diately observed me, and started in pursuit. The sharpshooters being now also again on my track, firing incessantly, and
yelling like bloodhounds, I had but one way left; so, urging
my horse* some distance higher up the river, and forcing him
to a tremendous leap from the high bank into the deep
stream, I crossed it swimming, the Yankee bullets like hail-
stones slashing the water all around me. I was received with
great enthusiasm and loud cheering by our own men, who
had witnessed the whole scene, full of anxiety for my fate.
Rosser also reached us safely with his command some hours
later, but he had been obliged to cut his way through, with
the loss of several of his men and two of his officers.

A heavy cannonade was kept up for the remainder of the
day by the enemy's batteries, which took position on the
opposite bank of the river, and were answered with spirit by
Jackson's guns, but little damage was done on either side. The
Yankees employed here a shell which, being closed by a
peculiar screw, made in its flight a most extraordinary noise,
very like the high notes of the mocking-bird. This excited the
lively merriment of our careless fellows, who greeted every
one of these melodious missiles with a loud piping imitation
from one wing of our army to the other.

22d August

The darkness of the night had not yet given way to dawn,
when we again set out for active operations, with portions of
Fitz Lee's and Robertson's brigades and our horse-artillery,
numbering about 2000 men. A strong demonstration was to
be made in the direction of Wellford's Ford on the Rappa-

---

*This was the same charger which saved me at Verdiersville by his fleetness, an
excellent coal-black Virginia horse, of medium size, well-bred and strongly

hannock, to divert the attention of the Federals, and facilitate the daring raid we were afterwards to undertake. Accordingly, we marched about five miles northward, crossed the Hazel river, a tributary of the Rappahannock, and arrived about eight o'clock at Wellford's Ford, where the opposite banks of the latter stream were occupied by the Yankees in great numbers. The enemy's artillery was soon engaged in a brisk duel with our two batteries of horse-artillery, which suffered severely, losing many men and horses, in consequence of the superior positions and greater weight of metal of their antagonists. About ten o'clock we were relieved by Jackson's batteries, and, withdrawing from the field without the knowledge of the enemy, proceeded in rapid trot eight miles higher up the river to Waterloo Bridge, where we crossed it, and continued our march to Warrenton. Late in the evening we entered this little town, and were received with the liveliest demonstrations of joy by the inhabitants.

We were now again exactly in the rear of the Federal army, the right wing of which we had marched round; and our bold design was nothing less than to capture the Commander-in-Chief and his headquarters, which, as our scouts reported, had been established at Catlett's Station, a point on the Orange and Alexandria Railroad. After an hour's rest to feed our horses, we left Warrenton behind us, continuing our march with great caution. Night was now rapidly approaching, and the angry clouds, which had been gathering in the sky throughout the afternoon, soon burst upon us in a tremendous thunderstorm and the heaviest rain I ever wit-

---

built, but one of the fleetest and best jumping horses I ever rode. I could fire from his back as accurately as on foot, and the animal seemed to understand perfectly his master's intentions, so that whenever I raised my revolver, my faithful black, however excited he might have been the moment before, stood as quiet as possible, one fore-foot raised from the ground, scarcely breathing

nessed. The narrow roads became in a short time running streams of water, and the little creeks on our route foamed and raged like mountain torrents. But this was the very condition of the elements we could most have desired. The enemy's pickets, in the fury of the storm, indifferent to everything but their own personal comfort, were picked up, one after another, by our advanced-guard to the last man, and we had thus arrived within the immediate neighbourhood of the main body of the enemy without the least information on their part of our approach.

Having been sent back by General Stuart with some orders to the rear of our column, I had, on my return, a very amusing adventure. In passing one of the farmhouses on the road, my sharp eye discovered, behind the curtains of one of the windows, a Federal officer, who disappeared on my approach. Instantly dismounting, I knocked at the door, ordering it to be opened at once; but instead of this, I heard tables and chairs moved hurriedly against it, which so much provoked me that I threw my whole weight upon the light frame. The door gave way with a loud crash, and hurled my Yankee, with all his chair-and-table fortifications, over upon the floor of the little parlour. Before I could lay hands upon the poor fellow—who, being unarmed, and seeing himself at the mercy of so powerful-looking an adversary, had risen from his humiliating position with the drollest expression of extreme terror on his face—a very pretty young woman came out of the adjoining room, bearing a waiter in her hands with a bottle of wine and other refreshments, which she offered me in the most graceful manner possible, placing herself at the same time between me and my victim. Tactics like these were so novel to me that for a moment I quite lost my self-

---

until the shot had been fired, and then bounding forward with all his native animation.

possession; but, very soon recovering my wits, I thanked her politely for her hospitality, which I should be very ready to accept after I had done my duty. But approaching again and again my prisoner, I encountered again and again this charming obstacle, so that we played for a good while the juvenile game of fox-and-goose. The scene of action had in the mean time shifted towards a broad door-like window, which opened upon the garden side, and from the gathering darkness, and its proximity to the surrounding forest, afforded a very fair opportunity of escape; so seeing no other way of bringing the interview to a satisfactory conclusion, I levelled my pistol at the officer's breast, and said, "Madam, if you cannot bear separation from the enemy of your country, I will leave him with you, but not alive." This had the desired effect. The fair creature abandoned her position, and in the midst of her bitter tears and pathetic appealings, which my sense of duty alone enabled me to resist, I bore my prisoner off. He was a handsome young man, a lieutenant in an infantry regiment, and had contracted an engagement of marriage with his protectress before the war commenced.

The rain was still pouring in torrents at eleven P.M., when we came directly upon the Federal encampment, which extended about a mile in length on either side of the railroad. We halted at the distance of about two hundred yards to form our long lines and make our dispositions, which we accomplished without attracting the notice of our adversaries in the heavy rain and amid the incessantly-rolling thunder. The sound of a single trumpet was the signal for nearly 2000 horsemen to dash, as they did with loud shouts, upon the utterly paralysed Yankees, who were cut down and made prisoners before they had recovered from their first astonishment. I myself had instructions to proceed with a select body of men to General Pope's tent, which was pointed out to us by a negro whom we had captured during the day, and who had been "impressed" by one of Pope's staff-officers as a servant. Unfortunately for us, the Commander-in-Chief had, for once, this day his "headquarters in the saddle"—an intention which he had so boastfully announced at the commencement of his campaign—and had started a few hours before our arrival on a reconnaissance, so that we found only his private baggage, official papers, horses, &c. &c. I obtained as booty a magnificent field-glass, which was afterwards of great service to me. The scene had become in the mean time a most exciting one, and the confusion, which is always the consequence of a night attack, had reached its highest point. The Federal troops on the other side of the railroad, which was not so easily accessible, had recovered from their panic, and, reinforced by some companies of the so-called Bucktail Rifles, commenced a vigorous fire upon our men, who were scattered all over the field burning and plundering to their hearts' content. In the background our reserves were actively employed in firing the immense depots and waggon-trains and the railway bridge; and the flames, rising from a hundred different points at once, reddened the dark cloudy night. It was difficult to recognise friend or foe. Shots fell in every direction—bullets whizzed through the air on all sides—no one knew where to strike a blow or where to level his revolver—no one could be certain whether the man riding at his elbow was Federal or Confederate.

Having received orders from General Stuart to cut the telegraph wire, I proceeded with twenty men to the execution of this purpose; but just as we had reached a pole, I saw suddenly, by the vivid illumination of a flash of lightning, a whole company of the enemy drawn up in line not fifteen steps from us; and I had just time to call out to my men to lie down, when a rattling volley sent a shower of bullets over our heads. I galloped back to the General asking for a squadron to assist me in carrying out his orders. The squadron was immediately granted. Attacking the Federal infantry myself in front, while Colonel Rosser took them in flank, we succeeded in driving them farther back. But they still maintained a rapid fusillade, and to climb the pole and cut the wire was a very dangerous undertaking. A young fellow of not more than seventeen volunteered to perform the daring feat, and, using my shoulders as a starting-point, he ran up the pole with the agility of a squirrel; the wire, severed by a stroke of his sabre, was soon dangling to the ground; and the brave boy escaped unhurt, several bullets, however, having struck the pole during his occupation of it.

About three o'clock in the morning the work of destruction at Catlett's Station was complete, and the order was given to re-form and start upon our return. The alarm had been spread over a great part of the Federal wing, and troops were marching against us from several directions. Our success, in spite of the great confusion of the midnight attack, had been very decided. We had killed and wounded a great number of the enemy; captured 400 prisoners, among whom were several officers, and more than 500 horses; destroyed several hundred tents, large supply-depots, and long waggon-trains; secured, in the possession of the Quartermaster of General Pope, 500,000 dollars in greenbacks, and 20,000 in gold; and, most important of all, had deprived the Federal Commander of all his baggage and private and official papers, exposing to us the effective strength of his army, the disposition of his different *corps d'armée*, and the plans of his whole campaign. Our loss was comparatively small; and after a rapid march, impeded only by the deluge of water still pouring down upon us, and compelling us to swim several creeks which were ordinarily but a few inches in depth, we reached Warrenton, with all our prisoners and booty, at eight o'clock the following morning.

We had but a few minutes' rest in the little town of

Warrenton, when our rear-guard reported a strong force in pursuit of us, and a heavy cannonade from the direction of Jackson's position summoned us to move on. These few minutes, however, we employed to advantage. Wet by the rain of twelve hours, and chilled by the sharp air of the morning, we found grateful reinvigoration in the viands that were offered us by the kind citizens of the place, who heard with the greatest delight of the success of our expedition. I was enjoying some delicious coffee, served by the fair hands of a lovely and accomplished young girl, whose acquaintance I had made the previous day, when, hearing that we had taken Pope's Quartermaster, she laughed heartily, and told us that when he had been quartered at her father's house a few days before, he had, in boasting of the magnificent army of Pope, declared his intention of entering Richmond before the end of the month, and that she had made him a bet of a bottle of champagne that he would not. She now regarded her wager as lost, as the Quartermaster would doubtless enter Richmond before the time specified—earlier, indeed, but under other circumstances, than he had expected—and she begged me to obtain permission from General Stuart to pay the champagne. General Stuart, of course, readily acceded to the playful request; and as our column passed along she stood at the garden gate of her home, with a malicious smile on her face and the bottle in her hand, and paid her wager most gracefully to the Yankee Quartermaster, who took the joke very well and the champagne very willingly, declaring that he should always be happy to drink the health of so charming a person.

23d to 26th August

We were soon out of sight of Warrenton. The glowing radiance of the sun breaking at last through the parting clouds brought life and cheer to our drenched and chilled column. About twelve o'clock we reached the scene of action, where there had been only a heavy artillery-fight, and not, as we had supposed, a general engagement. Our pursuers having stopped at Warrenton, we had therefore a short period of welcome inactivity, and the orders to dismount and feed the horses were received with pleasure by every man of our fatigued command. As soon as I had taken the proper care of my horse, and emptied my long cavalry boots of several quarts of water they contained, I fell fast asleep in the shade of a gigantic hickory-tree, from which refreshing slumber I was suddenly aroused some hours later by a spirited cannonade. The enemy were advancing, and the guns of Robertson's brigade had engaged a Federal battery. One of our squadrons, going forward to support the artillery, and being unnecessarily exposed by their captain, suffered here severely by a single well-directed shell, which, bursting at the head of the column, killed and wounded fourteen men. The fighting ceased at night, and we encamped upon the ground occupied by us during the day. At daybreak on the 24th, the enemy still advancing in heavy force, we marched rapidly towards the Rappahannock, which we found much swollen, but which we crossed in safety at eight o'clock.

General Stuart now galloped over to the headquarters of General Robert E. Lee, about five miles distant, and ordered me to proceed with the Staff and couriers to Waterloo Bridge, six miles higher up the river, near which a portion of our cavalry was to encamp. This bridge was now the only one left which for a considerable tract of country afforded a passage across the Rappahannock, and its preservation was therefore of great importance to our future military operations. Just as I reached the bridge an orderly galloped up to me at full speed, reporting that a strong body of the enemy, consisting of infantry, cavalry, and artillery, was rapidly advancing upon us, and was at that moment not more than a mile from the spot. The position of a senior staff-officer in the Confederate army was a very important and responsible one, and General Stuart had given me instructions, in his absence, to issue any necessary commands in his name; so I immediately des-patched a courier to the commanding officer of the nearest regiment, the 7th Virginia Cavalry, with orders for him to proceed with all haste to the river, and post his men as dismounted sharpshooters on the woody cliffs on both sides of the bridge; and galloping myself after our artillery, which had marched some distance to the rear, and taking back with me the first two pieces I fell in with, I arrived at the bridge just in time to receive the dense column of the approaching Federals with a destructive fire of canister from my light howitzers, which for a little while effectually checked their advance. It was not long, however, before they threw their skirmishers forward, and a brisk fusillade was rattling along the line. Their batteries also opened heavily upon us, and were answered gallantly by my howitzers. Matters were proceeding thus favourably when, about twelve o'clock, General Stuart, whom I had informed by an orderly of the state of affairs, arrived with reinforcements, expressing his great satisfaction with what had been done, and thanking me for having saved the bridge. The fight now became more and more general. The enemy brought several brigades of infantry into action, and opened upon us with several new batteries. In the mean time all the guns of our horse-artillery had arrived upon the ground, and were pouring their deadly missiles into the Federal ranks. Twice did the Yankees succeed in setting fire to the bridge with incendiary shell, but the flames were instantly extinguished by our gallant men. Several times their storming columns, advancing at a double-quick, got nearly across to our side of the river; but again and again were they hurled back, leaving their dead and wounded behind them, by the well-directed fire of our sharpshooters and of our field-pieces, which were now concentrated upon the narrow path. The darkness of the night at last put an end to the conflict, and we found ourselves with small loss masters of the situation against vastly superior numbers.

Early on the morning of the 25th the contest was renewed, and for several hours we had very hot work, until about eleven A.M. we were relieved by our infantry, and enabled to take some rest from our exhausting duties. During the afternoon I received from Fitz Lee's Quartermaster, Major Mason, as a mount for my negro servant William, an excellent grey mule, which was among our captures at Catlett's Station, and will often be mentioned in succeeding portions of this narrative. It will be recollected that some of the *spolia opima* of Catlett's Station were greenbacks and gold. As these were contained in solid iron safes, of which the key had been lost, it was not the easiest matter in the world to get at them. It was thought, however, a profitable employment of our earliest leisure to investigate General Pope's sub-treasury, and our men had been hammering away at the safes for some time without result, when General Stuart turned round to me and said, laughingly, "If nobody can open these strong boxes, we must call on Major *Armstrong* (a nickname he had given me) to assist us." Accepting the banter at once, I delivered a few heavy blows upon the safes with a serviceable axe, which laid them open, amid the loud cheers of our soldiers, who, with their accustomed idle curiosity, had formed a large circle round us. Two boxes of excellent cigars, which the Yankee Quartermaster had kept in this place of security, doubtless as the Cockney at the French custom-house expressed it, "pour fumigation luimême," fell to me as my share of the spoil—a great luxury indeed, to one who had long been deprived of the aromatic Havana weed.

In the evening I was sent over to General Robert E. Lee's

headquarters to carry thither the captured despatches and papers; and being invited by the General to partake of his modest supper, I had to relate many particulars of our recent raid, to which he listened with great interest. There was a good deal of merriment among the young staff-officers at headquarters concerning one of our Catlett's Station prisoners, whom I had taken over with me under charge of a courier for further instructions—and who, just as we were sending off the main body of these prisoners to Richmond, had been discovered to be a good-looking woman in full Federal uniform. In order that she might follow to the field her warlike lord, she had enlisted as a private soldier in the same company with him, and now claimed to be excepted from the rest of the prisoners as a privilege of her sex. It was decided, however, that this modern Jeanne d'Arc must share the fate of her comrades for the present, and further decision in the case was left to the Richmond authorities. The whole of Longstreet's corps had now been removed from Richmond to Culpepper, and occupied the line of the Rappahannock opposite the Federal army. Jackson's troops had been quietly withdrawn from the front, and his corps had been in motion during the whole of the afternoon, marching nobody but General Lee and his Lieutenant knew where. I also went back to General Stuart with marching orders for himself and the greater part of his cavalry.

26th and 27th August

The line of our march lay directly in the tracks of Jackson's troops, who, by the extraordinary rapidity of their movements, had gained the title of the "Foot-Cavalry" of the army, and who had now been taken by their great leader upon an expedition in flank of the enemy, which was brilliantly successful, and insured the failure of Pope's whole campaign. Our column consisted of nearly 6000 horse and our flying artillery. Starting at daybreak, we forded the Rappahannock near Hinzen's Mill, eight miles above Waterloo Bridge, and proceeded with great caution all day through the extensive forests of the county of Faughire, taking by-paths in the woods, where we were often compelled to ride in single file. Passing near the little town of Orleans, we reached Salem late in the afternoon, where at last we overtook Jackson's corps, but where we did not tarry, pushing forward in advance to Gainesville, at which place we arrived after night-fall. Here a squadron was left behind on picket, and here I received orders from General Stuart, who had continued his march to Bristow Station, on the Orange and Alexandria Railroad, to remain and keep open the communications between himself and Jackson. At Gainesville we passed a most exciting and unsatisfactory night. As the day had been excessively hot, I had given orders to my men to unsaddle, that our weary horses might be refreshed; and I had just taken the saddle off my own steed, when our pickets, who had been posted about a mile outside the village towards Centreville, came in at full gallop, reporting the enemy's cavalry in close pursuit of them. We had barely time to get ready for action when the Yankee advance-guard came thundering along through the darkness of the night. They were received with a sharp fire from the revolvers of myself and my staff of couriers; but in a moment, supported by our charging squadron, we threw ourselves upon them, driving them back in confusion, and taking several of their number prisoners. The enemy made no further effort to dislodge us; but our pickets, excited by the suddenness of the first attack, rode in five or six times during the night with false alarms, which brought us into the saddle, and I hailed with great satisfaction the daylight, which relieved me from my anxiety. I now pushed rapidly forward to Bristow Station, which our cavalry had already left, after having accomplished their work of destruction. They had torn up the track of the railroad for a long distance, captured four trains and a considerable number of prisoners, and demolished everything that could be of the least value to the enemy. There was now no time to be lost by us. From the plains of Manassas, about seven miles distant, rolled the thunder of cannon, and I hurried on as fast as our horses could carry us, crossing the memorable stream of Bull Run, just in the neighbourhood where the first battle of the war had been fought, and reaching Manassas about nine o'clock in the morning.

The plateau of Manassas presents an area of about three miles square, over which the Yankees had built an irregular town of storehouses, barracks, huts, and tents, which was fortified on all sides by continuous redoubts. Here were collected stores and provisions, ammunition and equipments for an army of 100,000 men (besides an enormous quantity of luxuries unknown to warfare), the capture of which was a most important success to our arms. The sight that was presented to me at the moment of my arrival was truly a magnificent one. In front, rapidly advancing, were the long lines of our cavalry, their pennons fluttering gaily in the morning air, and moving in company with them might be seen the horse-artillery, from whose pieces, as well as from the guns we had captured in the redoubts and were now serving with admirable effect, dense clouds of white smoke were spread over the plain; on the left Jackson's veteran columns were pushing forward at a double-quick, while in the distant view the blue masses of the enemy were in rapid flight towards the glimmering woods. I found General Stuart exceedingly delighted with his success. He had taken the troops guarding the place completely by surprise, capturing the greater part of them and twelve pieces of artillery in the redoubts without much fighting, and had just routed three brigades of infantry that had been sent from Alexandria as reinforcements. The enemy in their flight had left behind their dead and wounded and more than 1500 runaway negroes—men, women, and children. The quantity of booty was very great, and the amount of luxuries absolutely incredible. It was exceedingly amusing to see here a ragged fellow regaling himself with a box of pickled oysters or potted lobster; there another cutting into a cheese of enormous size, or emptying a bottle of champagne; while hundreds were engaged in opening the packages of boots and shoes and other clothing, and fitting themselves with articles of apparel to replace their own tattered garments. The liquors, with a proper degree of precaution, were at once seized by the Quatermaster and placed under a strong guard, to avert the consequences of immoderate indulgence. There was a good deal of jealousy between Jackson's artillery and our own with regard to the disposition that was to be made of the captured horses. Among other prizes of this description we had taken a Yankee sutler's waggon—one of those large gaudily-painted vans drawn always by four excellent horses; and General Stuart desired me to trot rapidly over with the waggon to our horse-artillery, assign the horses to the nearest battery, and dispose of the contents as I thought proper. It gave me great pleasure, after I had changed the four stately bays into stout artillery-horses, to divide the plunder among our brave cannoneers, who soon collected round the waggon in large numbers, and received the contents with loud demonstrations of delight. The different boxes were speedily opened by my sword, and were found to contain shirts, hats, pocket-handkerchiefs, oranges, lemons, wines, cigars, and all sorts of knick-knacks. I helped myself only to two boxes of regalias, which I managed to tie securely to the pommel of my saddle.

We were occupied throughout the day in collecting as

much of the booty as we could carry off with us, and preparing the rest for destruction. During the afternoon we received reports that the Federal army was moving rapidly upon us from various points, and very soon Ewell's division, which formed Jackson's rear, was hotly engaged with their advance-guard. The main body of our infantry commenced now to march off quietly in the direction of Centreville, turning afterwards towards the Stone Bridge and Sudley's Mill, while the cavalry remained on the plains to apply the torch to the captured property as soon as this might be necessary. All the storehouses and depots were filled with straw and hay, and combustibles were also placed in forty-six railway cars, which had been pushed closely together. The battle had in the mean time become fierce—the thunder of cannon and the roar of musketry rolling incessantly; but although the enemy in vastly superior numbers attacked us with vigour, and although the old hero Ewell lost a leg in the conflict (a casualty which disabled him for a long time from again taking the field), they were wholly unable to break the lines of those veterans who had given their commander the name of Stonewall, and who held their ground until night put an end to the slaughter. Then they withdrew from their position and joined the main body of their corps.

Just as the sun was disappearing behind the range of distant hills that formed the western horizon, the flames were rising from a hundred different points of the plain, bringing out vividly each one of a legion of dark figures which were moving about, in the midst of the conflagration, to assist in spreading the fire, and fanning it into fury wherever it languished. The glow reflected from all these burning buildings, tents, and railway cars, with the red glare from the mouths of the cannon, and the sparkling of the bursting shells as seen against the darkening forest, made up a spectacle of strange mysterious splendour. After all that we wished to preserve had been secured, and all that we wished to destroy had been laid in ashes, we followed the route of our retreat towards Centreville. In the confusion of the moment, and the increasing darkness of the night, I had become separated, with several other members of the Staff and a number of couriers, from General Stuart, with no hope of finding him until morning, so we bivouacked in a small pine grove in the neighbourhood of Centreville, which place had already been passed by the greater portion of our troops.

28th and 29th August

At an early hour of the following day we set out to join General Stuart at Sudley's Mill, a place about eight miles north of Manassas, where Jackson's corps was drawn up in line of battle, expecting a fresh attack of the enemy, and where the prisoners taken during the last few days, about 1800 in number, were collected; but the indefatigable Stuart had already started, at the time of our arrival, with his cavalry upon a new enterprise in the enemy's rear, leaving orders for me to follow him to the village of Haymarket. I pushed forward immediately with Lieutenant Dabney and two couriers, several of the other members of the Staff being obliged to remain behind on account of the weary condition of their horses, and soon discovered that the journey we had to perform was an exceedingly difficult one. Since General Stuart had left Sudley's Mills, several hours before our own departure from that place, the position of the hostile army had been a good deal changed, the left wing having shifted more to our right, and the cavalry patrols were crossing the country in every direction, so that at many points of our progress we were informed that bodies of Federal horse had passed along but a few minutes before our approach. About two o'clock in the afternoon there was a heavy cannonade and continuous musketry-fire heard in the direction of Jackson's position, announcing that the enemy had commenced their attack; but, at the same time, we heard a cannonade in the direction of Haymarket, and believing Stuart to be there at work, I regarded it as my duty to continue my march. Very soon, however, we heard firing all around us, and I was convinced that we had been misled by the sound, and the great number of narrow unfrequented bridle-paths in the woods. As it was impossible to decide where we should find friend or foe, our situation became a very critical one. About dusk we discovered in a small opening before us a negro on horseback, who had no sooner seen us than he galloped off in hurried flight, but was overtaken after a short chase by one of our couriers. It was difficult to make him believe that we were not Yankees, and his delight was indescribable when at last he recognised us as friends. He told me that a squad of Federal cavalry was at that moment engaged in pillaging his master's house, which he pointed out to us not more than three-quarters of a mile distant—that he had saved himself on one of the horses in the stable—that the enemy were all around us—and that Haymarket was occupied by them in strong force. Of Stuart and his cavalry the faithful negro had not seen or heard anything. Being perfectly at a loss, and nearly cut off from our army on all sides, I resolved to attempt returning by the same route we had come, and, protected by the darkness of the fast-coming night, to endeavour to rejoin Jackson's men. Silently we rode along the narrow lane for several hours, each one of us fully conscious of the danger of our situation, when suddenly the tramp of a body of horsemen sounded right in front of us—a scouting party as we could scarcely doubt, of the Federal cavalry. I explained to my companions that there was no choice left but to cut our way through. Our plan hastily formed was this.

The two couriers were to ride on either side of Dabney and myself, and to fire right and left with their revolvers, leaving us to open the way in the centre with our sabres. The advancing party having now arrived within twenty-five steps from us, I gave the customary order, "Halt! one man forward!" and, this being disregarded, the loud command, "Charge!" Just at this moment several voices cried out, "That is Major von Borcke! halt, halt: we are friends!" which at once checked our furious onset, and we found, to our great surprise and delight, and amid hearty laughter on all sides, that we had been on the eve of attacking the remaining part of General Stuart's Staff and escort, who had also been separated from the General, and, like ourselves, were in search of him. We heard now that the way to Jackson, who had repulsed the enemy after a sanguinary conflict, was perfectly unobstructed, and that one of our cavalry regiments, the 1st Virginia, was encamped a couple of miles farther to the rear. Thither we at once determined to ride, that we might refresh our weary horses, and seek rest for ourselves for the few remaining hours of the night.

We joined General Stuart early on the morning of the 29th at Sudley's Mill, where Jackson had established his headquarters in a building which was used, at the same time, as an hospital for several hundred of the wounded of the previous day's battle. Stuart was exceedingly amused at our story, and laughed very much at the adventure of the night before, confessing, however, that it was through his fault that I had become involved in the difficulty. At seven o'clock on the morning of the 29th the attack was renewed by General Pope, who tried his best to crush Jackson before Longstreet, who was rapidly approaching with his strong corps, could arrive. As old Stonewall had already gone to the front at the time of my arrival, I was sent to him by General Stuart to get orders for the disposition of the cavalry; and to my question at starting, "Where shall I find General Jackson?" my chief replied, with a smile, "Where the fight is hottest." So I galloped forward over the battle-field, still strewn with the dead of yesterday's conflict, towards a point where twenty pieces of our artillery, concentrated into one battery, were hotly engaged with an equal number of Federal guns. Here I felt sure of finding Jackson himself. The Yankee batteries were firing much too high, throwing their shot and shell in rapid succession upon a piece of soft swampy ground about a quarter of a mile beyond our position, over which I must ride if I did not choose to make a long circuit around it. My horse had already been sinking several times a little in the bog, when suddenly the ground beneath him, which was covered with a treacherous surface of verdure, gave way entirely, and my brave bay sank till half his body was buried in the morass. I leaped from his back just in time to gain a secure footing myself, but every effort to extricate the animal was in vain. Meanwhile shells were plunging and bursting nearer and nearer to me, throwing upon myself and horse a heavy shower of mud and dirt, excited by which, and not a little insulted, the noble beast made renewed exertions to get free, each time sinking deeper and deeper in the mire. I had already decided to abandon my steed and execute my orders on foot, when a body of our infantry marching by came very readily to my assistance, and, by dint of spades, ropes, and poles, managed to liberate the animal, which emerged from the bog perfectly black, and trembling in every limb, as I jumped again into the saddle. Without further accident I reached General Jackson, who, looking at me with astonishment, said, with his quiet smile, "Major, where do you get your dye? I could never have believed that a bay horse might be changed so quickly into a coal-black one." Then, upon my explaining my mission, he gave me orders for Stuart, who was to operate with his cavalry on the right flank, and hold the enemy in check until Longstreet could take his place.

On my return to Sudley's Mill I found everything changed, and great excitement prevailing there. Two brigades of the enemy had suddenly appeared in our rear, just where our provision and ammunition trains had been stationed. General Stuart had only a small portion of his cavalry and one battery of his horse-artillery at hand, but he was making every effort to save the trains, which were of the first importance to our army. There was the greatest confusion possible among the waggon-drivers: many of whose teams were "hitched on," and were driving off at the top of their speed; others had to be held back by main force to the performance of their duty, and made to put the horses to the waggons. All this time a rattling hail of the enemy's bullets was falling all around us. The quartermaster in charge of the trains, and many others, had already been killed. A little coolness and energy on the part of our commander, however, soon wrought a great improvement in the situation. Our sharpshooters were quickly dismounted and placed behind a fence, where they received the enemy with a very well-directed fire; while Pelham, who had come up at full gallop with his guns, threw from a favourable position such a deadly shower of grape and canister upon the advancing lines of the foe, as brought them suddenly to a halt.

Having been ordered to place the right wing of our sharpshooters, I was brought very conspicuously to the notice of the enemy as the only man on horseback at this part of the field, and several bullets had already whistled past me in uncomfortable proximity to my person, when one of the Yankee marksmen sent a ball, to my infinite annoyance, crashing right through a box of regalia cigars which, it may be remembered, I had tied to the pommel of my saddle as my part of the spoils of the sutler's waggon taken at Manassas

Plains. I was just expressing my displeasure in pretty round terms, and directing the attention of some of our men to the impudent fellow who had fired the shot, when General Stuart rode up and directed me to ride in full haste back to Jackson, and make report of the state of affairs, and order, in his name, the first troops I should meet on the way to his immediate assistance.

After a rapid gallop of a few minutes I met two brigades of A. P. Hill's division, which I ordered to proceed at a double-quick to the point of danger. Very soon I encountered General Hill himself, to whom I made the necessary explanations, and who at once proceeded in person to the threatened position. Meanwhile the cannonade had become fearful, more and more batteries had joined in the action, and from a hundred pieces of artillery the thunder of the battle roared along our lines. In the dense smoke that enveloped the field, and amid the bursting of innumerable shells, it was not easy to find General Jackson, whom I discovered at last sitting comfortably on a caisson, quietly writing his despatches. After I had made my report, I remarked to the General that it had been very difficult to find him, and that this was rather a hot place for him to be in. "My dear Major," he replied, "I am very much obliged to you for the orders you have given. Hill will take care of the enemy in the rear. I know what they are; there cannot be more than two brigades of them. And as for my position here, I believe we have been together in hotter places before." The great hero then calmly resumed his writing, cannon-shot ploughing up the ground all around him and covering his MS. with dust, so that, like one of Napoleon's generals under similar circumstances, he was in no need of sand to dry up his ink. In the mean time the trains had been saved, and the bold Yankees that had attacked our rear had been driven back with fearful loss, leaving the greater part of their number prisoners in our hands.

It was now about mid-day, and the engagement had become general. The Federal Commander-in-Chief again and again attempted to break Jackson's line, but again and again his forces had to recoil with wasted ranks from the STONE WALL in front of them. We were pressing slowly forward on our right, where our horse-artillery, under the gallant Pelham, did excellent service. Our cavalry was also here actively employed, one regiment alone, the 5th Virginia, under Colonel Rosser, taking 500 prisoners. Many of the enemy's wounded having fallen into our hands, we had erected a temporary hospital in a shady grove, near a cool clear spring, where several hundred of them had been received. It may have been that the enemy by accident fired too high, or they may have mistaken this group of men for a body of our troops, but suddenly a heavy fire was concentrated upon this point, and it was indeed a sickening sight to see shot after shot strike in among them, shell after shell explode over this dense mass of sufferers, who, with limbs shattered or lacerated by ghastly wounds, attempted to crawl out of the way, cursing their own friends for the agonies they had to endure.

The enemy, finding that they could not dislodge us, did not renew their attack later than four o'clock in the afternoon, and at five the advance of Longstreet's corps made its appearance, amid loud cheering all along our lines. These troops took up their position in line of battle on Jackson's right wing as fast as they arrived, and before sundown the last division of the corps, Hood's Texans, had come up, forming the extreme right of Longstreet's line. Yet farther on was Stuart with a portion of his cavalry—Fitz Lee, with the larger part of his brigade, having been detailed to Jackson on the extreme left. General Robert E. Lee had also now arrived, and the men of our army, throughout its entire extent, were cheered by the confident belief that on the following day a great victory would be gained for our arms.

Shortly before dusk we had yet a brisk little cannonade between some Federal batteries and a section of the famous Washington Artillery, which occupied a space intervening between Hood's Texans and our own position. While this was going on, a body of Federal cavalry impudently trotted over an open field quite within range of our guns, which opening opportunely upon them, and dropping a shell or two that exploded directly among their ranks, the whole squadron scattered in every direction, amidst the derisive cheers of the gunners and all of our troops who witnessed their rapid disappearance. After nightfall the Texans became engaged in a very heavy skirmish, which sounded for some time like a general conflict, but which ended, without much loss on either side, in their driving the enemy from a small piece of ground in our front. Late in the night I was requested by General Stuart to bear him company in a little reconnaissance outside our lines, which came very near terminating disastrously, as on our return, in the thick darkness, we were received with a sharp but fortunately ill-aimed fire from our own men. The rest of the night we slept by the side of our guns, and as we could not unsaddle our horses, I had nothing for a pillow but a cartridge-box which I had picked up on the ground.

30th August

The two great armies were now in full force confronting each other. Each numbered from 50,000 to 60,000 men, though Pope's may have a little exceeded the latter number, as he had been drawing reinforcements from Alexandria, where his reserves of 20,000 men had been collected. The early morning and forenoon of this memorable day passed in comparative quiet, yet before set of sun was to be fought one of the most sanguinary conflicts of the war. From time to time the rattle of slight skirmishing sounded along the lines, as it always does when two hostile armies are brought so closely together, and at long intervals the boom of cannon broke, like a sullen warning, through the hazy, sultry air. On our right was a body of Federal cavalry operating with great audacity, and as some of their skirmishers approached our position with what I regarded as excessive impudence, I determined (with the consent of General Stuart) to give them a lesson. At my request General Hood detailed to me several of his Texan marksmen, who moved forward with alacrity and pleasure to this exciting little enterprise, crawling through the high grass and along the fences with the suppleness of serpents, in a manner that might have excited the envy of the cleverest Indian on the war-path. The Federal cavalryman seemed not a little surprised to see me, as being on horseback I was the only one of the party visible to them, and were evidently quite undecided what to do when I halted at a distance from them of about 200 yards. Among my riflemen, one had been pointed out to me as the best shot, who was a Prussian by birth, but who had lived for many years on the prairies of Texas. He was the first to fire. Raising his rifle, he said to me with a certain pride, a smile lighting up his brown weather-beaten features, "Now, Major, you shall see what an old Prussian can do." An instant afterwards the crack of the rifle was heard, and the foremost of the Yankees rolled in the dust, then a second victim fell pierced by the bullet of another Texan, and the bold body of Federal cavalry galloped off as if a legion of demons were in chase of them, amidst the tumultuous shouts of Hood's men, and of our own cavalry and cannoneers, who had been looking on with great interest. Unfortunately we could not lay hold of the riderless horses, which rapidly followed their vanishing companions; but nothing could prevent my Texans from getting their spoils from the dead—a booty, in their opinion, richly merited by them.

About two o'clock in the afternoon the oppressive stillness of the situation gave place to commotion and activity. Adjutants were galloping to and fro. General Stuart was hastily summoned to General Lee's headquarters, where Jackson and Longstreet were already in council with our Commander-in-Chief. Strong reserves were posted in the centre, and forty pieces of cannon were concentrated there. Our horse-artillery was in readiness for action; and Colonel Rosser, who commanded the 5th Virginia Cavalry, but was an artillerist by education, had four batteries temporarily placed under his charge, with which he trotted to the front. Every one now saw that we were on the eve of great events, and a strange feeling of anxiety, as is often the case just before a battle, came over many a stout heart—a feeling which can be compared only to the heavy sultry silence that precedes the thunderstorm.

The greater part of the two hostile armies were separated by a narrow open valley of about three miles in length and half a mile in breadth, shut in by two parallel ranges of wooded hills, which fell away on the left into a wide wooded plain occupied by the outermost divisions of Jackson's corps, and closed on the extreme right by overlooking heights, which were held by our horse-artillery. It had been reported to General Lee that the enemy had massed large forces opposite to his centre, or the lower part of the little valley just described, which induced him to suppose that General Pope had determined to try one of Napoleon's *manœuvres de force,* and would attempt, by overwhelming numbers, to break through the centre in a sudden attack, trusting to dispose of the two wings easily thereafter. Our noble leader had not been deceived, and his measures to frustrate the plans of the enemy had been admirably concerted.

About three o'clock in the afternoon the close columns of the Yankees emerged suddenly out of the dark green of the opposite forest at a double-quick, five extended lines, at intervals of sixty yards, comprising at the least 15,000 men. Their colours were borne proudly aloft, and they advanced across the open space before us in beautiful order. Nearer and nearer they came, each one of us looking on with hushed anxiety at the imposing columns which moved towards the Confederate position as a water-spout moves over the deep. The silence was something appalling, when, at the instant, forty pieces of artillery poured a withering shower of shells into the very midst of the advancing host, while, at the same time, their first line was received with a perfect sheet of fire from our triple infantry line concealed in the dense under-growth of the forest. The artillery was in charge of Colonel Stephen D. Lee, and the accuracy with which the shells exploded in the very faces of the foe testified to the admirable service of the guns. It was as if an annihilating bolt out of the thunder-cloud had let loose its fury upon those doomed men, who until now had been pressing onward like moving walls, and they now wavered and swayed to and fro as if the very earth reeled beneath their feet. Again and again roared the thunder of our guns, again and again deadly volleys sent their hail of bullets into the dense ranks of the enemy, until all at once this splendidly-organised body of troops broke in disorder, and became a confused mass of fugitives. The Federal officers did their best to reanimate them. With the utmost energy and courage they brought their men forward to three several assaults, and three times were they hurled back, leaving hundreds of their number dead and wounded on the plain. At last physical strength and moral endurance alike gave way before the terrible effect of our fire, and the whole force fled in disorderly rout to the rear, a flight which could no longer be checked. At this moment the wild yell of the Confederates drowned the noise of the guns. As far as the eye could reach, the long lines of our army, with their red battle-flags, lit up by the evening sun to a colour like blood, were breaking over the plain in pursuit. It was a moment indeed of the intensest excitement and enthusiasm. With great difficulty could the cannoneers be kept back to their pieces. Scarcely could we, the officers of the general Staff, resist the impulse to throw ourselves with our victorious comrades upon the retreating enemy.

Thus the running fight was kept up for nearly two miles, our men, flushed with success, driving everything before them, and taking many prisoners. Suddenly, however, their headlong advance was vigorously checked at the village of Groveton, situated on a range of hills, now held by the main body of Pope's army, from which more than 100 pieces of artillery hurled their terrible missiles upon the Confederates exposed in the open plain and exhausted by the pursuit. In their turn they staggered, halted, and fell slowly back; but before the shouts of triumph of the Federals had died away, the onset was renewed and continued until we had brought the last man of our reserves into action. As the sun sank behind the heights of Manassas, the enemy, after a very gallant struggle, was driven entirely from the field, retreating towards Centreville in great confusion, leaving behind them many thousands of dead, wounded, and prisoners, besides many pieces of cannon and regimental standards, and a considerable quantity of small arms.

In the mean time our cavalry had been pressing forward on the right flank, driving the Federal horse with little resistance before them over a rolling wooded ground, from which we could see plainly the progress of the battle. Our horse-artillery, acting in concert with Rosser's four batteries, and advancing on a line parallel with that taken by the cavalry on the Groveton side, had been pouring a destructive flank-fire on the dense ranks of the Yankees. This fire was energetically returned by the numerous batteries of the enemy, which, firing too high, threw their shells all over the woods through which we of the cavalry were passing, breaking and shattering trees and branches in every direction, and inflicting much injury on men and horses. I myself received several slight injuries from the splinters and flying limbs with which the air was filled, and made a very narrow escape from serious damage, as one of the enemy's shells exploded between my horse's legs, striking, strange to say, neither rider nor animal.

After the taking of the Groveton heights, as the enemy was retreating in the direction of Centreville—all except their cavalry, which fell back towards Manassas Plains—our main line of battle had to move as on a pivot, the right wing advancing rapidly, and the whole standing nearly perpendicular to our former position. As the retreat led through a densely-wooded country, where cavalry could be of little use, only Fitz Lee's brigade joined our army in the pursuit— General Stuart pushing forward with Robertson's brigade to drive off the strong force of Federal cavalry which had been there brought together, and which would otherwise have operated successfully on our exposed flank. The 2d Virginia Cavalry, under the gallant Colonel Munford, was in the advance, and arrived at the plateau of Manasses before the two other regiments of the brigade had come up. Here they found the Yankee horse in far superior numbers, drawn up in two magnificent lines of battle, one behind the other. Without waiting for the arrival of their comrades, the brave fellows of the 2d, their intrepid Colonel at their head, threw themselves upon the foe. They succeeded in breaking the first line by their impetuous charge, but having been thrown into some disorder by the length of the attack, the second line of the enemy, using well its opportunity, made a counter-charge in splendid style, and drove them back in confused flight, shooting and sabering many of the men, the rallied Yankee regiments of the first line joining in the pursuit. At this moment we arrived with the 7th and 12th at the scene of the disaster, and, receiving our flying comrades into our ranks, we charged furiously the hostile lines, scattering them in every direction, recapturing all our men who had fallen into their hands, killing the commander of the entire force and many other officers, among whom was the Major who had given me such a run at Verdiersville, besides killing and wounding a large number of their soldiers, and taking several hundred prisoners and horses. The pursuit was not abandoned until we had chased them over the stream of Bull Run; and we heard later that the stampeded horsemen had continued their flight into the fortifications of Centreville. Our loss was comparatively small in killed, consisting mostly of wounded, among whom was the brave commander of the 2d, Colonel Munford, who had received several sabre-cuts on the head.

Night had now set in, and as we approached the field of battle on our return to the main body of our army, we found that fighting and pursuit had entirely ceased, darkness having at last checked our victorious progress. It was exceedingly unfortunate for the Confederates that the battle had been commenced so late in the afternoon, as two hours more of daylight would have rendered the result of the day yet more disastrous to the Federal army. Their loss, however, during the several days' fighting which terminated with the battle of Groveton, had been immense, amounting to at least 20,000 men in killed, wounded, and prisoners, 30 pieces of artillery, about 40,000 small arms, many standards, and uncounted stores of ammunition and provisions. The Yankee troops were totally demoralised, and had lost all confidence in their commanding general; and the Government at Washington, not less than the whole people of the North, looked with the greatest terror and anxiety into the future. Our loss had also been heavy, estimated in the last battle alone at 6000 in killed and wounded. Many a noble fellow breathed his last sigh for the South on the slippery heights of Groveton.

The little military family of our own Staff had specially to grieve for the loss of one of our number—Captain Hardeman Stuart, a nephew of our General, who had charge of the Signal Corps* of our cavalry. Poor Stuart, having been surprised with his party on the morning of the 30th by a body of Federal horse, was only able to escape with two of his men, leaving their apparatus and horses behind. Reaching the Confederate lines on foot just as the battle was commencing, and not being able to render more important service, these three heroes seized each one of the muskets which had been thrown down in large numbers by the enemy in their retreat, and joined the ranks of the 18th Mississippi infantry, which were just moving at a double-quick towards the Groveton heights. There they fell in glorious companionship after the regiment had captured several of the enemy's batteries. We encamped on the field of battle, and were occupied during the greater part of the night in carrying water to the wounded, and otherwise ministering to the wants of the sufferers to the extent of our ability.

We rested but a few hours after the fatigues of Groveton, and I was roused at peep of day by General Stuart, who desired me to accompany him on a little expedition to reconnoitre the position of the enemy. It was a dark cloudy morning, and a sharp wind drove a drizzling rain, which had

---

*The Signal Corps is an institution peculiar to the American armies, organised for telegraphic communications between distant points by the waving of flags of various colours in the daytime, and of lights of various colours at night. It is somewhat similar to the old semaphore system, and in campaigning can only be employed to advantage in a hilly region of country, where the signals can be made from elevated spots.

been falling throughout the night, right in our faces, so that we found the ride through the small pine thickets that lay in our way exceedingly disagreeable. Of the enemy we could discover nothing ourselves. From our scouts, and from the Federal prisoners that were still coming in every half-hour in squads of eight or ten, we learned that the army of General Pope had made a halt in and around Centreville. I was now asked by General Stuart to ride over to Jackson's headquarters, on the left of our lines, to make report and carry him important papers, and to proceed thence yet further to the left to Sudley's Mill, with orders for General Fitz Lee with his brigade, which had bivouacked there during the night, to march at once along the Little River turnpike in the direction of Fairfax Court-house, to a point where General Stuart himself, with Robertson's brigade, taking a short cut across the fields, would join him in the afternoon.

The headquarters of Jackson were at least five miles distant on our extreme left, and I had to ride along the entire line of our army, which at this moment was somewhat irregular. As the surface was much broken and covered with dense forests, I ran a narrow hazard of losing my way, and was compelled to make frequent inquiries of the different bodies of troops I passed *en route*. My appearance in the saddle was not a little *bizarre*, as I pushed onward through the rain, which still continued to descend soakingly. For protection against the storm I had wrapped myself up completely in my black oil-cloth cloak, at the same time turning down the wide brim of my slouched hat so as wholly to conceal my face. If these precautions kept me comparatively dry, they made it difficult for any one to distinguish me from a Yankee cavalier, and thus involved me in a ridiculous adventure, which might have had a tragical result. I had been questioning an infantry quartermaster as to the whereabouts of General Jackson, and my interlocutor, forming some grave suspicions from my appearance and foreign accent, took his measures accordingly. A few minutes after I had left him, two men on horseback came up, placing themselves on either side of me, and commenced a conversation which could not have been more impertinently inquisitive if they had learned to ask questions in Connecticut. I very soon wearied of this cross-examination, and so informed my companions, adding that if they desired anything at my hands they might express themselves fully. Whereupon they made polite apologies, declaring that they desired nothing beyond the pleasure of my company; but as at this moment three other horsemen came riding towards us, their manner underwent a sudden change, and they demanded my surrender as a Yankee, and called upon me to hand over to them any papers that might be in my possession. Exceedingly annoyed at this, I threw open my oil-cloth cloak, disclosing my grey uniform, and said to them, with some disgust, that if they still doubted my confraternity, one or two of them might ride with me to General Jackson's headquarters, when they would soon be convinced of their mistake; but that under no circumstances whatever would I expose to their inspection important papers which had been committed to my charge, and that, if need were, I would defend them with my life. This, however, wrought no change of opinion in my pertinacious accusers. They replied that any stranger might tell the same story; and that, as for my grey coat, it was a common Yankee trick to assume the Confederate uniform—it was just what a spy would naturally do. Losing all patience, I now drew my shining Damascus blade, and, driving my spurs into the flanks of my steed, I separated myself by a sudden leap from my disagreeable companionship, and continued in a quiet walk upon my journey. The quartermaster's troopers were taken completely by surprise by this determined movement, but they drew their revolvers, and, as if undecided what steps to take in the matter, slowly followed me at the distance of twenty or thirty yards. Fortunately I soon met an officer of my acquaintance, who was exceedingly diverted at my predicament, and quickly satisfied my would-be captors of their error. I was still so provoked, however, that I sent my card to the suspicious quartermaster, inviting him to meet me at General Stuart's headquarters, where I should be most happy to give him a good lesson for his future conduct. But he never came, and I never heard of him again.

After a long and weary ride over the battle-fields of the last few days, which were still cumbered with the unburied corpses of the slain, I at last found Jackson, who was just returning with General Robert E. Lee from a little reconnaissance beyond the Stone Bridge over Bull Run. Here they had been fired at by the advance pickets of the enemy, but had fortunately sustained no injury. They received me very kindly, and laughed at the recital of my recent adventure; but our interview was a short one, as I had to hasten after General Fitz Lee, who had already been ordered by Jackson to proceed with his command in the direction of Fairfax Courthouse, and was thus several hours ahead of me. A disagreeable gallop through the intricate bridle-paths of the forest enabled me to overtake our horsemen at the end of five or six hours. They had just come to a halt, as our advanced-guard had surprised and taken to the last man a picket of the 2d U.S. Cavalry, regular army, and two of our squadrons were on the point of starting to attack the Yankee picket reserves, who, having no idea of our approach, had bivouacked carelessly in and around a farmyard about a mile and a half higher up the road. Fitz Lee had been a lieutenant in the 2d U.S. Cavalry* before the war, and he was greatly delighted at

---

*General Robert E. Lee had been the Lieutenant-Colonel of this fine regiment, and many other Confederate officers had formerly served in it.

making prisoners in this way of many of his old comrades. For myself, being badly in want of a new horse, the steed I then bestrode having been very nearly broken down by the fatigues of the campaign, I joined with alacrity and pleasure the attacking detachment. There was but little fighting to be done. We rushed so suddenly and unexpectedly upon the Yankee reserves that they had not even time to mount, and two full companies with their officers fell into our hands. We captured also their horses, from among which I lost no time in exchanging a noble bay for my own worn-out animal. The officers gave their parole not to escape, and were treated by us with the utmost courtesy, being allowed to ride their own horses, and accompany our Staff at the head of the column. They had served in former days both with Fitz Lee and Stuart; and it was curious, as an illustration of the war, to hear these quondam companions-in-arms talking and laughing over the olden time. Late in the afternoon we were joined by Stuart with Robertson's brigade, and continued our march towards Fairfax Court-house.

We had been informed by our scouts that a large waggon-train of the enemy was moving on a parallel turnpike two miles distant from us, in the same direction with our column, and the shades of night were just closing in upon us when the heavy rumbling of the convoy, which was several miles in length, became distinctly audible. As the escort protecting this train consisted of several brigades of infantry, General Stuart did not regard it as prudent to hazard a direct attack, and concluded to pay them only a distant salutation. This was very handsomely done by our horse-artillery, which, being well posted on an eminence, soon began to perform great execution on the long line of waggons, whose white tops we could see, through the dusk of evening, winding slowly along the road like a gigantic snake. The confusion in a few minutes became bewildering, as the balls from our guns went crashing through the heavily-laden vans, and the loud cries of the drivers vainly endeavouring to get out of range commingled in tumultuous din with the disorderly commands of the officers of the supporting force, who did not seem to know from what quarter to expect the attack, or how to meet it; and by the time they had formed their line of battle, and were pushing bravely forward upon our position, we had proceeded already several miles upon the back-track towards the small village of Chantilly, which we reached about 10 o'clock, and where our cavalry encamped for the night.

Some six miles distant from Chantilly—in very unsafe proximity, it must be admitted, to the enemy's lines—lived on their plantation of family who were old and dear friends of Stuart. Finding himself in their neighbourhood, and not having seen them for a considerable time, our General could not resist the opportunity afforded by our night's halt in bivouac of paying them a visit, and the members of his Staff determined to keep him company. A brisk canter through the dark woods brought us about midnight to the mansion, where all were fast asleep except two ferocious dogs that tried unsuccessfully to resist our entrance to the immediate grounds. Stuart proposed that we should arouse the slumbering inhabitants with the dulcet-notes of a serenade; and the serenade was attempted; but the discordant voices that joined in the effort sounded so very like the voices of the wild Indians in their war-whoop, that the proprietor, at once awakened and fully persuaded that his peaceful residence was surrounded by a party of marauding Yankees, carefully opened a window and begged most anxiously that the building and the lives of its inmates might be spared, promising that he would do his best to satisfy our demands. His surprise and delight, when at last he recognised "Jeb" Stuart's voice, cannot be described. In a few minutes the whole household, young and old, were aroused, and we remained talking with our kind friends, until the morning sun, stealing through the curtains of the drawing-room, reminded us that it was time to be off. And so, after a hasty but hearty breakfast, we took leave of the hospitable family and rode back to our command.

Meanwhile the Federal army had halted in the neighbourhood of Fairfax Court-house, and was there throwing up intrenchments. Our Generals, however, did not suppose that they really intended to make a stand at that point, and their further retreat towards Alexandria was confidently expected. As they had received strong reinforcements from Alexandria and Washington, General Lee did not deem it advisable to press them vigorously the day after the battle of Groveton. Our own army had suffered severely in fight and from fatigue during the recent continuous engagements and marches, and fresh troops from Gordonsville and Richmond were hourly looked for. Our men, therefore, had been employed only in burying the dead, and collecting the ample spoils of victory. The small arms lying about everywhere were picked up and cleaned. Thus the morning of the 1st of September passed off quietly enough.

Stuart and I rode off to Jackson's corps, which was stationed at Ox Hill, and found Old Stonewall with his outposts very much amused at the effect of the rifle practice of some of his marksmen upon a squad of Yankee cavalry who had been advancing imprudently, and were just galloping off in a hurry across an open field. About noon the cavalry received orders to proceed cautiously along the road to Fairfax Court-house, Jackson's corps following at a short distance behind. The beautiful weather of the early morning had now changed into a drenching downpour of rain, and our column marched slowly onward, the 5th Virginia in the lead, with whose commander, Colonel Rosser, I was riding in front of the regiment. We were discussing our late fights and adventures, when suddenly the few men who formed our extreme advance and were riding a few rods ahead of us, came back at full gallop, and at the same moment rattling volleys from the thick pine-woods which lined the turnpike on either side sent a shower of balls over our heads. We had fallen into an ambuscade, which, if the Yankees had waited a little longer before firing, might have turned out very disastrously for us; but as only the head of our column was visible to them, and as they fired much too high, the damage done was inconsiderable, only a few men and horses being wounded. The order to wheel about was quickly given and quickly executed. Volunteering to ride back and report to General Stuart, I galloped rapidly to the rear, the 5th Virginia following in haste, and the Yankees still delivering their fire, which was now wholly ineffective, the bullets clattering through the forest. Two pieces of our horse-artillery, which had been detailed to the 5th, and which had loitered a little in the rear, I brought to a halt on a slight eminence in the road, and ordered to open fire as soon as the road was clear of our cavalry, the main body of which I arrested. A few minutes afterwards, I met Jackson and Stuart, who had been summoned to the front by the firing and the halting of the column. Old Stonewall made his dispositions with his usual celerity. He ordered Stuart to move along the by-roads towards Fairfax Court-house, and ascertain if the Federals were only making a demonstration, or if this was a general advance. For himself he was determined to stop the farther progress of the Yankees at once, and before we had turned off into the dark narrow path through the woods, the leading division of his corps had formed line of battle, and, advancing at double-quick, was soon hotly engaged with the enemy.

The rain was still pouring in torrents. The appearance of our column as it made its tortuous way through the dripping woods was not inspiriting, nor was its temper as buoyant as it might have been under happier auspices of sky and surroundings. The rattling of musketry and the roar of the cannonade on our left becoming every moment louder and fiercer, we could not but entertain some anxiety as to the result, for in case of Jackson's defeat, our situation would be rendered exceedingly precarious. Late in the evening, however, our patrols and scouts reported the bulk of General Pope's army in full retreat towards Alexandria; and the approaching darkness making our further advance impracticable, General Stuart determined to return. We were warranted now in believing that Jackson had been victorious, but as we had no information of the enemy's position, or of the strength of the force they had sent against him, it was necessary to march back with great circumspection. After several false alarms, we reached an outpost a little past midnight, wet and chilled to the very bones. Jackson's fight had been a sanguinary one, but the Yankees had been driven back with heavy loss, leaving behind them their dead and wounded, and 1000 of their number as prisoners in our hands. Among their dead were two Generals, one of whom, the famous warrior Phil Kearney, had years before left an arm on one of the battle-fields of Mexico. His body was respectfully taken care of, and sent, with all military honours, into the Federal lines under flag of truce the next day.

We pitched our camp in a dense pine-grove near Chantilly, and for the remainder of the night were occupied in drying our drenched garments by the heat of roaring wood-fires. On the morning of the 2d September we were agreeably surprised by the arrival of Hampton's splendid brigade, which had been retained on picket duty on the James, Chickahominy, and Pamunkey rivers, and our loud cheering was heartily responded to by the dashing horsemen of the Carolinas and Mississippi, who had long been anxious to meet the enemy under the lead of the gallant Stuart. As yet they had seen no fighting under his direct orders. Their desire was very speedily to be gratified. The main body of the Federal army had retreated towards Alexandria, but a strong cavalry force with horse-artillery still held Fairfax Court-house and its neighbourhood, and Stuart had been directed to drive them off.

The sun of the following day had just begun to exert its reinvigorating power upon our shivering limbs when we again set out for action. In the advance were Hampton's brigade, with the flying artillery attached to it, and the latter soon became hotly engaged with some of the enemy's batteries. From point to point we drove the Yankees slowly before us, until late in the afternoon they offered more determined resistance on a ridge about two miles in front of the Court-house. Hampton was now ordered to make a little circuit to the left to take the enemy in flank, and as soon as we heard the thunder of his guns we pressed forward with Fitz Lee's force, driving the Yankees in rapid retreat from their position. Stuart and I reached the abandoned heights, far ahead of our troops, just in time to see the long blue lines of the Federals trotting through the village, and their track marked by blazing farmhouses to the right and left in the fertile fields around it. The General, justly exasperated at the sight, turned round to me and said, "Major, ride as quick as you can, and bring up some of Pelham's guns at full gallop, that we may give a parting salute to these rascally incendiaries." Not less eager than he, I reached the artillery in a few minutes, and, getting the pieces into position without loss of time, we sent several shells with so much accuracy into the rear of the hostile column that, leaving their dead and wounded, they galloped off in the greatest confusion.

The magnificent lines of Hampton's brigade now appeared in brisk pursuit on the left, our Virginia horsemen, under Fitz Lee, had just joined us, and every one burned with the desire to throw himself forward upon the enemy. Stuart and myself took the lead: waving our battle-flag, which I had taken from the standard-bearer, high over my head, I echoed the loud yell of our men that came thundering after us, our artillery meanwhile firing shot after shot, which hurtled through the air above us; and so we entered the village of Fairfax Court-house at the moment that the last of the Federal cavalry, in headlong flight, galloped out on the opposite side. It was a moment of the wildest joy and excitement. The delirious joy and gratitude of the inhabitants, who for more than a year had been under Yankee rule, cannot be described when I planted the Confederate colours upon a little open space in the centre of the village, and thus took formal possession of it again. As night was approaching, and we knew, from the freshness of their horses, there was little chance of overtaking the fugitive Yankees, only two squadrons were sent in pursuit of them, and the rest of our command halted and encamped around the Court-house. Amid all the confusion and intoxi-cation of the hour I did not lose the opportunity of capturing a very good and well-equipped Yankee horse that was galloping about riderless, his master having been killed by a shell from our artillery. One gets a sharp practical eye for such things after a little experience of active warfare.

General Stuart established his headquarters at the house of a citizen whose daughter he had previously known, and regarded as a young lady of very ardent patriotism. Her subsequent conduct did not justify this opinion. In a playful imprudent manner the General had bestowed upon her a sort of honorary commission upon his Staff, which caused her to be arrested at a somewhat later period by the Federal authorities; but long before the termination of the war she managed to marry a Yankee officer, and took the oath of allegiance to the Northern Government, thus doubly dis-crediting the title of Virginian. After half an hour's rest,

Stuart requested me to ride with him to the headquarters of General Jackson, who had bivouacked only a few miles from the Court-house. A rapid gallop soon accomplished the distance, and we arrived just in time to partake of his simple supper, consisting of coffee and corn-bread.* At the conclusion of the repast, the night being already far advanced, we accepted General Jackson's invitation to sleep for a few hours till dawn beneath his small tent-fly. Wearied out by the exertions of the previous day, I was still deeply wrapt in slumber when I felt the pressure of a light touch on my shoulder, and a mild voice said to me, "Major, it is time to rise and start." Before I was yet fully awake, my caller placed a basin of water and a towel on a camp-stool near my head, and continued, "Now, Major, wash quickly; a cup of coffee is waiting for you, your horse is saddled, and you must be off at once." To my utter surprise, I now discovered that my attentive servitor was the great Stonewall himself—the light touch had been given by the iron hand, and the soft voice was that which had been heard in short energetic sentences so often amid the tumult of battle. I shall never forget the smile that broke over his kindly face at my amazement in recognising him.

General Stuart was himself already in the saddle, and in a few minutes we galloped back to the Court-house, the newly-risen sun just touching the tops of the tall hickory-trees, and the whole forest exhaling the most delicious odour, for the delight and refreshment of only such "early birds" as ourselves. Half an hour after our return to the village, our

---

*This article of food formed so much the most considerable part of our commissariat during the whole of my campaigns, that it may be well to explain that in America "corn-bread" invariably means bread made of Indian meal, and not of wheat flour. The Virginians are especially skilled in its preparation, and the old negro cook of the planter's family used to produce several varieties of this bread which were exceedingly palatable and nutritious.

whole command was mounted and on the march to the little town of Drainsville. We rode in advance with Hampton's brigade, which had some slight skirmishing with small bodies of Federal cavalry that from time to time made their appearance, but were driven back with little difficulty. The part of Virginia through which we were passing abounds with delicious peaches, and as this fruit was just ripening, it was a very grateful attention in the proprietors of the different farms and orchards on the road to invite us to partake of it freely. At one point of our day's march there came out to the highway, from a neighbouring mansion which was decorated with the Confederate flag, a little cavalcade, consisting of an old gentleman with grey hair, and three very pretty daughters. Galloping up to the column, the old gentleman addressed himself accidentally to Stuart, begging that he would be good enough to point out the famous cavalry leader whom he and his fair daughters were so anxious to see. Stuart, after having maintained for a while his incognito, at last acknowledged that he was himself the man, and the surprise of *pater-familias* and the blushing confusion of the young ladies, amused us not a little. They all insisted upon our stopping for a short time at their house, where luncheon had been prepared for the General and Staff; and I must admit that, in my breakfastless condition, I awaited Stuart's consent, which was only hesitatingly given, with some impatience.

Soon after this we witnessed a most touching scene. At the portico of a modest, cheerful dwelling by the roadside, there stood, as we rode along, an elderly lady in deep mourning, who held by the hand a fair-haired boy of about fifteen years of age, and who asked of the General that she might be permitted to bless our battle-flag. Having invoked the favour of heaven upon our colours in a manner as earnest as it was unaffected, she told us that she was a widow who had lost already two sons in the war, but that she was ready to sacrifice her last child for the sacred cause of her country. The eyes of the boy brightened up, and his fist was clenched at this; and tears fell down on our beards as we turned the heads of our horses towards the passing column. During the afternoon we rode over the ground, in the immediate neighbourhood of Drainsville, where Stuart in the year 1861 had fought his first fight. He showed me with pleasure the different positions which he and the enemy had occupied, and explained how differently he would have acted at that time, had he been favoured with the benefit of his present experience.

We encamped in and around Drainsville, our headquarters being established in the ample garden of a hotel in the centre of the village. Here, for the first time since we had left Hanover Court-house, were we enabled to reinforce our very dilapidated wardrobe from our long-missed portmanteaus, which we found in the waggons belonging to the cavalry staff. The following day was one of strange, blessed, uninterrupted quietude at Drainsville, the first day of rest after three weeks of continuous hard fighting. I have no power to convey the feeling of enjoyment with which, after a refreshing bath and the investment of the outward man in clean clothing from head to foot, I lay stretched upon my blanket beneath the shade of a wide-spreading hickory-tree. The day was delicious. The breeze came to me burdened with the fragrance of the latest summer flowers, lifting gently my hair, and whispering to me from the swaying branches overhead. Even the horses seemed to join in the general lassitude of the camp. They lay around us in the deep rich grass, which they were too lazy to crop, the very types of perfect physical satisfaction. And so we rested at headquarters—the officers, the soldiers, the negroes, the horses, the mules, all wrapped in the *dolce far niente* which marked the termination of our eventful summer campaign in Virginia.

CHAPTER VI

THE AUTUMN CAMPAIGN IN MARYLAND — GRAND BALL AT
URBANA — START FROM URBANA — FIGHTS NEAR FREDER-
ICK AND MIDDLETOWN — MARCH TO HARPER'S FERRY —
FIGHT AT CRAMPTON'S GAP — EXCITING TIME IN PLEASANT
VALLEY — SURRENDER OF HARPER'S FERRY — MARCH TO
SHARPSBURG — BOMBARDMENT OF SHARPSBURG — THE
BATTLE OF SHARPSBURG OR ANTIETAM — DAY AFTER THE
BATTLE, AND RECROSSING THE POTOMAC.

GENERAL Lee had now decided not to attack the enemy
in their strong fortifications around Alexandria, but
boldly to carry the war into the enemy's territory, or at least
into the fertile plains of Maryland. Many advantages, it was
hoped, might be secured by this policy. For a considerable
period he would be able there to subsist his army, relieved
from the necessity of protecting his lines of communication
for supplies. The confident belief was also entertained that
our army would be increased by 20,000 to 25,000 recruits,
who were supposed to be only awaiting the opportunity of
taking up arms against the Federal Government. Being so
reinforced, our commander-in-chief doubted not that he
might easily strike a blow against Baltimore, or even Washington, or transfer the theatre of military operations across
the border into the rich agricultural region of Pennsylvania.

On the morning of the 5th September there was again presented throughout the Confederate camps a scene of bustling activity. Every regiment was preparing for the march, officers were riding to and fro, and the long artillery-trains were moving off along the turnpike, their rumbling noise combining with the rattle of the drums and the roll of the bugles to wake the echoes for miles around. Our direction was *northward*, and as we rode onward towards the little town of Leesburg, inspirited by this fact, our horses exhibiting new life from yesterday's repose, many a youthful hero looked forward to his triumphant entry into the Federal capital, or to a joyous reception at the hands of the fair women of Baltimore, whose irrepressible sympathies had been always with the South.

After a march of several hours the column reached Leesburg, and the streets of the village were at once so compactly filled with troops, artillery, and waggon-trains, that General Stuart determined to make a detour with his cavalry, which had been halted about a mile distant, in preference to proceeding through the place. It was necessary, however, for the General to repair for final instructions to the headquarters of General Lee in the town, and in this ride he was accompanied by his Staff.

Leesburg, the county seat of Loudoun, is a town or village of about 4000 inhabitants, some four miles from the Potomac river, and, as might be readily supposed from its proximity to the border, was alternately in the possession of the Yankees and the Confederates, having undergone a change of masters several times during the war. General Lee's headquarters was set up in the commodious dwelling of a prominent citizen. Jackson and Longstreet had both already arrived there, and our great commander was soon engaged in a council of war with his lieutenants.

While this conference was going on, I went across the

street, with several other members of the Staff, to partake of an early dinner at the invitation of an old gentleman who lived directly opposite headquarters. Our venerable host had some time before been paralysed, and now spent the greater part of every day in a cane chair of immense proportions, seated in which he received us. This chair—so big as to resemble rather a summer-house or a cottage—came, through the chances of war, to a violent comico-tragical end. Some months after our visit, during one of the numerous fights that took place around Leesburg, our excellent old friend was seated in his favourite *fauteuil*, patiently awaiting the result of the conflict, when suddenly a shell crashed through the ceiling of the apartment, and bursting immediately under the chair of cane, tore it to atoms. The attendants, after recovering from their fright, looked around for the mangled remains of its late occupant. Strange to relate, the old gentleman had sustained not the slightest injury, and could complain of nothing beyond the somewhat rude manner in which he had been tossed upon the floor.

About two o'clock in the afternoon we received orders to move on, and after a dusty and very much impeded march of two hours, winding through infantry columns, and compelled frequently to halt, we reached the Potomac at White's Ford, where the cavalry were to cross. The banks of this noble river, which is of great width at this point, rise to the height of about sixty feet above the bed of the stream, and are overshadowed by gigantic trees of primeval growth, the trunks and branches of which are enwrapped with luxuriant vines, that, after reaching the very top, fall in graceful streamers and festoons to the ground, thus presenting tangles of tender verdure rarely seen in the forests of Europe. At White's Ford the Potomac is divided into two streams by a sandy strip of island in the middle. This island is half a mile in length, and offered us a momentary resting-place half-way in our passage of the river. It was, indeed, a magnificent sight as the long column of many thousand horsemen stretched across this beautiful Potomac. The evening sun slanted upon its clear placid waters, and burnished them with gold, while the arms of the soldiers glittered and blazed in its radiance. There were few moments, perhaps, from the beginning to the close of the war, of excitement more intense, of exhilaration more delightful, than when we ascended the opposite bank to the familiar but now strangely thrilling music of "Maryland, my Maryland." As I gained the dry ground, I little thought that in a short time I should recross the river into Virginia, under circumstances far different and far less inspiring.

The passage of the Potomac by the cavalry column occupied about two hours, and was attended with some difficulty to our artillery, as the water in many places rose quite up to the middle of the horses' bodies. Having safely accomplished it, we continued our march towards the little town of Poolesville. The inhabitants of Maryland whom we met along the road, with some exceptions, did not greet us quite so cordially as we had expected, this portion of the state being less devoted than others to the Confederate cause. It was different, however, at Poolesville. We reached this place about nightfall, with Fitz Lee's brigade; but just before entering it, our advanced-guard had a brisk little engagement with a squadron of Federal cavalry stationed there, which they dispersed by a sudden attack, killing and wounding several, and capturing thirty prisoners, with an equal number of horses. We remained in Poolesville about an hour, and in this brief space the enthusiasm of the citizens rose to fever heat. The wildest and absurdest questions were eagerly asked by the honest burghers concerning the strength of our armies, our intended movements, &c. &c. A number of young men became so much excited that they immediately mounted their horses and insisted upon joining our ranks. Two young merchants of the village, suddenly resolving to enlist in the cavalry, announced the peremptory sale of their extensive stock of groceries upon the spot for Confederate money. Our soldiers cleared out both establishments during the hour, to the last pin. Soldiers, on such occasions, are like children. They buy everything, and embarrass themselves with numberless articles which very soon afterwards are thrown away as useless. I myself could not resist the temptation of purchasing a box of cigars, a parcel of white crushed sugar, some lemons, and a pocket-knife, in the possession of which treasures I felt as happy as a king.

We bivouacked for the night about two miles from Poolesville, where we were fortunate enough to get an abundant supply of clover, hay, and Indian-corn for our horses. The following day we pushed on to the village of Urbana. On our march thither we saw, on the top of an isolated mountain of considerable height (known as the "Sugar Loaf"), a Yankee signal-station, where a company in charge were making signals to some of their colleagues at a distance with great rapidity. A small detachment was immediately sent after these industrious fellows, and speedily returned, bringing with them several officers and men, and an entire apparatus of beautiful instruments. We entered Urbana about noon. Around this place the cavalry had orders to encamp. My own instructions from General Stuart were to establish his headquarters, and afterwards to seek him at the headquarters of Jackson, who had bivouacked near the town of Frederick, eight miles farther on, having crossed the Potomac at fords higher up than the point of our passage, and by a forced march outstripped us by this distance.

Urbana is a pretty village of neat white houses, situated half-way between Poolesville and Frederick, in the midst of a smiling and prosperous country. The simple arrangements for our headquarters were quickly made, a few tents were pitched in the garden of a modest dwelling in the very centre of the village, the horses were picketed around, and in a few minutes the smoke rising from a dozen or more camp-fires gave pleasing assurance that the negroes were busy with their kettles in the occupation of all others most suited to their genius and temper—the preparation of dinner. Unfortunately, I could not wait to profit by the results of their culinary talent, and before my comrades of the Staff had commenced their meal I was trotting along the broad turnpike towards Frederick.

This town, which has a population of about 15,000, occupies a charming site in one of the most fertile valleys of Maryland, and is approached from Poolesville by a road lined on either side by rich estates, whose mansions are built round with the green verandahs of the South. At the point where the road sweeps suddenly down from a higher elevation to the vale of the Monocacy the view is really grand. Well-tilled fields stretch away for miles to purple ranges of mountains in the far distance; in the middle of the plain lies the city, with its domes and steeples, and in the intermediate space flows the brawling, limpid stream of the Monocacy, spanned by lofty bridges and the noble viaduct of the Baltimore and Ohio Railway. Frederick was a depot of supplies for the Federal army during the war, and in a strategetical point of view was a place of considerable importance.

Jackson's corps had taken the town completely by surprise, and a portion of the troops stationed there had been captured, besides two hospitals containing several hundred wounded men, and immense stores of medicines, provisions, and equipments. As General Stuart, always uncertain in his movements, was not at Jackson's headquarters, and was supposed to have gone into the town, I determined to ride there myself in the hope of finding him. Entering the good old city of Frederick, I found it in a tremendous state of excitement. The Unionists living there had their houses closely shut up and barred; but the far greater number of the citizens, being favourably disposed to the Confederate cause, had thrown wide open their doors and windows, and welcomed our troops with the liveliest enthusiasm. Flags were floating from the houses, and garlands of flowers were hung across the streets. Everywhere a dense multitude was moving up and down, singing and shouting in a paroxysm of joy and patriotic emotion, in many cases partly superinduced by an abundant flow of strong liquors.

Every officer who wore a plume in his hat was immediately taken for Jackson or Stuart: all averments to the contrary, all remonstrances with the crowd, were utterly useless. The public would have it their own way. So it happened that I was very soon followed by a wild mob of people, of all ages, from the old greybeard down to the smallest boy, all insisting that I was Jackson, and venting their admiration in loud cheers and huzzas. Ladies rushed out of their houses with bouquets. In vain did I declare that I was not Jackson. This disclaimer, they said, was prompted by the well-known modesty of the great hero, and afforded them the surest means of recognising him. The complication grew worse every minute. To escape these annoying ovations I dismounted at last at a hotel, but here I was little better off. It was like jumping into the mill-pond to get out of the rain. The proprietor of the establishment being a German, many of Germania's sons were there assembled, immersed in beer and smoking like so many furnaces. I am quite sure that most of them were very decided Yankee sympathisers, but as a grey uniform was right among them, and many others were not far off, they talked the hottest secession, and nearly floored me with their questions. One who had seen Jackson's columns on the march, affirmed they numbered not a man less than 300,000.

Another was only in doubt as to the day and hour when we should victoriously enter Washington, Baltimore, Philadelphia, and New York. All were sure that 30,000 Marylanders were ready to follow in the next few days our invincible army, a large proportion of whom were at that moment in Frederick, waiting only for arms, &c. &c.

I was exceedingly glad to break away from all this and get back to Urbana, there to rest my weary limbs on the soft carpet of grass at headquarters. As it was evident that we should be stationed at Urbana for some days, General Stuart, in order to establish a regular line of outposts, separated the different brigades of his command. Fitz Lee's was sent to the little town of Newmarket, about ten miles off; Robertson's, under Colonel Munford, was ordered to the neighbourhood of Sugar Loaf Mountain; while Hampton's remained in the immediate vicinity of Urbana. The following morning we were waited upon by the dignitaries of the place, and received an invitation for dinner from a Mr C., with whom and his pleasant family we soon became intimately acquainted.

There were several very charming and pretty young ladies staying at Mr C.s house, and among them one from New York, a relation of the family, on a visit to Urbana, whom General Stuart, from her warm outspoken Confederate sympathies, jokingly called the New York Rebel. In the agreeable conversation of these ladies, in mirth and song, the afternoon of our dinner-party passed lightly and rapidly away; and then came night, queenly and beautiful, with a round moon, whose beams penetrating the windows suggested to our debonnair commander a promenade, which he at once proposed, and which was carried *nem. con.* Leaving to our fair friends the choice of their partners, we were guided by them to a large building, crowning the summit of a gentle hill on the edge of the village, from which a broad avenue of trees sloped downwards to the principal street. This building had been occupied before the breaking out of the war as an academy, but was now entirely deserted and dismantled, and our footsteps echoed loudly as we walked through its wide, empty halls, once so noisy with human voices. Each storey of the house had its ample verandah running round it, and from the highest of these we had a magnificent view of the village and the surrounding country. The night was calm, the dark blue firmament was besprinkled with myriads of stars, and the moon poured over the landscape a misty bluish light that made it all look unreal. One might have thought it a magical scenic effect of the theatre, or been carried back in imagination to the Thousand and One Nights of Eastern fable, had not the camp-fires of our troops and the constant neighing of the horses reminded him of the realities by which he was surrounded.

We were indulging in the dreamy sentiment natural to the hour, when the gay voice of Stuart broke in—"Major, what a capital place for us to give a ball in honour of our arrival in Maryland! don't you think we could manage it?" To this there was a unanimous response in the affirmative, which was especially hearty on the part of the ladies. It was at once agreed that the ball should be given. I undertook to make all necessary arrangements for the illumination and decoration of the hall, the issuing the cards of invitation, &c., leaving to Stuart the matter of the music, which he gladly consented to provide.

A soldier's life is so uncertain, and his time is so little at his own disposal, that in affairs of this sort delays are always to be avoided; and so we determined on our way home, to the great joy of our fair companions, that the ball should come off on the following evening.

There was great stir of preparation at headquarters on the morning of the 8th. Invitations to the ball were sent out to all the families in Urbana and its neighbourhood, and to the officers of Hampton's brigade. The large halls of the Academy were aired and swept and festooned with roses, and decorated with battle-flags borrowed from the different regiments. At seven in the evening all was complete, and already the broad avenue was filled with our fair guests, proceeding to the scene of festivity according to their social rank and fortune—some on foot, others in simple light "rockaways," others again in stately family coaches, driven by fat negro coachmen who sat upon the box with great dignity. Very soon the sound of distant bugles announced the coming of the band of the 18th Mississippi Infantry, the Colonel and Staff of the regiment, who had been invited as an act of courtesy, leading the way, and the band playing in excellent style the well-known air of Dixie. Amid the loud applause of the numerous invited and uninvited guests, we now made our grand *entrée* into the large hall, which was brilliantly lighted with tallow candles. As master of the ceremonies, it was my office to arrange the order of the different dances, and I had decided upon a polka as the best for an animated beginning. I had selected the New York Rebel as the queen of the festival, and had expected to open the ball with her as my partner, and my surprise was great indeed when my fair friend gracefully eluded my extended arms, and with some confusion explained that she did not join in round dances, thus making me uncomfortably acquainted for the first time with the fact that in America, and especially in the South, young ladies rarely waltz except with brothers or first cousins, and indulge only in reels and contre-dances with strangers. Not to be baffled, however, I at once ordered the time of the music to be changed, and had soon forgotten my disappointment as to the polka in a very lively quadrille. Louder and louder sounded the instruments, quicker and quicker moved the dancers, and the whole crowded room, with its many exceedingly pretty women and its martial figures of officers in their best uniforms, presented a most striking spectacle of gaiety and enjoyment. Suddenly enters an orderly covered with dust, and reports in a loud voice to General Stuart that the enemy have surprised and driven in our pickets and are attacking our camp in force, while at the same moment the sound of shots in rapid succession is distinctly borne to us on the midnight air.

The excitement which followed this announcement I cannot undertake to describe. The music crashed into *a concordia discors*. The officers rushed to their weapons and called for their horses, panic-stricken fathers and mothers endeavoured in a frantic way to collect around them their bewildered children, while the young ladies ran to and fro in most admired despair. General Stuart maintained his accustomed coolness and composure. Our horses were immediately saddled, and in less than five minutes we were in rapid gallop to the front. Upon arriving there we found, as is usually the case in such sudden alarms, that things were by no means so desperate as they had been represented.

Colonel Baker, with the splendid 1st North Carolina regiment, had arrested the bold forward movement of the Yankees. Pelham, with his guns in favourable position, was soon pouring a rapid fire upon their columns. The other regiments of the command were speedily in the saddle. The line of battle having been formed, Stuart gave the order for a general attack, and with great rage and fury we precipitated ourselves upon the foe, who paid, with the loss of many killed and wounded, and a considerable number of prisoners, for their unmannerly interruption of our social amusement. They were pursued in their headlong flight for several miles by the 1st North Carolina, until, a little past midnight, they got quite out of reach, and all was quiet again.

It was about one o'clock in the morning when we got back to the Academy, where we found a great many of our fair guests still assembled, awaiting with breathless anxiety the result of the conflict. As the musicians had never dispersed, General Stuart ordered them again to strike up; many of our pretty fugitives were brought back by young officers who eagerly volunteered for that commendable purpose; and as everybody was determined that the Yankees should not boast of having completely broken up our party, the dancing was resumed in less than half an hour, and kept up till the first glimmer of dawn. At this time the ambulances laden with the wounded of last night's engagement were slowly approaching the Academy, as the only building at Urbana that was at all suited to the purposes of an hospital. Of course the music was immediately stopped and the dancing ceased, and our lovely partners in the quadrille at once became "ministering angels" to the sufferers.

Captain Blackford and I went down with our New York Rebel to an ambulance in which there was a poor fellow fearfully wounded by a ball in the shoulder. His uniform jacket was quite saturated with blood, and the tender white hands of our charming friend had just become fairly employed in the compassionate office of staunching the wound and cooling the inflammation with applications of cold water, when her strength broke down and she fainted away. When after a few minutes she had recovered, we did our best to persuade her to go home; but with a courage equalling that of the warrior on the field of battle, she replied, "I must first do my duty." This she did bravely and tenderly, until the wounded man, greatly relieved by her ministrations, expressed his gratitude with tears streaming from his eyes, and begged her now to take care of herself. Blackford and I accompanied the noble creature to the house of Mr C., and left her with the highest admiration for her tenderness and fortitude.

The sun was high in the heavens when we rose from our camp pallets the following day. The soldiers' slumber was naturally profound after the fatigues and adventures of a night when the ball-room had been so quickly deserted for the battle-field, and sanguinary conflict had in a moment succeeded to the dance. My first duty was to send back to the respective regiments their battle-flags, and I made all haste to discharge it. For once our troops had been called into action without their colours, and already many anxious inquiries had been instituted as to their safety.

General Stuart and myself were invited to dine with the doctor of the place, at whose pleasant dwelling we passed a few hours most delightfully. The universal verandah looked out upon the same beautiful landscape that we had admired from other points, and afforded us a cool retreat for cigars and conversation. I became very much interested here with a young vagabond Indian about fourteen years of age, who was pertinacious in his efforts to sell me a pet grey squirrel which he had tamed. As the fellow seemed homeless and masterless, I had some idea of taking him along with me as a servant, and perhaps might have done so but for the earnest remonstrances of General Stuart, who, from his life in the prairie, was well acquainted with the Indian character, and knew only too well what incorrigible thieves the Redskins always prove.

At a late hour of the afternoon the air was startled by the thunder of distant cannon, and we soon received a report from General Fitz Lee that he had been engaged in a brisk skirmish with the enemy's cavalry near the village of Barnesville. This, however, did not prevent us from spending the evening with our fair friends at Mr C.'s, nor from paying them the compliment of a serenade. But the time of inactivity for us was now soon to be over. Urbana was not to be our Capua, and the second day afterwards we bade adieu to what a punning member of the Staff called its Urbana-ties with regret.

One day more of rest at headquarters, the 10th, which gave

some occupation, however, to Robertson's brigade at Sugar Loaf Mountain, where Colonel Munford engaged the Yankees in a sharp but unimportant skirmish.

On the morning of the 11th we received marching orders. The aspect of military affairs had undergone a sudden but great change. General M'Clellan, who had again been intrusted by the Federal Government with the command of the Army of the Potomac, had collected together the remains of the army of the unfortunate Pope, and been largely reinforced by Burnside's corps from North Carolina, the troops around Washington, and the new levies. With a well-equipped and formidable force, he hurried forward to the relief of the garrison of Harper's Ferry, which stronghold had been closely invested by Jackson. General Lee, with Longstreet's corps, had left the vicinity of Frederick, and was slowly retreating in the direction of Middletown and Boonsboro'. The cavalry, as the rear-guard of our army, had orders to retard and embarrass as much as possible the forward movement of the enemy, and to follow slowly the road taken by General Lee. The fighting of the preceding two days had occurred with the cavalry of M'Clellan, which was a full day's march ahead of the main body of his army.

A steadily falling rain, which gave us some discomfort in the saddle, added much to the dejection of spirits with which we got in readiness to move away from Urbana. About 11 A.M. Fitz Lee's brigade passed through the village on its way to Frederick; Hampton's soon followed; and only Robertson's, under command of Colonel Munford, remained behind, covering the retreat, and holding in check, at a distance of about five miles from the place, the rapid advance of the Yankee cavalry. Meanwhile I was kept riding to and fro directing the retreat in the name of the General, who, with the other members of the Staff, to my intense disgust, still lingered in the verandah with the ladies.

About 2 P.M. our brave horsemen were pressed back by overwhelming numbers, at a point not more than half a mile from the village. The crack of the carbines was distinctly audible, and several shells, aimed too high, exploding just around the mansion, made it clear that the final moment of separation had indeed arrived. Great excitement now prevailed among the ladies, so soon to be again in the power of the detested Yankees, who, they had too much reason to fear, would punish severely the kindness and hospitality they had shown us. As for Mr C., he at once determined to ride off with us, and so we galloped out of the village, in the direction of Frederick, amid the tears of women and children, who stood waving handkerchiefs to us as long as we were in sight. Ten minutes later, Urbana was in the hands of the enemy.

Having crossed the Monocacy, we took up a new position on the opposite bank of the river. As the enemy did not advance that day beyond Urbana, the greater part of our cavalry encamped between that point and Frederick. About half a mile from the latter place we fixed our headquarters at the farm-house of an old Irishman, who amused us very much with his "buthiful brogue," and with whose pretty daughters—spirited Irish girls they were—we had a lively little dance at night. Early the next day (12th September) our scouts and patrols reported the enemy slowly advancing in strong force on the turnpike from Urbana, and we received orders to retreat through Frederick over the mountains to Middletown, but to retard the Federal column as long as possible at Monocacy bridge, which was to be burned at the last moment. As they were moving so slowly that at 2 P.M. their advance-guard was not yet in sight, General Stuart rode with his Staff into Frederick, where he had been invited by several prominent citizens to dine.

The appearance of the city had greatly changed since I had last seen it. The patriotic frenzy had completely subsided, and given place to an oppressive anxiety; most of the houses were shut up, and the inhabitants, with sorrowful faces, were wandering about the streets, credulous of every idle rumour, and asking at every corner the most ridiculous questions. Such of them as sympathised with the enemy could ill conceal their satisfaction at his approach; and one of these, a Mr F., was impudent enough to hoist a Union flag from the flat roof of his three-storey house, where he might be seen making with it undeniable signals. Very much provoked at his treasonable conduct, I posted two of our best marksmen on the opposite side of the street, sending at the same time my best compliments to Mr F., with the message that I had given my men orders to shoot him if for a minute longer he continued his offensive course. Federal ensign and ardent Yankee sympathiser now disappeared very rapidly together, but I have every reason to believe that, later in the day, when we were compelled to leave the city in some haste, he expressed his thanks to me in a charge of buckshot, which rattled from the front door of his house around my head.

Towards evening the enemy arrived in the immediate neighbourhood of Monocacy bridge, and, observing only a small force at this point, advanced very carelessly. A six-pounder gun had been placed in position by them at a very short distance from the bridge, which fired from time to time a shot at our horsemen, while the foremost regiment marched along at their ease, as if they believed this small body of cavalry would soon wheel in flight. This favourable moment for an attack was seized in splendid style by Major Butler, who commanded the two squadrons of the 2d South Carolina cavalry, stationed at this point as our rear-guard. Like lightning he darted across the bridge, taking the piece of artillery, which had scarcely an opportunity of firing a shot, and falling upon the regiment of infantry, which was dispersed in a few seconds, many of them being shot down, and many others, among whom was the colonel in command, captured. The colours of the regiment also fell into Major Butler's hands. The piece of artillery, in the hurry of the moment, could not be brought over to our side of the river, as the enemy instantly sent forward a large body of cavalry at a gallop, and our dashing men had only time to spike it, and trot with their prisoners across the bridge, which, having been already fully prepared for burning, was in a blaze when the infuriated Yankees arrived at the river's edge. The conflagration of the bridge, of course, checked their onward movement, and we quietly continued the retreat, which had been begun by the main column, under the annoyances only of a spirited shelling, which did us very little harm, and of an irregular fusillade kept up by bush-whackers and citizens from the houses.

The country between Frederick and Middletown is charming. The finest view of it is obtained from the Middletown Path, at the highest point of a wooded spur of the Blue Ridge Mountains that separates the two wide fertile valleys which are named from these towns. We could not resist stopping for a short time to look upon these beautiful and peaceful plains, which were so soon (in a few hours) to be the scene of an obstinate and sanguinary struggle. Our headquarters were now established at a farmhouse near Middletown, where that evening we very much enjoyed a plum-pudding, which had been hurled as a beneficent bomb at Captain Blackford by a philanthropic young lady of Frederick during our retreat through the streets of that city.

The boom of artillery summoned us to the saddle at an early hour of the 13th, and we rode as rapidly as possible to the front, where Hampton with his brigade had been gallantly defending the Middletown Path since daylight against vastly superior numbers of the enemy, and had, up to that moment, successfully repelled every attack. The position was extremely favourable for defence. No other passage to the right or the left led across the mountain-spur, and our two batteries, posted to great advantage, played with telling effect upon the numerous guns of the enemy in the open flat below, which, not being able to get the necessary elevation, proved almost harmless to us. Nevertheless it was evident that our small body of men would be soon obliged to give way before the overwhelming odds of the Yankees, who, just at the time we reached the spot, were preparing for a renewal of the assault under cover of an energetic fire from five or six batteries. At this juncture I was ordered by General Stuart to take one of our mountain howitzers—very light guns, which often did excellent service upon difficult ground, and could easily be drawn by two horses—and try to find an eligible place on our extreme left from which we could open fire with it upon the dense columns of Yankee infantry. With a good deal of trouble, and after we had been obliged several times to cut our way through the thick undergrowth, I found a little plateau, of perhaps fifty feet in diameter, and in a few minutes the rapid discharges of our little gun announced to General Stuart that I was at work.

The extended view from this plateau, which was the loftiest point of the mountain, rising from 1500 to 2000 feet above the rolling country below, was strikingly beautiful under all favourable conditions of atmosphere, but was now animated in the extreme. Frederick lay before us, distinctly seen through the clear air of the morning. The valley beneath, stretching away from the immediate base of the mountain, was literally blue with the Yankees. All at once their long columns of infantry with a waving glitter of bayonets, their numerous bodies of cavalry with "many a flirt and flutter" of gay flags and pennons, their imposing artillery-trains with the sunlight reflected from the polished brass pieces, and their interminable lines of waggons containing all the supplies for M'Clellan's army, broke upon my sight.

Directly beneath my feet the masses of the enemy were as busy as a swarm of bees. Two lines of sharpshooters were advancing in excellent style; the cavalry galloped hither and thither, seeking to get out of range of our cannon, while their numerous batteries, under the galling effect of our fire, were every moment changing position. The fire of my howitzer from a point hitherto regarded as inaccessible, plunging at this short range with fearful execution into the compact ranks of the enemy, greatly augmented the commotion. Several batteries at once opened upon us, but so far overshot their mark that at every fire my cannoneers threw their kepis into the air with loud yells of derision.

Meanwhile I had sent an orderly to General Stuart, reporting the state of affairs, and expressing my opinion that the time had come for our retreat. The General soon arrived upon the spot and gave orders for the withdrawal of the mountain howitzer; but as he had not seen the lines of the advancing infantry skirmishers, who had already disappeared in the thick underwood below us, he did not share in my opinion as to the danger of our situation. The firing of small-arms now became louder and louder on our right, and seemed to proceed from a point even a little to the rear of the place we occupied. Annoyed at my continued remonstrances, Stuart at last said—"Major, I am quite sure those shots come from our own men, who are firing at far too great a range; ride over there at once and order them to reserve their ammunition until they can see the whites of the Yankees' eyes." I knew very well that it was rushing into a wasp's nest, but orders were to be obeyed, and, making my way as quickly as the nature of the ground would admit, I proceeded to the scene of action, giving my orders in a loud voice as I heard several men breaking down the tangled thicket near at hand.

In a moment the bushes before me parted, and a Yankee, as blue as ever I saw one, emerged from them. At the same instant a bullet tore the bark from a tree behind me at a very few inches from my head, and several other tirailleurs made their appearance; and I had just time to turn my horse and gallop back to General Stuart, who now fully credited my report, and made off with me as fast as our charges could carry us over the rocky surface of the mountain. The Yankees, knowing very well that there was a noble game afoot, now advanced their whole line at a run, and with loud cries of encouragement, towards an open space over which we must ride, and where a shower of bullets fell around us, fortunately without touching a rider or a horse. The order for our general retreat was now given, and executed at a quick trot. I expected every moment to hear the roar of the Yankee artillery, which from the heights behind us must have inflicted very serious loss upon our column; but General Hampton, with admirable foresight, had so well barricaded the roads that we were out of range before they had gained our former position. It was now two o'clock in the afternoon, and as the fighting had commenced at four in the morning, we had for ten hours, with a few thousand horse and ten pieces of artillery, resisted the advance of the whole Federal army, with considerable damage to them and little to ourselves.

Near Middletown we took up a new position. The 1st North Carolina regiment, under Colonel Baker, and two pieces of artillery, were placed in front of the village, the other regiments and guns on the opposite side, behind a little stream known as Kittochtan Creek. The covered wooden bridge which spanned the stream was prepared with combustibles for destruction. General Stuart and myself rode forward a short distance in the direction of the enemy, whom we saw winding down from the mountain and stretching out over the plain in a mighty moving mass of blue. The fight was soon recommenced. The thunder of cannon roared incessantly, and as the enemy's guns had now the advantage of more favourable positions, which admitted of their being effectively employed in yet greater number, we suffered severely from their fire. At the same time the wings of the Yankee army, thrown rapidly forward, overlapped us on either flank, and our brave North Carolinians were thus subjected to a most destructive cross-fire before General Stuart gave the order for retreat, which, in consequence of the murderous tempest of shot and shell that raged around them, was not conducted in a very orderly manner. In my judgment our admirable General here betrayed a fault which was one of the few he had as a cavalry leader; and the repetition of the error on several occasions, at later periods of the war, did us material damage. His own personal gallantry would not permit him to abandon the field and retreat, even when sound military prudence made this clearly advisable. There was no necessity whatever, here, for the safety of the main body, to sacrifice a smaller command, for we might have withdrawn with honour long before the enemy's fire had so cruelly thinned our ranks.

I was one of the last horsemen that galloped through the town, and had a painfully accurate sight of the confusion and destruction that attended the retreat. The Yankee artillery threw a withering hail of shells along the main street of Middletown, from every by-street whistled the bullets of the sharpshooters, in our rear thundered the attack of the pursuing cavalry, while from the houses the Unionists fired at us with buck-shot and small-shot, and many fallen horses and riders impeded the road. The panic reached its height when we arrived at the bridge and found it blazing, through the premature execution of his orders by the officer in charge. Many of our horsemen leaped into the rapid stream and gained the opposite bank by swimming. For myself, with many of my companions-in-arms, I forced my horse through fire and smoke across the burning bridge, which, very soon after we had passed over it, fell with a loud crash into the water.

The hotly-pursuing enemy were now received upon the opposite bank with a deadly fire from our well-posted sharpshooters, and showers of canister from our artillery, which brought them to a stop; and after a heavy cannonade that lasted for more than an hour, we continued our retreat quietly towards the South Mountain, in the direction of Boonsboro'. The Federal cavalry managed the crossing of the Kittochtan with commendable expedition, and were soon again on our tracks, but the two pieces detached to our rear-guard kept them at a respectful distance by occasional discharges of grape and canister. We reached the part of the South Mountain known as Bradlock's Gap in the evening, and, just as we were taking another new position, were relieved by our infantry, which soon afterwards became hotly engaged with the enemy in a serious conflict. The foremost brigade of troops that relieved us was commanded by a dear friend of mine, General Samuel Garland, whom I met riding to the front, in buoyant spirits and confident of success. Ten minutes later he fell a corpse while trying to rally his men, who had momentarily given way at the first assault of the enemy. He was killed instantly, a bullet having pierced his brain.

Hampton, with his brigade, was now sent in the direction of Harper's Ferry, and had several encounters on the way with the Federal cavalry, against which the Georgia regiment of his command made a most brilliant and successful charge near the little town of Burkettsville, led by the gallant Lieutenant-Colonel Young, who was unfortunately wounded. General Stuart and his Staff rode to Boonsboro', which we reached at nightfall, and where we rejoined a portion of Fitz

Lee's brigade. Here we were greatly distressed at learning that the leader of our horse-artillery, Major Pelham, who had marched with Fitz Lee, had been cut off, and was a prisoner in the enemy's hands. He turned up, however, the next morning, having cut his way through the Yankee lines, and saved himself by his never-failing coolness and intrepidity. Our headquarters were established near Boonsboro', and we were glad enough to rest our weary limbs and exhausted horses after the fatiguing work of the day.

We moved on the 14th, making an early start, in the direction of Harper's Ferry, to reunite with Hampton's and Robertson's brigades, the latter of which had been already two days on the march for that point. Harper's Ferry is a stronghold of no little importance, most picturesquely situated on the Virginia side of the Potomac, just where this noble river receives the bright waters of its tributary the Shenandoah, and, augmented in volume thereby, breaks through the Blue Ridge. Here the United States Government had, many years before the war, established a very large arsenal and manufactory of small-arms. The Baltimore and Ohio Railway runs along the Potomac past the place, crossing from the Maryland to the Virginia bank at the immediate point of confluence of the two rivers; and a railway, connecting Harper's Ferry with Winchester, skirts the margin of the Shenandoah, and reaches its terminus at the extensive wayside station of the great line of communication between the Chesapeake and the Ohio. Around the workshops of the arsenal and the sheds of the railways a little town had grown up, built partly upon a narrow tract of level ground but little elevated above the rocky bed of the Potomac, and partly upon a lofty hill looking down upon either stream. This eminence is itself commanded on the Maryland side by the towering cliffs of the Blue Ridge known as the Maryland Heights, a position which had been strongly fortified, for the obvious reason that whoever became master of it might with little difficulty obtain possession of Harper's Ferry and all that it contained.

Jackson, after leaving Frederick with his corps, had crossed the Potomac with a large portion of it, and closely invested this stronghold, with its garrison of nearly 13,000 men, on three sides. A division of Longstreet's corps, under M'Laws, had been sent to attack and shut it up on the Maryland side, and now occupied the fertile tract of country which is enclosed by the continuation of the Maryland Heights and the South Mountain spur of the Blue Ridge. The two ranges run nearly parallel for a little distance from the river, with an intervening space of about two miles in breadth, but the South Mountain branches off in the neighbourhood of Boonsboro', forming what is called the "Pleasant Valley."

At Boonsboro', General Lee found himself, with the remaining portion of his army under Longstreet, confronting the bulk of the army of M'Clellan, which was rapidly advancing to the succour of Harper's Ferry. The passes over the South Mountain were all held by us, and were easily defensible. General Stuart had orders with two of his brigades to unite with M'Laws, and to reconnoitre and watch the enemy's movements, the other brigade, Fitz Lee's, having been detached from his command to the corps of Longstreet.

We reached Pleasant Valley in the afternoon, and our cavalry encamping there, General Stuart and I rode over to the headquarters of Brigadier-General Pryor, who commanded the left wing of M'Laws's division nearest to Harper's Ferry. General Pryor was just starting on a little reconnaissance, and we very readily accepted his invitation to bear him company. A proper degree of caution compelled us to go on foot. Creeping through the tall grass, we climbed the mountain occupied by our farthest outpost, from the summit of which we had an unobstructed view of the whole fortification. We could see the stir and bustle within the walls, mark the steps of each man, and even count the pieces of artillery. The look-out from this lofty perch would well have rewarded the toil of the ascent in the inactive time of peace; but the preparation and excitement of war, whose busy scenes we gazed in the distance, now combined with nature in her grandest mood to make the sight magnificent.

At a later hour of the evening Stuart rode off to the headquarters of General M'Laws, leaving me to await his return as General Pryor's guest at dinner. Among General Pryor's orderlies there was a handsome young fellow of about fourteen years of age who greatly interested me. He was a midshipman in the navy, who, making a visit to our lines at this exciting period, had volunteered his services, and had behaved on several occasions, as I was informed, with great gallantry. He was now galloping about on a little pony, and seemed highly elated with his temporary position. Two days afterwards the brave boy was killed in the battle of Sharpsburg (Antietam).

About dusk we were joined again by General Stuart, and I was just about to ride away with him to select a convenient spot for our night's rest, when the thunder of cannon, which had been sounding all the evening from M'Laws's right, grew fiercer and fiercer; and an orderly galloped up to us at full speed, reporting in a very excited manner that the enemy had repulsed our troops at Crampton's Gap, one of the passes of the South Mountain, broken through our lines, and already thrown several thousand men into the valley, thus cutting us off completely from Longstreet's corps. We started immediately, as fast as our horses could carry us, for the point where the disaster had occurred. In a very short time we were called upon to witness a scene of the most mortifying panic and confusion. Hundreds of soldiers, many of them wounded, were arriving in disorderly array from the fight, while guns

and caissons, huddled together with waggons and ambulances, moving towards the rear, blocked up the road. We at
once posted a strong guard along the road, with orders to
arrest every man who was not too badly hurt to renew the
conflict, and, taking the artillery with us, continued our ride.
After about an hour's progress we reached the spot, where
General C., an ex-politician and agriculturist, who had
commanded the troops at Crampton's Gap, was vainly
endeavouring to rally the remainder of his brigade. The poor
General was in a state of the saddest excitement and disgust
at the conduct of his men. As soon as he recognised us in the
dusk of the evening, he cried out in heartbroken accents of
alarm and despair, "Dismount, gentlemen, dismount, if your
lives are dear to you! the enemy is within fifty yards of us; I
am expecting their attack every moment; oh! my dear Stuart,
that I should live to experience such a disaster! what can be
done? what can save us?" General Stuart did his best to
comfort and encourage his disconsolate friend, assisted him
in rallying his scattered troops, and quickly placed in position
all the artillery. Then turning to me, he said, "Major, I don't
believe the Yankees are so near at hand, but we must be
certain about it; take two couriers with you, and find out at
once where the enemy is." My General was very fond of
sending me on these ticklish expeditions, and much as I
appreciated the honour thus paid me, I did not feel greatly
obliged to him on this particular occasion, as I rode forward
into the darkness, feeling that I should run a narrow chance
of being shot by our men on my return, if, indeed, I escaped
the bullets of the Yankees. Cautiously I proceeded, fifty yards,
a hundred, two hundred yards,—everything quiet; not a
trace of the enemy: at last, after a ride of more than a mile, I
discovered the long lines of the Federal camp-fires, where
Messieurs the Yankees had halted, and were busily employed
in cooking supper; and at sixty yards' distance I could see in

the road a cavalry picket, clearly defined against the glare of the fires, horse and trooper, who seemed to have no idea of our approach. Leaving the hostile sentry undisturbed, we rode quietly back to our lines, where the Generals awaited my return with the greatest interest and anxiety. In the mean time General M'Laws had arrived with reinforcements, our line of battle was formed, and several batteries in favourable position were ready for action. As it was evident, however, that the enemy did not intend making any further forward movement until the next day, General Stuart and I soon galloped back to our cavalry, with whom we bivouacked during the remaining hours of the night.

The air was sultry when at daybreak of the 15th September we marched towards the front, with hearts oppressed by the uncertainty of the events of the next few hours. Our position was indeed a perilous one: shut up in a narrow gorge, the garrison of Harper's Ferry, 13,000 strong (which, should Jackson fail in his siege, a matter to be decided before sunset, would inevitably fall upon us), in our rear, an enemy vastly superior in numbers on our front, we must gain the doubtful victory or perish in Pleasant Valley, the very name of which might mock our ruin. Every man felt this, and our lines, generally hopeful and cheery before an engagement, looked glum and desperately resolute to-day. The heavy silence of the march was broken only by the measured tramp of the column, the rumbling of the artillery-waggons, and the booming of the heavy guns from Harper's Ferry, which reverberated like rolling thunder through the surrounding mountains.

General Stuart, who moved with the cavalry to the extreme left, ordered me to remain and establish myself with twelve of our couriers on an elevation near our centre, from this point to reconnoitre the enemy's movements as much as possible, and to send him information every five minutes. About 10 o'clock the Federals commenced to move; their cavalry skirmishers advanced, and the lines of their infantry tirailleurs came in sight. The decisive moment had arrived, and every hand closed more firmly round its weapon. Already shots began to be exchanged, when suddenly a cry of joy, louder than the roar of cannon, commenced by our reserves and answered from one end of our lines to the other, brought delight to our hearts and carried despair to the foe, whose insolent advance it brought quickly to a halt—*"Harper's Ferry has surrendered to Jackson!"* In a few moments, an officer galloping towards us, his horse covered with foam and reeking with sweat, brought the official intelligence, which, passing from mouth to mouth with the rapidity of the wind, had already reached us by rumour. I at once sent a courier with the information to Stuart, and I had no occasion to enjoin upon him celerity in his movements. The faithful fellow speedily returned, and, with features lighted up by intense gratification, said to me, "Major, that was the quickest and the happiest ride of my life."

The enemy seemed completely paralysed by the shouts of our troops, and as we soon received reinforcements from Jackson's corps, and began to assume the offensive, they retreated rapidly along the road by which they had advanced. Stuart now came back to us, and was so delighted that he threw his arms round my neck and said, "My dear Von, is not this glorious? you must immediately gallop over with me to congratulate old Stonewall on his splendid success." Captain Farley, Captain Blackford, and Lieutenant Dabney joined us, and after a short and rapid ride we reached the magnificent scene of our magnificent victory, just in time to witness the formal ceremony of the surrender of the garrison, a sight which was certainly one of the grandest I ever saw in my life.

From what I have already said of Harper's Ferry, the reader who has never visited the spot may have learned that in regard to natural beauty it is exceeded by few localities on the surface of the globe. From the bed of the two rivers which here mingle their sparkling currents, the mountains rise precipitously to the height of several thousand feet. Within the fortifications is an extensive plateau, from which these bold headlands are seen in all their magnitude and majesty. Here the entire garrison of 13,000 men was drawn up in imposing lines, presenting, with their well-kept equipments, their new uniforms and beautiful banners, a striking contrast to Jackson's gaunt and ragged soldiers, who formed opposite to them, and whose tattered garments and weather-beaten features showed only too plainly the hardships they had undergone. To the long roll of the drums, the two armies came to a "present arms," and then the Federal troops laid down their standards and weapons, which were at once taken possession of by my men. The spoils captured at Harper's Ferry were enormous. Besides this large number of prisoners, there fell into our hands 70 pieces of artillery, about 30,000 small-arms, and an immense quantity of ammunition, provisions, tents, waggons, ambulances, machinery in machine-shops, horses, and mules.

Colonel Miles, the commanding officer at Harper's Ferry, a short time before the surrender, had lost both his legs by a cannon-ball, and died soon after sustaining this severe injury. A strong regiment of cavalry, numbering about 1100 men, had made good its escape the previous night by a road along the river bank, very little known, which M'Laws, against Stuart's urgent advice, had neglected to picket. General Jackson appeared quite satisfied with his success, but when I congratulated him upon it, he said, "Ah, this is all very well, Major, but we have yet much hard work before us." And indeed we had. That same evening the troops were again on the march to Sharpsburg, where General Lee was rapidly concentrating his army, and where a great decisive battle was expected to be fought during the next twenty-four hours. We had yet to learn how great a misfortune was the escape of the cavalry regiment the night before the surrender. During the night, under its bold leader, Colonel Davis, it came accidentally in contact with Longstreet's ordnance trains, capturing and destroying a great number of the waggons and stampeding the whole of the teams.

Riding over the plateau from point to point, I witnessed a ridiculous scene, which nearly proved tragical to a Yankee officer. Jackson had granted to the officers of the garrison permission to retain their side-arms and horses. Some of our men, ignorant of this fact, had just surrounded a Federal captain, summoning him to dismount and give up his arms. The captain, highly offended, had drawn his revolver from the holster, declaring, in a very excited manner, that he would kill anybody that approached him. He did not know with whom he had to deal, and did not see the uplifted musket of a wild-looking fellow from a Mississippi regiment who was just about to shoot him down. Fortunately I arrived just in time to save him by explaining to the soldiers the mistake they had committed.

What with riding about the fortifications and looking at this and that object of interest, the day wore quickly away, and it was five o'clock in the afternoon when I fell in with Captain Blackford and Lieutenant Dabney and some of our couriers, who told me that General Stuart had gone off some hours before with Hampton's and Robertson's brigades, proceeding along the tow-path of the canal on the Maryland side of the river to Sharpsburg, leaving orders for us to join him there during the night. We started immediately, and taking the shorter and more agreeable route on the Virginia side to Shepherdstown, where the river might be easily forded, and only a few miles from our destination, reached the ford after nightfall, where the scene presented to the eye was wild and beautiful beyond description. On either bank of the noble stream, here half a mile in width, had bivouacked the troops of Jackson's corps, whose thousands of camp-fires were reflected in the water, and threw a bright glare over the fantastic figures of the soldiers, bringing also into strange and vivid relief the gigantic trees that edged the shore, with their swaying foliage and their gracefully pensile vines. In the ruins of a large mill which had belonged to a friend of mine, Col. A. R. Boteler, and which had been burned by the enemy, a Mississippi regiment had taken up its quarters, and I could not help being reminded by the wild-looking long-bearded men, with their slouch hats, their blankets thrown over their shoulders, and their polished arms glittering in the red glow of the bivouac-fire, of the rude robber and gipsy of the olden time.

We managed the fording of the Potomac without trouble or delay, and arrived late in the night at the little town of Sharpsburg. General Stuart had fixed his headquarters at the house of Dr G., where we stretched our weary limbs on the floor of the entrance-hall, using our saddles for pillows.

16th September

General Lee was now in readiness to meet the mighty Federal host. Longstreet having retreated from Boonsboro', where his corps had a severe engagement with the enemy's advance, towards Sharpsburg, had there united with Jackson's troops, which had come down during the night from Harper's Ferry; and our army was in line of battle on the morning of the 16th, about half a mile in front of the town towards Antietam Creek, the right wing extending about a mile in a north-easterly direction, the extreme left resting on the Potomac. M'Clellan, moving forward from Boonsboro', was still on the opposite side of the Creek, but his attempt to cross and the consequent battle were hourly expected. A mistake has been made here by several writers who had not the advantage of taking part in the events they describe, in stating that none of Jackson's forces had effected a junction with Lee before the battle of Antietam. Our great leader had been too cautious to neglect the concentration of his troops, which had been partially accomplished by forced marches. A portion of Jackson's corps had, indeed, been left by the main body at Harper's Ferry, but they arrived on the field the night preceding the general engagement. M'Laws's division, which had also remained behind, did not join in the conflict, by reason of the slowness of its commander, until the latter part of the day. General Stuart started on the morning of the 16th, the day before the great battle, with a part of his cavalry, on a reconnaissance up the Potomac, leaving me with ten of our couriers at headquarters, with orders to receive and open all reports and despatches addressed to him, and to forward any important information to Generals Lee, Jackson, and Long-street.

Sharpsburg is a pretty little village of perhaps two thousand inhabitants. It presented, during these memorable September days, a busy scene of military life. Waggon-trains blockaded its streets, artillery rattled over its pavements, orderlies were riding up and down at full speed. The house of Dr G., one of the largest in the place, was situated just opposite the principal church, and was still occupied by his hospitable family, who awaited with an indifference peculiarly American the momentous events that were so close upon them. About 11 A.M. the enemy began to throw shells into the town, which, being aimed at the church steeple, fell all around their dwelling in such perilous proximity that I felt it my duty to order the ladies into the cellar, as the safest place of refuge. This order they obeyed, but, impelled by feminine curiosity, they were running up-stairs every five minutes to witness the effect of the cannonade. I had frequent occasion during the war to observe how much stronger is curiosity with women than the fear of danger. Accordingly, while the fire was every moment growing hotter, it was not long before the whole of Dr G.'s family were again assembled in the room I occupied. All at once, while they were looking out of the windows at some wounded men carried by, a shell fell with a terrific crash through the top of the building, and sent them in precipitate flight to the security of the vaults. About noon the bombardment became really appalling, and the explosion of the innumerable projectiles stunned the ear. Still deeming it obligatory on me to remain at my post, I was seated on the sofa engaged in writing in my journal, when a shell, piercing the wall of the room a few feet above my head, covered me with the debris, and, exploding, scattered the furniture in every direction. At the same moment another missile, entering the upper part of the house, and passing directly through, burst in the courtyard, killing one of our horses, and rendering the others frantic with terror. Regarding further exposure of my own life and the lives of my couriers as now unnecessary, I gave orders for our immediate departure; but it was not easy, amid the blinding dust and smoke out of doors, to find my horse, nor, after I had found him, to get into the saddle, so furiously did he rear and plunge, as if fully conscious of the danger of his situation.

In the street there was the greatest confusion. Dead and wounded men and horses lay about in every direction, in the midst of waggons and ambulances overturned in the hurry and anxiety of everybody to get out of the village, where cannon-balls whizzed incessantly through the air, and pieces of bursting shells, splinters of wood, and scattered fragments of brick were whirled about in the dense cloud of powder-smoke that enveloped all things. After an exciting ride of a quarter of an hour, during which my nerves were strained to the utmost, I gained an eminence beyond the town, and was happy to find that my followers, one and all, had, like myself, escaped death as by a miracle. My horse had been the only sufferer. A piece of shell had struck him in the right hind leg, and he went lame and bleeding.

Everybody was under the impression that this bombardment was the signal for a general battle; but after the batteries all along the lines had been engaged in a spirited artillery duel, and on our right even the roll of musketry had been heard for some time, the din of conflict gave way to a dull, drowsy silence, interrupted only at intervals by a random cannon-shot booming through the hot evening air. With great difficulty I at last found General Stuart, late in the evening, at the headquarters of General Lee. He appointed to meet Captain Blackford and myself in an hour's time, at a church about two miles from Sharpsburg, to which place of rendezvous we repaired; but the General came not. Having waited long for him, we finally rode off a short distance, and made our bivouac for the night on some stacks of straw, which seemed to offer the most comfortable spot for repose.

17th September

We obtained but little sleep. Occasional shots were fired all night in our neighbourhood. To add to our discomfort, a fine drizzling rain, which began to fall about daybreak, wet us to the skin, and, chilled as we were, we had no breakfast to reinvigorate us for the field. In the morning we discovered General Stuart, who had bivouacked quite near us, and, at his request, I rode with him along our line of battle, which stretched out, nearly four miles in length, over several of the little hills so frequent in this rolling country, and sheltered from the enemy's view by many patches of wood and extensive corn-fields. The strength of Lee's army was always over-estimated throughout the war, but more so at Sharpsburg than in any other great battle that he fought. I have it from our great commander's own lips that he had less than forty thousand men with him in the conflict; and as M'Laws's division, numbering 7000 men, and some other small detached bodies of troops, did not join in the action until a late period of the day, he commenced this tremendous struggle with not more than 30,000 men, the Federal army, according to General M'Clellan's own statement, amounting to not less than 90,000. Our force had been greatly reduced by the continuous fighting of the campaign, by the long and wearisome marches it had made, and the cruel hardships it had undergone. From these several causes it had happened that a great multitude of stragglers were left behind on the Virginia side of the Potomac, of whom thousands had been collected together in the immediate neighbourhood of Leesburg alone. I could not help expressing to General Stuart, as we passed the thin lines of our ragged, weather-beaten soldiers, many of them without shoes, that I did not think our army equal to the impeding contest, and that I felt great anxiety as to the result; but he was in good hope, and said, with his accustomed cheerfulness, "I am confident that, with God's assistance and good fighting, we shall whip these Yankees badly enough."

Jackson commanded our left wing. General Lee himself had taken charge of the centre, and Longstreet commanded the right. Of our cavalry, Robertson's brigade, under Colonel Munford, was detached to the extreme right, Fitz Lee's and Hampton's were held in reserve on the extreme left, which, as before stated, rested on the Potomac. The fighting commenced soon after daybreak, and was raging in full fury on the left with Jackson's corps at seven o'clock in the morning.

From the nature of the ground, our cavalry could take but little part in the active operations of the day; but the indefatigable Stuart, always eager to be at the place of most imminent danger, had obtained from Jackson, who had unbounded confidence in him, the charge of the left wing of his corps, and having concentrated there about twenty-five pieces of cannon, consisting principally of our horse-artillery, pressed boldly forward with his guns, and, by a most effective flank fire, did great damage to the enemy. The Yankees soon responded fiercely to this cannonade, and with such terrible effect that I was in constant anxiety for the life of my general, who was always where the carnage was greatest, and at whose side two of our best couriers had already been killed.

The enemy concentrated the whole weight of his attack upon Jackson's centre, which for a time gave way, and was driven back through a large patch of forest that had been gallantly defended. But the grim Stonewall soon rallied his men, and, having been reinforced, drove back the Yankees in his turn for several miles with great slaughter. About mid-day I was sent by General Stuart to our cavalry with orders that they should press forward, in corresponding movement with the infantry, up the bank of the Potomac. At the moment of passing the 3d Virginia Cavalry, as I was exchanging some friendly words with its gallant commander, Colonel Thornton, a piece of a shell tore off his left arm very near to the shoulder, from which wound he died in great agony a few hours afterwards. By the time I had returned to my general, the fighting in Jackson's front had ceased a little, and both the combatants seemed to be taking breath after the terrible struggle that had been maintained with such resolution for hours; but on our right, where, up to this moment, all had been comparatively quiet, the firing grew louder and more continuous. Longstreet, hard pressed by the superior numbers of the enemy, had been giving way slowly, but defending the ground, like a wounded lion, foot by foot, until, receiving reinforcements at the outskirts of Sharpsburg, he recovered his lost ground after a severe and sanguinary combat.

The little town of Sharpsburg was unfortunately set on fire by the Federal shells, and a portion of it utterly destroyed; and throughout the evening the sky was reddened by the glare of the conflagration. Our centre was much less engaged than the two wings, and the fighting there consisted mainly in a terrible connonade, during which our guns, advantageously posted, poured a most destructive fire into the enemy's ranks. In Jackson's front, the conflict was only moderately renewed during the later part of the day, and was carried on principally with artillery. Here, and elsewhere along the lines, all was going on so favourably for our arms, that we might well claim to be victors when the sunset streamed over the ensanguined field, and the rapidly-following darkness put an end to the fearful strife. Every inch of the ground lost by Longstreet at noon had been recovered. Our centre had greatly gained ground. On our left the enemy had been pushed back for nearly two miles. And we remained masters of the entire field of battle covered with the enemy's dead and wounded.

The victory would certainly have been more complete, had not General M'Laws failed to obey orders in bringing his division of nearly 7000 men earlier into the fight, and by the tardiness of his movements to a considerable extent thwarted the combinations of his commander-in-chief. Our troops fought better than ever on this glorious day; and it was astonishing to see men without shoes, whose lacerated feet often stained their path with blood, limping to the front to conquer or fall with their comrades. The spoils of the victory were not great. A few prisoners and guns were taken. As for our loss, it had indeed been heavy, amounting to not less than 2000 killed and 6000 wounded; including among the former, two general officers, Generals Branch and Starke. The Federals having been the assailants, their loss was yet more severe, reaching the terrible aggregate of 12,000 dead or disabled men. Their sacrifice of officers had been serious. Generals Mansfield and Reno were killed, and twelve other generals were among the wounded. Late in the evening, I received orders from General Stuart to take with me a regiment of infantry and some squadrons of cavalry, and establish a double line of pickets on our extreme left, along the margin of the Potomac, there to reconnoitre the position of the enemy, and await the arrival of fresh troops to relieve my command, upon whose coming I was to follow him to Sharpsburg. The night was far advanced when a brigade of infantry took the place of my weary soldiers, who had fought all day, and the "small hours" had succeeded when with two of my couriers I entered the village.

It was a sad spectacle of death and destruction, as seen by the light of the yet glowing embers of its habitations, the greater number of which had been swept away by the flames. The unburied corpses of men and horses lay on every side in the streets, while helpless women and children, who had lost their homesteads, were moving about amid the smouldering ruins seeking shelter for the night. The mansion of Dr G., after having been completely riddled by shells, had been consumed; but a small summer-house in the garden had escaped injury, and here the family found a temporary refuge. The Doctor himself was quite calm and composed. He congratulated me on my escape, and said that he derived consolation from the hope that we should whip the Yankees as badly the next day as we had done already. As usual, General Stuart, having once separated himself from his aides, was not to be found, so for the remainder of the night I rested with my couriers in a small cow-stable, on the top of which we were fortunate enough to discover some hay for the horses.

Several shots fired in rapid succession about day-light, very near to our little dormitory, roused us from sleep with the idea that the fighting had been renewed in the streets of the village; but, on going out of the cow-stable, I found, to my surprise and relief, that they came from some of our men, who were amusing themselves with shooting the pigs and chickens, which, rendered homeless by the fire, were wandering about in a distracted condition. "Poor little things," said our troopers, with a dry sort of humour, "they have nowhere to go, and we ought to take care of them." Already, at several points among the ruins of the houses, commodious sheds had been hastily erected, and the savoury smell of roast meat, wafted to me on the fresh air of the morning, brought very forcibly to my mind and stomach the indisputable and melancholy fact that for more than forty-eight hours I had been wholly without food. This was indeed the case with the greater portion of our army, which, for several days preceding the battle, had been living on green apples and ears of Indian-corn picked up on the roadside and roasted. Nevertheless, I felt obliged to rebuke a Texan, who, only a few steps from me, had just rolled over, by a capital shot, a porker galloping across the street at sixty yards distance, for his wanton disregard of the rights of property. With a look of utter astonishment, he turned to me, and asked, "Major, did you have anything to eat yesterday?" and, upon my answering in the negative, said, "Then you know what it is to be hungry; I haven't tasted a morsel for several days." I had nothing more to say, and mounting my horse, I rode forward to the front, where our army, in line of battle, was momentarily expecting the renewed attack of the enemy.

I found General Stuart much sooner than I had hoped for, on our left flank, and at his request rode with him over the battle-field to reconnoitre the enemy's lines. It was a sickening sight. None of the corpses had yet been buried, and in Jackson's front the Federal dead lay around in great numbers, while many wounded men still remained untended in their agony in out-of-the-way spots of the woods and corn-fields. The outposts of the two armies were separated from each other by only a few hundred yards, and frequent shots were exchanged between them whenever an enterprising fellow went forward to pick up a gun or strip a dead body upon the intermediate ground. After having completed our reconnaissance, and when several Yankee sharpshooters had rewarded our curiosity with the whizzing of their bullets, we proceeded towards the point where Jackson was supposed to be, and found old Stonewall, near a battery of twenty-five guns, stretched out along a fence, and enjoying the luxury of a cup of coffee, quite hot, which his trusty servant had prepared from the contents of a Yankee haversack, and of which we were kindly invited to partake.

General Lee soon arrived upon the spot, and leaving these three great men to their council of war, I moved off a short distance, and, throwing myself at full length upon the soft turf, gave way to deep reverie. I had heard much and read much, in my own German and elsewhere, of the presentiment of approaching death, and had often speculated upon the matter, its verity, and the mental and physical conditions that might superinduce it, &c.; but this morning I was taken hold of, rather than oppressed, by the conviction that I should be killed before night in the coming battle, and I should have regarded any one as a profane sceptic who had tried to argue me out of it, and prove the foreboding nonsensical upon philosophical principles. Whether the famished state of my body, or the excitements of the last two days acting on the brain, had wrought the presentiment in the mind, it is not worth while to consider: certain it is that I made the most mournful entry in my notebook, at which I cannot now look without laughing, and which is too absurd to be repeated here. I only revert to the fact to show that while in some instances presentiments of death are afterwards verified, in others that we do not hear of, probably the greater number, they have no subsequent realisation.

Hour after hour passed away in anxiety and watching for the enemy's attack, but the perfect quietude of the morning was interrupted only by a flag of truce sent in by the Yankees asking permission to bury their dead. This was of course granted, and the work occupied them until the afternoon, when it became evident that the battle would not be renewed, and that my misgivings for the day had been utterly idle. My annoyance at having indulged them was greatly mitigated when, with the evening, came my negro, William, mounted on my beautiful little grey mule "Kitt," and, with a grin all over his black face, offered me tomatoes, apples, and roasted ears of corn, which he had promptly seized the earliest occasion of stealing from a neighbouring farm.

In the mean time our great commander-in-chief had decided to recross the Potomac, and transfer his weakened army again to the soil of Virginia. Nothing could be accomplished by remaining longer in Maryland. Even had the battle been renewed with the most satisfactory results for our arms, General Lee had not men enough for the continued occupation of the country. General Lee has often been censured for having fought the battle of Sharpsburg at all; but he was compelled to do so in order that he might save the immense booty taken by Jackson at Harper's Ferry, which was of the very greatest importance to us, and well worth a great sacrifice. Besides, it was not known how much the enemy had exhausted his strength in the conflict. Not until some time afterwards did we learn from General M'Clellan's own statement that there was but one single corps of the whole numerous Federal army that could well have been brought into action again. The retreat of our army was in preparation throughout the day, was commenced at night, and was executed in a masterly manner when one considers that it was conducted along a single road, that, except three hundred men who were too severely wounded to bear transportation, nothing was left in the enemy's hands, and that they were wholly ignorant of our disappearance until the next morning, when our entire army was on the Virginia shore.

General Stuart started with his Staff about ten o'clock at night, and I can safely say that the ride to the Potomac was one of the most disagreeable of my life. A fine rain, which had been falling all the evening, had rendered the roads so deep with mud and so slippery that it was difficult to make any progress at all, and I fell with my horse not less than five times. The way was everywhere obstructed by waggon and artillery trains, and marching columns; and the darkness was so great that one knew not where to direct his doubtful steps. General Stuart made a narrow escape from being crushed to death. His horse fell with him directly under the wheels of a heavy army waggon, which must inevitably have gone over him had I not fortunately been able to arrest its motion. The General was in great haste, and was calling out continually to those in front of him in somewhat angry tones, which were often answered, to my great amusement, in a sufficiently rough manner by the soldiers and waggon-drivers, who did not recognise his voice. At last we reached the Potomac, crossed it in safety, and after moving about for some time in the darkness on the opposite bank, and being compelled to lead our horses over the rocky precipitous ground near Shepherdstown, came shortly before daylight to a halt, and sought on a wet but hard place in the open an hour's rest preparatory to starting upon a new enterprise—unlooked-for finale to the autumn campaign in Maryland.

CHAPTER VII

DEMONSTRATION INTO MARYLAND — OUTPOST-DUTY AND
FIGHTS ON THE POTOMAC — RENEWED FIGHTING, AND
PASSAGE OF THE POTOMAC BY NIGHT — CAMP AT MARTINS-
BURG AND CHARLESTOWN — VIRGINIA PARTRIDGES AND
A VIRGINIA PLANTATION — ESCAPE OF A SPY — ADVANCE
AND REPULSE OF THE ENEMY — VISITS TO NEIGHBOURS.

GENERAL Stuart had received orders from General Lee
to march at once, with two of his brigades (Hampton's
and Robertson's), two regiments of infantry, and his horse-
artillery, to the little town of Williamsport, about fifteen miles
higher up the Potomac, cross again into Maryland, and by a
vigorous demonstration induce the enemy to believe that a
large portion of our whole army was manœuvring against
them at that point. Accordingly, we had scarcely fallen asleep
when the order was given to mount, and we commenced our
rapid march through the chill fog of the morning, cold,
hungry, and wet to the skin. But a few hours of hard riding,
the genial warmth of the sun breaking through the watery
sky, and more than all else, a luxurious breakfast, which was
quickly prepared for us at a hospitable house on the roadside,
the first regular meal that we had enjoyed for many days,
revived and refreshed us. About noon we reached the Potomac opposite Williamsport, forded the river, and drove a

squadron of Federal cavalry stationed there out of the place towards Hagerstown, a village some six miles distant. A mile beyond Williamsport we halted, throwing out our pickets and videttes. It was not long before the enemy returned with reinforcements, and a lively skirmish ensued, with even a spirited cannonade; for we made, of course, as a part of our plan, as great a display of our forces and as much noise as possible.

I had here a very striking example of how little effect is often produced by volley-firing. Two companies of one of our infantry regiments which were stationed on the turnpike running to Hagerstown, and had hastily thrown up a small intrenchment across the road, were charged in a very dashing manner by some squadrons of the Federal cavalry. The intrenchment was concealed from view by a slight elevation of ground about forty steps in front of it, so that the Yankees came upon it quite unexpectedly. The infantry officer in command had given orders to his men to reserve their fire till the last moment, and the dense ranks of the horsemen had arrived within close range when suddenly the volley thundered upon them, making them turn and fly precipitately. Having been myself with the infantry, I galloped forward, believing that at least half of the assailants had been brought to the ground, but found to my surprise that not a man or a horse had been struck down, the leaden hail having passed far above their heads. On several subsequent occasions I had a similar experience. The haste and uncertainty of volley-firing, even with the improved firearms now in use, made it possible in a few cases for our cavalry successfully to attack and ride down unbroken infantry—an attempt which, with accurate dropping fire, I regard as out of the question.

During one of the pauses of the fight, when the enemy had retired some distance, General Stuart requested me to reconnoitre their position and further movements. Having done this closely, I sent my report by an orderly I had taken with me, and was riding slowly along the turnpike on my return, when I passed a modest-looking farmhouse, in the garden of which was a trellis of such superb grapes that I could not resist asking of the proprietor, who stood in his doorway, permission to pluck some of the branches which hung in such tempting profusion. The request was not only granted at once, but the hospitable farmer invited me to alight and join him at dinner, which was just about to be served. As everything now seemed perfectly quiet, and the enemy no-where at hand, I did not think it imprudent to accept his kind offer, otherwise so entirely consistent with my inclination; so tying my horse to the garden-gate, about twenty steps from the building, I entered the drawing-room, which was already pervaded by the appetising smell of the coming meal. The farmer's wife, seeing some ugly rents in my dilapidated uniform coat, kindly proposed to mend them for me, and, waiving the etiquette of a major remaining in her presence in his shirt-sleeves, had just commenced her task, when I heard the heavy clatter of hoofs on the turnpike, and saw, at the same moment, a whole squadron of Yankees approaching at a full gallop. With one bound I cleared the drawing-room, leaving coat and dinner behind, and ran to my horse, which, participating in his master's alarm, was jumping and plunging so furiously that it was quite an acrobatic feat to mount him. Meanwhile the hostile dragoons had arrived within twenty steps of me, brandishing their sabres and yelling like demons; and it seemed likely enough that the grapes which had seduced me with their sweetness would prove sour enough in the sequel. At this critical moment, a couple of shells from two of our guns, which had been put in position on an acclivity commanding the turnpike, a mile off, whizzed close over my head, and with admirable aim exploded in the very midst of the advancing foe, emptying several saddles. At the same instant was heard the war-cry of a squadron of our Virginia horsemen sent by General Stuart to my relief. Their onset and the terrible effect of our artillery made the Yankees wheel and run much faster than they had come; and thus was saved my life and liberty, coat and dinner. Joining our men in the pursuit, I had the satisfaction of overtaking and capturing several of the recent disturbers of my peace. Passing the farmhouse on my return, the excellent mistress of the establishment, with a pleasant smile upon her honest face, handed me across the garden-gate my repaired garment, saying that she had kept my dinner for me. I accepted her attentions with many thanks, but preferred at this time to enjoy dinner and grapes on horseback.

One of our guns on this occasion had been fired off by a fair young lady of Williamsport, re-enacting the part of the Maid of Saragossa. She had solicited the honour from General Stuart, and the cannon was ever afterwards called by our artillerymen "The Girl of Williamsport." During the afternoon we drove the enemy back for a considerable distance, and our line of pickets was established about four miles from the Potomac, on the roads leading through Maryland into Pennsylvania. Late in the evening I received orders from General Stuart to make a reconnaissance with two squadrons of the Georgia regiment of Hampton's brigade, along the turnpike leading to Hagerstown, and ran against a strong body of the Federal cavalry, whom we at once attacked and chased into the suburbs of the town. Here large reinforcements received us with so galling a fire that we were obliged to give up the pursuit. At night General Stuart was invited with his Staff to a little party in Williamsburg, where we had a capital supper, and where, with music and the dance, in the society of some very charming young ladies, the time went merrily by, till we joined our troops, at a late hour, in their bivouac.

20th September

Our regiments moved early to the front the following day, as our scouts had reported the enemy, largely reinforced, to be advancing slowly upon our outposts. At General Stuart's request, I accompanied him on one of those little reconnoitring expeditions outside our lines, of which he was so fond, and which were always likely to terminate disastrously, as in this instance was so near being the case. We observed the precaution in the start of keeping as much as possible concealed by the dense undergrowth of the forest, but we had nevertheless been observed by some of the Yankee pickets, and a body of about twenty-five horsemen had been quietly sent to our rear, cutting us off completely from our command. We were riding along at our ease, when my sharp ear detected the little clinking sound which a sabre-scabbard often makes in striking against a tree in a ride through the woods; and, believing that one of our couriers was approaching, I turned leisurely round, and saw the long line of the hostile cavalrymen, each man riding at about twenty steps interval from his neighbour, a short distance behind us. A few quietly uttered words informed General Stuart of the impending danger, when, putting spurs to our horses, we galloped off, feeling confident that a hot pursuit would follow, in the confusion of which we might make good our escape. Accordingly, we had a regular fox-chase. The whole body of the Yankees broke forward in a run, calling out to each other, and firing their revolvers in every direction. But we were too well mounted, and too much accustomed to riding through the tangled thickets of the forest, to be overtaken; so in a short time, when the Federal troopers had been a good deal scattered by their rough and rapid motion, we slipped through them and got over to our lines again before the astonished blue-jackets had recovered from their amazement and chagrin.

General Stuart now placed me in command of the left wing of our forces, proceeding himself, with the other members of his Staff, to the extreme right. My principal care was to guard a broad turnpike road leading from Williamsport into the interior of Maryland, along which an advance of a considerable body of the enemy was expected, and where small parties of their cavalry had already appeared. I had two pieces of artillery very favourably posted, and two companies of infantry, which, to prevent a sudden dash of the Yankee horsemen, I employed in making a barricade across the road, flanked by small intrenchments stretching out about fifty yards on either side. From time to time I had to check the impudent advance of the Federal cavalry by a shot from my two guns, but altogether there was comparative quiet for several hours.

One of the Yankee officers, who, as I was later informed, was the colonel of the regiment that had effected its escape from Harper's Ferry, had attracted my attention the previous day by his gallantry and the excellent dispositions he made of his troops. Here I saw him again, galloping very near us on a handsome grey horse, quickly discovering our weak points, and posting and instructing his men accordingly. After having left him undisturbed for some time, I thought it necessary to put a stop to his proceedings, and, selecting a couple of my infantrymen who had been pointed out to me as the best shots, I made across the open space in front of our lines directly towards him. Having arrived within reasonable distance, I ordered my sharpshooters to fire at the daring colonel, who was moving along at an easy gallop, without paying me the slightest attention. After several bullets had whistled quite close to him, he suddenly halted, and, turning round, advanced a few steps and made me a military salute in the most graceful manner possible. Then calling out to one of his men to hand him a carbine, he raised the weapon, took a deliberate aim at me, and sent his ball so close to my head that I thought it had carried away a lock of my hair. I saluted him now on my part, and, wheeling round quietly, both of us rode back to our respective lines. So are courtesies sometimes exchanged in the midst of hostile conflict.

During the afternoon, Pelham, who for the present had but little occupation with his artillery, and had been reconnoitring the enemy, rode up to me and told me that he had discovered, at five hundred yards' distance, an orchard of very fine peaches, a spot which was well worth visiting, because, while enjoying the fruit, we could obtain there a near view of the movements of the Federal cavalry, which were in considerable strength hard by, and thus combine the *utile* with the *dulce*. As all was quiet in my front, I readily consented to accompany him to the orchard upon a reconnaissance which promised to be so fruitful in its results, and we were soon seated amid the branches of a large peach-tree, eating and looking out to our great satisfaction. The Federal cavalry, only a few hundred yards from us, was already four regiments strong, and farther off the rising clouds of dust indicated the approach of yet larger columns, so that it was evident our demonstration into Maryland had not failed of its desired effect, and that we occupied the attention of a considerable portion of M'Clellan's army.

I now returned to my former position, and sent an orderly with my report to General Stuart, from whom I received orders to transfer my present command to Major Pelham, and join him without delay on the right. Here also the enemy's forces were heavily massed in front of us, and our scouts reported large columns of infantry, with cavalry and artillery, advancing upon all the roads leading towards Williamsport. In my opinion the time for our retreat had now arrived, but Stuart believed he could still hold his ground, and seemed determined not to give up until he had shown fight. As usual, he was exceedingly desirous of closely observing the enemy's movements himself, and forming his own judgment concerning them; and as he and I were riding very close upon their lines, we were several times chased by small bodies of Yankee horse, whom we only escaped by jumping the fences, which crossed the country on every hand, and which were rather too high for Northern horsemanship.

In front of our centre, occupied by Hampton's brigade, no signs of the Yankees were to be observed, which led Stuart to the opinion that it would be practicable for his command to move forward under cover of the darkness of the night, make a circuit round Hagerstown, operate in the enemy's rear, and recross some ten miles higher up the Potomac. General Hampton, whose patrols had made prisoners of men belonging to several different divisions of the Federal army, believing that a very large portion, if not the whole, of M'Clellan's force was stretched out in a semicircle before him, regarded this operation as impossible, and remonstrated against it. But Stuart resolutely insisted on the execution of his daring design, and sent me back to Hampton with peremptory orders to march at once. This intrepid General instantly gave the command to move forward to what he so justly considered certain destruction, saying to me, "Good-bye, my dear friend; I don't think you will ever see me or a man of my brave brigade again." Agreeing with him perfectly as to the impossibility of the undertaking, I felt sad and oppressed as, galloping back, I saw the last of the gallant horsemen disappearing in the darkness behind the hills.

General Stuart had sent one of his batteries across the river, which, occupying the high banks opposite Williamsport, was, in case of necessity, to cover our retreat; the rest of the guns he posted on an eminence a mile from the town, around which the remaining part of our command had been concentrated. Night had set in fairly when I returned to him, and the enemy commencing to press upon us with cavalry, infantry, and artillery, a deafening cannonade ensued, filling the air with solid shot and shell, one of which latter missiles burst so near my head that for several minutes I was completely stunned.

Stuart soon discovered the mistake he had committed with regard to Hampton's brigade; and hoping it might not yet be too late to save them, he said to me, "Major, you are the only man who will perhaps be able to find Hampton and reach him in time; ride to him as quickly as your horse can carry you, and order him to return at once and recross the Potomac." I was very well aware of the danger of this commission. The night was pitch dark, the enemy's troops were spread out over the whole country, the ground was broken and difficult, and but partially known to me; but, more discouraging than all, my horse had been so worn down by the continued fatigues of the last few days, that I could scarcely spur him into a gallop. So long as the true cavalier has a good fresh horse under him, he recks little of danger, and confronts it gaily; but with the giving in of his charger's strength the *élan* disappears, and the sense of honour and duty alone urges him forward. Silently I pressed the hand of my chief as a last farewell, then, driving the spurs into the flanks of my exhausted steed, I rode off into the night. After half an hour I heard the sound of hoofs in front of me, and had just put myself in readiness for the probable rencontre, when, to my surprise and delight, my challenge for "Halt! who are you?" was answered, "It is I, Major—Captain Hamilton, of Hampton's Staff. Where can I find General Stuart?" He then informed me that Hampton had tried at several points to break through the enemy's lines, but had been met everywhere by overwhelming numbers, and being well convinced of the utter hopelessness of doing so, had on his own responsibility ordered a retreat. I despatched Captain Hamilton at once to General Stuart, to make report to him, and proceeded myself to join Hampton, whose column I could hear close at hand, trotting along the turnpike. Whoever has been himself in so perilous a situation, and has unexpectedly found hope and relief again, can understand the joyous emotion with which I greeted my chivalrous friend, who was as much pleased to receive as I was to deliver General Stuart's orders.

Without further accident we reached the banks of the Potomac, and as I was well acquainted with the somewhat difficult ford, I piloted the brigade across the broad stream, and having satisfactorily accomplished this, returned to General Stuart, who had in the mean time been pressed hard by the enemy, and was just directing his troops towards the river. Our battery on the Virginia side, joined by the other pieces as they were successively brought over, now opened a spirited fire in the direction where the enemy was supposed to be advancing, which was answered vigorously by the Federal artillery. This passage of the Potomac by night was one of those magnificent spectacles which are seen only in war. The whole landscape was lighted up with a lurid glare from the burning houses of Williamsport, which had been ignited by the enemy's shells. High over the heads of the crossing column and the dark waters of the river, the blazing bombs passed each other in parabolas of flame through the air, and the spectral trees showed their every limb and leaf against the red sky.

About 11 P.M. the crossing had been safely effected, and we all felt thankful to regain the soil of Virginia, after a loss in killed and wounded comparatively trifling when considered with the dangers to which we had been exposed. The pursuit was not continued by the enemy across the river, and we marched quietly about six miles further in the direction of Martinsburg, and bivouacked for the remainder of the night near the large plantation of Mr C., whose abundant supplies of corn and hay gave sufficient food for the fatigued and hungry horses of our whole command.

On the beautiful clear morning of Sunday, the 21st of September, we continued our march to Martinsburg, a small town on the Baltimore and Ohio Railway and the Winchester turnpike, which we reached about noon, and around which our troops bivouacked. Here we received the earliest intelligence of a decided victory, won by Jackson's corps the previous day, over a portion of the enemy's forces. General M'Clellan, finding the fords of the Potomac but slightly guarded, determined upon a forward movement into Virginia, and had already crossed the river with a considerable body of his troops at Boteler's Mill. General Lee, foreseeing this, had put Jackson in charge of his rear, and old Stonewall, having allowed as many Yankees to come over as he thought convenient, suddenly broke upon them, in his rapid and vigorous way, routing them entirely, killing and wounding large numbers, and taking 2000 prisoners. Such as were not placed *hors de combat* by his impetuous charge, he drove into the waters of the Potomac, which for hours floated down the corpses of men killed in the middle of the stream by bullet or shell, or whelmed beneath the waves in attempting to escape. Thus the retiring lion had taught a severe lesson to his pursuer, and attempts to follow our army into Virginia were for some time abandoned.

An old friend and comrade of Pelham's, Captain A., living in Martinsburg, invited the Major and myself to dine, and we spent a delightful evening with him and his amiable family, it being a late hour of the night when we joined the rest of our headquarters party in bivouac about a mile from town. During the forenoon of the following day, we received information that our waggons had halted five miles from us in the direction of Williamsport, at the small village of Hainesville, where General Stuart subsequently decided to establish his headquarters. The main body of our army had gone in the mean time in the direction of Winchester, the right wing, under Longstreet, encamping near that town; the left, under Jackson, remaining half-way between Martinsburg and Winchester, near the hamlet called Bunker Hill. The cavalry had to cover the line along the Potomac from Williamsport to Harper's Ferry, Hampton's brigade being stationed near Hainesville, Fitz Lee's near Shepherdstown, and Robertson's under Colonel Munford, near Charlestown, opposite Harper's Ferry; which latter stronghold, after everything valuable had been removed from it, had been given up to the enemy. We rejoiced greatly at coming up with our waggons again after so long a separation from them, and at having our negro servants to wait on us and fresh horses for use. Our tents were soon pitched in the garden of a little tavern; and having performed our ablutions, and indulged in a change of linen, we felt once more clean, comfortable, and happy.

In the evening, Pelham and I, mounting our mules, rode very proudly over to the camp of the 1st North Carolina regiment, where we had been invited by its officers, Colonel Baker and Major Gordon, to join them—rare luxury indeed—in a bowl of punch, and where we had a very pleasant symposium, laughing and talking over the adventures of our recent campaign. The next day passed as quietly as if there had been no enemy within a hundred miles of us, and we became assiduously lazy, lying about on the soft grass, smoking the pipe of placid contentment, if not the calumet of peace. After an early dinner, I determined to make myself useful in providing for the next morning's breakfast-table of our mess; and, with my trusty double-barrel gun, which, with the necessary ammunition, I always carried along in the waggons, I sought the partridges which were said to abound in the large fields around the village.

The American partridge in its habits closely resembles the partridge of Europe, but is much smaller in size, and different in plumage, reminding one more of the European quail. It consorts in large coveys, which, after having been dispersed, collect together again by a musical whistle, piped in a high key. Frequently, during the winter months, when the ground is covered with snow, and sometimes even in summer, they take to the trees; and more than once I have seen whole coveys of them fly out of the tufted top of a pine. The meat is white and has not much of a game flavour, but that of the young birds is very tender and delicious. I found a great many in the high grass, but having no dogs with me, I lost several that I had shot, and brought but four home with me in my bag. In the evening I galloped over to Martinsburg, and paid a second visit to Captain A. and the agreeable ladies of his household, returning after midnight to my soft bed in the tent.

Quite unexpectedly I received orders next morning from General Stuart to proceed with half of the Staff and couriers to Charlestown, nearly twenty miles off, and to establish near there, until further instructions, a second headquarters, to which reports from Robertson's brigade, forming the right wing of our line, should be sent, and from which, in case of urgency, they should be transmitted by me to General Jackson, at Bunker Hill. Our route lay through Martinsburg, where a well-dressed man, mounted on a good-looking horse, was turned over to me by the town authorities as a spy. He had been arrested there, and it was said the evidence was pretty clear that he had been engaged in this disgraceful business for a long time. I placed him between two of my couriers, giving them orders to shoot him down should he make any effort to escape.

In due time we reached Charlestown, a charming village, the county seat of one of the richest and most fertile counties of Virginia—Jefferson—and fixed our headquarters upon the farm of Colonel D., about half a mile from the town, immediately informing the commanding officer of Robertson's brigade, Colonel Munford, of my presence. Colonel D.'s plantation was one of the most extensive and beautiful I had seen in America. The stately mansion-house stood in the midst of fair lawns, and orchards prodigal of the peach and the apple; a little removed from which were large stables and granaries, and all around an amplitude of rich, cultivated fields, with a background in the distant landscape of dense forests of oak and hickory. The family consisted of the proprietor—whose military title of Colonel had been derived from the militia—his wife, daughter, and son-in-law, all of whom received me with the greatest courtesy and hospitality. The Colonel was good enough to conduct me all over the estate, where many things interested me; among others the large cider-press, then in full operation, pouring out the sweet juice of the apple, of which everybody, white and black, was permitted to drink as much as he pleased. Colonel D. took much pride in showing me his stock of Cashmere goats, the first pair of which he had himself imported many years before, at a cost of several thousand dollars. It is sad to know that all these valuable animals, at a later period of the war, were killed and devoured by the ruthless Yankees.

I was not a little embarrassed at headquarters by my prisoner, and was compelled to ask Colonel D.'s permission to use one of the rooms of a house in his garden as a jail for the night, to which I had the spy transferred, with orders that he should be bound hand and foot. It was very soon reported to me, however, that he made a very obstinate resistance to this treatment, and it became necessary for me to proceed in person to the lodge to have my orders carried out. While the work of securing him was going on, the spy broke out in a most excited manner against me, saying that he was a gentleman, and that he should not fail hereafter in making me personally responsible, and punishing me for my conduct. I begged him, very politely, to be quiet, assuring him that if I could but follow my own convictions of propriety, I should save him from the inconvenience and discomfort of his bonds by hanging him before the next morning. I regretted afterwards that I had not done so.

Colonel D. being obliged to make use of the temporary prison the following morning, I had the delinquent released from his manacles, and placed him in charge of a trusty young courier, named Chancellor, in whom I had the fullest confidence, and who had always accompanied me on expeditions of peculiar peril. About half an hour later, as I was just making the latest entry in my journal, Chancellor rushed into the room in the wildest excitement of range and mortification, and informed me, with the tears actually streaming from his eyes, that the spy had escaped. Having imprudently permitted him to walk out near a large field of Indian corn, then fully in tassle, he had profited by a momentary inattention on the part of his keeper to jump into the thicket of green stalks, and vanished behind their luxuriant blades before poor Chancellor was able to fire a shot at him. In a few minutes, I myself and most of my men were in the saddle, searching the fields narrowly, but without success; and I was obliged to relinquish the game, and return to headquarters, as the boom of artillery, sounding over from beyond Charlestown, announced that there was other work to be done.

On my way to the scene of action, I met a courier from Colonel Munford, who reported that the enemy had driven back our pickets opposite Harper's Ferry, and was advancing towards Charlestown in considerable strength. I found the brigades drawn up across the broad turnpike leading to the river, on a slight range of hills beyond Charlestown, and our artillery well posted and already hotly engaged with two Federal batteries. A large number of our men were dismounted as sharpshooters, and the firing ran briskly along our whole line. The combat grew for a time fiercer and fiercer, and the Yankees seemed determined upon driving us off; but during the afternoon we assumed the offensive and repulsed them heavily, chasing their flying columns into the protecting fortifications of Harper's Ferry. Our loss in killed and wounded was small; that of the Federals must have been large, for, besides those left upon the field, many of their wounded were carried off in their ambulances, which I had seen moving to and fro all the morning. We took twenty-five prisoners. Late in the evening I returned to the hospitable mansion of Colonel D., where the whole family awaited in great anxiety the result of the conflict, and heartily congratulated me on our success. The spy's horse, a fine mare five years old, which he left behind him, I took in charge, and it was afterwards formally turned over to me by General Stuart.

The next two days, 26th and 27th September, passed in perfect quietude, and I greatly enjoyed the glorious autumn weather, riding over all the country with Colonel D.'s son-in-law, and visiting the neighbouring plantations, which, almost without exception, were large, fertile, and beautiful. Among others, I visited the mansion of Colonel Lewis Washington, a descendant of George Washington, who had in his possession the sword which Frederick the Great of Prussia had given to his ancestor, with the inscription, "From the oldest living general to the greatest." We also visited the noble estate of Mr T., who had travelled much in Europe, and who gave us an excellent dinner, where we passed some pleasant hours over the walnuts and the wine. All around the

dwelling were magnificent hickory-trees, which were inhabited by innumerable tame grey squirrels that were great pets
of Mr T., and amused me exceedingly with their nimble and
graceful antics. On the way home we passed a large plantation which, I was told, belonged to a free negro, one of the
richest men of the county, who was himself the owner of
numerous slaves. My pleasant companion took care also to
show me, with a certain pride, what he called an old ruin—
a dismantled church, a short distance from Charlestown,
which had seventy or eighty years ago been burned down,
and which looked quite picturesque, with ivy trailing from its
shattered walls and Gothic windows. Upon me, long accustomed to the century-stained ruins of Europe, the "old"
church of Jefferson did not make the desired impression.

CHAPTER VIII

GENERAL Stuart had meanwhile shifted his headquarters to a point exactly in rear of the centre of our outpost lines, and much nearer to Jackson than my own position at Charlestown, thus rendering my further detached duty unnecessary. Accordingly, on the morning of the 28th, orders reached me to join him at "The Bower," a plantation eight miles from Martinsburg, and about ten from Charlestown. Two-thirds of our march thither had been already accomplished, and we were just entering the little village of Leetown, when a heavy cannonade was heard from the neighborhood we had left, and Stuart soon came galloping towards us. His orders now were that I should return with him at once to the scene of the conflict.

Riding at full speed, in an hour's time we reached the spot, where our troops were hard pressed by the far superior numbers of the foe. General Stuart immediately sent instructions to Fitz Lee to come with all haste to his support, and determined upon trying to maintain his position until his reinforcements should arrive. Munford and his men had been fighting with their accustomed gallantry; but the Yankees receiving again and again fresh troops from Harper's Ferry, and their numerous batteries pouring upon us a most destructive fire, we were compelled to retreat and abandon Charlestown, which was instantly occupied by the enemy, who halted there, and did not seek to push their success farther. Their possession of the town, however, was of very short duration; for Fitz Lee suddenly appearing on their right flank at the same moment that we attacked them vigorously in front, they were now driven in turn to their stronghold of Harper's Ferry; and before nightfall we had regained our old lines and re-established our pickets. As a renewed attack on the morrow was not to be expected, General Stuart with his Staff and escort started at dusk for our new headquarters in the elysian fields of "The Bower," of the beauty of which spot my comrades had given me such glowing accounts, that I waited with great impatience and curiosity the light of the morning, arriving there, as we did, after midnight in utter darkness.

When I arose from my grassy couch at sunrise on the 29th, I found, indeed, that the half had not been told me of "The Bower." Our headquarters were situated on a hill beneath a grove of lofty umbrageous oaks of primitive growth, which extended, on the right, towards the large mansion-house, the thick brick walls of which, in the blush of the early sunlight, were just visible in little patches of red through the rich verdure of the embosoming garden. At the foot of this hill, skirting a main road to which the slope was smooth and gradual, ran the bright little river Opequan, its limpid waters breaking through and tumbling over cliffs and rocks, thus forming a cascade of considerable height, with rainbows in its spray as the sun changed every falling drop into a ruby or a diamond. This lovely *entourage* was now enlivened and diversified by the white tents of our encampment, the General's, with its fluttering battle-flag, in the centre, by the smoke of the camp-fires where the negroes were busily engaged in cooking breakfasts, by the picturesque groups of officers and men who were strolling about or cleaning their arms, and by the untethered horses and mules which were quietly grazing all over the ground. One may be pardoned some extravagance of language in attempting to describe a scene which brought a feeling of thankful happiness to the soldier, weary of the excitement, the toil, the hardships, and the anguish of war. We had now plenty of food for our exhausted animals, which had undergone so much fatigue and privation, and our own commissariat was far more abundant than it had been for many weeks. The long mess-table, at which we dined together in the open air, was loaded with substantials that seemed dainties and luxuries to us, who often for days together had gone without food, and at best could secure only a meagre repast.

The plantation of "The Bower" had been long in the possession of the family of Dandridge, one member of which, more than a century ago, was the pretty widow Martha Custis, *née* Dandridge, afterwards the wife of George Washington, whose beauty and amiability have been preserved in history and fiction, who was delineated by the pencil of Stuart in one generation, and the pen of Thackeray in another. Nowhere, perhaps, in the wide limits of the State, could one have formed a better idea of the refined manners and profuse hospitable life of dear old Virginia, and before the breaking-out of the war "The Bower" had rarely been without its guests. The proprietor at the time I knew the place was a kind-hearted intelligent gentleman of fifty or thereabouts, whose charming wife retained, in a remarkable degree for America, the personal attractiveness of her youthful bloom. The rest of the numerous family consisted of grown and growing sons and daughters and nieces. Of the boys, three were in the army fighting bravely for cause and country. The girls, some of whom were exceedingly handsome, and all of whom were pleasing and accomplished, remained beneath the rooftree of the old homestead. With these amiable people I soon contracted a very intimate friendship, which time nor distance can ever weaken.

Frequently, when the mocha, of which we had captured a large supply from the enemy, was smoking invitingly on our breakfast-table, we had the pleasure of greeting the proprietor as a welcome guest at our morning meal at headquarters; later in the day a lady's skirt might even be seen in the streets of our encampment; but regularly every night we proceeded with our band to the house, where dancing was kept up till a late hour. The musical director of our band was a private of one of our regiments, whom Stuart had detached to his military family for his musical talent alone, Bob Sweeney, a brother of the celebrated banjo-player, Joe Sweeney, forerunner of all the Christy's;—Bob Sweeney, who also played this favourite instrument of the family with amazing cleverness; who knew sentimental, bibulous, martial, nautical, comic songs out of number; who was carried about with him by the General everywhere; who will have a conspicuous place in some of our later adventures; and who, after having safely passed through many accidents of war, died at last of small-pox, regretted by everybody, but most of all by "Jeb. Stuart." Bob was assisted by two of our couriers who played the violin, musicians of inferior merit; but his chief reliance was in Mulatto Bob, Stuart's servant, who worked the bones with the most surprising and extraordinary agility, and became so excited that both head and feet were in constant employment, and his body twisted about so rapidly and curiously that one could not help fearing that he would dislocate his limbs and fly to pieces in the midst of the break-down. General Stuart was himself always the gayest and noisiest of the party, starting usually at the close of the festivity the famous song—

> "If you want to have a good time,
>   Join in the cavalry,
>   "Join in the cavalry," &c.—

the whole of the excited company, young and old, uniting in the chorus, the last notes of which sounded far through the still air of the night as we walked back to our tents. General Stuart did not like it at all if any one of his Staff officers withdrew himself from these innocent merry-makings, after the fatigues of the day, to seek an early rest, and would always rouse him from his slumbers to take part in the revelry.

On the 29th Stuart turned over to my care and attention a Federal deserter, who pretended to have been an officer of Engineers in the Prussian army, and professed a competent knowledge of topography, but who turned out to be a great humbug, of whom I got rid as soon as possible. I have recently seen in the Northern newspapers that this fellow was used as a witness for the Federal Government in the great conspiracy trial at Washington.

I had now taken up my quarters in the same tent with my comrade, Captain Blackford, who had a wonderful talent for making himself comfortable; and in a short time we had so improved our *habitat* that is was quite a model establishment. My former tent (one of the so-called dog-tents), which was very narrow and contracted, insomuch that when I lay in it at full length either my head or my feet must be exposed to the night air and the dews, I turned over to our two negroes

William and Gilbert, who enlarged it greatly, and it now stood immediately in the rear of our own.

The first day of October brought a sudden change in our life of happy quietude and social enjoyment. At an early hour we received a report from our pickets near Shepherdstown that the enemy were showing themselves in large numbers on the opposite bank of the Potomac, to which about noon succeeded the intelligence that several brigades of Federal cavalry under General Pleasanton had crossed the river, driven in our pickets, and were rapidly advancing upon Martinsburg. This put us at once in the saddle, and we proceeded at full gallop to the headquarters of Colonel William H. F. Lee (son of General Robert E. Lee), who was temporarily in command of the brigade of his cousin Fitz Lee, this officer having a few days before received a kick on the leg from a malicious mule, which disabled him for a considerable time. Colonel Lee had already hastened towards Martinsburg, whither we followed him, and where General Stuart found, to his intense disgust, that the place had been abandoned,—a fact first made apparent by the whizzing bullets of the Yankee sharpshooters on approaching the outskirts of the town. Colonel Lee had retired a short distance upon the turnpike leading to Winchester; General Hampton with his brigade rested on the road leading to Hainesville, both commands still keeping up a connection with each other. General Stuart sent at once for the brigade commanders, and, expressing his great dissatisfaction, said, "Gentlemen, this thing will not do; I will give you twenty minutes, within which time the town must be again in our possession." Lee's brigade was ordered to open the attack in front, supported by a corresponding movement of Hampton's command on the enemy's right flank. Our brave horsemen, who were happy to have their bold commander with them again, received us as we galloped up to their lines with tremendous cheers, which struck terror into the hearts of the Federals.

Our column of attack (column of platoons, as the road leading into Martinsburg, being lined on either side by stone walls, rendered the formation in line impossible) was soon formed, the sabres leapt rattling from their scabbards, and with a loud yell the mighty body of many hundred horsemen dashed forward at a full gallop down the turnpike. Hampton starting simultaneously on the Hainesville road, and our horse-artillery opening a spirited fire over our heads, the effect was too much for the Yankees, who turned in rapid flight in the direction of Shepherdstown.

I was the first of our command to enter Martinsburg, but determinedly as I spurred my horse, I arrived there only in time to see the last of the blue-jackets disappearing on the opposite side of the village. Hampton now received orders to occupy Martinsburg and gradually re-establish his pickets, Lee's brigade continuing the pursuit, followed by Pelham with four of his guns, which he posted on a hill a mile beyond the town, and opened with them a rapid and very effective fire upon the dense columns of the enemy.

Stuart would have given a great deal to capture the commander of the Federal horse and annihilate his command. He had been with General Pleasanton at West Point, and they had there been bitter enemies. Pleasanton had annoyed Stuart greatly in the olden days by his foppish vanity, and in the latter days by his dash and enterprise. But this was not to be. The Yankees in their flight, recovering from their panic, often turned round and showed determined fight; and their numerous horse-artillery, which was admirably served, by its destructive fire covered excellently well their retreat. The increasing darkness also interfered much with the celerity of our movements; but the indefatigable Stuart, leading everywhere in person, carried his men forward again and again, driving the enemy through Shepherdstown into the waves of the Potomac. The rear-guard of the Federals was, by a determined attack at the last moment, completely dispersed; but, protected by the intense darkness of the night, most of the men made their escape, and only thirty prisoners fell into our hands. But the killed and wounded of the Federals must have reached a large figure.

On our return through Shepherdstown, we stopped for an hour at the house of a lady, a friend of General Stuart, Mrs L., who had lost her husband, one of his former classmates, at the first battle of Manassas. To her and her sisters I was presented; at a later period I became well acquainted with them. The General's presence was no sooner known in the village than a mob of young and pretty girls collected at Mrs L.'s house, all very much excited—to such an extent, indeed, that the General's uniform was in a few minutes entirely shorn of its buttons, taken as souvenirs; and if he had given as many locks of his hair as were asked for, our commander would soon have been totally bald. Stuart suffered all this very gracefully, with the greater resignation as every one of these patriotic young ladies gave him a kiss as tribute and reward. This latter favour was unhappily not extended to the Staff-officers, and it may be readily imagined that it was tantalising for us to look on and not take part in the pleasant ceremony. We arrived at "The Bower" at a late hour of the night, but found our kind host yet awake, the excitement and anxiety of the day having prevented him from retiring. Here we obtained compensation for the loss of our dinner in an abundant supply of cold meat, and cut into a capital Virginia ham with a greater amount of destruction than we had done during the day into the ranks of the enemy.

The following day there came some important documents and letters from General R. E. Lee to be transmitted to General M'Clellan, and I had the honour to be selected by our commander-in-chief as the bearer of them into the Federal lines. To make a favourable impression upon "our friends the enemy," I fitted myself out as handsomely as the very seedy condition of my wardrobe would allow; and as all my own horses were, more or less, broken-down, I borrowed a high-stepping, fine-limbed chestnut from one of my comrades of the Staff for the occasion. General Stuart took advantage of the opportunity to send under my charge a batch of prisoners for exchange, and, intrusting me with some private messages to M'Clellan, bade me proceed as far as possible into the enemy's lines, and employ all my diplomacy to obtain a large insight into his positions—to as great an extent, at least, as was consistent with the proprieties of my mission. About ten o'clock in the morning, my fifty or sixty Yankee prisoners were turned over to me by Colonel W. H. F. Lee at his camp, and at noon I reached the Potomac near Shepherdstown, escorted by a cavalcade of our officers, who were interested in accompanying me as far as the river with my flag of truce. This imposing ensign consisted of a white pocket-handkerchief on a long pole, and was borne most loftily by one of our couriers, a handsome martial-looking fellow, who crossed the river with it, and soon brought me the permission to come to the opposite shore. I was greatly amused, during our passage of the ford, by the bitter complaints of the Yankee prisoners, that they were forced to wade through the cold waters of the Potomac, which wet them from head to foot. I answered them, that I was not myself unmoved by the cruel compulsion, and that I should be yet more deeply affected by it, had not all the boats along the river been seized and burned by their army. On the Maryland shore I was received by a major, who was in command of the outposts at this part of the Federal lines, who handed me his proper written acknowledgment for the prisoners, and said, that as for the papers and documents I might deliver them to him, and he would forward them at once. This, of course, I politely declined, giving him to understand that despatches of such importance I could only deliver to General M'Clellan, or, should this be impossible, to some other general of his army; and adding, that as I supposed General Pleasanton to be supreme in command of this portion of the lines, I should be glad to be conducted to him. The Major here betrayed some embarrassment, and spoke of impossibilities, &c., but at last concluded to send off a mounted officer for further instructions.

Meanwhile all the Yankee soldiers who were not on duty came running towards me, impelled by curiosity to see the "great big rebel officer," in such numbers that the Major was compelled to establish a cordon of sentries around me to keep them at a respectful distance. The only camp-stool that could be produced having been politely offered me for a seat, I soon found myself engaged in a lively and pleasant conversation with a group of Federal officers. Upon one matter only that was brought into the discourse we were unable to agree. They claimed the battle of Sharpsburg as a brilliant victory for their arms. I could not see it in that light.

At length, after a weary time of waiting, came the answer to the Major's message that I might proceed; and a good-looking young cavalry officer was reported to me as guide and protector. Eager to anticipate a disagreeable and awkward formality, I now asked to be blindfolded, but this was politely waived. Starting from the ford, I took a tall and singularly shaped pine-tree, which reared itself far above the tops of its neighbours, as a landmark, and with this constantly in sight, it was not difficult for me to discover that I was purposely carried about in a circle, up hill and down dale, through dense woods and vast encampments of troops. The Federal army at this time certainly appeared to the greatest advantage in its camps. Everywhere was observable the most beautiful order. The soldiers were well dressed, and had the look of being well fed; their arms were in excellent condition; and the whole of their cantonments spoke of a high degree of military discipline, the absence of which I had so often regretted in our own bivouacs.

My companion proved to be a very pleasant young gentleman but inexperienced officer, who, during a ride of eight miles, which brought us to somebody's headquarters, voluntarily gave me much information that he should have kept to himself. Here I saw at a glance a considerable display of the pomp and circumstance of war. What a contrast it presented to the headquarters of our general officers, especially to the simple encampment of our great commander-in-chief, who, with his Staff and escort, occupied only a few small tents, scarcely to be distinguished from the tent of a lieutenant! Here a little town of canvass surrounded the magnificent marquee of the General, from which floated the stars and stripes in a reckless extravagance of bunting; numerous sentries were pacing their beats; mounted officers, resplendent with bullion, galloped to and fro; and two regiments of Zouaves in their gaudy uniforms were drawn up for parade.

I had already found out that this was General Fitzjohn Porter's headquarters, and it was evident enough that some very great personage was expected there. Adjoining the General's marquee there had been erected a beautiful pavilion, under which was stretched out a long table laden with luxuries of every description, bottles of champagne in silver ice-coolers, a profusion of delicious fruit, and immense bouquets of flowers. A balloon (I have mentioned before that this means of observation was much in use with the Federal army) was rising every few minutes to the height of several hundred feet, the car, secured by ropes, filled with officers, who, with all kinds of glasses, were looking out narrowly in the direction of Harper's Ferry. I was not mistaken in my conjectures. As I afterwards learned, no less a dignitary than President Lincoln was momentarily looked for. Escorted by General M'Clellan, the President had already inspected a great portion of the Federal army of the Potomac; and as this was to be kept a secret, my visit was necessarily to be a short one.

During the time my young companion was announcing my presence to General Porter, I directed my eye towards the river, and there stood my pine-tree, not more than three miles distant in a straight line, plainly in view.

From General Porter's tent I could now hear the sound of voices in excited conversation; indeed, I caught several very angry expressions before my guide returned with a flushed face, in which one could read plainly the reprimand that had been given him, and desired me to enter. General Porter, as he rose to receive me, I found to be a man of rather above the middle height, with a frank and agreeable face, the lower part of which was covered with a luxuriant black beard, and in his whole bearing and appearance the soldier. The floor of his ample tent was carpeted, easy-chairs and a couch offered their accommodations, and his headquarters had all the comfort of a well-furnished drawing-room. After a brief interchange of salutations, ensued the following colloquy:—

Federal General.—"You will allow me to express my regret that you have been brought here, and to say that a grave fault has been committed in your coming."

Confederate Major.—"General, I have been long enough a soldier to know that a grave mistake *has* been committed, but I also know that the fault is not on *my* side."

Fed. Gen.—"You are right—I ask your pardon. But why did you inquire for General Pleasanton, and what in the world induced you to suppose that he was in command here? I do not myself know where General Pleasanton is—at this moment he may be on your side of the Potomac."

Confed. Major. — "Where General Pleasanton is to-day I am certainly not able to tell; but as I had the pleasure of seeing him with my own eyes last night returning with considerable haste to *this* side of the river, I had the right to suppose that he was here."

Fed. Gen. (laughing). — "I can have no objection to your conjecture. When do you think to join General Stuart again?"

Confed. Major. — "Should I ride all night, I may hope to reach him some time to-morrow morning." (I was dancing at half-past ten o'clock that same night at "The Bower.")

Fed. Gen. (again laughing). — "You seem to enjoy riding at night."

Confed. Major. — "Very much, at this delightful season of the year."

The General now very courteously offered me some refreshments, which I declined, saving and excepting a single glass of brandy-and-water. I then delivered my despatches, pocketed my receipt for them, and took leave of a man whom I could not help admiring for his amenity of manners and high soldierly bearing. General Fitzjohn Porter proved to be too much of the gentleman for the Northern Government. He was very soon afterwards dismissed from the service for faults alleged to have been committed during Pope's campaigns, but I have pleasure in bearing my testimony (that of an enemy) to his qualities as a gallant soldier and an excellent fighter.

I availed myself of this opportunity of writing from the tent of the Adjutant-General a private note to Major Von R., a former brother officer of mine in the Prussian army, who was serving on M'Clellan's Staff, looking to an interview, possibly under similar circumstances as had now brought me into the Federal lines, which interview, however, never took place. Starting now upon my return, I could not help expressing to my escort how very much I regretted he should have incurred the displeasure of his general by conducting me to him. He had the amazing effrontery to deny that this was the case; but I knew better. Soon afterwards he offered me a cigar, which I thankfully accepted, and, finding it excellent, praised very highly; whereupon he said, that having a large supply of them, he should be only too happy if I would consent to take a few boxes as a present, adding that he believed we were entirely cut off from luxuries of this kind. I thanked him cordially, but declined his friendly proposal, assuring him that he was altogether mistaken as to this matter, inasmuch as the steamers that were constantly running the blockade kept us abundantly provided with havannas. This was not strictly true, and I made the little sacrifice to pride with an almost broken heart.

We had the same long roundabout ride on our return, and it was late in the evening when we arrived on the bank of the Potomac, through whose waters I was conducted half-way by my friendly foe, who, as we shook hands at parting, regretted that we were enemies to each other, and said that he hoped we should meet again, "when this cruel war was over," under happier circumstances. I thanked him for his kindly feeling, and begged him to take a lesson from me as a farewell offering. Showing him my pine-tree on the Maryland shore which had served me as landmark, I said to him—"My young friend, General Fitzjohn Porter's headquarters in a straight line are not three miles from that tree—he is in command of your right wing: to deceive me, you have conducted me all around the country, but I have always known where I was, and I have passed three divisions of your army; moreover, an important personage is every moment expected at General Porter's tent, and this personage is no other than President Lincoln." My courteous adversary laughed heartily at this, and said, "Well, I did not believe that in any other nation of the world there was a man who *could fool a Yankee*; you have shown me the contrary, and I accept the lesson." We then shook hands for the last time, and returned to our respective lines.

Darkness had already set in as I reached Shepherdstown; nevertheless I stopped for a short time at the house of Mrs L., where the recital of my adventures greatly interested a crowd of young ladies. It was half-past ten o'clock when I arrived again at "The Bower," from the brightly illuminated windows of which there came the merry sound of music and the dance. General Stuart listened with great amusement and satisfaction to my report and the particulars of my interview with General Porter; and upon my concluding, said, "My dear Von" (one of his many forms of salutation to me), "you shall have thirty minutes' dancing, and then a fresh horse shall be saddled for you, and you must be off at once to make your reports to Generals Jackson and Lee." I used my thirty minutes well, and had just taken my place opposite a very pretty girl in a Virginia reel, when J. E. B. suddenly usurped it, saying, "Be off, my dear fellow; I will do your duty here." And he did, what time I was galloping through the woods in the darkness of the night.

One o'clock had passed when, after a ride of fourteen miles, I reached Jackson's headquarters, where everybody was fast asleep. The lightest touch of my hand awoke old Stonewall, and, recognising my voice, he cried out, "Ah! there you are, my dear Major; you must bring us important news from the Yankees." I replied that I did, but that fortunately I had nothing alarming to report. Then, availing myself of the General's kind invitation, I stretched myself on the blanket by his side and quietly told my story, to which he listened attentively, interrupting me several times in his peculiar way with "Good, good!" which was always the highest expression of his satisfaction. Thanking me much for my report, he said that he would himself ride over to General

Lee's headquarters at daybreak, and thus save me the ride there for the present; that some time during the day I could proceed to Falling Waters, but above all things he desired my immediate return to Stuart, that he might be summoned to an interview at General R. E. Lee's. The sun had just peeped above the eastern horizon as I galloped up the hill to the tent of General Stuart, whom I had great difficulty in rousing from his slumbers. The General proposed to me to ride back with him as soon as his horse was saddled, but this I respectfully declined, saying that I desired first to get the few hours' sleep which I was under the impression I had richly deserved.

The day was already far advanced, when, after long and ineffectual efforts on the part of my negro William to bring me into a waking condition, I was at last stirred to consciousness by the aroma of my morning cup of coffee. The rich sunlight of October lay full over the landscape, as, refreshed by a hearty breakfast, I again rode along the highway towards Winchester. General Lee's headquarters were exactly in the centre of our army in its encampment, about midway between Bunker Hill and Winchester, at a little place called Falling Waters. On either side of the turnpike stretched for miles the camps of our troops, who plainly showed, in their healthy appearance and by their jokes and songs, how soon they had forgotten the fatigues and hardships of the recent campaign. I reached General Lee's tents in the afternoon, and was cordially greeted by my comrades, the officers of his Staff, whom I had not seen since the battle of Sharpsburg. The Commander-in-Chief himself received me at once with his invariable kindness, and heard my report of yesterday's proceedings with the liveliest interest.

The Quartermaster of the army, Colonel Corley, having received a large supply of common English boots of yellow leather for officers and men, I seized the opportunity of purchasing a pair for the very moderate sum of sixteen dollars, and threw them across the pommel of my saddle, where they seemed almost as huge as the seven-league boots of the pantomime. Just as I was returning home I had the good fortune to encounter Lieutenant Channing Price, of our Staff, who had come to headquarters on a special boot-mission of his own, and we enjoyed a most delightful ride back to "The Bower" through the woods, then gay with autumnal tinges.

For days afterwards there was perfect quiet at our head-quarters. No cannonade shook the air, and the lazy, listless life we led was in harmony with the serenity of the season, which charmed us with the repose and loveliness of the American *Fall*. The wooded hills and rich fields around "The Bower" abounded in game—partridges, pheasants, wild turkeys, hares, and grey squirrels—so that I could indulge to the fullest extent my passion for sport. Unfortunately for my bag, my ambition led me to direct my attention chiefly to the wild turkey, which is by no means so easy to kill as I had imagined. It differs very much from the domestic turkey, having a taller and slighter frame, with plumage of varied tints from a rich green to a darkish brown. These birds live in flocks of from six to eight, or even more where several families unite. The hen lays her eggs during the month of April in the nest, which is usually built in the open fields, and the young are fully grown abut the end of October, at which time they are quite fat from the abundant nourishment they have derived from the fields of Indian corn. The meat is much darker and of more decided flavour than that of the domestic turkey. The best way of getting a shot at them in the autumn is to call them, but a very good way is to hunt them with dogs, which must be trained for the purpose, and which, as soon as a flock has been started, disperse it and pursue the single birds so long and with such loud barking that they fly in affright to the tree, where the sportsman finds it a simple matter to bring them down. They fly only when pressed in this manner or when suddenly driven out of a thicket, but they run with the celerity of the greyhound, and are extremely wary and cunning. If in Europe one uses the proverb "As stupid as a turkey," in America one says "As smart as a wild gobbler." The American pheasant is a fine bird, about the size of the English grouse, but the meat is far superior, and I thought it the best game I had ever eaten. The Virginia hare is of very small size, and resembles the European rabbit in habits and appearance. It is an easy prey for any fast pointer dog, but the meat is of very inferior quality.

Very near "The Bower," on the opposite side of the Opequan, I had discovered a charming little valley, through which ran a sparkling rivulet, a tributary of the larger stream. This valley was nearly two miles in length, with a breadth of from fifty to one hundred yards, and was enclosed by high rocky cliffs, covered with a dense growth of oaks and pines. In the ravine the richest grass grew abundantly, and alternated with little patches of thick undergrowth and groups of paw-paw trees, the banana-like fruit of which was just ripening. On the immediate banks of the creek gigantic tulip-poplar, hickory, and walnut trees rose to an immense height, interlacing their branches so as to form a leafy arch over the sequestered glen. Here I found always a large quantity of game, especially the wild turkey, which came at sunrise and at dusk for water; and here I often directed my steps, or rather the steps of my pretty grey mule "Kitt." This very small but exceedingly strong animal I used always for my shooting excursions, and I was often laughed at by my comrades as I made my appearance upon her with my legs dangling nearly to the ground. But "Kitt" carried me excellently well for all that, and, with my weight of fifteen stone ten, took all the ordinary fences and ditches with the greatest ease. She stood perfectly quiet when I shot from her back, and I could throw the reins on her neck and go off for hours together, with the assurance that on my return she would be found grazing or lying down composedly at the spot where I had left her. Sometimes Bob Sweeney, the banjo-player, accompanied me on my expeditions with the fowling-piece. Bob had the good sense to confine his efforts to the grey squirrels and the partridges, of which he killed large numbers, while I was running my legs off after the larger game. Nevertheless I enjoyed even my unsuccessful turkey-hunting very much, and was frequently rewarded for my trouble by bagging a pheasant or a hare. But we had other diversions during this period of military inactivity. Pelham and I had got hold of a yellow-painted army waggon, captured from the Yankees, to which we hitched our horses and drove about all over the country, though the rapid motion of the vehicle with its hard springs over the rough rocky roads nearly shook our souls out of our bodies.

At headquarters we had some very agreeable guests, among whom were Colonel Bradley T. Johnston, and an intimate friend of General Stuart and myself, Colonel Brien, who had formerly commanded the 1st Virginia Cavalry, and had resigned his commission in consequence of his failing health. Every evening before starting for the mansion-house we all assembled—guests, officers, couriers, and negroes—around a roaring wood-fire in the centre of our encampment, where Sweeney, with his banjo, gave us selections from his *repertoire*, which were followed by a fine quartette by some of our soldiers, who had excellent voices, the *al fresco* concert always concluding with the famous chorus of "Join in the cavalry" already mentioned, which was much more noisy than melodious. But every evening the negroes would ask for the lively measures of a jig or a breakdown—a request invariably granted; and then these darkies danced within the circle of spectators like dervishes or lunatics—the spectators themselves applauding to the echo.

On the 7th, a grand ball was to take place at "The Bower," to which Mr D. had invited families from Martinsburg, Shepherdstown, and Charlestown, and in the success of which we all felt a great interest. As an exceptional bit of fun, Colonel Brien and I had secretly prepared a little pantomime, "The Pennsylvania Farmer and his Wife," in which the Colonel was to personate the farmer and I the spouse. Accordingly, when the guests had all assembled and the ball was quite *en train*, the immense couple entered the brilliantly lighted apartment—Brien enveloped in an ample greatcoat, which had been stuffed with pillows until the form of the wearer had assumed the most enormous proportions; I dressed in an old white ball-dress of Mrs D.'s that had been enlarged in every direction, and sweetly ornamented with half-a-bushel of artificial flowers in my hair. Our success greatly outran our expectations. Stuart, exploding with laughter, scrutinised me closely on all sides, scarcely crediting the fact that within that tall bundle of feminine habiliments dwelt the soul of his Chief of Staff. Again and again we were made to repeat our little play in dumb show, until, getting tired of it and wishing to put a stop to it, I gracefully fainted away and was carried from the room by Brien and three or four assistants, amid the wild applause of the company, who insisted on a repetition of the fainting scene. When, in a few moments, I made my appearance in uniform, the laughter and applause recommenced, and Stuart, throwing his arms around my neck in a burlesque of pathos, said, "My dear old Von, if I could ever forget you as I know you on the field of battle, your appearance as a woman would never fade from my memory." So the joyous night went on with dancing and merriment, until the sun stole in at the windows, and the reveillé sounding from camp reminded us that the hour of separation had arrived.

From a long rest, after the dissipations of the past night, I was roused about noon by General Stuart, with orders to ride, upon some little matters of duty, to the camp of General Jackson. I was also honoured with the pleasing mission of presenting to old Stonewall, as a slight token of Stuart's high regard, a new and very "stunning" uniform coat, which had just arrived from the hands of a Richmond tailor. The garment, neatly wrapped up, was borne on the pommel of his saddle by one of our couriers who accompanied me; and starting at once I reached the simple tent of our great general just in time for dinner. I found him in his old weather-stained coat, from which all the buttons had been clipped long since by the fair hands of patriotic ladies, and which, from exposure to sun and rain and powder-smoke, and by reason of many rents and patches, was in a very unseemly condition. When I had despatched more important matters, I produced General Stuart's present, in all its magnificence of gilt buttons and sheeny facings and gold lace, and I was heartily amused at the modest confusion with which the hero of many battles regarded the fine uniform from many points of view, scarcely daring to touch it, and at the quiet way in which, at last, he folded it up carefully, and deposited it in his postmanteau, saying to me, "Give Stuart my best thanks, my dear Major— the coat is much too handsome for me, but I shall take the best care of it, and shall prize it highly as a souvenir. And now let us have some dinner." But I protested energetically against this summary disposition of the matter of the coat, deeming my mission, indeed, but half executed, and remarked that Stuart would certainly ask me how the uniform fitted its owner, and that I should, therefore, take it as a personal favour if he would put it on. To this he readily assented with a smile, and having donned the garment, he escorted me outside the tent to the table where dinner had been served in the open air. The whole of the Staff were in a perfect ecstasy at their chief's brilliant appearance, and the old negro servant, who was bearing the roast-turkey from the fire to the board, stopped in mid-career with a most bewildered expression, and gazed in wonderment at his master as if he had been transfigured before him. Meanwhile, the rumour of the change ran like electricity through the neighbouring camps, and the soldiers came running by hundreds to the spot, desirous of seeing their beloved Stonewall in his new attire; and the first wearing of a fresh robe by Louis XIV., at whose morning toilet all the world was accustomed to assemble, never created half the sensation at Versailles, that was made in the woods of Virginia by the investment of Jackson in this new regulation uniform.

Reaching our camp again in the evening, I was informed by General Stuart that he was to start the next day with a portion of his cavalry on an extended military expedition, and that, much as he regretted being constrained to leave me behind, it was yet necessary that I should remain, to fill his place in his absence, to act for him in case of emergency, and to keep up frequent communications with General Lee. With how much pain and discontent I received this information, I do not care to say; but I had profited too much by my experience in that excellent school of military discipline, the Prussian army, to make any remonstrance.

CHAPTER IX

THE EXPEDITION INTO PENNSYLVANIA — LIFE AT "THE BOWER" DURING GENERAL STUART'S ABSENCE — THE GENERAL'S OWN REPORT OF THE EXPEDITION — CAMP LIFE AT "THE BOWER" CONTINUED, AND THREATENED FINAL DEPARTURE, WITH AN INTERLUDE OF TWO DAYS' FIGHTING NEAR KEARNEYSVILLE — A VIVACIOUS VISITOR — MILITARY REVIEW — AT LAST WE BREAK UP CAMP AT "THE BOWER."

THE day came, the 9th of October, and with its earliest streakings of light the bustle of preparation for departure. Arms were cleaned, horses were saddled, and orderlies were busy. About eight o'clock the bugle sounded to horse, and soon afterwards I, and the rest of my comrades who had been left with me behind, saw, with great depression of spirits, the long column disappear behind the distant hills. We determined, however, with a soldier's philosophy, to accept the situation, and to forget our disappointment by indulging, as much as was compatible with the performance of duty, in rides, drives, shooting, and social visiting at "The Bower." So I resumed my field-sports with very great success, except in respect of the turkeys, often accompanied by Brien, who was an excellent shot.

I had now also the satisfaction of greeting on his return

to headquarters my very dear friend and comrade, Major
Norman Fitzhugh, who had been captured, it will be recollected, near Verdiersville in August, and had spent several
weeks in a Northern prison. There was much for us to talk
over in the rapid vicissitudes which had been brought about
by the progress of the war during our separation. Fitzhugh
had been pretty roughly handled at the beginning of his
captivity, and the private soldiers of the enemy that took
him—provoked, probably, by his proud bearing—had ill-
treated him in the extreme; but he soon met officers whom he
had known before the war in the regular army, and afterwards fared better. On the 10th arrived Major Terrell, who
had formerly served on General Robertson's staff, and was
now under orders to report to General Stuart, and we had
again a pleasant little military family at our headquarters.

From General Stuart we heard nothing for several days.
There were some idle rumours, originating doubtless with the
Yankee pickets, that he had been killed, that his whole
command had been dispersed, captured, &c. Though we
certainly did not in the least credit this nonsense, we were yet
not without a good deal of anxiety as to the result of the
expedition; and as I was under the necessity, in any event, of
inspecting our line of outposts, I rode on the 12th to
Shepherdstown, in the hope of obtaining some more trust-
worthy information. Here I received the earliest tidings of the
General's successful ride through Pennsylvania, the capture of
Chambersburg, and his great seizure of horses, and also
learned that our daring band of horsemen was already on its
rapid return to Virginia. I availed myself of the opportunity
while in Shepherdstown of paying my respects to Mrs L., by
whom and the other ladies of her household I was welcomed
with the utmost kindness.

On the morning of the 13th General Stuart arrived again
safely at "The Bower," heralding his approach from afar by

the single bugler he had with him, whose notes were somewhat oddly mingled with the thrum of Sweeney's banjo. Our
delight in being again together was unspeakable, and was
greatly enhanced by the glorious issue of the expedition.
Many prisoners had been taken; he had secured large numbers of horses and mules, and he had inflicted great material
damage upon the enemy. All my comrades had mounted
themselves on fresh horses, and they came back with wonderful accounts of their adventures across the border, what
terror and consternation had possessed the burly Dutch
farmers of Pennsylvania, and how they groaned in very agony
of spirit at seeing their fine horses carried off—an act of war
which had been much more rudely performed for months and
months, not to mention numberless barbarities, never sanc-
tioned in civilised warfare, by the Federal cavalry in Virginia.

General Stuart gave me a gratifying proof that he had been
thinking of me in Pennsylvania, by bringing back with him an
excellent bay horse which he had himself selected for my
riding.

As I am fortunate enough to have General Stuart's own
official report in MS. of this memorable enterprise among my
papers, I give it here, in the belief that the reader will be glad
to follow our horsemen upon their journey in the words of
the dashing raider himself.

"HEADQUARTERS, CAVALRY DIVISION,
October 14, 1862.

"To General R. E. Lee,

"Through Colonel R. H. Chilton, A.A. General, Army of
Northern Virginia.

"Colonel,—I have the honour to report that on the 9th
inst., in compliance with instructions from the Commanding

General, Army of Northern Virginia, I proceeded on an expedition into Pennsylvania with a cavalry force of 1800 men and four pieces of horse-artillery, under command of Brig.-Gen. Hampton and Cols. W. H. F. Lee and Jones. This force rendezvoused at Darkesville at 12 o'clock, and marched thence to the vicinity of Hedgesville, where it camped for the night. At daylight next morning (October 10th) I crossed the Potomac at M'Coy's (between Williamsport and Hancock) with some little opposition, capturing two or three horses of the enemy's pickets. We were told here by the citizens that a large force had camped the night before at Clear Spring, and were supposed to be *en route* for Cumberland. We proceeded northward until we reached the turnpike leading from Hagerstown to Hancock (known as the National Road). Here a signal station on the mountain and most of the party, with their flags and apparatus, were surprised and captured, and also eight or ten prisoners of war, from whom, as well as from citizens, I learned that the large force alluded to had crossed but an hour ahead of me towards Cumberland, and consisted of six regiments of Ohio troops, and two batteries under General Cox, and were *en route, via* Cumberland, for the Kanawha. I sent back this intelligence at once to the Commanding General. Striking directly across the National Road, I proceeded in the direction of Mercersburg, Pennsylvania, which point was reached about 12 o'clock. I was extremely anxious to reach Hagerstown, where large supplies were stored, but was satisfied from reliable information that the notice the enemy had of my approach, and the proximity of his forces, would enable him to prevent my capturing it. I therefore turned towards Chambersburg. I did not reach this point till after dark in a rain. I did not deem it safe to defer the attack till morning; nor was it proper to attack a place full of women and children without summoning it first to surrender. I accordingly sent in a flag of truce and found no military or civil authority in the place; but some prominent citizens, who met the officers, were notified that the place would be occupied, and if any resistance were made the place would be shelled in three minutes. Brigadier-General Hampton's command being in advance, took possession of the place, and I appointed him Military Governor of the city. No incidents occurred during the night, throughout which it rained continuously. The officials all fled the town on our approach, and no one could be found who would admit that he held office in the place. About 275 sick and wounded in hospital were paroled. During the day a large number of horses of citizens were seized and brought along. The wires were cut and the railroad obstructed, and Colonel Jones's command was sent up the railroad towards Harrisburg to destroy a trestlework a few miles off. He, however, reported that it was constructed of iron, and he could not destroy it. Next morning it was ascertained that a large number of small-arms and munitions of war were stored about the railroad buildings, all of which that could not be easily brought away were destroyed—consisting of about 5000 new muskets, pistols, sabres, and ammunition; also a large assortment of army clothing. The extensive machine-shops and depot buildings of the railroad and several trains of loaded cars were entirely destroyed. From Chambersburg I decided, after mature consideration, to strike for the vicinity of Leesburg as the best route of return, particularly as Cox's command would have rendered the direction of Cumberland, full of mountain gorges, exceedingly hazardous. The route selected was through an open country. Of course I left nothing undone to prevent the inhabitants from detecting my real route and object. I started directly towards Gettysburg, but, having passed the Blue Ridge, turned back towards Hagerstown for six or eight miles, and then crossed to Maryland by Emmettsburg, where, as we passed, we were hailed by the inhabitants with the most enthusiastic demonstrations of joy. A scouting party of 150 lancers had just passed towards Gettysburg, and I regretted exceedingly that my march did not admit of the delay necessary to catch them. Taking the route towards Frederick, we intercepted despatches from Colonel Rush (Lancers) to the commander of the scout, which satisfied me that our whereabouts was still a problem to the enemy. Before reaching Frederick, I crossed the Monocacy, and continued the march throughout the night, *via* Liberty, New Market, and Monrovia, on the Baltimore and Ohio Railroad, where we cut the telegraph wires and obstructed the railroad. We reached at daylight Hyattstown, on M'Clellan's line of communication with Washington, but we found only a few waggons to capture. and pushed on to Barnesville, which we found just vacated by a company of the enemy's cavalry. We had here corroborated what we had heard before, that Stoneman had between four and five thousand troops about Poolesville and guarding the river fords. I started directly for Poolesville, but instead of marching upon that point, I avoided it by a march through the woods, leaving it two or three miles to my left, and getting into the road from Poolesville to the mouth of the Monocacy. Guarding well my flanks and rear, I pushed boldly forward, meeting the head of the enemy's force going towards Poolesville. I ordered the charge, which was responded to in handsome style by the advance squadron (Irvine's) of Lee's brigade, which drove back the enemy's cavalry upon the column of infantry advancing to occupy the crest from which the cavalry were driven. Quick as thought Lee's sharpshooters sprang to the ground, and, engaging the infantry skirmishers, held them in check till the artillery in advance came up, which, under the gallant Pelham, drove back the enemy's force upon his batteries beyond the Monocacy, between which and our solitary gun there was a spirited fire for some time. This answered, in connection with the high crest occupied by our piece, to screen entirely my real movement quickly to the left, making a bold and rapid strike for White's Ford, to force my way across before the enemy at Poolesville and Monocacy could be aware of my design. Although delayed somewhat by about 200 infantry strongly posted in the cliffs over the ford, they yielded to the moral effect of a few shells before engaging our sharpshooters; and the crossing of the canal (now dry) and river was effected with all the precision of passing a defile on drill—a section of the artillery being sent with the advance and placed in position on the Loudoun side, another piece on the Maryland heights, while Pelham continued to occupy the attention of the enemy with the other, withdrawing from position to position until his piece was ordered to cross. The enemy was marching from Poolesville in the mean time, but camp up in line of battle on the Maryland bank, only to receive a thundering salutation, with evident effect, from our guns on this side. I lost not a man killed on the expedition, and there were only a few slight wounds. The enemy's loss is not known, but Pelham's one gun compelled the enemy's battery to change its position three times.

"The remainder of the march was destitute of interest. The conduct of the command, and their behaviour towards the inhabitants, are worthy of the highest praise. A few individual cases only were exceptions in this particular. Brigadier-General Hampton and Colonels Lee, Jones, Wickham, and Butler, and the officers and men under their commands, are entitled to my lasting gratitude for their coolness in danger and cheerful obedience to orders. Unoffending persons were treated with civility, and the inhabitants were generous in their proffers of provisions on the march. We seized and brought over a large number of horses, the property of citizens of the United States. The valuable information obtained in this reconnaissance as to the distribution of the enemy's force, was communicated orally to the Commanding General, and need not be here repeated. A number of public functionaries and prominent citizens were taken captive, and brought over as hostages for our own unoffending citizens, whom the enemy has torn from their homes, and confined in dungeons in the North. One or two of my men lost their way, and are probably in the hands of the enemy.* The results of this expedition, in a moral and political point of view, can hardly be estimated, and the consternation among property-holders in Pennsylvania was beyond description. I am specially indebted to Captain B. I. White (C.S. Cavalry) and to Messrs Hugh Logan and Har-baugh, whose skilful guidance was of immense service to me. My Staff are entitled to the highest praise for untiring energy in the discharge of their duties. I enclose a map of the expedition, drawn by Captain W. W. Blackford to accompany this report; also a copy of orders enforced during the march.

"Believing that the hand of God was clearly manifested in the signal deliverance of my command from danger and the crowning success attending it, I ascribe to Him the praise, the honour, and the glory.—I have the honour to be, most respectfully, your obedient servant,

(Signed) J. E. B. Stuart,
Major-General Commanding Cavalry."

All now went merrily again at "The Bower." General Stuart, who had been blessed with the satisfaction of "winning golden opinions from all sorts of people," was the lightest-hearted of the whole company. On the 15th another ball was given in honour of the expedition, and the ladies of the neighbourhood were brought to the festivity in vehicles captured in the enemy's country, drawn by fat Pennsylvania

---

* "I marched from Chambersburg to Leesburg, 90 miles, with only one hour's halt, in thirty-six hours, including a forced passage of the Potomac—a march without a parallel in history."

horses. Stuart was, of course, the hero of the occasion, and received many a pretty compliment from fair lips.[†] Yielding to the urgent solicitations of the ladies and the General, Brien and I again produced our popular extravaganza, which was received, as at its first representation, with the greatest applause.

The beams of the morrow's sun were just making their way through the intricacies of foliage above our heads, as we lay in camp resting from the fatigues of the night's dancing, when a blast of the bugle brought the whole command to their feet, with its summons to new and serious activity. The enemy in strong force, with cavalry, infantry, and artillery, had crossed the Potomac during the latter part of the night, had driven in our pickets, and were resolutely advancing upon the main body of our cavalry, which, having been duly advised of their approach, confronted the far superior numbers of the Yankees in a tolerable position on the turnpike between Shepherdstown and Winchester, near the small hamlet of Kearneysville. General Stuart had already with great promptness reported their advance to Generals Lee and Jackson, asking for reinforcements; our horses were now saddled, and we soon passed at a full gallop the mansion-house of "The Bower," where only a few hours before the violin and banjo had sent forth their enlivening strains, riding forward to the scene of action, which already resounded with wilder music.

We found a full division of the Federal infantry moving upon us in admirable order, their cavalry operating on either flank, and their artillery seeking to get into position upon some heights in our front, where several pieces had already

---

[†]The ladies of Baltimore presented General Stuart at this time with a pair of golden spurs, as a token of their appreciation, whereupon he adopted for himself the *nom de guerre*, "Knight of the Golden Spurs," signing his name, in private letters of his, sometimes "K.G.S."

arrived and had opened a brisk and annoying fire upon our horsemen. Large clouds of dust rising all along the road towards Shepherdstown indicated the approach of other bodies of the enemy, and it was quite plain that our resistance to odds so overwhelming could be only of short duration.

A great part of our men had been dismounted as sharp-shooters, and General Stuart and myself endeavoured to place them to the greatest advantage, and to animate them to the utmost obstinacy in the fight by our own example, on horseback as we were, and exposed to the continuous fire of the Federal tirailleurs; but we were compelled to withdraw from position to position, all the time happily well protected in our retreat by the excellent service of our horse-artillery under the untiring Pelham. During the afternoon we were reinforced by a brigade of infantry, which aided in checking for a time the onward movement of the enemy, but which did not accomplish as much as we had hoped for, and the order for a still further retreat had just been given, when about dusk the Federals came to a halt, and, to our infinite surprise, turned slowly back for a mile and a half, where we soon saw the main body go quietly into bivouac, and became con-vinced from their numerous camp-fires that no further attack was to be apprehended during the night—if, indeed, satisfied with their success, they had not determined to return the following day into Maryland.

General Stuart himself directed the placing of a strong double cordon of outposts, and, having planted two pieces of artillery on a crest of the road, gave orders for the remainder of his troops to bivouac and cook their rations. The General then proceeded with his Staff to headquarters at "The Bower," which was only a few miles distant. Before we reached there we were overtaken by a drenching shower of rain, and we thankfully accepted Mr D.'s kind invitation on our arrival to dry our dripping garments and warm our chilled bodies before a roaring wood-fire in his large and comfortable family drawing-room. Here we found two Englishmen, the Hon. Francis Lawley, the well-known Richmond correspondent of the 'Times,' and Mr Vizetelly, who was keeping the readers of the 'Illustrated London News' informed of the events of the war with pen and pencil, with both of whom we were to spend many pleasant hours in camp. These gentlemen were at the time guests at General Lee's headquarters, and had undertaken the long ride to "The Bower" for the satisfaction of one day with Stuart. This satisfaction had been greatly marred by the troublesome advance of the Yankees; but by snatching a few hours from the night, we secured time enough for a delightful parley, of which the news from the old country formed a considerable part.

The fighting was renewed at an early hour the next day; and, as the enemy was also reported to be advancing in strength upon Charlestown from Harper's Ferry, it appeared to be a general movement of the whole Federal army. At "The Bower" the breaking up of our camp seemed to indicate a final departure from our soldier's paradise. The tents were struck, the waggons were packed, and every preparation was made for starting at any moment. Our amiable guests, who had come only for a day, had now an additional reason for taking leave, as they were not prepared for accompanying us upon any extended military adventure.

The Yankee, fully conscious of their own strength and our comparative weakness, were pressing slowly forward, and General Stuart had given orders to our troops to offer only a feeble resistance, and retired deliberately to an easily defensible position, about a mile and a half from "The Bower," where our artillery had been eligibly posed on a range of hills forming a wide semicircle. About nine o'clock General R. E. Lee arrived at this point; A. P. Hill's division was on the march to reinforce us; and it seemed clear that the further progress of the Federals, certainly any attempt on their part to cross the Opequan, would be energetically opposed. At this time I received orders from General Stuart to proceed with a number of couriers at once to the little town of Smithfield, about twelve miles distant, where we had a small body of cavalry, to watch the enemy's movements on our right, and establish frequent communications with Jackson at Bunker Hill only a few miles off. *En route* I had to pass in the immediate neighbourhood of "The Bower," where I found the ladies of the family all assembled in the verandah, in a state of great excitement and anxiety. I did my best to console my fair friends, who wept as they saw me; but I could not help feeling a good deal of solicitude with regard to their position, since they would certainly be within range of the artillery fire; and should the enemy get possession of the place by any accident, it could hardly be hoped that they would not revenge themselves savagely upon the household for all the kindness we had received at their hands.

It was about mid-day when I reached Smithfield, which I found occupied by a squadron picketing the turnpike to Shepherdstown and Harper's Ferry. Our brigade stationed at Charlestown had evacuated the place before the superior numbers of the enemy, and retired in the direction of Berryville, so that there was nothing in the way of the Federal advance but these our pickets, and the dreaded blue uniforms were expected by the excited inhabitants to make their appearance every minute. Accordingly, I had not been more than an hour in the village, when our outposts from the Shepherdstown road came galloping along in furious haste, reporting a tremendous host of Yankee cavalry right behind them in hot pursuit. I rode forward immediately with about fifty men to meet the enemy, but found, as is usual in such cases of alarm, that the danger was by no means so imminent as had been represented, the Yankees having halted on a little hill about two miles from town, and their whole force consisting of a squadron of horsemen, which turned back on my approach, and moved off when a few carbine-shots had been exchanged. This squadron had come from Harper's Ferry, along a by-road which struck the turnpike at a point about midway between Kearneysville and Smithfield, which point they had reached just ten minutes after General Lee with a very small escort had passed by. Our Commander-in-Chief had thus very narrowly escaped falling into the hands of the enemy, and I thought it necessary to despatch a courier at once to General Stuart to inform him that the road was not clear.

During the afternoon the alarm was renewed, this time in the direction of Charlestown; but industriously as I endeavoured to discover the whereabouts of the Yankee infantry, who had been plainly seen advancing along the turnpike with glistening bayonets, and the dust rising on their line of march, I could obtain no trace of them whatever, after a ride of four miles towards their supposed quarter of approach. Late in the evening I received a report from Colonel Jones, now commanding Robertson's brigade, that the hostile forces were retreating again towards Harper's Ferry, and that he hoped to be again in occupancy of Charlestown even before his message could reach me. The firing in the direction of "The Bower" had now ceased; and as I felt well assured that the two Federal columns were in corresponding movement, I rightly conjectured that the Yankees were also retreating there. So I established my men and myself at the house of an interesting young widow, who, with her sister, enlivened our evening with songs and spirited discourse.

Agreeably with my expectation, I received orders early next morning to return to "The Bower," which not a little delighted me. It was a sparkling, beautiful morning of autumn, and I enjoyed the ride home the more for being fortunate enough—firing from my horse's back with my revolver—to kill a grey squirrel, which, as our mess arrangements had been thrown into utter disorder by the events of the last two days, was gladly welcomed the same evening on our dinner table. Meanwhile our tents had been again put up at "The Bower," and no one who had not visited the place in our absence would have supposed that any change had occurred in the interim. The Federal army, after considerable fighting the previous day, had recrossed the Potomac, their rearguard being badly cut up by a dashing charge of Lee's cavalry. The Federal newspapers called the movement a "grand and successful reconnaissance in force," and it had evidently been undertaken to counteract a little the effect, and abate the ill-feeling, that had been produced all over the North by Stuart's expedition into Pennsylvania.

Once more established in quietude at "The Bower," we received from our kind friends, Mr D. and his family, numberless proofs of their great satisfaction in having us near them. In accordance with his promise, Mr Vizetelly came now to pay us a longer visit, unaccompanied, however, to our regret, by Mr Lawley, who had been obliged to go to Richmond for the purpose of sending off his regular letter to the 'Times.'

Our new guest was an old campaigner, who accommodated himself very readily to the hardships of camp life, and was soon established in his own tent, which I had caused to be erected for him in the immediate neighbourhood of that of Blackford and myself. He was not long in becoming a general favourite at headquarters. Regularly after dinner, our whole family of officers, from the commander down to the youngest lieutenant, used to assemble in his tent, squeezing ourselves into narrow quarters to hear his entertaining narratives, which may possibly have received a little embellishment in the telling, but which embraced a very wide circle of human experience, and had a certain ease and brilliancy beyond most such recitals. The "ingenuous youth" of our little circle drank in delightedly the intoxications of Mabille and the Chateau des Fleurs, or followed the story-teller with eager interest as he passed from the gardens and the boudoirs of Paris to the stirring incidents and picturesque scenery of the Italian campaign, which he had witnessed as a guest of Garibaldi. V. was greatly pleased with our musical entertainments; and when, after talking for several hours, he had become exhausted, and when, from the gathering darkness, we could only distinguish the place where he was reclining by the glow of his pipe, and thus lost all the play of the features in his rehearsal, we proceeded to our great central camp-fire, there to renew the negro dances to the music of the banjo—scenes which Vizetelly's clever pencil has placed before the European public in the pages of the 'Illustrated London News.' Less successful was our friend in his efforts to improve the *cuisine* of our negro camp cook, and we often had the laugh upon him—especially when one day he produced in triumph a roast pig, with the conventional apple in its mouth, which we found to be raw on one side and burned to a cinder on the other. This work of art had been prepared under his own personal management, and was served as *cochon à l'Italienne*, but it proved by no means so happy an accident as the original roast pig, done *à la Chinoise*.

Our supplies now began to fail in the country around "The Bower." The partridges had grown exceedingly wild, and we were obliged, each in his turn, to make long excursions into the woods and fields to keep our mess-table furnished. I was therefore very much gratified when my friend Rosser appeared early one morning at my tent, with the news that there was to be a large auction sale of native wines and other supplies that very day, at a plantation only eight miles off in the direction of Charlestown. As all was quiet along our lines, we at once determined to attend the sale, so the horses were hitched to the yellow-painted waggon, and we were soon proceeding at a rapid trot over the rocky road, amid the loud outcries and bitter complaints of my gallant Colonel of the 5th Virginia Cavalry, who declared that he had never in his life experienced such joltings. Arrived at the place of destination, we bought largely, making frequent trials and tastings of Corinth and blackberry wines, and returned to camp with our waggon well filled with stores of various kinds. Among our purchases was an immense pot of lard, which we placed in the back part of the waggon, regarding it as an acquisition of great value for our camp biscuit-bakery. We had not, however, counted on the melting influence of the sun upon the lard, and the consequences was that with every jolt of the waggon over the frequent stones in the road, the fluid mass sent its jets of grease in a fountain over the hams, potatoes, and apples that covered the bottom of the vehicle. This annoyance, provoking as it was, little disturbed our temper, which had been somewhat mellowed by the frequent inhibitions of the country wine (in the way of tasting); and we continued our drive at a rattling pace, varying our discourse from the gay to the sentimental. We had just reached the topic of the tender passion, when, all unheeding the roadway before us, I bumped the waggon against a large stone with so severe a shock that Rosser was thrown out far to the left, while I settled down, after a tremendous leap, far to the right. Fortunately, beyond some slight contusions, neither of us sustained any damage by this rude winding-up of our romantic conversation. The horses were reasonable enough not to run off, and we quietly continued our drive to headquarters, but we talked no more sentiment on the way.

Major Terrell, having been ordered to Winchester in

attendance on a court-martial, had left his excellent horses to my exclusive use, and my own animals, enlarged in number by the addition of the stout Pennsylvanian, had very much improved by their long rest and rich grazing, so that my stable was now extensive, and we had many a pleasant ride with our fair lady friends. On Sunday, the 26th of October, there was a grand review of Hampton's brigade, which was attended by the ladies from far and near, and as the day was lovely, it proved a fine military spectacle. When the review was over, the officers of our own and Hampton's Staff assembled to witness the trial of a diminutive one-pounder gun, which turned out to be of very little account, and afterwards we had some equestrian sports, matches in horse-racing, fence-jumping, &c. Captain Blackford, who, with a thoroughbred chestnut mare, attempted to take a high fence just in advance of Stuart and myself, had a severe fall, which was fortunately unattended with serious consequences. Re-marking upon it, that, in my opinion, the fault lay not so much with the horse as with the rider, Stuart said, "Hear old Von, how grand he talks!" Then turning to me, he added, in a banter, "Why don't you jump the fence yourself, if you know how to do it better?" I had never leaped my heavy-built Pennsylvanian as yet, and I was in doubt whether he was equal to the lofty barrier, but as there was no possible escape from Stuart's challenge, I struck my spurs into his sides, and over he went like a deer, amidst the loud applause of the General himself and other spectators. I had now the laugh on my side, and very soon afterwards the opportunity of ban-tering Stuart, when he could say and do nothing in reply. Returning to camp, we took, as a short cut, a road that led through a field of Indian corn; upon getting to the farther end of which, we found that the fence, usually pulled down at this place, had been recently put up, making a formidable barrier to our farther progress. Stuart and others observing this, turned off to the right, towards the main road; but seizing my opportunity, I cried out to him, "General, *this* is the way;" and clearing the five-barred fence in a splendid leap, I arrived at headquarters several minutes in advance of my comrades, whom I welcomed upon their approach, rallying my chief very much for not having followed my example.

Our long and delightful sojourn now drew rapidly to its close. Guest after guest departed, and every day the indications of a speedy departure became plainer. At length, on the 29th of October, a hazy, rainy autumn day, the marching orders came, and the hour arrived for the start. A number of the Staff did not fail to indulge in the obvious reflection that nature wept in sympathy with us at the separation. With heavy hearts indeed, we left the beautiful spot, and bade adieu to its charming, kindly inhabitants. Silently we rode down the hill, and along the margin of the clear Opequan stream, musing on the joyous hours that had passed away— hours which those few of our dashing little band of cavaliers that survived the mournful finale of the great war, will ever hold in grateful remembrance.

CHAPTER X

GENERAL M'Clellan, the Federal Commander-in-Chief, having largely reinforced his army with regiments from the new levy of 300,000 volunteers called out for nine months, and having brought it to a strength of 140,000 men, well equipped in every respect, had at last determined upon a forward movement, all unknowing at the time that the supreme command was soon to be taken from him by the Government at Washington. The right wing of the Federal forces, by a strong demonstration towards Harper's Ferry, made a show of invading Virginia from this point, but the great bulk of the army crossed the Potomac about fifteen miles lower down, near the little town of Berlin. General Lee, having been opportunely informed by his vigilant cavalry of the enemy's operations, had commenced, in the mean time, a movement on the opposite side of the Blue Ridge, in a nearly parallel direction towards Front Royal, being about a day's march ahead. Longstreet's corps was in the advance, Jackson's troops following slowly, covering the rear, and still holding the passes of the Blue Ridge, Snicker's, Ashby's and Chester Gaps. The cavalry under Stuart had orders to cross the Ridge at Snicker's Gap, to watch closely the movements of the enemy, retard him as much as possible, and protect the left flank of our army.

So we rode quietly along in the tracks of our horsemen, who, before the Staff had left "The Bower," had proceeded in the direction of Berryville. Our mercurial soldiers were as gay as ever, and even the most sentimental members of the Staff had rallied from the despondence incidental to departure from our late encampment, when during the afternoon we reached *en route* the little town of Smithfield, where, under Bob Sweeney's direction as *impresario,* we managed to get up a serenade for the amiable widow who had entertained me with such hospitality.

Meanwhile the rain, which had been falling when we rode off from "The Bower," had ceased, a keen north wind had set in, and it had begun to freeze hard, when, late at night, we reached Berryville, chilled, wet, and hungry. The provisions of the country had been more or less consumed by the troops who had preceded us on the march, and it was therefore regarded as exceedingly apropos that we were invited to supper by a prominent citizen, at whose pleasant house we greatly enjoyed a warm cup of tea, a capital old Virginia ham, and afterwards a pipe of Virginia tobacco before a roaring wood-fire.

Our troops bivouacked about two miles from town; and as on a march, for the sake of the example, we never took up our quarters beneath a roof, we left our hospitable entertainer about midnight, and established ourselves in an open field under some old locust-trees, near several large fodder-stacks, which furnished us with abundant food for our horses. It was a clear, cold, starlight night, and as we had no protection from the frost but our blankets, we kept in lively blaze several tremendous fires, the wood for which each and every one of us had assisted in collecting. General and Staff were all fast asleep, when, on a sudden, we were aroused by a loud crash, which startled even the feeding horses and mules. One of the old hollow trees, against the trunk of which our largest fire had been imprudently kindled, after smouldering for hours, had at last yielded to the force of the wind and fallen heavily to the ground, fortunately without doing any damage whatever.

In the early morning, when we awoke to the *reveillé*, the fires had quite burnt out, a white hoar-frost lay thickly over every object around us, and the shivering officers of our military family expressed in every feature their ardent desire for a good warm breakfast. As we were discussing the probabilities of such a thing, we were most agreeably surprised by the kind invitation of a neighbouring planter to satisfy ourselves at his hospitable board, an invitation which we did not hesitate to accept. To provide against a future want of breakfast, when a good Samaritan might not be so near at hand, our careful mess-caterer, the portly doctor of our Staff, availed himself of the opportunity of purchasing a quantity of hams and bacon, which, being deposited for safety in an army-waggon, were stolen before two hours had elapsed by some of our rascally negro camp-followers.

The sun shone down with the warmth and glory of the soft Indian summer, a season of peculiar loveliness in America, when we reached the Shenandoah, our passage of which was extremely picturesque. The banks of this beautiful stream are often bold, and sometimes even majestic, the current breaking through gigantic cliffs which rise to the height of several hundred feet on either side, or flowing placidly along between wooded shores, whose stately trees, where the river is narrowest, almost intermingle their branches. The forests skirting the course of the Shenandoah were now glowing with the gorgeous hues of the American autumn, which the landscape-painter cannot adequately reproduce nor the writer properly describe. The light saffron of the chestnut-trees was in effective contrast with the rich crimson of the oaks and maples, while the trailing vines and parasites displayed every tint from the palest pink to the deepest purple. Upon the opposite shore, at a distance of only a few hundred yards from the margin of the river, rose the mountain-range of the Blue Ridge thickly covered with forest, within whose depths the head of our column was just disappearing as we arrived at the bank. The main body was passing the stream, while here and there a single trooper might be seen watering his horse or quietly examining his weapons.

On the summit of the mountain we found a portion of our Maryland cavalry, which, having been stationed there to guard Snicker's Gap, had been engaged in a sharp conflict with a party of Federal cavalry that disputed its possession, and had driven back their opponents with severe loss. Dead bodies of men and animals, lying still unburied along the road, gave evidence of the obstinacy of the fight on both sides. The Federal army in its forward movement had meanwhile made but slow progress, the main body having proceeded no farther than Leesburg and its immediate neighbourhood, only a few detachments of cavalry having advanced beyond that point. So we continued our march wholly without interruption all the beautiful autumn day through the smiling county of Loudoun, one of the fairest and most fertile regions in Virginia, passing many fine estates with extensive corn-fields and large orchards, until we arrived in the evening in the vicinity of the little village of Upperville, where we bivouacked, and without difficulty obtained abundant provisions for our men and forage for our animals.

The counties of Loudoun and Fauquier had known but little as yet of the devastations of the war, and abounded in supplies of every description, which were eagerly offered for sale by the farmers at moderate prices, and might have subsisted our army for six months. Instead of being permitted to profit by this plenty, we had been compelled for the past two months, through the mismanagement and want of experience of the officials of the Quartermaster's Department at Richmond, and against the earnest remonstrances of General Lee, to draw all our supplies from the capital, whence they were sent by rail to Staunton, there to be packed into waggons and deported beyond Winchester, a distance of more than one hundred miles after leaving the railroad. The subsistence which was so near at hand was thus left for the enemy, by whom it was afterwards used to the greatest advantage. The importance, nay the necessity, in a war of such magnitude, carried on over so vast and thinly-populated a territory, of establishing great magazines for the collection and storage of provisions for the army, very often occurred to me during the struggle in America, and I have, on several occasions, expressed my opinion with regard to it. Had the Confederate authorities, following Napoleon's example, established at the beginning of the war (when it might easily have been done) large depots of army-supplies at points not exposed, like Richmond, to raids of cavalry, I am convinced that it would have had a material influence on the final issue of the great conflict. The difficulties that were experienced during the last two years of the war in supporting the army, and the terrible privations to which men and animals were subjected in consequence of early maladministration and neglect, can be known only to those who were eyewitnesses of the misfortune and participants in the suffering.

Having sent out a strong cordon of pickets from our place

of bivouac near Upperville, General Stuart yielded to the urgent solicitations of Dr Eliason, our staff-surgeon, to ride with him to his home in the village, and spend the evening and night at his house. As I was included in the invitation, I bore them company. We were received very cordially by the ladies of the doctor's family, and many others, who, as soon as our arrival was known, had flocked to the mansion. I very quickly secured for myself the friendship of Dr Eliason's little daughter, a child of ten years of age, who suffered under the sad infirmity of blindness. With the most eager interest she listened to the words of the foreign soldier, whom she required to give her an exact description of his personal appearance; and I was deeply touched as I looked into those tender, rayless blue eyes which gave back no answering glance to my own, and which were yet bent towards me with such seeming intelligence. How little I thought, as I enjoyed the hospitality of these kind people, that nine months later I was to be brought to their house prostrated by a wound which the surgeons declared to be mortal, and that I was to be received by them with an affectionate sympathy such as they could only be expected to manifest for a near and dear relative!

31st October

Our horses stood at the door of Dr Eliason's house at the hour of sunrise, and a short gallop brought us to the bivouac of our horsemen, whom we at once aroused to activity with orders for immediate saddling. As Messieurs the Yankees were so long in finding us out, General Stuart had determined to look after them; and in a few minutes our column, animated by the hope of again meeting the enemy, was in motion along the road leading to the little town of Union, about midway between Upperville and Leesburg, near which latter place we were quite sure of encountering them. We reached Union at noon, where we came to a halt, sending out in various directions scouts and patrols, who speedily reported that the main body of the Federal cavalry were at Aldie, where they were feeding their horses, having arrived there since morning, but that a squadron of them was three miles nearer to us at a farm known as Pothouse. Towards this squadron we started immediately, and, moving upon by-roads, arrived within a few hundred yards of them before they had any idea of our approach. Their earliest warning of danger was the wild Confederate yell with which our advance-guard dashed upon them in the charge. They belonged to the 3d Indiana Cavalry, a regiment which we had often met in battle, and which always fought with great steadiness and courage. I could not resist joining in the attack upon our old enemies, and was soon in the midst of the fight. This lasted, however, only a few minutes. After a short but gallant resistance, the Federal lines were broken, a great part of the men were cut down or taken prisoners, and the rest of them driven into rapid flight, pursued closely by the Confederates.

Captain Farley* and myself, being the foremost of the pursuers, had a very exciting chase of the captain commanding the Federal squadron, who, at every demand that we made for his surrender, only spurred his horse into a more furious gallop, occasionally turning to fire at us with his

---

*Captain Farley, who served as a volunteer aide-de-camp on the Staff of General Stuart, was a very remarkable young man. He was by birth a South Carolinian, but he entered the service quite independently of all State military organisations. Promotions and commissions had been frequently offered him by the General, but he refused them all, preferring to be bound to no particular line of duty, but to fight, to use an American phrase, "on his own hook." He

revolver. But each moment I got nearer and nearer to him; the long strides of my charger at last brought me to his side; and I was just raising myself in the saddle to put an end to the chase with a single stroke of my sabre, when, at the crack of Farley's pistol, the fugitive, shot through the back, tumbled from his horse in the dust.

Yet a little further Farley and myself continued in pursuit of the flying Federals, and then returned to rejoin General Stuart. While slowly retracing my steps, I discovered the unfortunate captain, lying against the fence on the roadside, apparently in great agony, and evidently enough in a most uncomfortable situation. Desirous of doing all that I could to alleviate his misery, I alighted from my horse and raised the poor fellow into an easier recumbent position, despatching at the same time one of my couriers to our staff-surgeon, Dr Eliason, with the request that he would come to me as speedily as possible. The wounded officer seemed to me in a state of delirium, calling out, as he did, to every passing horseman, that the rebels who had killed him were about to rob him also, and scattering his personal effects, his watch, money, &c., in the road, so that I had some difficulty in saving them for him. One of our orderlies, who had galloped up, begged me to give him the captain's canteen, it being a very large and handsome one. This of course I refused, the more decidedly as the poor fellow had been crying out continually for drink, and, resting upon my arm, had already nearly exhausted the canteen of its contents. In a few moments Dr Eliason came up, and, having examined the

---

was accustomed to go entirely alone upon the most dangerous scouting expeditions. With his own hand he had killed more than thirty of his country's enemies, and had never received the slightest injury, until June 1863, when, in the great cavalry battle at Brandy Station a shell from a Federal battery terminated his heroic exploits with his life. Captain Farley was of medium stature, but he was sinewy, and strongly built, and capable of great endurance.

wound, said to me, "Major, this man is mortally wounded, but what you have taken for delirium is nothing more than a very deep state of intoxication, which had commenced before the shot was received." I did not at once fully credit this medical opinion, and my surprise was therefore great when, taking a smell of the canteen, which I had supposed to contain water, I found that it had been filled with strong apple-brandy, which the unfortunate man had snatched at in his dying moments. When the next morning I sent his efforts to the temporary field-hospital, to which he had been conveyed over night, I received the report that he had died before day-break, still heavily intoxicated. Fortunately, we were enabled to find out his address, and had the satisfaction of sending his valuables to his family in Indiana.

Our squadron that had been sent in chase of the Yankees, having continued the game into the village of Aldie, and having been much scattered by the length of the pursuit, was met at that place by a fresh body of Federal horse, and easily repulsed. But our main column was very soon at hand for its protection, and reached a range of hills overlooking the village, in time to see a force of several thousand of the enemy's cavalry advancing in beautiful lines across an open field on the right. The fight was at once opened with great spirit by Pelham's guns, which met with a furious response from several Federal batteries, and we were soon hotly engaged all along our line of battle. The enemy's resistance was obstinate; charges and counter-charges were made over the plateau in our front, and for a time the issue seemed doubtful, no decided advantage having been gained on either

---

His expression of countenance was singularly winning, and had something of feminine tenderness; indeed, it seemed difficult to believe that this boy, with the long fair hair, the mild blue eyes, the soft voice and modest mien, was the daring dragoon whose appearance in battle was always terrible to the foe.

side. At last, however, we succeeded in driving the Yankees back into the woods, and before sunset they were in full retreat, by the road they had come, towards Leesburg. Our flying artillery, under the intrepid and energetic John Pelham, whom I have so often had occasion to mention in these memoirs, had, as usual, done admirable service, disabling several of the enemy's guns, and contributing greatly, by the terror it carried into their advancing columns, to the final result.* About dusk in the evening we marched back along the road to Middleburg, near which place General Stuart intended to encamp, having ordered me to gallop ahead of the column into the village to make the necessary arrangements for food and forage with the Cavalry Quartermaster stationed there.

Middleburg is a pleasant little place, of some 1500 inhabitants, which, by reason of its proximity to the Federal lines, had often been visited by raiding and scouting parties of the enemy, and had suffered specially in the shameless barbarities committed by those Yankee robbers, Milroy and Geary. The citizens had awaited the result of our late combat with the greatest anxiety, and manifested their satisfaction at our success in loud expressions of rejoicing. Riding up the main street of the village, I was brought to a halt by a group of very pretty young girls, who were carrying refreshments to the soldiers, and invited me to partake of them, an offer which I was not strong enough to decline. In the conversation which followed, my fair entertainers expressed the greatest desire to see General Stuart, and were delighted beyond measure to

---

*The famous "Stuart Horse Artillery" was made up of volunteers of many nationalities, and embraced Englishmen, Frenchmen, Germans, Spainards, and Americans. Many of these men had not brought to the standard under which they served an immaculate reputation, but they distinguished themselves on every field of battle, and established such an enviable character for daring and good conduct that the body was soon regarded as a *corps d'élite* by the whole

hear that the bold cavalry leader was my personal friend, and that I should probably have little difficulty in persuading him to devote a quarter of an hour to their charming company. This spread like wildfire through the village, so that half an hour later, when Stuart galloped up to me, I was attended by a staff of fifty or sixty ladies, of various ages, from blooming girlhood to matronly maturity. The General very willingly consented to remain for a while that every one might have an opportunity of seeing him, and was immediately surrounded by the ladies, all eager to catch the words that fell from his lips, and many with tears in their eyes kissing the skirt of his uniform coat or the glove upon his hand. This was too much for the gallantry of our leader, who smilingly said to his gentle admirers, "Ladies, your kisses would be more acceptable to me if given upon the cheek." Thereupon the attacking force wavered and hesitated for a moment; but an elderly lady, breaking through the ranks, advanced boldly, and, throwing her arms around Stuart's neck, gave him a hearty smack, which served as the signal for a general charge. The kisses now popped in rapid succession like musketry, and at last became volleys, until our General was placed under as hot a fire as I had ever seen him sustain on the field of battle. When all was over, and we had mounted our horses, Stuart, who was more or less exhausted, said to me, "Von, this is a pretty little trick you have played me, but in future I shall detail you for this sort of service." I answered that I would enter upon it with infinite pleasure, provided he would permit me to reverse his mode of procedure, and commence with

---

army, and it came to be considered an honour to be one of them. I have often seen these men serving their pieces in the hottest of the fight, laughing, singing, and joking each other, utterly regardless of the destruction which cannon-shot and musket-ball were making in their ranks. They were devoted to their young chief, John Pelham, whom an English writer, Captain Chesney, justly styles "the boy hero;" and as they knew my intimacy with him, and as in many

the young ladies. The General and Staff bivouacked with the cavalry near Middleburg, while for me was reserved the agreeable duty of riding on special business to Upperville, where, beneath the hospitable roof of Dr Eliason, I passed some pleasant hours with the family circle, to whom I had to recite fully the events and adventures of the day.

---

engagements we had fought side by side, they extended something of this partiality to myself, and whenever I galloped up to the batteries during a battle, or passed them on the march, addressing a friendly salutation in English, French, or German, to such of them as I knew best, I was always received with loud cheering. They called Pelham and myself, in honourable association, "our fighting Majors," and after my dear friend's death, and when I had myself been disabled by wounds, I often received letters from the *braves* of the "Stuart Horse Artillery" written in a style sufficiently inelegant and extraordinary, but expressive of the sincerest sympathy and attachment.

CHAPTER XI

THE following morning we received reports that the enemy in heavy force was advancing from Leesburg in the direction of Union. Thither we marched at once, arriving just in time to occupy a naturally strong position about a mile and a half from the little village. Scarcely had our artillery got ready for action, when the Yankees made their appearance, and there began a lively cannonade with spirited sharpshooting, the latter doing little damage to either party, as the high stone fences which enclose the fields in this part of Virginia afforded protection to both sides. The Federal cavalry being far superior in numbers to our own, and our scouts reporting the approach of a strong infantry force, whose glistening bayonets, indeed, we could already see in the far prospect, it seemed almost certain that, after some little resistance, we should be compelled to retire. The Yankees, however, appeared to have their reasons for not moving too rapidly forward, and so the day passed in comparative inaction, the whole resembling, with its slow manœuvring of troops and regular firing, the operations of a sham-fight or a field-day of volunteers.

Stuart and Fitz Lee, with the officers of their respective

Staffs, had taken their position on a gigantic rock, from which they had an excellent view of the movements of the Yankees, and could observe with perfect security the effect of the incessant explosions of the shells that were exchanged between our own guns and those of the enemy. We had the opportunity here of witnessing one of those daring feats which Pelham was so constantly performing. He had been greatly annoyed during the day by a squadron of Federal cavalry which operated with great dash against his batteries, rapidly throwing forward their sharpshooters and as rapidly withdrawing them, after their muskets had been discharged, behind a piece of wood which completely hid them from view. This they did before Pelham could get a shot at them, and they had already killed or disabled many of his horses, when our gallant major, losing all patience, suddenly advanced with one of his light howitzers at full gallop towards the wood, where the horses were unhitched and the piece drawn by hand through the impeding undergrowth which rendered further progress of the horses impossible. From our position, which was some distance to the right of the batteries, we could plainly see the Yankee squadron, which had come very quietly to a halt without the slightest suspicion that a cannon loaded with a double charge of canister was directed upon them from a point only a few hundred yards off. All at once, the thunder of the howitzer was heard, and its iron hail swept through the ranks of the Yankees, killing eight of their number, among whom was the colour-bearer, wounding several others, and putting the rest to flight in hopeless stampede. Pelham and his cannoneers now emerged from the wood in a run, bringing with them many captured men and horses, and the Federal standard, amid loud shouts of applause. Before the Yankees could recover from their astonishment, the howitzer was removed, the horses were hitched to it again, and it had arrived safely at the battery.

With the approach of evening the firing ceased, and as the smoke of the camp-fires rising all along the Federal lines clearly indicated that it was not the enemy's intention to push on further during the night, Stuart gave orders for his command to encamp about a mile beyond Union, after having established a strong cordon of pickets in front of the village. The General and his Staff bivouacked near the extensive plantation of a Mr C., at whose house we supped luxuriously, our host serving up for us a gigantic saddle of Virginia mutton which might have rivalled any of the famous southdowns of Old England.

Peacefully broke the morning of Sunday the 3d of November, a rich, soft day, with all the splendour of the autumnal sunshine, and all the quietude of the Christian Sabbath, till, instead of the sweet church-bells from the neighbouring village calling us to the house of God, we caught the summons to the field in the rattle of musketry and the roar of cannon. It would have been exceptional, indeed, if, confronting the enemy so closely, we had not been compelled to fight on this "day of rest," for it is remarkable that many of the most important and sanguinary engagements of the war in America—Chancellorsville and others—were fought on Sunday.

The enemy commenced his attack on us at an early hour with great vigour. A double line of tirailleurs advanced in excellent order; four batteries opened upon our guns from different points; the air shook with the continuous roar of the cannonade; on every side the bullets buzzed like infuriated insects; on the whole, the outward signs were rather those of a great battle than of a mere cavalry combat. This day the enemy's artillery was admirably well served, and its effect was very dreadful. Just as I rode up to a battery, which was answering as rapidly as possible the Yankee fire, a hostile shell blew up one of our caissons, killing and wounding several of the men, and stunning me completely for several minutes. For some time the fire was terrific at this spot. In less than half an hour one battery alone lost fifteen men killed and wounded, and I was obliged to force the frightened ambulance-drivers to the assistance of their suffering and dying comrades, by putting my revolver to their heads and threatening to shoot them if they did not go.

On our right the sharpshooting grew warmer and warmer, the enemy bringing line after line of their dismounted men into action, and I was despatched thither by General Stuart to watch the movements of the Yankees, and to animate our soldiers to an obstinate opposition. Here I found my dashing friend Rosser stationed with his brave fellows of the 5th Virginia Cavalry. In reply to my question as to how he was getting along, he said, "Come and see for yourself." So, to obtain a good look at the enemy, we rode forward together through the wide gaps in the stone fences, which had been made to admit of the passage of cavalry and artillery, and presently discovered, somewhat late, that we had got much nearer to our antagonists than we had intended. Suddenly the Yankee sharpshooters emerged from behind rocks and trees, sending their bullets in most alarming proximity to our ears, and running forward to cut us off from our line of retreat. Fortunately, we were both well mounted, and our horses had escaped a wound, so that we were able to clear the stone fences where they stood in our way, without difficulty. This steeplechase afforded great amusement to Rosser, who seemed delighted at having got me into what he called "a little trap," but what I regarded as an exceedingly ticklish situation.

As the far superior numbers of the enemy's cavalry, which up to this time we had successfully opposed, began now to be reinforced by infantry, General Stuart at last decided to fall back upon a new position. The retreat through Union was admirably covered by Pelham with his artillery, and was executed with great steadiness and order under a perfect hail of shot and shell, which, crashing through the houses of the little village, had already set on fire several stables and straw-ricks. The furious flames, leaping from one to another of these great masses of combustible material, and the dense volumes of smoke that rolled from them, added to the terror and confusion of the scene, which now became truly frightful. On a ridge, behind a small creek where we had encamped the previous night, about a mile and a half beyond the town on the road leading to Upperville, we halted and again confronted our assailants, who did not keep us long in waiting for their attack, and ere half an hour had elapsed the thunder of cannon again shook the air, and the sharpshooters on either side were hotly engaged.

The enemy here, by a resolute and united charge, drove a portion of our dismounted men back in some confusion through the woods; and the officer in command, the gallant young Captain Bullock of the 5th Virginia, in the attempt to rally them, had his horse shot under him, and, before he could get on his legs again, found himself surrounded by the Yankees, who demanded his surrender. Bullock, however, responded with two shots of his revolver, killing two of his adversaries, and then endeavoured to save himself by flight. The whole incident having taken place within fifty paces of Stuart and myself, we could see, and even distinctly hear, the Yankees as they gave chase to our poor captain. Taking some of our couriers, and such of the tirailleurs as had recovered from their stampede, with us, we galloped forward at once to the assistance of our brave comrade, whom we succeeded in rescuing from his pursuers, but in a state of such utter exhaustion that we had to lift him to the back of one of the led horses that chanced to be on the spot.

After a short but spirited resistance we were again compelled to retire, turning round and showing fight wherever the nature of the ground would admit of it, until late in the afternoon we took a new position near the large estate of Colonel Dulaney, which was of some strategical importance. Preparing for a more serious opposition to the movements of the enemy, Stuart and myself had halted on an eminence which afforded an extensive view of the surrounding country, when a squadron of Federal cavalry, which came trotting along over an open field in beautiful lines as if on parade, and which seemed quite disdainful of the opposing host, attracted our attention. Stuart turned to me, and said, "Major, pray amuse yourself with giving these gentlemen a lesson: take two of Pelham's guns, place them in such position as you think best, and receive our impudent friends with a proper salute." Our cannoneers followed me with loud expressions of joy, bringing with them the two howitzers, to a small hill, where dense bushes concealed our preparations from the enemy's notice. The guns were carefully aimed, and when the hostile squadron came within easy range, both shots sounded simultaneously, the shells exploding with wonderful accuracy right in front of the foe, emptying several saddles, and driving our contemptuous adversaries into headlong fight, along the line of which we sent several missiles from the howitzers with less effect.

All our pieces were now concentrated on a wooded acclivity, and were soon brought into a spirited cannonade with four or five hostile batteries. As usual, General Stuart and his Staff exposed themselves for several hours continuously to the hottest fire—shells and solid shot fell around us on all sides, covering us with dust and dirt, and tearing the splinters from the trees right and left; and I could not comprehend how any of us escaped death. The scene was one of the wildest and grandest confusion and destruction. Men were falling, killed or wounded, on every hand, wounded horses galloped hither and thither, and the numerous herds of cattle, which had until that Sunday grazed peacefully in their wide pastures, wrought up to the highest pitch of brute frenzy by the first battle they had ever known, ran about in frantic terror and excitement.

In the very fury of the cannonade, one or two little incidents excited our surprise and amusement. A shell, falling in the midst of a large flock of sheep, exploded there, and we thought that the greater part had been converted into mutton; but when the dust and smoke had cleared away, we saw the frightened animals scamper off, not one of their number missing, and all apparently unhurt. A few minutes afterwards, a stout young bullock, out of a herd of oxen that had been galloping up and down for a considerable time before our batteries, suddenly threw a sommersault, and lay, to all seeming, dead upon the field, but presently got on his legs again, and after reeling and tumbling about for a little while in a drunken sort of way, started off all at once with the speed of an arrow. I have already mentioned cases of prostration by "windage" of cannon-balls. A more diverting instance occurred, in a later fight, with one of our soldiers, a North Carolinian, who, lying flat on his back, apparently badly wounded, answered to General Stuart's inquiry whether he was hurt, "Oh, General, I shall soon be all right again, but I am dreadfully demoralised by a bomb-shell;" the fact being, that a cannon-ball, passing very close to his head, had knocked him over.

With the darkness of evening, our situation became critical. Our artillery had lost many men and horses; our cavalry, having been exposed all day to a murderous fire, had also suffered severely, and our sharpshooters were unable any longer to resist the double and triple lines of Federal tirailleurs, which were again and again sent against them. General Stuart accordingly determined to retreat to Upperville, and ordered me to recall our dismounted men all along the line. To obey this order, I had to ride to our extreme right, where Captain Farley, with a small body of riflemen, occupied some hay-stacks, which he had held all day against the vastly superior numbers of the enemy. As I was the only man on horseback in range of the Yankee carbines, I was exposed for the whole distance to a heavy fusillade; but returning was yet more perilous, for having to ride between the enemy and our own troops, the former hotly pursuing, and the latter, in their dogged retreat, returning with spirit every shot that was sent after them, I was subjected to two fires, and was in as much danger of being killed by friendly as by hostile bullets.

The Yankees did not continue their pursuit after nightfall, and allowed us to retire quietly to the vicinity of Upperville, about a mile from which place we bivouacked. A feeling of devout and fervent thankfulness possessed my heart, as I lay down on my blanket for a short night's rest, and recalled the innumerable dangers through which I had safely passed on that exciting eventful day. These smaller combats with the enemy are far more dangerous than great battles. Especially is this true as regards the staff-officer, who, having to be constantly in the saddle, remains throughout the day exposed to the enemy's particular attentions. In a general engagement there is much more rattle of musketry and thunder of cannon, but the fire is not so much concentrated upon a small tract of ground, and four-fifths of the balls and bullets which wound or kill, find their mark accidentally.

3d November

Fighting was renewed the following morning, and the tremendous hosts of the Yankees advancing upon us across the fields, which I could compare only to a mighty avalanche, seemed likely to crush everything before them; but the gallant fellows of Fitz Lee's brigade stood the shock of their attack nobly, and succeeded for a time in checking the onward movement of their columns. Stuart perceiving, however, that he could not long maintain his ground, sent me off in the direction of Paris to select a new position, where the nature of the country would facilitate further resistance. This I soon found near Ashby's Gap, a few miles from Upperville, where a range of mountains, spurs of the Blue Ridge, accessible for a long distance only by a single road, made successful opposition to a far superior force possible. On my return to the General, the conflict had reached its height, and, in my opinion, the urgent necessity of immediate retreat was patent to all. Nevertheless, Stuart was for continuing the struggle. Again and again animating his men by his presence and the exposure of his own person, he led our admirable soldiers to the conflict. Not until one of our caissons had been exploded by a well-aimed shot; not until Colonel Wickham, temporarily commanding Fitz Lee's brigade, had been wounded at my side, a fragment of shell striking him in the neck; not until the hostile infantry was outflanking us on either side,— was the order given for the withdrawal, which, in consequence of the long delay of our commander in issuing the order, was managed, I am sorry to say, with a great deal of haste and confusion, and came very near being a rout. The dismounted sharpshooters, running back hurriedly to their horses, upon gaining them, rode off, without forming, in every direction; the regiments themselves, exposed to a concentrated withering fire of the enemy, galloped confusedly, and in precipitation, through the narrow streets of Upperville, followed by the hostile cavalry in eager pursuit.

General Stuart and myself were the last of our column to ride through the village, escaping almost miraculously the Yankee balls and bullets that whistled after us, and both receiving slight injury from a falling chimney, which, at the very moment of our passing by it, was struck by a shell, and toppled over by the explosion, the shattered stones and bricks flying far and wide. We had not left the village when the enemy entered it on the opposite side; and yet many heroic young ladies, regardless of the great danger, ran out of the houses to wave a last farewell to us with their cambric handkerchiefs, and what was better still, to seek out, amidst this fearful tempest of shells and bullets, our poor wounded, who, unable to follow their flying comrades, were lying about, in their agony, anywhere in the dusty streets.

Too much credit cannot be given to Pelham for the great forethought and coolness with which he had taken his artillery along a little by-path around the village to a point about a mile distant, where, placing his guns in a favourable position, he skilfully covered our retreat, and, by the accuracy and rapidity of his firing, saved us from greater disaster. My brave friend was himself hard at work in his shirtsleeves, taking a hand with the cannoneers in loading and aiming the pieces. Meanwhile the united efforts of General Stuart and the members of his Staff had availed to put a stop to the stampede; our regiment were re-formed, and our lines re-established. But the scene was still frightful. Wounded men on foot were limping to the rear, or riding two on one horse; wounded animals were galloping wildly over the field; ambulances and army-waggons were being hurried along the road, on which was concentrated a heavy fire of the hostile batteries, and over which canister and shell were howling in the air, or ricochetting on the hard dry ground.

Pelham's guns were now in a very dangerous situation, a squadron of Federal cavalry having advanced against them at a gallop, and having dismounted and placed a number of men behind a stone fence not more than 200 yards distant, from which they poured a fatal carbine fire upon the gunners and artillery-horses. I tried my best to lead two squadrons of one of our regiments forward to a charge, and I might drive the Yankees from this position; but after following me at a gallop to within eighty yards of the wall, they broke into rapid flight at the murderous volley of the sharpshooters. Pelham was doing his best, in the mean time, to dislodge the bold riflemen, by firing canister at the wall, but this had not the desired effect in consequence of the thickness of the barrier, so I shouted out to him, "Try solid shot!" which he did at once, and with the best results. Every ball demolished large sections of the fence, scattering the fragments of the stones all around, killing and wounding many of the sharpshooters behind it, and driving off the rest, whom we pursued, cutting down and taking prisoners nearly all of them.

About six o'clock in the evening we arrived at the heights near Ashby's Gap, from which we could overlook the whole lower country towards Upperville. In the waning light of the day we could plainly discern that for a considerable distance it was covered with the dark masses of the enemy, with their long cavalry columns and artillery-trains, so that we had no reason to indulge chagrin at having been put to flight by numbers more than ten times superior to our own. The exceeding narrowness of the approach, and the two mountain-ridges stretching out on either side of it, made defence an easy affair; not to mention the fact that D. H. Hill, with his division, was only a few miles farther back, ready to come to our assistance at any moment that this might be necessary.

The hostile batteries, occupying the heights near Upperville, kept up an incessant firing upon our troops ascending the mountain, but not being able at so great a distance to get the necessary elevation, their shells fell, and exploded innocently, at the base of the ridge, and our own batteries did not any longer respond. Only a 12-pounder Whitworth gun, which yet held its position half a mile in our rear, maintained the fight, and here stood its very first trial magnificently. Being on the higher part of the mountain, watching closely the enemy's movements with my trusty field-glass, I had the full opportunity of witnessing the wonderful efficiency and accuracy of this fine gun. When the wholly ineffective bombardment of our position had been carried on for some time by the Federal batteries, I heard all at once the sharp clear report of the Whitworth, and distinctly saw the ball strike, at a distance of four miles from the gun, right in the midst of the enemy's artillery, which, changing its position again and again as the Whitworth missiles became more and more destructive, at last altogether retired. Firing ceased entirely with the coming darkness; and as we saw by the Yankees going into camp that the pursuit would not be continued by them until the following day, we determined to give rest to our weary men and horses, and the glow of our bivouac-fires was soon reflected from the mountains around us.

CHAPTER XII

NIGHT-RIDE TO JACKSON'S CAMP — RETURN ACROSS THE
MOUNTAINS — WE ARE CUT OFF BY THE ENEMY — FIGHT
AT BARBER'S CROSS-ROADS — RETREAT TOWARDS ORLEANS
AND ACROSS THE RAPPAHANNOCK — FIGHTS NEAR WATER-
LOO BRIDGE AND JEFFERSON — CROSSING OF THE HAZEL
RIVER — BIVOUAC IN THE SNOW — SCOUT WITH GENERAL
STUART — HEADQUARTERS NEAR CULPEPPER COURT-
HOUSE — RECONNAISSANCE IN FORCE, AND FIGHT NEAR
EMMETSVILLE.

4th November

THE deep sleep which succeeded to the fatigues of the previous day had hardly fallen upon me, when I was aroused by the touch of Stuart's hand upon my shoulder. The General's wish was that I should bear him company, with several of our couriers and Dr Eliason, who was well acquainted with all the roads in the neighbouring county, to the headquarters of General Jackson, who had encamped about twelve miles off, on the opposite side of the Shenandoah, near the village of Millwood. The command of our cavalry had been temporarily transferred to Colonel Rosser, who had instructions to hold his position as long as possible, and to keep General Stuart informed by frequent messengers of the progress of the impending fight.

A cold wind was blowing in our faces as we trotted through the village of Paris in the direction of the Shenandoah, and it was freezing hard when we reached the stream, about midnight, at a point where ordinarily it was easily fordable, but where we found it so much swollen by the recent rains in the mountains that we were compelled to cross it swimming. We reached the opposite bank in safety, but chilled through and with soaking garments. Such was the intensity of the frost, that in a very few minutes our cloaks and blankets were frozen quite stiff; and the water, as it dripped from the flanks of our horses, congealed into icicles, and the legs of the animals were rough with ice. But a sharp ride, as it promoted the circulation of the blood, kept us tolerably warm, and at two o'clock in the morning we arrived at Jackson's encampment. Stuart, being unwilling in his great tenderness for Old Stonewall to disturb his slumbers, proposed that we should seek rest for the remaining hours of the night; but in our frozen condition, it being first necessary that we should thaw out our garments before we could dry them, we preferred building a huge fire of logs, around whose cheerful blaze we sat and smoked our pipes, though, with teeth chattering like castanets, this was smoking under difficulties. Jackson, who, in accordance with his usual habit, awoke with the easiest glimmer of day, no sooner discovered us than he expressed his regret at our evident discomfort, but gave us the readiest consolation by ordering breakfast to be immediately prepared. Nothing was better calculated to restore our good spirits than the summons to the General's large breakfast-table, where the aroma rose in clouds of vapour from an immense coffee-pot, and where stood a magnificent haunch of venison, cold, a present from a neighbouring planter.

The good cheer had the happiest effect on Stuart, who enlivened our repast with abundant anecdote and the recital of many a joke at the expense of his companions-in-arms. It was his special delight to tease me on account of the little mistakes I still frequently committed in speaking the English language, which he always cleverly turned so as to excite the merriment of his auditors. During one of our many conversations concerning Old Stonewall, his personal traits and military character, while intending to say, "It warms my heart when he talks to me," I had employed the expression, "It makes my heart burn," &c. Stuart now took occasion to repeat my remark, and presented me most absurdly as having declared that "it gave me the heartburn to hear Jackson talk," which of course provoked the roaring laughter of our little company. Jackson himself alone did not participate in the boisterous mirth. Looking me straight in the face with his large expressive eyes, and pressing my hand warmly across the table as just the faintest smile broke over his features, he said, "Never care, Major, for Stuart's jokes; we understand each other, and I am proud of the friendship of so good a soldier and so daring a cavalier as you are." I was conscious of a blush reddening my cheeks under my beard at this, but I felt also a glow of pride, and I would not at that moment have exchanged the simple, earnest tribute of the great warrior for all the orders and crosses of honour of Europe. "Hurrah for Old Von! and now let us be off," said Stuart, and slapping me on the back to conceal his own slight embarrassment, he rose from the table, followed by his companions. In a few minutes we rode off at a gallop to fresh scenes of excitement and activity.

In Virginia the vicissitudes of temperature are great and sudden, the weather frequently changing from biting frost to genial warmth in a few hours; and we experienced this pleasant alternation as we rode forth into the brilliant sunshine of the clear November morning. To avoid the disagreeable passage of the river by swimming our horses,

General Stuart had determined to cross higher up, where the Shenandoah might be forded without difficulty, and we continued our ride through the rich country on the left bank, passing the pleasant little hamlet of White Post on our route, until mid-day, when we made an easy ford, and soon after partook of a hasty dinner at a hospitable mansion most picturesquely situated on the very margin of the beautiful stream. Here I could not resist purchasing for our mess-table two of a flock of fat turkeys, which, tied together by the legs, I carried for a while thrown across the pommel of my saddle. The fowls gave me so much annoyance, however, by the flapping of their wings, that I was glad to give them in charge to one of our couriers, who quieted their motions very speedily by the simple expedient of cutting off their heads with his pocket-knife.

The son of the gentleman who entertained us at dinner, being thoroughly familiar with the bridlepaths across the mountains, offered himself as our guide to save us the long detour of the common highway, and his services were thankfully accepted. So we pursued our course along the rough mountain-side, but seldom touched by human foot, and, as we rode, enjoyed frequent opportunities of admiring the wild and wonderful scenery of the majestic Blue Ridge. Climbing up steep banks and skirting dizzy precipices, we were often obliged to cut our way with our sabres through the dense entanglement of bushes and vines, many of the latter heavy with clusters of small dark-blue grapes. A rolling cannonade, borne to us from the direction of Ashby's Gap, hurried us on our toilsome and difficult way, and about five o'clock in the afternoon we reached the summit of the mountain. The view we obtained from this point was surely the most magnificent I have ever witnessed. For many, many miles beneath us lay the sumptuous valley, in the full gorgeousness of its rich and varied autumnal hues, spread out like an immense gaily-coloured Persian carpet, and through the middle space, like a stripe of green, ran the emerald-tinted Shenandoah, winding away to the remote distance where the plain was fringed by a range of wooded mountains, whose soft, waving line of horizon was reddened and gilded by the sunset. Our admiration of this glorious prospect gave place to something like bewildered astonishment when, immediately below us, only a few thousand feet from the spot we occupied, we discovered the dark masses of the enemy with glittering arms and fluttering pennons, and beyond them the rapidly-disappearing lines of our horsemen, the smoke rising at many points from the muzzles of our guns as the artillery covered the retreat of their comrades. Stuart gave me a significant look, and said very quietly, "The Yankees have taken Ashby's Gap—Rosser is retreating, and we are completely cut off." Our situation was indeed full of danger. The enemy was so near us that we might expect to come upon one of their scouting-parties at any moment; our volunteer guide had no knowledge of the mountain-roads on our right; to procure other guides was a matter of great difficulty, as only a few herdsmen lived so high up on the mountain, and these would have been restrained by no sense of patriotic duty from betraying us into the hands of the Yankees; and to ride back to Jackson and join our horsemen again involved a circuitous and fatiguing journey of sixty or eighty miles, could we even make this without interruption. Yet it was of the utmost importance that Stuart should be with his command again before morning.

Meanwhile, as night was rapidly approaching, we recognised the necessity of coming to some conclusion, and it was finally determined that we should disperse over the ridge in various directions, in the hope that some one of our party might fall in with a mountaineer whom we should force to guide us, and that a whistle twice repeated should be the signal for reuniting at a point where Stuart himself should remain that he might watch closely the movements of the enemy. After much unsuccessful riding about over the rocks and through the forest, I was fortunate enough to pick up a fellow of exceedingly wild and haggard appearance, with garments "all tattered and torn," who, upon my approach, endeavoured to slip away from me in the bushes, but who came to a better mind when he saw my revolver levelled at his head. At the appointed signal we soon came together again, when General Stuart explained to my trembling captive that if he would guide us over the mountains on our right to a point from which we could reach Barber's Cross Roads, the supposed new position of Fitz Lee's brigade, without bringing us in contact with the Yankees, he should receive an ample reward; but that should he intentionally mislead and betray us, he should be shot down without hesitation. Under the joint influence of fear and avarice, the poor devil became voluble with promises of fidelity, and we started at once on our hazardous march, one of us riding just before and another just behind the guide with cocked pistols, to prevent his escaping into the dense undergrowth on either side of the narrow path. In many places the road was barred by immense boulders or became too steep to ascend on horseback, so that we were compelled to dismount and lead our horses. The briars and brambles scratched our hands and faces, and made sad work with our uniforms.

The night had now deepened into great darkness, and we expected momentarily to lose our way or tumble over one of the frightful precipices along the verge of which we had to pass. But, surmounting all difficulties and escaping all dangers, we at last reached the foot of the Blue Ridge, near the small village of Macon, at a short distant from which place we saw a large camp-fire, and in the glare of the flames discovered a group of soldiers around it. We halted, of course, at once, and with a proper precaution sent forward on foot one of our couriers to ascertain whether the men before us were friends or foes. After a few minutes of extreme anxiety on our part, the courier came back with the pleasing intelligence that all was right, as the picket in sight consisted of soldiers belonging to the division of General D. H. Hill, who had retired in the direction of Front Royal, but was still holding Manassas Gap. Dr Eliason being now fully acquainted with the neighbourhood, we dismissed our mountaineer, who evinced great delight when General Stuart handed him a fifty-dollar note for his services.

The perils of our journey, however, were by no means yet over, as we had still a long distance to ride outside our own, and very near the enemy's, lines, whose numerous camp-fires were often plainly to be seen on the mountain-side; but after our advance-guard of two couriers had several times brought us to a halt through false alarms, and, blinded by the intense darkness of the night, had fired again and again at imaginary Yankees, we arrived without further adventure, about midnight, at Barber's Cross Roads. Here we learned, to the surprise and indignation of General Stuart, that tony one of our squadrons was on picket at the place, and that Colonel Rosser, with the rest of his brigade, had fallen back seven miles farther, to the immediate vicinity of the small town of Orleans. Wearied out of the fatigues of the day, I was just looking out for a suitable spot for my night's rest, when Stuart, who was in no good humour, called to me, saying, "Major, I desire that you will ride at once to Colonel Rosser, and order him to report to me instantly in person, leaving instructions for Lee's brigade to follow without delay, that we may be ready to receive the enemy at this place at daylight. I am determined not to retire without fighting, and shall give battle to the Yankees here to-morrow." Thinking of the fifteen long miles that my faithful but exhausted charger must yet perform, I started rather unwillingly and slowly; but I had not gone two hundred yards when a courier rode up to me with the message from Stuart to go on as rapidly as possible, regardless of the life of my horse. So I drove the spurs into his flanks, and went off at a gallop through the dark pine-forests that skirted the road on either side, until I reached Orleans, and with some difficulty found the headquarters of Colonel Rosser. This officer was exceedingly annoyed at being aroused from his comfortable repose, having gone into bivouac under the impression that he had operated with great wisdom and circumspection. The urgency of my instructions, however, soon brought him into the saddle. His adjutants quickly conveyed the necessary orders to the regiments of his brigade, and the Colonel and I trotted off together ahead of the column to Barber's Cross Roads.

Rosser had been compelled, after a gallant resistance, to give way before the superior numbers of his assailants, having sent during the day reports to General Stuart by several couriers, all of whom had either missed their way or fallen into the hands of the enemy. Upon our arrival at the Cross Roads, we found Stuart, and our comrades of his Staff, wrapped in the profoundest slumber upon the portico of a small farmhouse. When I had succeeded in awakening my chief, and had taken due care of my horse, I drew my blankets closely around me, and, wearied with a ride of more than fifty miles, stretched my limbs on the hard ground, in the hope of gaining some refreshment for the inevitable rough work of the coming day.

5th November

The bugle sounding to saddle cruelly cut short my slumbers with the dawn, and a few minutes afterwards we galloped up to Fitz Lee's brigade, which, according to orders, occupied its position on the cross road. We now found, to our inexpressible delight, that Hampton's brigade, which, having been detached to our infantry, had been separated from us during the past week, had also arrived on the spot; and the hearty welcome we gave them attested the new hope and confidence as to the issue of the impending conflict which their presence inspired.

General Hampton had been ordered to form the right wing of our line of battle, and I accompanied him upon a little reconnaissance to a slight eminence, from which we could narrowly watch the approach of the vast numbers of the enemy. With his battery he had two 15-pounder brass guns, imported by him from Europe at his own expense, that were remarkable for their long range and accuracy of aim, but were too heavy for flying artillery. These pieces, being at once placed in position at our point of survey, speedily commenced the fight, and their fire being energetically returned by the Yankees, there ensued a tremendous cannonade. Ere long Stuart joined us, with all the other members of his Staff, and our group of horsemen attracting the attention of the enemy's artillerists, we were honoured forthwith with several cannon-balls, which came whistling high over our heads, and gave us small concern. Suddenly, however, a percussion shell whizzed very close to us, and, striking a small locust-tree at a distance of about twenty yards, sent its iron hail right into the midst of our party. We looked at each other with startled apprehension, scarcely deeming it possible but that some one of our number had been struck. In the most wonderful way all had escaped. My horse was the only sufferer, as one of the fragments of the shell had cut a deep gash in his right hind-leg. Finding that fortunately no bone or sinew had been injured, I staunched the wound by tying my pocket-handkerchief around the limb, and I was thus able to ride my brave animal, despite his lameness, throughout the day.

The fight soon became very spirited, and our sharp-shooters repulsed with great success and fatal effect the repeated charges of the Federal cavalry. One squadron of the Yankees especially was severely punished for their audacity in charging up the turnpike road upon a strong barricade which we had hastily erected. In front they were received with a most destructive fire, while a detachment of our horse attacked them at the same moment in the rear, sabring or taking prisoners the larger number of these dashing dragoons. The enemy continuing to be largely reinforced from time to time, General Stuart gave about mid-day the order for the retreat towards Orleans, which was commenced under the heaviest fire of the enemy's batteries. Here occurred a very curious incident. One of the horsemen of our retiring column was so instantaneously killed by a bullet through the brain, that his rapidly-stiffening limbs held him for a considerable time in the saddle, and he was sitting bolt upright upon his horse dead—stone dead—several minutes before his comrades on the right and left discovered that he had been struck. Frequently upon our retreat our pursuers pressed us so closely that we were compelled to turn round and engage them hand to hand; but they came at last to a halt, so that upon reaching Orleans we had an hour to rest the men and feed the horses. General Stuart and Staff were invited to dinner at a stately old country-house, half a mile from the village, where dwelt a venerable lady, Mrs M., whose native dignity of manner and kindliness of disposition greatly won our respect and gratitude. The following day this house was occupied by the Yankees, and a detachment of the New York Zouaves acted towards its inmates with the greatest barbarity. After the greater portion of the furniture had been broken to pieces and completely destroyed by them in mere wanton malice, one of these brutes demanded of the old lady where she had hid her silver, and upon her answering him quietly that it had been long ago sent to a place of safety, struck her a blow with the butt of his musket, under which she fell senseless into the arms of her daughters.

Throughout the afternoon we continued our retreat towards Waterloo Bridge, which we crossed at night, and in the vicinity of which our troops bivouacked. The General and Staff proceeded a mile farther on, and established their headquarters at the house of a Mr M., where we had at last an opportunity of cooking and devouring the turkeys of which mention has been made. Mr M.'s house was a few days later burned by the Yankees for the hospitality he had shown us.

During the night there came a telegram for General Stuart, which, in accordance with his instructions, habitually observed by me, I opened with his other despatches, and found to contain the most painful intelligence. It announced the death of little Flora, our chief's lovely and dearly-loved daughter, five years of age, the favourite of her father and of his military family. This sweet child had been dangerously ill for some time, and more than once had Mrs Stuart summoned her husband to Flora's bedside; but she received only the response of the true soldier, "My duty to the country must be performed before I can give way to the feelings of the father." I went at once to acquaint my General with the terrible tidings, and when I had awakened him, perceiving from the grave expression of my features that something had gone wrong, he said, "What is it, Major? Are the Yankees advancing?" I handed him the telegram without a word. He read it, and the tenderness of the father's heart overcoming the firmness of the warrior, he threw his arms around my neck, and wept bitter tears upon my breast. My dear General never recovered from this cruel blow. Many a time afterwards, during our rides together, he would speak to me of his lost child. Light-blue flowers recalled her eyes to him; in the glancing sunbeams he caught the golden tinge of her hair; and whenever he saw a child with such eyes and hair, he could not help tenderly embracing it. He thought of her even on his deathbed, when, drawing me towards him, he whispered, "My dear friend, I shall soon be with little Flora again."

6th and 7th November

The morning of the following day, to our great surprise, passed quietly, and we were enabled to take up our old line of defence at Waterloo Bridge, sending out scouts and patrols in the direction of the enemy. One of the latter was fortunate enough to capture and bring off a Yankee waggon, which gave us a good supply of Havana cigars, and contained, among other articles, a large number of fine bowie-knives. For a long time afterwards, each of us carried one of these knives in his belt, finding it extremely serviceable, not as an offensive weapon against the Yankees, but for the cutting of the very tough beef which, during the next month, formed the greater part of our rations. The bowie-knife occupied a somewhat conspicuous place in the earlier annals of the war, and we were often told of Louisianians, Mississippians, and Texans who threw away their muskets in the hottest of the fight, and fell upon the enemy with their favourite weapon; but I have always regarded these stories in the same fabulous light with the stories of the bayonet conflicts to which I have before referred, and certainly I have never seen the bowie-knife put to any other than a purely pacific and innocent use.

About mid-day we went across the river with one of our squadrons on a reconnaissance, and very soon afterwards met the advancing column of the enemy, which attacked us vigorously, and, to the great mortification of General Stuart and myself, drove our men in disgraceful stampede, despite all our efforts to prevent it, back over the bridge. Here our pursuers were checked by the fire of our artillery and sharp-shooters, and the fight ere long raged with full fury all along the lines, being kept up, especially in the vicinity of the bridge, with great spirit until late in the evening. At dusk, General Stuart decided to continue the retreat. The bridge, having been prepared with combustibles for this event, was set on fire, and its blazing timbers fell with a loud crash into the waters of the Rappahannock as our column turned off in the direction of Jefferson. This hamlet, which lay eight miles distant towards Culpepper Court-house, we reached soon after dark. Here, as the enemy did not follow up the pursuit, our troops bivouacked for the necessary pickets had been established.

The night was extremely cold, and about ten o'clock a snow-storm set in with such severity that the General and his Staff took refuge in a deserted old wooden house, where, having with great trouble collected the fuel, we built immense wood-fires in the tumble-down chimneys. But we obtained little sleep. The storm raged all night; and as it howled around the dilapidated building, it made every rafter shake so threateningly that we looked for the edifice to fall in ruins about our heads at any moment, while the wind swept in wrath through the windows, wholly destitute of glass, bringing the snow in swirls into the cheerless apartments, which were so densely filled at times with smoke driven down the chimneys that we had to beat a rapid retreat into the tempest to escape suffocation. At daybreak the temperature became a little less severe, but a fine rain was now mingled with the snow, which soon wet us to the skin, and rendered the roads slippery and horrible in the extreme. It may be imagined that our horsemen did not make a very proud appearance when our columns drew up to meet the advance of the enemy. Men and horses were muddy, draggled, and shivering, and both had been twenty-four hours without food.

The Yankees did not long keep us waiting for their attack, and at ten o'clock the fight was fully in progress, making us quite warm enough. Our resistance, however, was but a short one. General Stuart feared the rising of the Hazel river in his rear, and our artillery horses were scarcely able any longer to pull the guns through the miry roads. So greatly were we embarrassed on this account, that we had been obliged already to bury two of our pieces which we could not carry with us. About noon we again commenced the retreat, turning round and giving battle to the enemy whenever we were hard pressed by them. Late in the evening we reached the river, which we forded safely, but with some difficulty, and took a new position on the heights of the opposite shore, near the small village of Rixeville.

It was a sorry sight this crossing of the Hazel river. Our command, and especially Fitz Lee's brigade, had suffered severely from the continuous marching and fighting we had undergone, from the inclement wintry weather, and from scarcity of food. Many of our horses had been killed, and many more, broken down or lame, could only be led along. All the sick and disabled men, making up a body of nearly 500 non-combatants, were formed together into a corps which was jokingly called "Company Q," and had been put in charge of Fitz Lee's gallant quartermaster, Major Mason. I felt no little anxiety until I saw the last of this large squad of limping men, leading crippled horses, safely on the other side of the river. I had often to urge the stragglers along by saying, "The Yankees are close upon you," when they lingered to pluck the fruit of the numerous persimmon trees on either side of the road—fruit which the recent frosts had brought plentifully to perfection, and which furnished a welcome though meagre repast of our famished troopers.*

The Yankees not making their appearance on the opposite bank of the Rappahannock, we left behind several squadrons and two pieces of artillery to guard the two nearest fords, and went at nightfall with the main body of our troops a few miles farther back, establishing our bivouac in a dense forest of oak and pine. The night set in cold again, and the rain changed to a heavy fall of snow, giving us every prospect of a most uncomfortable time of it. But the accustomed wood-fire, with its immense pile of blazing logs, around which General and Staff and escort collected, kept us sufficiently warm. The bivouac itself was exceedingly picturesque. Many of the officers were enveloped in red blankets, worn in the Mexican fashion, falling from the shoulders, with a hole cut in the middle for the head of the wearer to come through. Others wore long overcoats, and wide-brimmed hats pulled over their faces. Among these groups were the negroes preparing supper; around us was the dark engirdling forest, the branches of the nearest trees white with the snow; and over all was thrown the rich red glow of the fire, producing the highest effects of light and shade. The never-failing pre-vision of my negro servant William supplied our evening repast with some excellent Irish potatoes, which he had contrived to pick up somewhere on the road, and which he roasted in such a manner as to produce a very pleasing result.

One of our couriers, whom we had sent off to the post-office at Culpepper Court-house, came in after supper, bring-

---

*The persimmon tree grows very abundantly in Virginia, and its fruit resembles somewhat the European medlar or the Asiatic date. In the green state the persimmon is exceedingly acrid and astringent, but it becomes mellowed by successive frosts, and in winter its taste is sweet and palatable. Very good beer is made from it, and the kernels were frequently employed by us in the preparation of a wretched substitute for coffee. The North Carolina troops

ing me the first letters I had received from home since my departure for America. Stretched out upon the damp ground, I became so much absorbed in reading them by the fitful glare of the fire, that my blanket caught from the embers without my perceiving it, and was in rapid combustion when Stuart called out to me, "Von, what are you doing there? Are you going to burn yourself like an Indian widow?"

8th, 9th, and 10th November

Early the following morning we left our beds of mud and snow, and moved to the Hazel river, where we awaited the further approach of the enemy in line of battle, on the high hills which line the Culpepper shore near Rixeville. But everything remaining perfectly quiet, Stuart and myself crossed the river to look after the enemy, whom we found to be encamped near Jefferson, manifesting no intention of a further advance. Having satisfied ourselves upon this, we at once returned to our command, the greater part of which was ordered back to the camp of the past night, only a few squadrons and some pieces of artillery being left behind to resist a sudden attack on the fords. Our pickets were thrown forward at the same time two miles on the opposite side of the river.

Our headquarters waggons having arrived meanwhile, and it appearing most likely that our stay in this part of the country would be of considerable duration, we pitched our tents on the edge of an oak wood, and our encampment was soon laid out in regular order. General Lee with the greater part of his army, had now arrived, and had gone into camp in

---

were often "chaffed" by their comrades from other States for being so fond of persimmons—a taste they had in common with the negroes and that remark-

the vicinity of Culpepper Court-house, General Longstreet, with his whole corps, having reached there several days before, followed by Jackson, who had left behind only one of his divisions under D. H. Hill, near Front Royal.

General Stuart went off next day on a little reconnaissance to Brandy Station and Rappahannock Bridge, but for once I did not accompany him, being detained in camp by domestic duties, arranging the interior of my tent, and building the customary fireplace and mud chimney. For the transportation of materials we employed our well-known yellow van captured from the Yankees, to which Pelham and I each harnessed one of our horse. The first time we attached the team, I had occasion to witness with indignation and punish with severity the brutal conduct of Pelham's negro Willis, who, at the moment my horse was making the greatest efforts to pull our heavily-laden waggon out of a mud-hole, struck him in a paroxysm of anger over the head with a hatchet, felling the poor animal to the ground, where it lay for several minutes apparently lifeless. I was fortunately close enough to reward the scoundrel's barbarity at once with his own horsewhip.

General Stuart returned in the evening, in time for our slender dinner of coffee and baked potatoes, telling us that on his way back he had called at the headquarters of General Lee, and received orders for going off the next day on a reconnaissance in force. He was to take with him Fitz Lee's brigade, one battery, and two regiments of infantry, the latter having been detached to him for this special purpose. We were roused at daybreak next morning by the roll of the drums of our reinforcements, and at eight o'clock we crossed Hazel river, sending one regiment of cavalry to the right towards Jefferson, and proceeding with the main column to

---

able animal the Virginia opossum, which is always fattest when the persimmon season is at its height.

the left towards the village of Emmetsville. About ten o'clock
our advanced-guard came up with the enemy, with whom we
were soon hotly engaged, the Yankees falling back slowly
before us. I could not help admiring on this occasion the
excellent behaviour of a squadron of the 5th New York
Cavalry, who received with the greatest coolness the heavy
fire of our battery, maintaining perfect order while shell after
shell exploded in their ranks, and saddle after saddle was
emptied—quietly filling the gaps in their lines, and finally
only giving way when we charged them with several squadrons.

During the earlier part of the fight the Federals had been
wholly without artillery, but several batteries now came to
their assistance, opening a vigorous and well-directed fire
upon our guns, which lost heavily in men and horses. I had
halted near two of our pieces, and was talking with Lieutenant M'Gregor, the officer in command of them, when a shell,
bursting within thirty feet of us, sent its deadly missiles in
every direction, several fragments of the iron passing directly
between us, and one of them shattering the leg of the brave
young fellow so that it dangled loosely from his side. He
insisted, however, on remaining with his guns, and it required
the joint persuasions of General Stuart and myself to induce
him to withdraw from the field and place himself in the hands
of the surgeon.

Our infantry now joining in the fight, we drove the
Yankees back to the neighbourhood of Emmetsville, when I
was ordered by my chief to reconnoitre the position there
before he could attempt pushing his success further. Climbing
a high hill about a mile on our right, I soon obtained a
magnificent view of the surrounding country, extending for
many miles towards the town of Warrenton, where numerous
encampments indicated the presence of the entire Federal
army. In the immediate front, towards Emmetsville, I could

see the force opposing us about being reinforced by three brigades of infantry and several batteries of artillery, which were advancing at a double-quick along the turnpike road. In full haste I galloped back to inform General Stuart of the danger of his position, but before reaching him I saw our troops falling back, my chief having himself quickly perceived the additional strength of his opponents.

The enemy's tirailleurs were now moving rapidly forward in admirable order, and by their spirited and accurate fire greatly harassed the retreat of our troops, which was covered by two pieces of our artillery and our cavalry sharpshooters. Stuart, seeing his cavalrymen rapidly driven back, and greatly provoked at the successful advance of the foe, called to him twenty-five or thirty of our infantry riflemen, and posted them at the corner of a wood, with orders not to fire until the enemy had arrived within two hundred yards of them, that they might punish effectively the impudence of the Yankees, as he called it. Stuart here, as usual, greatly exposed his own person on horseback, by riding out of the wood into the open field, and I felt it my duty to say to him that in my opinion he was not in his proper place, as in a few minutes the whole fire of the enemy would be concentrated upon him; but as J. E. B. was in a very bad humour, he answered me curtly, that if this place seemed likely to become too hot for myself, I was at liberty to leave it; where-upon I made response, that, my duty attaching me to his side, no place could be too hot for me where he chose to go. Nevertheless I changed my position, cautiously bringing a large tree, in front of which I had been standing, between myself and the enemy. In an instant the firing commenced, and three bullets struck the tree at just the height to show that, had I remained where I was, they would certainly have gone through my body. Looking at Stuart, I saw him pass his hand quickly across his face, and even at this serious moment I could not help laughing heartily when

I discovered that one of the numberless bullets that had been whistling round me had cut off half of his beloved mustache as neatly as it could have been done by the hand of an experienced barber.

The Yankees having kept up the pursuit for only a short distance, we continued our retreat quietly towards Hazel river. Altogether our reconnaissance had been highly successful. We had found out all we desired to know without much loss, while we had inflicted serious damage upon the enemy, and brought back with us thirty prisoners. Being ordered by General Stuart to report immediately to General Lee what had been done, I galloped rapidly ahead, about dusk, passing *en route* our headquarters, where those who had been left behind came running towards me to get news of the fighting, which I gave them in a condensed form, "All right!" and hurried onward without stopping. With some trouble I found General Lee's encampment on the opposite side of the town, where his modest tents had been pitched in a dense pine thicket. Supper was announced just as I arrived, and, having accepted the General's kindly invitation to join him at the table, I there recited to an eager audience our recent adventures. The Commander-in-Chief and the members of his Staff were all greatly amused at the loss of half of Stuart's mustache, a personal ornament upon which they knew our cavalry leader much prided himself. It was late at night when I got back again to our headquarters, where Stuart and my comrades of his Staff had arrived long before me.

CHAPTER XIII

ALL was quiet next day at headquarters, and we had the pleasure of seeing there Mrs Stuart, who had arrived at Culpepper Court-house the previous evening. She had come to spend some days with her husband, to share with him her sacred grief in the calamity that had befallen them both. It was a melancholy pleasure to see how well that admirable lady bore up under the weight of her affliction, in tender regard for her husband. Her manner was composed, but her eyes betrayed their frequent overflow of tears; and the warm pressure of the hand she silently gave me upon our meeting, indicated that words could not describe the agony she had endured. Mrs Stuart had brought with her to camp her son Jemmy, a stout little "three-year-old," who, in his vivacity, in his passion for horses, and in his whole appearance, strongly resembled his father. Whenever his mother or his negro "mammy" left him unguarded for a moment, Jemmy was immediately among the horses; and the greatest gratification

I could give him was to take him for a rapid gallop before me in the saddle. During the morning General Lee came over to our camp on a short visit, and I was touched by the gentle, sympathising way in which he talked with Mrs Stuart. Our friend Lawley having announced by telegram his coming in this day's train from Richmond, I drove over to the station at Culpepper Court-house to meet so welcome a guest, who had promised to give us the pleasure of his company for several days. To do him proper honour, I substituted on this occasion for the rough-going, yellow-painted waggon in which Pelham and I were accustomed to make most of our journeys, a top-buggy which Stuart had brought from Pennsylvania.

On the 12th the General started on a reconnaissance "to stir up the Yankees a little," as he expressed himself, in which he was accompanied by Lawley, who desired to get an idea of our mode of cavalry fighting. My orders were to remain at headquarters in the performance of some important duties there. I disliked this exceedingly, but I was soon compensated by the unexpected arrival of Vizetelly and Brien, who, after a very amusing ride through the valley and across the Blue Ridge, had at last found us again, and came into the encampment with the outburst of "Dixie," sung to new words, the composition of the versatile Vizetelly himself. Most heartily were these guests welcomed by the whole camp. The negroes especially were greatly pleased to greet "Major Telly" (a name and title they had adopted for the artist) once more at headquarters. During the evening General Stuart returned from his "stirring-up" expedition, which had been so successful that he brought back with him about thirty prisoners, among whom were several officers.

Dinner was soon after served, and though poor in viands it was rich in good fellowship, in mirth and anecdote and song. On this excursion, of which we had animated accounts from Stuart and Lawley, Captain Farley had executed another of those daring feats for which he was so famous, and the recital of it called forth the highest compliments of our whole dinner-party. Riding forward alone, as was his custom, through the woods in the direction of the enemy, he discovered a regiment of Federal infantry marching along the road, and observed the colonel and adjutant making a little detour to a neighbouring plantation-house, doubtless in the hope of obtaining eatables for themselves or forage for their horses. As soon as they had dismounted and entered the dwelling, Farley rode up, and, confronting the astonished officers with his revolver, said, "Gentlemen, you are my prisoners; make the least outcry to your men for assistance and I will blow your brains out." The brave colonel and adjutant, finding it was the best they could do, surrendered at discretion; and Farley brought them quietly into our lines, with their excellent and well-equipped horses, away from their regiment, which was marching along at a distance of only a few hundred yards. The astonishment of the regiment at this sudden and inexplicable disappearance of its commander may be imagined.

Fitzhugh and I having been invited to supper with Captain Dearing, a friend of ours commanding a battery of Pickett's division in Longstreet's corps, who was encamped about two miles off, started on foot, late in the evening, for this entertainment, and after losing ourselves in the darkness, and getting our boots full of water in a swamp, at last reached the camp of the gay artilleryman, where we found large company and little supper. The "spread," indeed, consisted only of a small piece of pork and a canteen of bad apple-brandy; but wit and good-humour make amends for the lack of dishes, and our songs re-echoed through the adjoining forests. Dearing soon proposed that we should send a courier for Bob Sweeney and his banjo, which was carried *nem. con.;* and before half an hour had elapsed, the joyous minstrel occupied the post of honour upon the large mess-chest at our great camp-fire, and the music of the banjo, the songs of the bivouac, and the dances of the negroes, amused us till a late hour, when we returned on Dearing's horses to our headquarters.*

On Sunday the 14th, General Stuart said to me that, as all was quiet along the lines, he wished me to go to Richmond for a few days on some matters of business. As I had never once asked for leave of absence since the commencement of my eventful campaigning, the General, at my request, very readily extended the term of my sojourn at the capital to ten days. Brien and Vizetelly having determined to accompany me, the gay trio soon rolled along in one of the most uncomfortable of railway carriages to our place of destination, where we arrived the same evening, and took lodgings at the well-known Spotswood Hotel. My personal appearance, after so long a period of rough service in the field, was somewhat out of repair for the streets of the metropolis. I looked, indeed, more like a bandit than a Staff officer. There were several large holes for ventilation in my hat, my coat was full of rents, and my riding-boots were soleless, so that, having worn for some time past my last pair of socks, my naked feet now touched the pavement as I walked. Not desiring to exhibit myself in this plight to the good people of Richmond, I was obliged to spend the greater part of the following day in my room, until my tailor could make me presentable again. The effect of dress upon the outward man has very often been dwelt upon by worldly philosophers.

---

*Captain Dearing, who was a very gallant and distinguished officer of artillery, was transferred at a later period of the war to the cavalry. He became the colonel of a North Carolina cavalry regiment, and soon afterwards a general of brigade, in which position he gained a high reputation for daring enterprise and celerity of movement. A Federal bullet ended at once his brilliant military career

When, in my new externals, I met Vizetelly in the afternoon, he barely recognised me, and assured me, with many polite bows, that he had not supposed it possible that I could have changed so much for the better.

I found Richmond very little altered; especially had its generous hospitality known no abatement. I was received in many houses with a cordial welcome. Of course, I did not fail to pay my respects to General and Mrs Randolph, who listened with the most flattering interest to the account of my adventures, and manifested their astonishment at my rapid progress in the English language. Very pleasant hours I spent at the charming residences of Mr P. and Mr W. H. M. With dinner-parties and business engagements, the time passed swiftly by, and I could scarcely believe that I had spent so long an interval of social enjoyment when the day of my departure arrived.

I had packed my portmanteau and taken leave of my kind friends of both sexes in Richmond, and the negro waiter at the Spotswood Hotel had just left my room, promising, with a grin upon his swarthy face, that I should certainly be called in time for the early train the following morning, when a telegram was brought me from General Stuart, ordering me to proceed by rail, not to Culpepper Court-house, as I had intended, but to the vicinity of Fredericksburg, to which place he was upon the eve of transferring his headquarters. General M'Clellan had already, on the 7th of November, been superseded as Federal Commander-in-Chief by General Burnside, who, ambitious of a glory that in his wild dreams his exalted position seemed to promise him, and vehemently urged by the Government at Washington to rouse himself from his inactivity, and undertake something conclusive with his largely

---

and his life, in one of the fights near Petersburg, a short time before the termination of the struggle.

reinforced and splendidly equipped army, had decided to try the shortest and most direct route to the long-coveted Confederate capital. Accordingly the new commander had moved the greater part of his force by rapid marches down the Rappahannock towards Fredericksburg, hoping to cross the river and occupy the town before Lee should be able to divine his intentions. But Mr Burnside had not counted on the vigilance of Stuart's cavalry, the untiring activity of our scouts, and the promptness of decision that belonged to our noble leader; and when he arrived opposite Fredericksburg, demanding, in grand words, the surrender of the place, he found Longstreet, to his great surprise, seriously objecting to this,—Longstreet who, by a movement parallel to his own, had reached the spot with his corps several hours too early for him. Whereupon the Federal General was fain, after many useless threats to shell the town, to postpone yet a little while his rapid "On to Richmond," thus giving General Lee time to move his whole force towards Fredericksburg, where, at the end of November, the two hostile armies were confronting each other.

This change of base gave me one day's longer leave of absence, as I could reach the vicinity of Fredericksburg by rail in twenty-four hours' less time than Stuart by marching across the country. There being nothing to detain me in Richmond, I took advantage of my additional holiday to visit my dear friends, Dr P———and his family, at Dundee, near Hanover Court-house, where I passed Sunday the 22d most delightfully, continuing my journey next day to Hanover Junction, which point I reached unfortunately too late for the passenger-train to Fredericksburg. Being thus compelled to take a freight train, and to ride in an open flat, I felt the sharp, eager wintry air intensely. The train moved at a very slow pace, stopping at every little wayside station, so that it was late at night when we arrived at Hamilton's Crossing, the last stopping-place before reaching Fredericksburg. Here we were obliged to bring the train to rest a quarter of a mile from the station, as it was within range of the enemy's guns, and the Yankees shelled it furiously whenever they heard the sound of an engine. I was thus landed in utter darkness in the depths of the forest, and found myself soon sitting on my portmanteau, with every reasonable prospect that I should remain in this position until morning. Fortunately there were a number of Confederate surgeons, who, having been released from the different hospitals within the enemy's lines, were *en route* to report again to their respective commands, and had left the train under the same unhappy circumstances with myself; and as a common misfortune always quickly unites those who are casually thrown together, it was not long before we were assisting each other in removing our luggage to a fire which at some distance glimmered through the woods. Here, to our great satisfaction, we found the camp of a quarter-master of the army, who was able to give us all the information we desired, and very promptly rendered us every assistance. As the bulk of our army was three or four miles, and Stuart's headquarters at least five miles distant, and we had no means of transportation, we determined to rest here for the night, and readily availed ourselves of a large tent-fly which the quartermaster was kind enough to offer us, beneath which we were soon sufficiently comfortable—each member of the party contributing, from the stores brought with him, to a supper that might have been called luxurious. The next morning we contrived to get hold of an ambulance, and made an early start on our roundabout journey to the different positions of our troops. My point of destination being the most distant, I had to wait until the last of my pleasant companions had reached his special command before I could turn the horses' heads directly to Stuart's headquarters, which I gained not until a late hour of the forenoon.

Our camp was situated in a small piece of pinewoods about five miles from Fredericksburg, on the Telegraph Road leading from that place to Richmond. The white tents gleamed pleasantly amid the dense umbrage of the evergreen pines; straight into the frosty air rose the columns of blue smoke from many chimneys, and the whole encampment wore so snug and comfortable an appearance, that it was far from affording me the least suggestion of the cold and hunger I should yet have to endure on this very spot. I had scarcely climbed out of the ambulance, the news of my arrival having been rapidly circulated through the camp, when comrades and couriers, Stuart foremost of them all, hastened to welcome me. My chief was so much delighted at my return that he threw his arms around my neck in a transport of affection, and the general manner of my reception greatly heightened the happiness I felt in being once more with my dear companions-in-arms. My tent had been already pitched; in the large chimney of it a generous fire was in full blaze, and I had no sooner entered my new abode than I felt entirely at home in it. But I had scarcely time to deposit my luggage and hang up my arms, when Stuart's ringing voice summoned me to his ample tent, which boasted, besides many little internal comforts, the phenomenal adjunct of two chimneys, and of which my chief seemed to be as proud as an Indian nabob of his sumptuous palace. Here all the members of the Staff soon gathered around me, and many more questions were asked of me in a few minutes than I could answer in an hour. The greater part of these questions referred to the pretty and accomplished young ladies I had seen in Richmond, the very mention of whose names caused the hearts of several of my younger comrades to beat quicker than the excitement of the field of battle. Dinner followed without loss of time; then came Sweeney with his banjo, and dancing with the music; and again I enjoyed the harmless, careless gaiety of our camp-life to the top of my bent. Late in the evening we had the pleasure of greeting our friends, Messrs Lawley and Vizetelly, for whom a tent was pitched at once, and whom, by dint of blankets and a roaring wood-fire, we endeavoured to make as comfortable as possible in the severe season of frost that was upon us. Nevertheless I had a hearty laugh the next morning, when, looking for our guests, I found my friend Lawley running up and down before his tent, shivering with cold, and trying, by the addition of a few sticks which he had collected one by one, to bring a large pile of wood into blaze. The wood long resisted his efforts to fan it into lively combustion, but a cup of hot coffee and a hearty breakfast in Stuart's double-chimneyed tent soon brought him into a sufficiently genial state to accept my invitation to drive Vizetelly and himself down to Fredricksburg, to take a good look at the town and at our Yankee friends on the opposite side of the river. So the celebrated yellow waggon, with two of my chargers hitched to it, was soon in readiness, and after an hour's drive, amid the plaintive outcries of my victims as we rattled along over the rough frozen road, we reached the elevated ridge in front of the town, from which we had an excellent view of the town itself, the valley wherein it is situated, and the white tents and swarming numbers of the enemy on the heights across the Rappahannock.

Fredericksburg, one of the oldest places in Virginia, was before the war a pretty town of about 5000 inhabitants, which enjoyed a considerable local trade, and was distinguished for the hospitality and refinement that belonged to its society. It was now comparatively deserted. The larger part of its citizens had been driven off by the continued threats of bombardment which had hung like a Damocles's sword above their heads for several weeks, and the few who had been compelled to remain behind plainly exhibited in their features that the apprehension of doom was pressing like an iron weight upon their hearts. The knowledge on their part that more than a hundred hostile cannon, planted on the dominating "Shepherd's Heights" of Stafford, over the river, bore directly on their unfortunate town, might well have given disquietude to this community of non-combatants. A lively contrast was presented, however, in the demeanour of Barksdale's Mississippi Brigade, stationed at Fredericksburg, the men of which were wandering carelessly about, talking and laughing, as if there were no Yankees within the radius of a thousand miles from them, or making themselves at home in several of the largest houses which had been quite converted into barracks. As the river was not more than 200 yards wide, we could distinctly see each one of the numerous Yankee sentinels who were pacing to and fro in their light-blue overcoats on the opposite bank, and who frequently engaged in amicable conversation with their adversaries across the stream, as it had been agreed that the firing by pickets at each other should be stopped for the time as a useless waste of ammunition. The Federals and Confederates were still nearer together at the site of the railway bridge which had been burnt at an earlier period of the war, leaving on either side the dismantled abutments and the timbers, extending to one or two piers, which were occupied by pickets; and I could not help feeling some solicitude for the safety of Vizetelly, who had quietly seated himself and was making a sketch of the ruins of the viaduct and of the Stafford shore, a picture which afterwards appeared in the 'London Illustrated News.' We were very soon at no loss to discover that the Yankees were under the impression that one of our engineers was drawing a plan of their position and fortifications, for we could see them talking together in suspicious groups; and after a little time several officers came up, who viewed our unconscious artist narrowly through their field-glasses; and had he not opportunely retired, at my instance, to a less exposed situation, a bullet from one of their sharpshooters would doubtless have demonstrated the impropriety or insecurity of his labours.

On our return we made a little detour to the headquarters of General Jenkins of South Carolina, commanding a brigade of troops from the Palmetto State in Longstreet's corps, who received us very courteously, and insisted on our dining with him—an invitation which, after some hesitation, we accepted. Poor Jenkins met with a sad fate, after having served through the greater part of the war with the greatest gallantry and distinction, and having reached the exalted rank of major-general, he was killed through misadventure by his own men upon the same unhappy occasion when Longstreet was so severely wounded.

It was late at night when we got back to our own headquarters, and I was not able to persuade our weary guests to join in a grand opossum-hunt, which the negroes had arranged to carry on in the adjoining woods. Opossum-hunting is a favourite sport with the negroes, and they rarely fail to make sure of their game. The meat of this ugly animal, which grows very fat in the latter part of the autumn, is quite similar to pork. The hunters go out always at night, when the opossum comes forth from his hole in quest of food; and the dogs, which have been carefully trained for the purpose, follow up the scent until they have made out in which tree the frightened fugitive has taken refuge, and commence at once a most dismal howling at the foot. The tree is then cut down, and the opossum, which invariably simulates death, falls an easy prey into the clutches of his enemies. (This ruse of the animal in appearing to be dead gives rise to the well-known American phrase of "playing 'possum," when any one affects unconsciousness.) The stranger, unaccustomed to the manner of hunting the opossum, might suppose, from the horrible din that assails his ears—the blowing of horns, the yell of human voices, and the furious barking of the dogs—that the wild jäger of Germany, or some equally ferocious beast of the European forest, had come over on a visit to the backwoods of America. Very frequently in the opossum-hunt the dogs start a racoon, which more closely resembles the fox, and makes always a gallant fight, at times punishing his assailants severely.

CHAPTER XIV

DISPOSITION OF OUR CAVALRY FORCE — PELHAM'S FIGHT
WITH GUNBOATS — GREAT SNOWBALL ENGAGEMENT —
ANOTHER ENGLISH VISITOR — AMUSEMENTS OF THE CAMP.

THE different brigades of our cavalry were now separated, guarding the numerous fords of the Rappahannock, which rendered necessary a picket-line of more than fifty miles in length. W. H. F. Lee's brigade was stationed on the Lower Rappahannock, near Port Royal; Fitz Lee's command, under Rosser, at a point some distance beyond our headquarters, at Spotsylvania Court-house; and Hampton's on the Upper Rappahannock, in Culpepper county. On the morning of the 27th November I galloped over to Rosser's headquarters upon some matters of business, which, having been duly transacted, the Colonel and I proceeded together to the estate of a neighbouring planter, Mr R., a noted fox-hunter, with whose hounds the officers of Fitz Lee's brigade, when duty would admit of it, were accustomed to engage in the exciting diversion of the chase. General Stuart and his Staff had been invited by Mr R. to take part in a fox-hunt, the arrangements for which had been fully made, and we had looked forward to it with no little satisfaction; but our hopes in this direction were frustrated by the important events which pressed upon us.

Returning to our headquarters, I learned that Stuart had gone with Pelham to Port Royal, to drive off some of the enemy's gunboats which had ascended the river thus far with the view of forcing their way through to Fredericksburg; and next morning Dr Eliason and myself followed them, to take part in the engagement which was in all probability to come off. Being little acquainted with the country, however, we missed our way completely; and as it seemed too late to proceed farther, in complete uncertainty as to where we were going, and, moreover, as General Stuart was expected to return that same night, we resolved to retrace our steps to camp, taking Fredericksburg in our route. Here we stopped at the house of a well-known old wine-merchant, Mr A., with whom Dr Eliason was personally acquainted, and in whose cellar, after a good deal of tasting, we purchased for our mess two demijohns of excellent old madeira. We regretted very much, a few days later, that we had not laid in a larger supply of this capital wine, which was worthy of a happier destiny than to fall into the hands of the Yankees. Getting back to camp, we were derided mercilessly by our companions of the Staff for having missed our way to Port Royal; but when next day we produced the madeira, there was an evident change in public opinion as to the ill-success of our expedition, and our little misadventure was set down as a most fortunate accident. Our purchase, indeed, met with a higher degree of appreciation than we had wished for, since, the news of it having been widely circulated, we had numerous visitors at camp; and several officers, whose names need not be given, plied the demijohns so industriously that we thought they would never be able to find their way back to their respective encampments.

On the morning of the 2d December I received by a courier information from Stuart that he had been unexpectedly detained in Port Royal, together with orders that I should join him there at once; so that I started a second time with my portly friend the doctor on our journey. It was a disagreeable ride enough. The cold was intense, the road rough, and the distance long. We had ridden already more than twenty miles, the icicles hanging from our beards and our horses' nostrils, when we met General Stuart returning to Fredericksburg. He laughed heartily at us for our former unsuccessful ride, and ordered us to turn back with him.

The fighting was over at Port Royal, and Pelham with his horse-artillery had met with his usual good fortune, inflicting much damage upon the enemy, and driving off the gunboats, which, from the narrowness of the stream and the height of the cliffs where our guns were posted, had scarcely been able to respond at all to the destructive fire which was pouring down upon them at so near a range. The return to camp was even more distressing than our ride of the morning, as a heavy snow-storm set in, which continued throughout the night; and we reached our headquarters, men and horses wet and chilled, and almost wearied out by a journey of more than forty miles.

The following morning we were enlivened by snowball fights, which commenced as skirmishes near our headquarters, but extended over the neighbouring camps, and assumed the aspect of general engagements. In front of our headquarters, beyond an open field of about half a mile square, Hood's division lay encamped in a piece of wood; in our immediate rear stretched the tents and huts of a part of M'Laws's division. Between these two bodies of troops animated little skirmishes had frequently occurred whenever there was snow enough on the ground to furnish the ammunition; but on the morning of the 4th, an extensive expedition having been undertaken by several hundred of M'Laws's men against Hood's encampments, and the occupants of these finding themselves considerably disturbed thereby, suddenly the whole of the division advanced in line of battle, with flying colours, the officers leading the men, as if in real action, to avenge the insult. The assailants fell back rapidly before this overwhelming host, but only to secure a strong position, from which, with reinforcements, they might resume the offensive. The alarm of their first repulse having been borne with the swiftness of the wind to their comrades, sharpshooters in large numbers were posted behind the cedar bushes that skirt the Telegraph Road, and hundreds of hands were actively employed in erecting a long and high snow-wall in front of their extended lines. The struggle had now the appearance of a regular battle, with its charges and counter-chargers—the wild enthusiasm of the men and the noble emulation of the officers finding expression in loud commands and yet louder cheering, while the air was darkened with the snowballs as the current of the fight moved to and fro over the well-contested field. Nearer and nearer it came towards our headquarters, and it was soon evident to us that the hottest part of the engagement would take place on our neutral territory. Fruitless were the efforts of Stuart and myself to assert and maintain the neutrality of our camp, utterly idle the hoisting of a white flag; the advancing columns pressed forward in complete disregard of our signs and our outspoken remonstrances, clouds of snowballs passed across the face of the sun, and ere long the overwhelming wave of the conflict rolled pitilessly over us. Yielding to the unavoidable necessity which forbade our keeping aloof from the contest, Stuart and I had taken position, in order to obtain a view over the field of battle, on a big box, containing ordnance stores, in front of the General's tent, where we soon became so much interested in the result, and so carried away by the excitement of the moment, that we found ourselves calling out to the men to hold their ground, and urging them again and again to the attack, while many a stray snowball, and many a well-directed one, took effect upon our exposed persons. But all the gallant resistance of M'Laws's men was unavailing. Hood's lines pressed resistlessly forward, carrying everything before them, taking the formidable fortifications, and driving M'Laws's division out of their encampments. Suddenly, at this juncture, we heard loud shouting on the right, where two of Anderson's brigades had come up as reinforcements. The men of M'Laws's division, acquiring new confidence from this support, rallied, and in turn drove, by a united charge, the victorious foe in headlong flight back to their own camps and woods. Thus ended the battle for the day, unhappily with serious results to some of the combatants, for one of Hood's men had his leg broken, one of M'Laws's men lost an eye, and there were other chance-wounds on both sides. This sham-fight gave ample proof of the excellent spirits of our troops, who, in the wet, wintry weather, many of them without blankets, some without shoes, regardless of their exposure and of the scarcity of provisions, still maintained their good-humour, and were ever ready for any sort of sport or fun that offered itself to them.

On the morning of the 5th, General Stuart and myself, with several other members of the Staff, again set out for Port Royal, where some of the Federal gunboats were renewing their demonstrations. The day was bitterly cold, and the road exceedingly slippery from the frost, so that the ride was anything but pleasant. All along our route we found our troops, chiefly those of Jackson's corps—Old Stonewall having established his headquarters midway between Fredericksburg and Port Royal, at the plantation of James Parke Corbin, Esq., known as "Moss Neck"—busily employed in throwing up fortifications, rendering our position as impregnable as it afterwards proved itself to be. They had greatly improved the highway also, erected lines of telegraphic communication to the headquarters of the different corps of the army, and cut military roads through the woods to various points along our lines. It was late in the evening, and darkness had overtaken us, when we reached the charming country-seat of "Gaymont," within a short distance of our place of destination, where a most cordial hospitality was extended to us, and where, in the snug library, before a glorious wood-fire, we warmed our half-frozen limbs, and remained in delightful conversation with the ladies till a late hour of the night.

The following day it was reported by our scouts and patrols that the gunboats had disappeared. It was Sunday, and we spent it as a day of rest, in the most blissful quietude. On Monday morning we reluctantly took leave of our kind hosts, and started on a reconnaissance up the river with General D. H. Hill, who with his division formed the extreme right of our infantry lines, and occupied a position where a crossing of the stream offered every kind of advantage to the enemy, though, strange to relate, they never availed themselves of it. The Yankees were in plain view on the other side of the river, and were evidently very active in erecting fortifications, marching and countermarching small bodies of troops, and in communicating with other parts of their lines by signal-flags.

Night was far advanced when we returned to our head-quarters, where we found, to our great delight, a pleasant addition to our little military family in an English guest, Captain Phillips, of the Grenadier Guards, who was profiting by a short leave of absence from his battalion, stationed at the time in Canada, to witness some of the active operations of the war on our side. The next day there was a review of the South Carolina Brigade of General Jenkins, in an open field within half an hour's walk of our camp, and I had the gratification of taking our new guest to see it. General Jenkins received us with his habitual courtesy, and manifestly felt great pride in showing off his magnificent brigade, which consisted of about 3500 men, veterans who had participated in nearly all the great battles of the war. Captain Phillips was highly pleased with the appearance of the brigade, and the material of which it was composed, saying, that while they would not do for a parade in Hyde Park, with their motley uniforms and their style of marching, the men looked like work. One of the regiments, the Hampton Legion, raised at the breaking-out of the war by the distinguished patriot and soldier whose name it bore, carried a flag displaying many rents of shot and shell, which had been presented to it by Mrs Hampton, who, with her own fair hands, had made it out of a robe worn by her several years previous at a "Drawing-Room" of her Majesty Queen Victoria.

We accepted General Jenkins's kind invitation to dine with him at his headquarters, where we passed some most agreeable hours, and were sent back to our camp by the General on his own horses, Captain Phillips riding a superb animal, a bay, which had been presented by the State of South Carolina to her gallant son.

Desirous of amusing our guest, and of making our rough camp-life as agreeable to him as possible, we had secured invitations to a country ball which was to come off the night following at a small plantation, about ten miles distant, and for which we had promised to provide the music. Accordingly, about six o'clock the next evening, the very-frequently-before-mentioned yellow waggon was again brought out, and four spirited mules of the medical department of our headquarters were harnessed to it. Sweeney reported himself with his banjo and two fiddlers, and very soon the whole company, consisting of Captain Phillips, Major Pelham, Major Terrell, Captain Blackford, Lieutenant Dabney, and myself, with our musicians, were settled on the rough wooden planks which constituted the improvised seats of our carriage, and the carriage itself was in rapid motion. General Stuart's mulatto servant Bob, who was to accompany the instrumental performance with his inimitable rattle of the bones, followed us with a led horse for Captain Phillips, in case the violent jarring of our vehicle should prove too much for one not accustomed to such rude transportation. As an expert driver I had taken the reins in my own hands, the mules being rather difficult to manage from having run off several times with their accustomed teamster. So we rattled along through the cold starlight night, waking the echoes of the woods with song, and creating a sensation in many encampments *en route*, from which the soldiers ran out and cheered us as we passed. All went well for a little time, when Major Terrell, who somewhat prided himself on his driving, proposed to take the reins—a change of position to which I consented the more readily, because I felt a great desire to unite in the animated conversation and merriment going on behind me. Our rate of progress now became greatly accelerated, and the rapid clatter of the hoofs of our fleet animals on the hard-frozen road, just covered with snow, struck pleasantly on the ear, as all began to partake of the agreeable excitement which great velocity of movement generally produces; when suddenly, with a loud crash and a heavy thump, the waggon, overturning, projected its inmates in various directions fully ten paces out upon the snow. Fortunately for us, the mules, struck dumb with astonishment most probably at this unexpected turn in affairs, remained very quietly in their tracks, while the scattered members of our party gathered themselves up to examine into the extent of the disaster. Nobody having received serious injury, though all were more or less bruised, we were in condition to be diverted at the accident, and heartily to deride Major Terrell, who had managed to upset us by driving directly against a stump several feet in circumference and as many feet in height.

The waggon having marvellously escaped, to all appearance, without a fracture, it was soon set up again, and Major Terrell, not without some cavil, having been reinstated as driver, away we went on our journey not less rapidly than before. But the severe thump against the tremendous stump had been, alas! the *coup de grace* for the dear old yellow-painted Yankee van, which was to carry us no more. After creaking and groaning very painfully for a mile or two, the back part of it all at once gave way everywhere, landing us rudely once more on the snowy ground. Captain Blackford was the chief sufferer from the casualty, one of the wheels, which had been violently detached from the axletree by the shock, having passed directly over his head, cutting so deep a gash in it that we had to employ all our pocket-handkerchiefs in making bandages to stanch the flow of blood. We were now no longer in a frame of mind to laugh over our misfortunes, for we were yet four miles from our place of destination; around us lay the wide forest of the Wilderness, with no human dwelling within striking distance, and above us was the intense wintry night. A return to camp was not to be thought of, as it would have subjected us to the endless ridicule of our comrades. A council of war was at once held over the ruins of the waggon. Our English guest, who had borne all the discomforts and mishaps of our journey with soldierly nonchalance, was left to decide upon our course, and his decision was that we should go on. Indeed, the unanimous vote of our party, including even poor wounded Captain Blackford, was to grin and bear it, and carry out the original expedition in the best way that we could manage. The two fore-wheels of the waggon, to which the mules still remained hitched, being uninjured, and securely connected by the axletree, Captain Phillips, Dabney, and myself seated ourselves on their narrow base; the four other gentlemen mounted the four mules, the musicians mounted the led horse, and so this extraordinary caravan proceeded on its way. After an hour of torture, during which the headlong speed of our team over the rough plank-road had given to the sufferers on the axletree the sensation of riding on a razor, we reached the scene of the evening's festivity. The mansion was brilliantly lighted up, many fair ones had already assembled, and the whole company awaited, with impatience and anxiety, the arrival of their distinguished guests and the promised music. Sweeney lost no time in his orchestral arrangements. In a very few minutes the banjo vibrated under his master hand, the two fiddles shrieked in unison, and Bob's bones clattered their most hideous din; and in the animated beat of the music, and the lively measures of the dance, we soon forgot the little *désagrémens* of our journey. Our English captain entered into the fun quite as heartily as any of us. If there was no magnificent hall, with the light showering down from a thousand wax candles on the brilliant toilettes of Europe, to fall forth our admiration, there were many pretty faces and sparkling eyes worth looking into; and it was quite delightful to see our foreign friend winding through the mazes of many bounding quadrilles and Virginia reels with an evident enjoyment of the same. After several hours of mirth and dancing, we accepted the kind offer of our host to lend us one of his own waggons for our return to headquarters, where we arrived a short time before daybreak, little thinking how soon we should be aroused by the notes of a very different music from that of Sweeney's orchestra.

CHAPTER XV

BOMBARDMENT OF FREDERICKSBURG — EVENTS PRECEDING THE BATTLE OF FREDERICKSBURG.

11th December

I had enjoyed but a few minutes or repose, enveloped in my warm blankets, when I was waked from sleep by a dull heavy noise, which, in the earliest moments of consciousness, I believed to have been produced by the thawing and sliding down of the snow that had accumulated on the top of my tent. I was quickly undeceived, however, by my negro servant Henry, who, appearing at my tent door, informed me in a single abrupt sentence of the true condition of affairs. "Major," said Henry, "de Yankees is shelling Fredericksburg. I done saddled your horse, and de General is ready for to start." This intelligence brought me in an instant to my feet. Inserting my legs into my huge cavalry-boots, I soon emerged from the tent, and in a few minutes I galloped off with the General and the other members of the Staff in full haste for the front.

For the reader's better comprehension of the events I am about to narrate, it will be necessary to describe the position of the two hostile armies, and the ground on which one of the most sanguinary battles of the present century was to be fought. The little valley in which Fredericksburg is situated in enclosed on the south side of the Rappahannock by a range of hills, which, directly opposite the town, are known as "Marye's Heights," and approach within half a mile of the river, and which, receding from it afterwards in a semicircular or crescent-like sweep of five miles to a distance of three miles from the stream, again trend towards it near Hamilton's Crossing, at which point the interval between them may be one mile and a half. Most of these hills are covered with a thick copse of oak, and only in front of the town are they quite bare of trees. The ground towards the Rappannock is open and flat, and is intersected only by some small streams—such as the Hazel and Deep Run—and broken immediately upon the river by several large and deep ravines, which afforded serviceable shelter to the Federal troops in their retreat under the fire of our artillery. This valley is cut nearly in half by the railway from Hamilton's Crossing to Fredericksburg, the high embankment of which was used by a portion of Jackson's troops as a breast-work. Nearly parallel with the railway runs the county turnpike road, which, at a distance of four miles from Fredericksburg, branches off, leading on the right to Hamilton's Crossing, where it crosses the railway, giving the name to the station, and on the left to Port Royal, where it strikes the Rappahannock. The turnpike road from Fredericksburg to the fork just mentioned, being carried for a considerable distance through deep cuts, formed a formidable defensive work for the Federals.

On this semicircle of hills, the relative position of which to the river, the railway, the turnpike, and the town I have endeavoured to render intelligible, our army, numbering in all about 80,000 men, was posted in order of battle behind a continuous line of intrenchments, concealed from the enemy's view by the thick underwood, which, except in a few small spaces, covers the ridge abundantly. Longstreet's corps formed the left, Jackson's the right, of our lines. Our extreme left, constituting Anderson's division, rested on a broad swampy ditch, which about two miles above Fredericksburg makes up from the Rappahannock; then came Ransom's and M'Laws's divisions, the right wing of the latter extending across the Telegraph Road, there joining Pickett's troops; and farther on Hood's division, which occupied as nearly as possible the centre of our whole line of battle, at a point where the hills open into a small valley for the passage of the creek, Deep Run; yet further on came Early's division of Jackson's corps. The extreme right was composed of A. P. Hill's division, holding in reserve the troops of Taliaferro. The splendid division of D. H. Hill, having been kept back by some demonstrations of the enemy in the direction of Port Royal, did not join us until the evening of the battle, the 13th, when it took its place on the extreme right. The cavalry, with the exception of Hampton's brigade, which was operating on the upper Rappahannock, and our horse-artillery, under Pelham, occupied the road leading from Hamilton's Crossing to Port Royal, our right extending to Massaponax Creek, and our line of battle thus stood nearly perpendicular to the lines of the main army. The bulk of the artillery, numbering about 250 pieces, was well posted all along the lines, but was principally concentrated into large batteries, on the extreme right, under Colonel Lindsay Walker, in the centre under Colonel Alexander, and on the left opposite Fredericksburg, on Marye's Heights, under Colonel Walton. The Rappahannock is closely lined on its northern bank by a range of commanding hills, on which the hostile artillery, consisting of more than 300 pieces, some of them of heavier calibre than had ever before been employed in the field, were advantageously posted. The greater part of them, especially those on the Stafford Heights, bore immediately on the town, but nearly all were in a position to sweep the plains on our side of the river. The entire strength of the Federal army in the battle amounted to not less that 150,000 men.

Reaching our lines, we found General Lee on an eminence which, rising considerably above the other heights, a few hundred yards to the right of the Telegraph Road, afforded a view over nearly the whole plain before him, and gave our great commander the opportunity of watching closely the operations of the enemy, and controlling the movements of his own army in accordance therewith. This hill having been occupied by General Lee during the entire progress of the battle, received his name, and to all future generations of Southerners it will be known as the spot from which their gallant forefathers were led on to victory. Longstreet and several other generals were also assembled here, looking anxiously towards Fredericksburg, as yet concealed from their sight by a dense fog which hung heavily over the little valley. Information had been received here that under cover of the fog the enemy had endeavoured to lay his pontoon bridges across the river, but that, by the accurate and effective fire of Barksdale's Mississippi brigade, the Federal engineers and working parties had been driven off with heavy loss, and all their efforts had been so far unsuccessful. The cannonade which had so rudely roused us from our slumbers had been nothing more than an artillery duel between some of the Federal batteries and a like number of our own, and had now ceased altogether; and the quiet of the morning was disturbed only by the repeated cracks of Barksdale's rifles sounding over from the river, from which we knew that the enemy's bridge-building was still resisted with spirit. The frequent reports which reached us from that quarter were as favourable as could be desired—"All right! the enemy have been driven back, with severe loss, from their pontoons."

So several hours passed wearily away, oppressing every one

of us with an anticipation of the sad spectacle we should soon be compelled to witness in the bombardment of the town. Already the Telegraph Road leading up to the heights from Fredericksburg was thronged with a confused mass of fugitives, men, women, and children, who had not been willing or able to leave their homesteads before, bearing with them such of their effects as they could bring away, and as they most wished to save, many of which, having been dropped in the haste and terror of their exodus, marked the line of their flight as far as the eye could reach. Ten o'clock came, and the hammers of the church-clocks were just sounding the last peaceful stroke of the hour, when suddenly, at the signal of a single cannon-shot, more than 150 pieces of artillery, including some of the enemy's most ponderous guns, opened their iron mouths with a terrific roar, and hurled a tempest of destruction upon the devoted town. The air shook, and the very earth beneath our feet trembled at this deafening cannonade, the heaviest that had ever yet assailed my ears. The thick fog still prevented us from obtaining a satisfactory view of the bombardment; but the howling of the solid shot, the bursting of the shells, the crashing of the missiles through the thick walls, and the dull sound of falling houses, united in a dismal concert of doom. Very soon the exact site of the unhappy town was indicated, even through the fog, by a rising column of smoke and dust, and the flames of burning buildings broke out of the dark overhanging canopy with reddening glare, while the bursting bombs flashed athwart the gloom like the arrowy lightning in a thunder-cloud. Our batteries did not respond to the guns of the enemy with a single shot. It was evident enough that nothing could be done to save the place from the desolation to which it had been fore-doomed by the wanton barbarity of the Federal commander. The horrible din lasted for two hours, and was succeeded by perfect silence—the silence of a solitude. About noon, a gentle breeze, springing up just as the roar of the latest guns died away, lifted the veil which had mysteriously shrouded the valley, and the sun, breaking through the clouds, seemed to mock with its garish splendour the smoking ruins it revealed. Sad indeed was the scene that presented itself to our gaze, and to the eyes, filled with tears, of the mournful fugitives whose once happy homes lay before them, shattered or smouldering; and every heart of the thousands of brave Confederate soldiers who witnessed it burned for revenge.

It may be supposed that we thought with great anxiety of our Mississippi brigade, which had all the time been exposed to this *feu d'enfer*; but the sharp crack of their rifles soon gave us the gratifying assurance that these gallant fellows, unmindful of the death and anguish which shot and shell had been spreading amid their ranks, had firmly maintained their ground, and were ready to meet the enemy's attack; and a little later we received the satisfactory report that a renewed attempt of the Federals to force the building of their bridges had been defeated. But General Lee knew very well that he would not be able to prevent the passage of the river by the Federal army; and having entertained from the beginning no idea of seriously contesting this, he now gave orders for Barksdale's brigade to withdraw gradually from the town, and to keep up only a feigned resistance. Accordingly, about 2 P.M., Fredericksburg was altogether abandoned by our men, after a sanguinary fight had been maintained for a considerable time in the streets. During the rest of the afternoon and evening, the pontoon bridges having been completed, the dense masses of the Federal army commenced to move over to our side of the river.

In the quietude that followed the hurly-burly of the day we exchanged felicitations upon the great blunder of the Federal commander in thus running right into the lion's mouth, and preparing to attack us in a position of our own choice, where his defeat was wellnigh certain—a lack of generalship on his part which we had scarcely dared to hope for. Even the face of our great commander Lee, which rarely underwent any change of expression at the news of victory or disaster, seemed to be lit up with pleasure at every fresh report that a greater number of the enemy had crossed the river. With the gathering darkness Stuart returned to our cavalry headquarters, attended by the members of his Staff, for a short interim of rest, each one of us looking forward with good confidence and certain hope, in common with our whole army, to the great battle which, in all human probability, would be joined at an early hour of the following day.

12th December

At an early hour of the morning we were again assembled on "Lee's Hill," viewing the plain beneath us, from which the fogs of the night were just rising, and where the rays of the newly-risen sun revealed many thousands of Yankees who had crossed from the Stafford side of the river since the previous afternoon. The enemy seemed as busy as bees. Long trains of artillery and ammunition and provision waggons were to be seen descending the heights on the opposite side, and interminable columns of infantry, blue in colour, and blurred by distance, flowed towards us like the waves of a steadily-advancing sea. On and on they came, with flash of bayonets and flutter of flags, to the measure of military music, each note of which was borne to us by the morning breeze, and we could distinctly observe them deploy into line of battle. From the many heavy batteries over the river rose, from time to time, little white puffs of smoke, and the deep, dull boom of the big guns was almost immediately followed by the angry whirr of a 50 or 100-pound shell, which falling, in the majority of instances, too short, did little or no damage. Our artillery, from different points along our line, occasionally answered the enemy's guns with just as little effect; and our confident belief that the great battle would be fought on the morning of the 12th was more and more weakened as the day wore on.

About eleven o'clock I was asked by General Stuart to accompany him on a ride along our line of battle to the extreme right, that we might look after our horsemen, reconnoitre the position and movements of the enemy in that direction, and ascertain whether the nature of the ground was such that a charge of our whole cavalry division during the impending fight might be profitably attempted. It was a pleasure and an encouragement to pass the extended lines of our soldiers, who were lying carelessly behind their earth-works, or actively engaged in throwing up new ones—some cooking, others gaily discussing the designs of the enemy, and greeting with loud cheers of derision the enormous shells, which they called "Yankee flour-barrels," as these came tumbling into the woods around them, and to read in every bronzed face of them all eagerness for the conflict, and confidence as to the result. The atmosphere had now again become obscure, and the fog was rolling up from the low swampy grounds along the margin of Deep Run Creek, in the immediate front of Hood's and Early's divisions. Here we turned off into a narrow bridle-path, which bore away some distance from our lines, but would shorten our ride by nearly a mile. We had proceeded but a few steps in a careless trot, when suddenly a long line of horsemen in skirmishing order appeared directly before us in the mist. I felt very certain they were Federal horsemen, but Stuart was unwilling to believe that the Yankees would have the audacity to approach our position so closely; and as the greater part of them wore a brownish dust-coloured jacket over their uniforms, he set them down as a small command of our own cavalry returning from a reconnaissance. So we continued upon our route yet a little farther, until, at a distance of about forty yards, several carbine-shots, whose bullets whistled around our heads, taught us very plainly with whom we had to deal. At the same moment ten or fifteen of the dragoons spurred furiously towards us, demanding, with loud outcries, our surrender; hearing which, we galloped in some haste back to our lines, where our bold pursuers were received and put to flight by Early's sharpshooters. A considerable number of our infantry skirmishers now moved forward to drive the dashing cavalrymen off; but the latter held their ground gallantly, and kept up so annoying a fire with their long-range carbines, that our men did not obtain any advantage over them, while Stuart and myself could not look without admiration upon the address and intrepidity our enemies displayed. General Hood, who had been attracted by the noise of the brisk fusillade, soon came riding up to us, and seeing at a moment what was going on, said, "This will never do; I must send up some of my Texans, who will make short work of these impudent Yankees." One of Hood's adjutants galloped off at once with an order from his general, and soon a select number of these dreaded marksmen, crawling along the ground, after their wild Indian fashion, advanced upon the Federal dragoons, who had no idea of their approach until they opened fire at a distance of about eighty yards. In a few seconds several men and horses had been killed, and the whole Federal line, stampeded by a galling fire from an unseen foe in a quarter wholly unexpected, broke into confused and rapid flight.

This opened the way for us, and we continued our ride without farther interruption. On the left wing of A. P. Hill's division, we had to pass a small piece of wood, extending in a triangular shape about six or eight hundred yards outside of our lines, with a base of about half a mile, offering, in my opinion, a great advantage to the enemy, and I remarked to Stuart that I thought it ought to be cut down. He did not regard this as necessary, as he did not believe that, under the sweeping cross-fire of our artillery, the Federals could ever advance so far. The events of the following day proved, however, that I had been right, as, under cover of this identical piece of wood, a hostile division approached so rapidly and unexpectedly that here alone our line was broken, and we suffered severe loss before the enemy could be driven back. We found our horsemen in good spirits, and occupying their position on the Port Royal road, where the right wing was engaged in a lively skirmish with a body of Federal cavalry, which ended in the withdrawal of the latter. Our comrades of the other arms of the service had indulged in some captious criticism of the cavalry for not having given the decisive finishing stroke to great battles by grand and overwhelming charges, as had been done in the times of Frederick the Great and Napoleon—criticism that was unwarranted and unjust, since the nature of the ground in Virginia did not favour the operations of cavalry, and since the great improvement in firearms in our day had necessitated a very material change in cavalry tactics. Still more unkind and uncalled-for did such animadversions appear when it was considered what important services had been rendered by the cavalry—the hard fighting they had done, the wearisome marches they had made, the fatigue and cold and hunger they had cheerfully endured. Nevertheless General Stuart was anxious, with every officer and private under his command, to show that we were able to do what other cavalry had accomplished before us; and all burned with the noble ambition of winning an enduring fame on so grand a theatre, with the eyes of the whole army resting upon us. The forty centuries that looked down from the Pyramids on the legions of the mighty Corsican did not inspire them with a more generous ardour. The open plain before us, cut by only a few ditches and with only here and there a fence running across it, seemed to offer us the arena for the realisation of our dreams of glory; but upon a closer survey of the ground we found it much too soft for a charge with any chance of success, as the horses, moving even at a moderate speed, would sink several feet into the mire. A sluggish artillery fire which had lasted all day, grew, about one o'clock, into a spirited cannonade all along the lines, in which the Federal light batteries on our side of the river took no part, it being altogether maintained by their heavier guns on the Stafford Hills. This continued until two o'clock, when the firing slackened again to the occasional boom of the largest pieces of ordnance.

On the road between Hamilton's Crossing and Fredericksburg, thousands of Yankees were working like beavers in digging rifle-pits, and erecting works for their artillery. Stuart being anxious to discover exactly what they were about, I rode with him in that direction to a small barn, where we dismounted and tied our horses, and thence carefully approached the hostile lines by creeping along a ditch which led into the main turnpike road, constituting the boundary of an inconsiderable plantation. Thus we proceeded until we reached a slight eminence only a few hundred yards from the Yankees, where two big posts, the remains of a dismantled gate, concealed us from their observation. Our own view was so satisfactory, that with our field-glasses we could distinctly mark the features of the men. It was evident enough to us that they were engaged in converting the simple road into a most formidable work of defence, and that in Jackson's front they were massing large forces of infantry and artillery, of the latter of which I counted thirty-two guns in one battery.

Quite content with what we had seen, we returned to our horses, and I received orders to ride at once to General Lee to make report of our reconnaissance, General Stuart himself galloping over to A. P. Hill. After a ride of a few minutes, I met Generals Lee and Jackson, who were taking a turn to inspect our own lines, and to reconnoitre those of the enemy. Upon hearing what I had to tell them, both generals determined at once to repair themselves to the point of look-out from which we had just withdrawn, and, leaving their numerous escort behind, accompanied only by an orderly, they rode forward under my guidance to the barn already mentioned. Here the horses were placed in charge of the orderly, and we made our way on foot to the gate-posts. Fearing to augment the danger of their situation by my presence, I retired to the roadside some twenty yards distant, and left the two great leaders to their conference and survey. I must confess I felt extremely nervous as regards their safety, so close to the enemy, who surely little suspected that the two greatest heroes of the war were so nearly in their clutches. One well-directed shot, or a rapid dash of resolute horsemen, might have destroyed the hopes and confidence of our whole army. The sensation of relief on my part was therefore great, when, after many minutes of painful anxiety and impatience, the generals slowly returned, and we reached our horses without accident.

We were now soon joined by Stuart, and all, except Jackson, who parted with us to regain the troops under his command, rode back to Lee's Hill, from which a desultory cannonade was still kept up. Here we found that one of our 32-pounder Parrott guns had burst only a few moments before—a disaster which was fortunately not attended with loss of life, but which came very near proving fatal to our English friend Captain Phillips, who was standing at the instant of the explosion quite close to the gun, huge fragments of which had been scattered with fearful violence all around him. The witnesses of the scene were full of admiration at the coolness displayed by our visitor on this occasion, and none of us could fail to remark the soldierly indifference to danger he manifested under heavy fire throughout the day. These Parrott guns had been manufactured in Richmond, and the iron of which they were cast was so defective that a second gun burst the same evening, wounding several of the gunners severely. At dusk the firing ceased altogether, and we returned to our headquarters, where our little military family, officers and guests, gathered around the glowing fires of Stuart's double-chimneyed tent to recite the adventures of the past, and discuss the chances of the coming day.

CHAPTER XVI

13th December 1862

THE darkness of night was just giving way before the doubtful light of morning, which struggled with a dense, all-obscuring fog, when the bugle sounded to horse at our headquarters. In obeying the summons, every man girded his sword more tightly around his waist, and looked with greater care than usual to the saddling of his horse and the loading of his revolver, feeling well assured that the hour of the momentous conflict had indeed arrived. Our guest, Captain Phillips, believing that he should obtain a more extended and satisfactory view of the engagement from Lee's Hill than from the position of our cavalry on the right flank, made up his mind to separate himself from us for the day, and at an early hour we parted with this portly grenadier, whose engaging manners had endeared him to us all. Our parting had just that little admixture of sadness in it which came from the involuntary misgiving that possibly we were bidding each other a final farewell. Captain Phillips had worn in camp a narrow red and blue striped necktie, consisting of a bit of a ribbon of his regiment, the Grenadier Guards, which, at the moment of leaving us, he handed to Pelham, with the request that he would wear it as a talisman during the battle, and return it afterwards to the owner to be preserved as a relique. The boy-hero, with the blush of modesty and pride suffusing his fair cheek, readily accepted the compliment, and, tying the ribbon around his cap, galloped off with us to the front, where we hastened to take our position on the extreme right. On our way we met General Maxey Gregg, a gallant officer from South Carolina, with whom I exchanged a few words of friendly greeting for the last time, as a few hours afterwards he was a corpse.

Jackson had chosen his own position on an eminence, within a few hundred yards of Hamilton's Crossing, which rose above the general elevation of the ridge in a similar manner to Lee's Hill on the left, and which has ever since borne the name of "Jackson's Hill," from its having been rendered historical by the presence of the great warrior during the fight. Here we first directed our horses, and here we found Stonewall and A. P. Hill, with their respective Staffs, looking out through the white mists of the morning into the plain below, from which arose an indistinct murmur, like the distant hum of myriads of bees, vaguely announcing to us its hostile occupation by thousands of human beings. Jackson and Stuart concurred in the opinion that it would be the best plan to make a sudden general attack upon the enemy under cover of the fog, which must have prevented the fire of the numerous Federal batteries on the other side of the Rappahannock, or caused that fire to be ineffective; but General Lee had decided in council of war against any offensive movement, preferring to fight behind his intrench-ments and to inflict a severe blow upon the enemy without the risk of fearful loss of life, even should the material result prove a less decided one. After remaining for half an hour upon Jackson's Hill, we rode down to the lines of our cavalry, and found our sharpshooters all along the Port Royal road, well posted in rifle-pits or behind the high embankments of the turnpike, the regiments themselves a little farther back in reserve, and Pelham's eighteen pieces of horse-artillery in favourable position, the young leader longing for the combat, and anxious to open the ball with some of his light guns.

Nine o'clock came, and still the vaporous curtain overhung the plateau, still the brooding silence prevailed, which always seemed the deeper just before the furies of war were to be unchained; and we slowly returned to the Crossing, almost despairing that the decisive action would be fought on that day. Here we dismounted to rest our horses, and I found a convenient seat on a large box, one of many filled with boots and uniforms for our soldiers, which had been deposited near the station for distribution among the respective commands of our army. I had been seated but a few minutes, when suddenly it seemed as though a tremendous hurricane had burst upon us, and we became sensible upon the instant of a howling tempest of shot and shell hurled against our position from not fewer than 300 pieces of artillery, which had opened all along the hostile lines, with a roar more deafening than the loudest thunder. Hundreds of missiles of every size and description crashed through the woods, breaking down trees and scattering branches and splinters in all directions. I was just calling out to the orderly who held my horse, and had been walking the animal up and down at the distance of a hundred yards, to return to me at once, when, about thirty paces from me, a young officer of artillery, struck by the fragment of a shell, fell with a groan to the earth; I immediately rushed to his assistance, but reached him only to receive his parting breath as I lifted him from the spot. This incident, sad as it was, saved my own life, for, a few seconds after I had left my seat, a huge shell, falling into a pile of boxes and bursting there, shattered them to atoms, filling the air with the debris of wood, leather, and clothing.

As this cannonade was in all probability to be immediately followed up by a general attack, we galloped to our post with the cavalry, which as yet had suffered not at all from the heavy fire of the enemy, this being concentrated chiefly upon our main line. And now the thick veil of mist that had concealed the plain from our eyes rolled away, like the drawing up of a drop-scene at the opera, and revealed to us the countless corps, divisions, brigades, and regiments of the Federal army forming their lines of attack. At this moment I was sent by Stuart to General Jackson with the message that the Yankees were about commencing their advance. I found old Stonewall standing at ease upon his hill, unmoved in the midst of the terrible fire, narrowly observing the movements of the enemy through his field-glass. The atmosphere was now perfectly clear, and from this eminence was afforded a distinct view of more than two-thirds of the battle-field, and the larger part of the whole number of the advancing foe, extending as far as the eye could reach—a military panorama, the grandeur of which I had never seen equalled. On they came, in beautiful order, as if on parade, a moving forest of steel, their bayonets glistening in the bright sunlight; on they came, waving their hundreds of regimental flags, which relieved with warm bits of colouring the dull blue of the columns and the russet tinge of the wintery landscape, while their artillery beyond the river continued the cannonade with unabated fury over their heads, and gave a background of white fleecy smoke, like midsummer clouds, to the animated picture.

I could not rid myself of a feeling of depression and anxiety as I saw this innumerable host steadily moving upon our lines, which were hidden by the woods, where our artillery maintained as yet a perfect silence, General Lee having given orders that our guns should not open fire until the Yankees had come within easy canister range. Upon my mentioning this feeling to Jackson, the old chief answered me in his characteristic way: "Major, my men have sometimes failed *to take* a position, but *to defend* one, never! I am glad the Yankees are coming." He then gave me orders for Stuart to employ his horse-artillery, and open fire at once on the enemy's flank.

Pelham was accordingly directed to prepare for action, but, being exceedingly anxious to go to work without a moment's delay, he begged Stuart to allow him to advance two of his light pieces to the fork of the road where the turnpike branches off to Fredericksburg, as from this point the masses of the enemy offered him an easy target. The permission being giving, Pelham went off with his two guns at a gallop, amidst the loud cheering of the cannoneers, and in a few minutes his solid shot were ploughing at short range with fearful effect through the dense columns of the Federals. The boldness of the enterprise and the fatal accuracy of the firing seemed to paralyse for a time and then to stampede the whole of the extreme left of the Yankee army, and terror and confusion reigned there during some minutes: soon, however, several batteries moved into position, and, uniting with several of those on the Stafford Heights, concentrated a tremendous fire upon our guns, one of which, a Blakely gun, was quickly disabled and compelled to withdraw. I was now sent by General Stuart to tell Pelham to retire if he thought the proper moment had arrived, but the young hero could not be moved. "Tell the General I can hold my ground," he said, and again and again pealed out the ringing report of his single gun, upon which at one time 32 pieces of the enemy's artillery were brought to bear in a sweeping cross-fire, which killed and wounded many of the men, so that at last Pelham had to assist himself in loading and aiming it. Three times the summons to retire was renewed; but not until the last round of ammunition had been discharged, and after spreading carnage for two hours in the ranks of the Federal infantry, did the gallant officer succumb to necessity in abandoning his position.*

The rest of our horse-artillery had in the mean time joined in the cannonade, and the thunder soon rolled all along our lines, while from the continuous roar the ear caught distinctly the sharp, rapid, rattling volleys of the musketry, especially in the immediate front of General A. P. Hill, where the infantry were very hotly engaged. The battle was now fully developed, and the mists of the morning were presently succeeded by a dense cloud of powder-smoke, out of which rose ever and anon the dark column from an exploding caisson. At intervals above the tumult of the conflict we could hear the wild hurrah of the attacking hosts of the Federals, and the defiant yell of the Confederates, as the assault was repulsed. Directly in our own front the cavalry sharpshooters had become occupied with long lines of hostile tirailleurs, and a vivid fusillade raged all along the Port Royal road, the shot and shell of our horse-artillery, which was in position in our rear, crossing in their flight the missiles of the enemy's batteries high in air above the heads of our men. The firing grew most animated near a number of stacks of straw, which a body of Federal infantry had taken possession of, and which offered them so efficient a shelter that all attempts to dislodge them had proved in vain. I had just been ordering our men not to waste their ammunition, and to fire only when they saw the person of a Yankee completely exposed, when close at hand I heard the dull thud of a bullet striking home, and turning

---

*For the gallantry displayed here, and his great services rendered during the latter part of the battle, Pelham was highly complimented in Stuart's, Jackson's, and Lee's reports, the latter of which styled him "the gallant Pelham"—a title which was adopted in a short time by the whole army, and which has often been employed in these memoirs. Several English writers have done justice to his

round saw one of our soldiers, a gallant young fellow whom I knew well, throw up his arms and fall heavily to the ground. Dismounting at once I hastened to his side, but finding that the ball had struck him right in the middle of the forehead, I regarded him as a corpse, and deemed all further assistance wholly unnecessary. Not many minutes had elapsed, however, before the apparently dead man began to move, and when the surgeon, who had already arrived, poured some brandy down his throat, to our infinite amazement he opened his eyes. A few hours later, miraculous to relate, when the bleeding from the wound had ceased, he had recovered sufficiently from the severe shock to return to his post of duty. According to the surgeon's statement, the ball, striking obliquely, had glanced, passing between cuticle and skull all around the head, emerging at last from the very place it had first entered!

The fury and tumult of the battle lasted all the forenoon and until two o'clock in the afternoon along Jackson's lines. A comparative quietude then succeeded, the infantry firing died away, and only a regular intermittent cannonade was kept up in our immediate front; but from the left opposite Fredericksburg there came to us the heavy boom of artillery and the distant rattle of small-arms, and we knew the fight still raged there with undiminished vehemence. So far all had gone favourably for us. The division of A. P. Hill had sustained the first shock of the Federal attack, which for a while had promised success to the enemy. On the left wing of this division, under cover of the fog and protected by the triangular piece of wood already described, the hostile column had fallen rather suddenly upon our men, the first line of whom, consisting of a brigade of North Carolina conscripts,

---

heroism on this special occasion. — See Chesney's 'Campaign in Virginia,' vol. i. p. 192; Fletcher's 'History of the American War,' vol. ii. p. 250.

gave way, reaching the second line in their retreat at the same moment nearly with their pursuers, with whom they became indiscriminately mingled, whereby was caused inevitable confusion and great loss of life on our side. Here the gallant General Gregg fell mortally wounded while attempting to rally his men. Our reserves speedily coming up, however, with the right wing of Early's division, the Yankees were repulsed with severe loss, and pursued far into the plain. The whole of Early's and Hood's divisions now soon became engaged, and after a short but sanguinary contest succeeded in driving back the enemy in like manner with fearful slaughter. Again and again, with the most obstinate courage and energy, did the Federals renew the attack, bringing more and more fresh troops into action; but their dense lines were so much shattered by the appalling fire of our artillery that, upon coming within range of our infantry and being there received with a withering hail of bullets, they broke and fled time after time, leaving the ground strewn with hundreds of their dead and wounded. Our men could with difficulty be held back in their intrenchments, and more than once followed the flying host far out upon the plateau, until the sweeping fire of the Yankee batteries put an end to their pursuit. Immediately in front of Jackson's Hill the fight had for a considerable period been fiercest, and our antagonists, repeating the onset with the greatest bravery, had on several occasions come up to the very muzzles of our guns. Here, opposite his great namesake, fell the Federal General Jackson. The troops under his command broke into disorderly flight after his death, and one of his regiments, from the State of Pennsylvania, was captured to the last man in the railway cut in front of our position, where they sought shelter from the tremendous fire of artillery and musketry that poured down upon them.

While the Yankees were thus suffering reverses in this

portion of the field, large masses of their troops had been concentrated near Fredericksburg, opposite Marye's Heights, where that stern and steady fighter Longstreet awaited their attack with his accustomed composure, and where our great leader Lee himself inspired the troops by his presence. This portion of our lines was unquestionably the strongest, and the folly of the Federal commander in sending his men here to certain death and destruction is utterly incomprehensible. All along Marye's Heights runs a sunken road, fenced in with a stone wall on either side, which in itself constituted a most formidable defensive work for our troops; a little higher up the hill there was a regular line of intrenchments, the defenders of which might fire over the heads of those below them, and the crest was occupied by the numerous pieces of the famous Washington Artillery, under their gallant commander Colonel Walton; so that the assailants were received with a triple sheet of fire, which swept them away by hundreds. The Federals certainly behaved with the utmost gallantry. Line after line moved forward to the assault, only to recoil again and again from the murderous tempest of shot, shell, and bullets, and to strew yet more thickly with dead and wounded the crimsoned field, which was afterwards most appropriately named "the slaughter-pen." Pickett's division was but little engaged here, the wider open space of ground giving ample opportunity to our artillery to play upon the hostile columns, scattering them and throwing them into disorder even before they could form their lines of attack.

About three o'clock in the afternoon there seemed to be a new movement preparing on the enemy's left, and General Stuart, suspecting it might be a movement on our right flank, ordered me to proceed with twenty couriers to our extreme right, reconnoitre the operations of the Yankees as closely as possible, and send him a report every five minutes. Captain

Blackford, who possessed a very good field-glass, volunteered to accompany me, and we at once trotted off together upon our hazardous expedition. Near to the point where the Massaponax Creek falls into the Rappahannock, and at about one hundred yards' distance from the larger stream, there rises a small elevation of ground thickly covered with cedar and pine trees, from which we were well assured there might be obtained a good view over the river, and the whole left wing of the Federal army. This hillock was quite outside of our lines, and there had been pushed forward towards it only a small body of our sharpshooters, whom we found lying concealed in the bushes below, for the Yankees, perfectly aware of the importance of this point of observation, had cleared the summit of its occupants by a severe fire whenever a grey uniform had been seen there. Leaving the couriers at the foot of the hill, Blackford and I dismounted and climbed cautiously up to the top, creeping along through the bushes and concealing ourselves behind some pine-trees that grew on the way. The view which here presented itself to our eyes far exceeded our expectations. The Yankees, not more than a thousand yards distant from us, were evidently enough preparing for a new advance; reinforcements were moving up at a double-quick and forming into line of battle as they arrived; troops that had been engaged in the battle and been repulsed were marching sulkily to the rear; wounded men were being carried off by hundreds, while there galloped up and down the lines general officers with their Staffs, some of whom we could personally recognise through our glasses. To the right we looked down upon the river for a considerable distance, and could plainly see and count the heavy guns on the opposite bank, and could even hear the conversation of the cannoneers. Cautious as we had been, however, the Yankees quickly discovered our presence, and a number of their sharpshooters, sent forward to dislodge us, commenced a sharp fire of exploding bullets, which, striking the objects around us, burst, with the noise peculiar to these projectiles, and scattered their fragments in every direction like small-shot. Well protected by the pine-trees we paid little attention to this fusillade, when suddenly I observed two pieces of artillery moving into position, and before Blackford finished uttering the words, "Von, the Yankees are going to shell us out of this," a missile, whizzing towards us, struck the topmost branches of one of the pines, and, exploding there, rained down upon us a shower of limbs and splinters. Other followed in rapid succession with increasing accuracy of aim, so that we concluded to evacuate the spot and seek shelter for a time on the opposite side of the hill. Breaking at once through the bushes, we thought it would be an easy matter enough to get to a place of security, but the enemy's gunners followed our movements with a nicety of calculation so admirable that shot after shot came yet nearer and nearer to us, and at the very moment that we supposed we had got out of their reach, a shell passed so near to our heads that my gallant friend and myself were precipitated headlong by the force of windage at least fifteen feet down the hillside, where we both lay motionless for a brief space, and then rose in a fit of uncontrollable laughter as we looked each in the other's blank and astonished face. Returning, as soon as the firing had ceased, to the spot we had so suddenly abandoned, we saw the Federal lines moving forward to their new attack, which was introduced and supported by a cannonade of several hundred pieces equal in fury to that of the morning. The balls fired from the opposite side of the river howled and hissed in their course over our heads, each shot of the heavy guns reverberating from the cliffs like rolling thunder, while the musketry soon became audible again, giving proof by its increasing vehemence that the hostile parties were now hotly engaged. An hour of anxiety and doubt passed away, until at five o'clock we saw scattered fugitives straggling to the rear, their numbers augmenting every moment, until whole regiments, brigades, and divisions, in utter confusion and bewildered flight, covered the plain before us. Blackford, as excited as myself, jumped from his hiding-place, and, throwing his hat in the air, cried out, "Thank God, they are whipped—they are running!" Yes; there was no doubt about it—they were running; and all the efforts of their officers, whom we could distinctly see using their sabres against their own men to check the precipitate retreat, were unavailing. All discipline was lost for the moment, and those thousands of troops whom an hour before we had seen advancing in beautiful military order, now presented the spectacle of a stampeded and demoralised mob. Having kept Stuart constantly informed of the enemy's movements, I was at this moment more careful to send courier after courier to apprise him that the Yankees were routed, and that in my judgment the time for our attack had arrived; but my general did not fully credit my report, until at my urgent request he galloped up to us in person to see, just a little too late, how correct my account of affairs had been. Off we now hastened to Jackson, who at once sent to General Lee the request that he might leave his intrenchments without further delay, fall upon the enemy, and render the victory complete. A single cannon-shot fired from our centre was to be the signal for the general attack by our whole line, at which movement Stuart was to press forward with his cavalry and horse-artillery vigorously upon the enemy's flank.

Returning to our position on the Port Royal road, we awaited in anxious silence the so much desired signal; but minute after minute passed by, and the dark veil of night began to envelop the valley, when Stuart, believing that the summons agreed upon had been given, issued the order to advance. Off we went into the gathering darkness, our sharpshooters driving their opponents easily before them, and Pelham, with his guns, pushing ahead at a trot, firing a few shots whenever the position seemed favourable, and then again pressing forward. This lasted about twenty minutes, when the fire of the enemy's infantry began to be more and more destructive, and other fresh batteries opened upon us.* Still all remained silent upon our main line. Stuart himself, as usual, was always in the extreme front, exposing his person to the hottest fire; one bullet had already pierced his haversack, and another torn the fur collar off his cape, and the wonder was that any one of us had escaped unhurt.

Our situation had become, indeed, a critical one, when a courier from General Jackson galloped up at full speed bringing the order for Stuart to retreat as quickly as he could to his original position. Our commander-in-chief, adhering to his earliest idea, still objected to a forward movement, for which, in my judgment, the golden moment had now passed, had he inclined to favour it. Under cover of the darkness of the night, we conducted our retrograde movement in safety, and reached our old position on the Port Royal road with but slight loss.

The division of D. H. Hill had now arrived at Hamilton's Crossing, and had been placed at once in the open field upon Jackson's right, where might be seen the glare of their hundreds of camp-fires, and where they were busily engaged in throwing up intrenchments. On our left wing the assault of

---

*It must be remarked here that the division of Federal infantry opposite to us had not as yet gone into the battle, and therefore had not been included in the rout, and that the Yankees had gained time enough to replace their demoralised troops with reserves drawn as rapidly as possible from the other side of the river.

the enemy had been renewed at dark, and had been attended with the same fatal result to them with their efforts elsewhere, and the ground in front of Marye's Heights was heaped with dead bodies, chiefly those of the brave Irishmen of Meagher's brigade, which went to the attack 1200 strong, and left 900 of their number upon this dreadful spot. About seven o'clock the battle ceased for the day; only random cannonshots were still interchanged, the flight of the shells distinctly marked in flaming curves across the dark firmament, and the shadows of evening fell upon a battle-field, the nameless horrors of which none of us had even measurably conjectured—a battle-field where thousands of mutilated and dying men lay in hopeless anguish, writhing in their wounds, and pitilessly exposed to the sharp frosty air of the winter's night.

Not one of our generals was aware of the magnitude of the victory we had gained, of the injury we had inflicted upon the enemy, and of the degree of demoralisation in the hostile army, everybody regarding the work as but half done, and expecting a renewal of the attack the following morning. Of our own army only one-third had been engaged, and our loss did not exceed 1800 in killed and wounded. Most of these belonged to A. P. Hill's division, and had fallen during the first attack in the morning on the spot where our lines had for some time been broken. We had to mourn the loss of two general officers, Maxey Gregg of South Carolina, and Thomas R. R. Cobb of Georgia, who fell on Marye's Heights. At his side General Cooke, a brother of Mrs Stuart, was dangerously wounded in the forehead. The Federal loss was not less than 14,000 in killed and wounded (we took only 800 prisoners), and in this frightful aggregate of casualties was to be reckoned the loss of many officers of rank. Among these there was the much-lamented General Bayard, a cavalry officer of great promise, who, far in the rear of his lines, was torn to pieces by one of our exploding shells while in the act of taking luncheon under a tree.

General Lee has been much criticised, and chiefly by English writers, for not having assumed the offensive in this battle; but every one who knows how exceedingly difficult it had become, already at that time, to fill the ranks of the Confederate army, and how valuable each individual life in that army must have been considered, and, on the other hand, what reckless prodigality of life characterised the Federal Government and the Federal commanders, caring little that 20,000 or 30,000 men should be killed in a campaign, when as many more Germans and Irishmen could be readily put in their places,—I say that every one who bears in mind these facts will agree with me in thinking that our commander-in-chief acted with great consideration and wisdom. There was scarcely an officer in the whole army who did not confidently believe that the attack would be renewed the next day; and where an opportunity was likely to be afforded of again inflicting serious damage upon the enemy with trifling injury to ourselves, it surely cannot be censured as a fault to have speculated upon the incapacity of the adversary. General Lee, who had been careful to strengthen the weaker portions of his line during the night, said in my presence on the following morning, "My army is as much stronger for their new intrenchments as if I had received reinforcements of 20,000 men." I regard it as almost certain that had the Federal commander been able to carry out his intention of renewing the struggle, the second day would have turned out even more disastrously to him than the first.

It was a late hour of the night when we returned to headquarters for a short rest. There we found Captain Phillips, who congratulated us heartily upon having safely passed through the perils of the day, and who spoke with enthusiasm of the magnificent view of the battle which he had obtained from Lee's Hill. With a modest smile, Pelham returned to the Captain the bit of regimental ribbon he had worn as a talisman during the fight, its gay colours just a little blackened by powder-smoke, for it had flaunted from the cap of the young hero in the very atmosphere of Death. Poor Pelham! he has been lying these three years in his early grave there in Alabama, whose Indian name, "Here we rest," has a pathetic significance as applied to the "narrow home" of one so young and so full of promise; and the record of his services to his country fills a few pages in the melancholy story of an unsuccessful struggle for national existence; but his memory is green in the hearts of friends that survived him, and a brave English soldier cherishes the ribbon he wore at Fredericksburg as one of the dearest souvenirs of the past in his possession.

We were greatly delighted at finding also at headquarters two of the younger members of the Staff, Lieutenants Hullyhan and Turner, who had just returned from a dangerous expedition into the enemy's lines on the other side of the Rappahannock. Several days before they had gone off with the hope of rescuing from the hands of the Yankees, Miss Mary Lee, the daughter of our commander-in-chief and a dear friend of General Stuart's, who, while on a visit to some friends in the county of Stafford, had been cut off from her home and family. This was an expedition after my own heart, but I was prevented from undertaking it by General Stuart's energetic opposition. The young lieutenants had reached in safety the house where Miss Lee was staying; but as her friends were afraid to allow her to accompany them on their return, they were compelled to come back without their expected precious charge—fortunately enough, indeed, for the lady, as they were very soon taken prisoners by a patrol of

Federal cavalry. During the night following their capture they found the opportunity of overpowering and killing two of their sentinels with their own carbines; and mounting, just in the nick of time, the horses of the Yankee guard, they made good their escape before the rest of their captors had recovered from their amazement at the boldness of the venture.

CHAPTER XVII

DARKNESS still prevailed when we mounted our horses and again hastened to Jackson's Hill, the summit of which we reached just in time to see the sun rising, and unveiling, as it dispersed the hazy fogs of the damp, frosty winter's night, the long lines of the Federal army, which once more stood in full line of battle about half-way between our own position and the river. I could not withhold my admiration as I looked down upon the well-disciplined lines of our antagonist, astonished that these troops now offering so bold a front to our victorious army should be the same whom not many hours since I had seen in complete flight and disorder. The skirmishers of the two armies were not much more than a hundred yards apart, concealed from each other's view by the high grass in which they were lying, and above which, from time to time, rose a small cloud of blue smoke, telling that a shot had been fired, before the report came feebly wafted to us by the light morning breeze.

As the boom of artillery now began to sound from different parts of the line, and the attack might be expected every minute, each hastened to his post. As on the previous day, our cavalry was briskly engaged with the hostile sharpshooters, and again the firing sounded loudest in the neighbourhood of the straw stacks already mentioned. That these should no longer offer a shelter, some of Pelham's well-directed shells soon set the dry material in a blaze, and the squad of forty or fifty Yankees who had sought the protection of the stacks, finding the place too hot to hold, scampered off in a body, accompanied by a loud cheer from our men, and a well-aimed volley, which brought down several of the fugitives. Hour after hour passed away in anxious expectation of the combat; but though the skirmishing at times grew hotter, and the fire of the artillery more rapid, long intervals of silence again succeeded. As usual, the hostile batteries were not chary of their ammunition; and whenever a group of officers showed itself plainly within range, it was at once greeted with a couple of shells or solid shot. Having to ride over to Fitz Lee, who, with the greater part of his brigade, was in reserve, I met Dr J., whose acquaintance I had made during one of our raids.

He was just driving up to the General in his buggy, which, besides its hospitable inmate, contained an excellent cold dinner and a bottle of whisky for our solace. We had scarcely, however, begun to unpack the chickens and biscuits, and the cork was still on its way through the neck of the whisky bottle, when, instead of the "cluck" announcing its complete extraction, our ears were greeted with a sound never pleasing at any time, but at this particular moment more than ever awakening disgust—the whizzing of a shell which plunged into the soft ground not more than twenty feet off, covering us instantaneously with an abundant coating of mud. This was too much for the nerves of our peaceful host, who drove off, carrying with him the much-coveted refreshments, which had delighted our eyes only to delude our remaining senses. We followed him, however, in eager pursuit, and succeeded several times in overtaking and arresting the flight of the precious fugitive, but each time our happiness was cut short by the enemy's artillery, whose aim pursued the buggy as tenaciously as ourselves, till at last we took refuge in a deep ravine, completely screened from the keen eyes of the Yankees, who, as we completed our meal, came in for a fire of maledictions for their want of common courtesy and consideration.

Thus did the day wear on to its close without any event of importance; and it becoming evident as the evening advanced that the attack would not be renewed on the 14th, we returned after nightfall once more to our short night's rest at headquarters. Things looked very little changed when, on the cold, clear morning of the 15th, we rode up to Jackson's Hill; and General Stuart deciding to remain until serious fighting should commence, we had an opportunity of having a good look at the devastations caused by the tremendous artillery-fire of the 13th. The forest was literally torn to pieces—trees more than a foot in diameter were snapped in two, large branches were shattered to splinters, and scarcely a small twig but showed marks of some kind of missile. In many places the ground was ploughed up by the cannon-balls, which together with pieces of shell, canister, and grape-shot, lay strewn in every direction. Most of our dead had already been buried, but the carcasses of the animals were still lying about in large numbers; the batteries of Walker's artillery on Jackson's Hill having lost not less than ninety horses during the first two hours of the terrific bombardment.

The morning passed slowly away, the anxious silence maintained being broken only but the firing from time to time of the heavy batteries; and many of our leaders, Stuart and Jackson foremost, began to give up any hope of a renewal of the attack. The latter general was still in favour of a night attack, and proposed that our men should be stripped naked to the waist, so that they might easily recognise each other in the darkness and confusion of the conflict. About twelve o'clock two mounted officers, followed by a small squad of cavalry, bearing a white flag, suddenly appeared riding towards us from the enemy's lines, and soon after General Jackson received a report that a flag of truce had arrived, with a request on the part of the Federal generals to be allowed to bury their dead and look after the wounded. To this Stonewall did not think proper to accede, as the application was not signed by the Federal commander-in-chief, an omission which, on several previous occasions, had opened the way to serious misunderstandings. Accordingly the Federal officers retired to obtain the signature of Burnside, and did not return until after a delay of nearly two hours, when the permission which humanity dictated being applied for in due form, was readily granted.

Being one of the officers appointed on our side to superintend the proceedings, I rode forthwith down to the plain, and thus had the first opportunity of inspecting the battle-field in our immediate front. The burial parties of the Federals were ready and in excellent order, and as soon as the truce was accepted, different columns, from 200 to 300 strong, moved forward in double-quick and went at once to work, taking up the wounded and burying the dead, assisted by a large number of our own men, who had long been anxious to bring help to the wounded sufferers outside our intrenchments, but were deterred from yielding to their humane impulses by the bullets of the enemy's sharpshooters. All had been going on thus smoothly for half an hour, when suddenly some of the batteries in the enemy's centre opened a heavy fire. The excitement and consternation caused by this was immense; the cry of treason ran along our lines; our men hurried back to their arms, while the Federal officers exerted themselves to maintain unbroken the peaceful relations which threatened for some little time to end in a sanguinary conflict. Fortunately, however, the firing soon afterwards ceased, and full explanations being given, proving the apparently treacherous act to have been a mistake, the work of humanity proceeded.

The carnage had raged most fiercely immediately opposite Jackson's Hill, and many hundred dead and wounded lay there intermingled. We had considerable difficulty in discovering the body of the Federal General Jackson, and it was at last found in a small ravine. Beside him lay his adjutant, a very fine-looking young man, who, riding a grey horse during the action, had attracted the attention of our men, and frequently elicited their admiration by his conspicuous gallantry. His noble charger, only a few steps from him, was pierced by several bullets, and had probably fallen at the same moment with his brave rider. The poor wounded were in a miserable state after their long exposure to cold and hunger, and many were dying simply from starvation and neglect. We held long and interesting conversations with the Yankee officers, and were not a little surprised at the freedom and severity of the criticisms they passed on their commander-in-chief, and the candid acknowledgment of the heavy losses and severe defeat they had sustained. These gentlemen asserted that General Burnside was perfectly incapable of commanding a large army; that his splendid troops had been sacrificed and slaughtered uselessly, but that the General himself had taken good care not to endanger his own life, having observed and directed the battle from Phillip's House, a point of safety on the Stafford side of the river. There being but a comparatively small number of our dead, they were soon buried; but the Federal were occupied all day with their mournful task, and had not half finished when darkness put an end to their operations. The approaching night brought with it a heavy storm and rain, and we were wet to the skin and shivering with cold when at a late hour we returned to headquarters. Stuart was in a very bad humour, and entertained no hope of a renewal of the fight the following day. "These Yankees," he said, "have always some underhand trick when they send a flag of truce, and I fear they will be off before daylight." This suspicion proved to be only too true. The next morning, when on our way to Hamilton's Crossing, we met a courier riding full gallop, who reported that the whole of the Federal army had disappeared from our side of the river.

The heavy rains and storm which raged all night favoured their enterprise. General Burnside had managed to remove his whole army over the three pontoon-bridges to the Stafford side; and his retreat was effected with such consummate skill, that our pickets had not the slightest knowledge of the movement until daybreak showed them that the whole of the large Yankee army, with all the artillery and waggon-trains, had disappeared from their front. On our arrival at the battle-field we found our men scattered over the plain, busy burying the dead, large numbers of which were still lying about. Reaching a place where about 300 corpses had been collected to be lodged in one common grave, some of our men showed a number of small torpedoes, which they informed us had been set in large numbers by the enemy all over the field. Fortunately the charge of powder with which these infernal machines were prepared had been so damped by the heavy rain that they did not explode, and by this failure a large number of our men were saved from destruction. Soon afterwards we were much amused by lighting upon the entire band of a Yankee infantry regiment, who, having encamped at some distance from their troops, had been quite forsaken, and were still fast asleep when they were taken prisoners to the last man by our Mississippians. They seemed but little troubled at their fate, and cheerfully struck up the tunes of Dixie, to the great delight of our men, who meanwhile set about preparing for them whatever comforts our rough hospitality could afford. After about an hour's ride we reached Lee's Hill, where we found Captain Phillips again, whom I invited to join me in a little tour to Marye's Heights and the field in front of them, the horrors of which had been depicted in the most vivid colours by all who had visited the dreadful spot. As the Federal batteries on the opposite side of the river were firing on every horseman who showed himself, I took Pelham's mulatto servant, Newton, who happened to be there, along with us, and, leaving our horses out of sight in his charge, we descended on foot to the plain. Here we met General Ransom, who had commanded one of the brigades on Marye's Heights which had sustained the principal shock of the assault; and the General's polite offer to show us the battle-field, and give us a description of the fight, was gratefully accepted.

The sight was indeed a fearful one, and the dead bodies lay thicker than I had ever seen before on any field of battle. This was chiefly the case in front of the stone wall which skirts the sunken road at the foot of Marye's Heights. The dead were here piled up in heaps six or eight deep. General Ransom told us that our men were ordered not to commence firing until the enemy had approached within a distance of eighty yards; but that from the moment they advanced within this, the hostile ranks had been completely mowed down by our volleys. The nature of the ground towards the town is open and flat, broken only by some plank fences, and dotted with a few wooden houses scattered here and there. All these objects, and even the very ground, were so thickly riddled with bullets that scarcely a square inch was without its dint; and it became incomprehensible to me how even that small few of the most dashing assailants, who had run up within fifteen paces of our lines, could have survived this terrific fire long enough to do so. Many of the Federal soldiers had found death seeking shelter in the small courtyards of the houses behind the wooden plank fences surrounding them, but which, of course, offered not the slightest protection; and heaps of the corpses of these poor fellows filled the narrow enclosures. On a space of ground not over two acres we counted 680 dead bodies; and more than 1200 altogether were found on the small plain between the heights and Fredericksburg, those nearest the town having mostly been killed by our artillery, which had played with dreadful effect upon the enemy's dense columns. More than one-half of these dead had belonged to Meagher's brave Irish brigade, which was nearly annihilated during the several attacks.

A number of the houses which we entered presented a horrid spectacle—dead and wounded intermingled in thick masses. The latter, in a deplorable state from want of food and care, were cursing their own cause, friends, and commander-in-chief, for the sufferings they endured. As we walked slowly along, Captain Phillips suddenly pressed my arm, and, pointing to the body of a soldier whose head was so frightfully wounded that part of the brain was protruding, broke out with, "Great God, that man is still alive!" And so he was. Hearing our steps the unfortunate sufferer opened his glassy eyes and looked at us with so pitiable an expression that I could not for long after recall it without shuddering. A surgeon being close at hand, was at once called to the spot to render what assistance was yet possible; but he pronounced the man in a dying condition, and observed that it was totally opposed to all medical experience, and could only be considered in the light of a miracle, that a human being with such a wound should have lived through nearly sixty hours of exposure and starvation.

In the mean time our little company had attracted the notice of the enemy on the other side of the river, and several shells had already bowled over our heads, when soon the firing grew so heavy, and the missiles struck and exploded in such increasing proximity to us, that we decided on getting out of range. So, shaking hands with General Ransom and thanking him much for his kindness, we returned to the place where we had left our horses; but mulatto and chargers had disappeared together; and after a lengthened search, we had nearly made up our minds that we must return on foot, when the fugitives were found at a considerable distance and hidden in a clump of bushes, the worthy Newton still trembling, and completely "demoralised" with the fright inspired by some of the shells which, fired too high, had exploded in his neighbourhood and induced his rapid retreat.

On our return to Lee's Hill we found a great number of the generals assembled around our Commander-in-Chief, all extremely chagrined that the Federals should have succeeded in so cleverly making their escape. The tranquillity in which the day passed off was interrupted only by the firing from the enemy's batteries, which, by the way, very nearly proved fatal to our friend Vizetelly. In the town of Fredericksburg a great many Yankees had been found straggling and lurking in the houses, either with a view to desertion, or too overpowered by the liquor they had stolen to leave with their army; and a body of those captives marching along the turnpike road escorted by a detachment of our soldiers, attracted the curiosity of Mr Vizetelly, who immediately rode down to meet them. Having reached the column, he had just entered into conversation with a corporal from a South Carolina regiment who commanded the detachment, when the hostile batteries, mistaking their own men for enemies, opened fire, and one of their very first shells, passing quite close to our friend, tore the head of the poor fellow with whom he was talking completely off his shoulders, scattering pieces of skull and brains in every direction. Horror-stricken at this sad incident, and having no call of duty to remain, the artist at once put spurs into his charger's flanks, and galloped off as fast as the noble steed could carry him. But the hostile gunners seemed to take particular pleasure in aiming at the flying horseman, and ever closer and closer flew the unpleasant missiles about his ears, while we who from Lee's Hill were spectators of the unenviable position in which our guest was placed, were for some time seriously alarmed that we should never again hear his merry laugh and joyous songs; but at last he reached us in safety, though much exhausted, and was received with loud cheering in our midst.

During the afternoon General Burnside renewed his request for the burial of the dead, which was at once granted; and the Federal troops destined to this duty, having crossed the Rappahannock in pontoons, went to work without delay. Having been again ordered to assist in the superintendence of the proceedings, I was painfully shocked at the inevitably rough manner in which the Yankee soldiers treated the dead bodies of their comrades. Not far from Marye's Heights existed a hole of considerable dimensions, which had once been an ice-house; and in order to spare time and labour, this had been selected by the Federal officers to serve as a large common grave, not less than 800 of their men being buried in it. The bodies of these poor fellows, stripped nearly naked, were gathered in huge mounds around the pit, and tumbled neck and heels into it; the dull "thud" of corpse falling on corpse coming up from the depths of the hole until the solid mass of human flesh reached near the surface, when a covering of logs, chalk, and mud closed the mouth of this vast and awful tomb.

On my return to Lee's Hill I saw President Davis and Governor Letcher with our Commander. They had come from Richmond to congratulate him and the troops under him on their success, and had been greeted all along the lines with the utmost enthusiasm. It was late at night when we returned to headquarters, where I stretched my weary limbs along my blankets, intensely soothed with the balmy reflection that I was about to enjoy a long spell of rest for my body, and relief for my mind from the racking anxiety and emotion with which the too familiar but never familiarised sight of death and destruction had so long and deeply affected it.

CHAPTER XVIII

QUIET CAMP LIFE — THE ARMY IN WINTER QUARTERS — A
VISIT TO THE OTHER SIDE OF THE RAPPAHANNOCK —
STUART'S EXPEDITION TO DUMFRIES — CHRISTMAS IN
CAMP — PURCHASE OF A CARRIAGE AND HORSES —
ENGLISH VISITORS.

NEITHER the thunder of cannon nor the sound of the bugle disturbed our peaceful slumbers on the morning of the 17th, and the sun stood high in the firmament when General Stuart's clear ringing voice assembled us again round the large common breakfast-table in his roomy tent. During the forenoon we had the pleasure of welcoming Mr Lawley and Captain Wynne among us, the latter of whom, a comrade and *compagnon de voyage* of Captain Phillips, had been detained in Richmond through illness. Amid his sufferings, he had eagerly listened to the rumours of the battle which had been fought and was expected to continue, and he had now hastened, though too late, to the scene of action. Both gentlemen expressed their sincere regret to have come a day after the fair, and envied very much Captain Phillips, whose better fortune had procured him the magnificent spectacle of the great conflict. Our new guests had brought with them from Richmond a case of champagne as a present to the officers of the Staff, although the General himself never took anything stronger than water; but finding no conveyance at Hamilton's Crossing Station, they had, as ill luck would have it, been obliged to leave the precious burthen there under charge of a South Carolina sergeant, acting as hospital steward near that halting-place.

The following day Captain Wynne and Lawley started, accompanied by several members of our military family, for a ride over the battle-field, I myself undertaking an expedition after the anxiously coveted case of champagne; for although I entertained but slight hope of its having escaped the attention of the soldiers, I considered that there was a bare possibility of recovery, sufficient to make it worth while to risk the trouble in so valuable a cause. Alas! my worst fears were destined to be realised. Not a vestige of the case or of the faithless sergeant to whose keeping it had been trusted could I light on, and I had to return all chapfallen from my vain errand, and announce to my comrades that they must make the best of water and good spirits as a substitute for the effervescent stimulant; and, indeed, so cheerily were we all disposed, that our indignation soon evaporated. Much to our sorrow, on the following day all our guests deserted us, and we were left to the unrelieved routine of camp life in all its dull and listless monotony. The bad weather, moreover, setting in with full force, the campaign might be regarded as completely at an end for the next two or three months; and as the hostile army was reported to have gone into winter quarters, our own soon followed the example.

The stroke of many axes rang through the surrounding forests and oak copses, and pine thickets dissolved from the view to give place to complete little towns of huts and log-houses, provided with comfortable fireplaces, from whose gigantic chimneys curled upwards gracefully and cheerily into the crisp winter air many a column of pale-blue smoke. Longstreet's corps remained opposite Fredericksburg and its immediate neighbourhood; Jackson's was stationed half-way between that place and Port Royal; and Stonewall himself had fixed his headquarters about twelve miles from us, near the well-known plantation of the Corbyn family, called Moss-Neck. The weather became now every day worse, snow-storms alternating with rains and severe frosts; and if officers and men were tolerably well off under the circumstances, it was not so with our poor beasts, whose condition, from want of food, exposure, and vermin, was pitiable indeed. The sheds and stables, improvised for them out of logs and pine-branches, offered but scant protection against the battering of wind, rain, and snow, which assailed them on all sides, penetrating through the lightly-thatched roofs, and the wretched quadrupeds stood for the most part knee-deep in water or slush. Ere long a disease bred out of this unhappy state of things showed itself, and spread rapidly throughout the camp, our cavalry and artillery losing more than one-fourth of their horses and mules. The symptoms of the malady became first visible just above the hoof, whence it gradually extended, eventually involving the entire limb. We received for forage a certain amount of Indian corn, which was supplied quite regularly; but hay and straw grew every day more scarce, and at last failed us altogether. I had in more opulent times prepared for myself a most luxurious couch of hay, on which I slept softly, as on a bed of eider-down; but the lamentations of my negro over the scarcity of "long forage," and, still more, the woeful aspect of my animals, soon prevailed on me to abandon this luxury, and lay the sacrifice in their troughs, to be hungrily devoured by my poor beasts. The mules withstood the effects of scarce fodder, cold, and wet, better than did the horses. Especially was this exhibited in the case of my grey mule Kitt, for in spite of hard times she looked as gay and sleek as ever; but it must be added that she displayed an omnivorous appetite. All was fodder to her impartial palate, from pine-leaves to scraps of leather, and even the blankets with which I covered my horses were not safe from her voracity.

On the 21st we had a visit from Custis Lee, son of our Commander-in-Chief, and aide-de-camp to President Davis, who wished to inspect the battle-field and the town of Fredericksburg; and at his request General Stuart and I gladly accompanied him on the expedition. I had thus the first direct opportunity presented to me of leisurely inspecting the ruins of poor Fredericksburg, which, with its shattered houses, streets ript open, and demolished churches, impressed me sadly enough. The inhabitants had nearly all deserted the place, the only visible exceptions being here and there a wretched pauper or aged negro, to whom no refuge elsewhere was open, creeping noiselessly along the silent street. The brave soldiers of Barksdale's brigade, however, who had so nobly resisted the first attempt of the enemy to cross the river, were re-established in the town, and comfortably installed in several of the large buildings now abandoned. The firing of the pickets having once more ceased, a network of friendly relations had begun again to connect them, and an inter-change of communications also of the necessaries of life recommenced. To carry on these the most ingenious devices were resorted to, at some of which I was vastly amused. On reaching the river we beheld quite a little fleet of small boats, from three to four feet in length, under full sail, with flying pennants, crossing backwards and forwards between the shores of the river, conveying tobacco and Richmond news-papers over to the Stafford side, and returning loaded in exchange with sugar and coffee and Northern journals. The diminutive craft were handled with considerable nautical skill, and rudder and sails set so deftly to wind and stream, that they always unerringly landed at the exact point of destination. Some days afterwards, this free-trade movement having outpassed the limits which were judged safe or convenient, a sudden embargo, in the shape of a severe and stringent order, was put upon the friendly traffic of foe with foe, to the mutual and unmitigated disgust of both sides.

Next day, under favour of a flag of truce sent by the Federals to negotiate an exchange of prisoners, I received a message from Baron H., an ex-officer of the Prussian army then serving on Burnside's Staff, appointing a rendezvous at Fredericksburg. Although I set off at once, I found on reaching the town that H., impatient of waiting, or giving me up, had returned to the other side of the river. Vexed to have had my ride for nothing, I was, in no very good humour, turning my horse's head towards home, when I fell in with Major Fairfax of Longstreet's Staff and the officers bearing the flag of truce. After expressing their sympathy with my disappointment, they invited me over to the other side, the truce not having yet expired. I replied that I should not be justified in complying with their invitation, as I had not, like Major Fairfax, any business to transact, and should be running the risk of remaining longer on the Stafford side than I desired. My cautious scruples elicited a hearty laugh, and, pledging their personal honour for my safe return whenever I chose, they again pressed their rather extraordinary invitation in a manner that would have made it very uncourteous to decline. On reaching the opposite shore, Fairfax and I were soon surrounded by a circle of Federal officers proffering every mark of politeness and hospitality, the latter being manifested by the production of several bottles of wine and whisky, which were soon in brisk circulation. Meantime a number of orderlies had been despatched in search of H.; but after an hour of fruitless waiting I returned with Fairfax, first emptying, as we took leave of our temporary hosts, a last cup of the speedy restoration of peace. On arriving at headquarters I was greeted with a good scolding from Stuart for my escapade; an old fox, he said, should never under any circumstances trust his head in the lion's mouth.

On the 23d we had the pleasure of welcoming once more among us General Hampton, the distant position of whose brigade on the Rappahannock had rendered him a rare visitor of late; but as his absence had been well occupied, his enterprise and activity having inflicted considerable damage on the enemy, it was the less to be regretted. Among his achievements was a raid across the river towards the end of November, with a small detachment of his brigade, when he surrounded and took prisoners to a man two squadrons of a Pennsylvanian cavalry regiment. Twice again, in December, he made similar expeditions to the rear of the Federals with equal success, capturing on the last occasion a large waggon-train laden with forage, provisions, and sutlers' stores, out of the latter of which he now brought us a quantity of luxuries as a Christmas present.

As General Hampton had not yet visited the battle-field, I had much pleasure in tendering my services as his guide and companion on the occasion, and we did not return from the long rambling ride we took over the ground till late in the evening. On the following day arrived Mrs Stuart from Richmond, taking up her residence at a plantation not more than half a mile from headquarters, in the hope of spending Christmas-day with her husband, but unfortunately without taking into her reckoning the extreme uncertainty of the General's movements, always, moreover, kept secret by him till the very last moment. Christmas-eve had been spent in calm unsuspicious enjoyment, amidst long gossips over old times and consultations on the preparations of the next day's festive fare; and we were slumbering peacefully in the early morning, when we were suddenly roused by the sound of the bugle. To my intense astonishment I learned from General Stuart that in an hour he would start on a wide-ranging raid in the rear of the Federal army. With bitter chagrin I found my poor horses reduced, by cold and hunger, to so miserable a condition that not one was fit for duty; two of them, indeed, perished within the next few days. All my efforts to procure a new charger failed, so scarce had horses become, and I had the mortification of seeing the General and those few of my comrades who happened to be in better plight than myself ride off without me to join the regiments, which had already, from an early hour, received marching orders. As usual, however, I did not allow my discomfiture to affect me long, and my vexed spirit soon yielded to the consolation of an excellent "egg-nogg"* and a roast turkey, which formed the mainstay of a dinner to which I had been invited by my friend Dearing, of the artillery. Encamped with his battery close to headquarters, in a dense pine thicket, he had, with the help of his cannoneers, built himself the snuggest little log-hut imaginable; and I was entirely restored to equanimity, after dinner, when I heard from my host that Major M., Longstreet's quartermaster, had two horses for sale, one of which would exactly suit my purpose.

Not to let slip so good an opportunity of a remount, I started, the first thing in the morning, for Major M.'s camp, where I found that, though I had been quite correctly informed, my purchase would be saddled with onerous and unexpected conditions. The horses were not to be sold separate; but, more than this, a lumbering family carriage was to go with them into the bargain. The conditions were absolute, both coach and horses having belonged to a friend

---

*Egg-nogg is an American drink which chiefly comes into notice at Christmas time, and in the good old days scarcely a house in Virginia was without a large bowl of this beverage standing in the hall on Christmas-day from morning till night for all to help themselves at. It consists of eggs beaten up with sugar, milk, and the indispensable ingredient of whisky or brandy. It is very agreeable to the taste, and has the dangerous property of concealing its strength under the guise

of the quartermaster, who, holding a plantation within the lines of the enemy, had, in wholesome fear of Yankee depredators, sent him the entire equipage. It was certainly an odd thing for a cavalry officer in the field to become owner of a stately family coach; nevertheless, I had no alternative, and so, having paid the comparatively cheap sum of 800 dollars for the whole concern, I drove off with my bargain. The laughter and wonderment which greeted my appearance at headquarters, gravely tooling my carriage and pair up to my tent, may be easily conceived.

This setting up of my carriage became an inexhaustible source of joking and bantering, to which I had to submit with the best grace I could; never did jest wear so well or so long; it outlasted by a long span the poor old carriage, its parent, which, after serving on many a merry expedition with the young ladies of the neighbourhood, gradually succumbed to the shocks of the rough roads and 'cross-country jaunts; and in a few weeks its frame had, bit by bit, resolved itself into its component parts. Only a heap of ruins at my tent door, and the cushions, which served me excellently for pillows, remained as outward and visible tokens of its existence. But the joke lived still, and even General Lee, by no means addicted to the jocular vein, would frequently, on parade or in the battle-field, come out with, "Major, where's your carriage?" and once, in the midst of fighting, he exclaimed, "If we only had your carriage, what a splendid opportunity to charge the enemy with it!"

On the evening of the same day I mounted my grey mule Kitt, the steed I generally selected for night excursions such as that I was bent on, and paid a visit to Longstreet's head-quarters, distant not more than a mile and a half. With the

---

of an innocent softness of savour, thus exerting its intoxicating influence on the inexperienced before the least suspicion is aroused.

officers of his Staff, as with the General himself, I was on excellent terms, and we used to assemble in a large tent which Major Latrobe, Major Fairfax, and Captain Rodgers occupied together, or else in a large hospital-tent in which the three doctors of the Staff—Cullen, Barksdale, and Maury—chummed together with a most harmonious result. The mess arrangements at Longstreet's headquarters were always more satisfactorily ordered than those of our own, especially in the matter of fluids, to which Stuart objected altogether, while I far from shared his aversion; so that, whenever I felt disposed to spend a sociable evening where the genial glass was not excluded, I took refuge with these cheerful companions, from whom I knew I could always reckon on a warm welcome.

Quickly did these pleasant evenings pass away, as we related the incidents by flood and field within our experience, or occasionally broke into song. In the latter respect Captain Rodgers was our chief performer; and when he was in thorough good-humour, he would enliven us with reminiscences of his stay among the Mormons, interspersed with select specimens of Brigham Young's psalmody. Whenever Latrobe's party fell short of liquor, the doctors were sure to be in a condition to supply the void; and when Kitt was sent over to them, with a polite invitation, it was generally answered by the simultaneous appearance of the three doctors in person, mounted one behind the other on the brave little mule, and bringing along with them the necessary materials for our social enjoyment. My return from these camp assemblies was invariably at an advanced hour of the night, and often did I owe my safe arrival at camp to Kitt's wonderful knowledge of the road. Once at my tent door, I would just relieve her of saddle and bridle, and let her gallop to the stable, whence the welcoming neigh of my black horse would soon after apprise me of the safe arrival of his intimate friend.

We were much cheered on the following day by the happy return of the waggons which had been despatched in charge of couriers to Loudoun County for provisions to furnish forth our Christmas dinner. The presence of some scouting Yankee cavalry on the road had delayed our messengers; but though too late to do honour to the Christian feast, not the less welcome were the good things they had brought. Among these were thirty dozen eggs, sweet potatoes and butter in abundance, and some score of turkeys. These last-named visitors to our camp were the object of the most polite attentions. In a few hours a magnificent mansion, built of small pine-trees and brushwood, was prepared for them by the united efforts of officers, couriers, and negroes, whose zeal was worthy of the occasion. Stuart's mulatto servant, Bob, was appointed major-domo and body-guard of the household and its inmates—an office which he discharged with no less skill than gallantry, when later the enterprising Texans encamped in our neighbourhood organised a regular succession of nightly marauding expeditions for the capture of our *raræ aves*.

The replenishment of our stock of provisions which had been thus effected appeared the more timely and valuable when, the same evening, we learned by telegram that Lawley would arrive the following day with two of his countrymen, the Marquess of Hartington and Colonel Leslie, both members of the British Parliament, on a voyage of inquiry, who intended to honour us with a visit. The preparations for their reception were rapidly made with that alacrity which distinguishes the hospitality of soldiers in camp, where all vie with each other in sacrificing their own comforts to render the entertainment of a visitor as agreeable as possible. I myself, having a large round Sibley tent, which, besides an ample fireplace, contained the luxury of a small iron stove, gave it up to be tenanted by the new-comers, and emigrated to a

smaller one in which I had scarcely room to turn. Others
contributed blankets, of which an abundance was forthcom-
ing. A table and camp-stool were supplied, and the equipments even included a small looking-glass, which dangled
from the tent-pole, giving altogether, with the rest of the
arrangements, an air of luxury and comfort which was quite
palatial.

It was close upon dinner-time when our visitors made their
appearance; and after their luggage was stowed in safety, and
they had been shown into their temporary domicile, we had
the pleasure of conducting them to their place at the long
camp dinner-table, the presence on which of a fat turkey and
some other dainties evidently created surprise, and exceeded
the expectations of our guests as to the manner in which they
were destined to fare. We had made every effort to procure
some liquor for the occasion, but all we succeeded in getting
was a large barrel of blackberry wine, captured by our
cavalry pickets. Whatever was thought by our visitors of this
extraordinary beverage, they were polite enough to pronounce it excellent. Lawley being already acquainted with the
members of the Staff, we soon became on good terms with his
two friends, and the night was far on ere we separated.

The moment we had finished breakfast next morning our
horses were in readiness, and we all started for a ride to
Fredericksburg, and over the battle-field, which presented
itself to the astonished eyes of our English friends still stained
with blood, and with the marks still fresh, in all their horror,
of the past work of desolation and destruction. The day
wound up with a great Fandango in Stuart's roomy tent,
enlivened with Sweeney's songs and banjo-playing to negro
dances; and a monster egg-nogg was prepared, in the mixing
of which even Lord Hartington and Colonel Leslie lent their
inexperienced hands in beating up the eggs—a part of the
preparation, by the way, which requires no little skill, and is,

moreover, intensely laborious; and when, after several hours of merriment, we separated at a late hour, both of them agreed that camp life was, after all, not so unendurable.

On the morning of the 30th our guests paid a visit to General Lee, where I joined them, and we rode off together to Moss-Neck, Jackson's headquarters, a distance, as has been mentioned, of twelve miles. We arrived about midday, and were received in a small pavilion attached to the main building, where the General had been prevailed upon, at the urgent request of the owner, to take up his abode. Old Stonewall so fascinated his English visitors by his kind and pleasant manners and the resources of his conversation, that, quite against their previous intentions, they accepted his invitation to dinner, and instead of a visit of twenty minutes, many hours were spent under the General's roof—hours that sped so rapidly, that when Lawley bethought himself to look at his watch, it was discovered to be very near the hour when we were all expected back to supper with General Lee. Away we started at full gallop; but though our horses were urged to their topmost speed, we reached headquarters far behind our time, and the General had long since taken his simple meal. To Lawley's excuses for our unintentional unpoliteness he laughingly replied, "Gentlemen, I hope Jackson has given you a good dinner, and if so, I am very glad things have turned out as they have, for I had given the invitation without knowing the poor state of my mess provisions, and should scarcely have been able to offer you anything."

The 31st was quietly spent at headquarters in the discharge of our camp duties and the enjoyment of the bright warm sunshine with which for the space of a few days the winter in Virginia is favoured. Our guests accommodated themselves with admirable facility and good-humour to the discomforts of a soldier's life, and insisted that we should not make any change for them in our ordinary routine, but let them fare exactly as the rest. Accordingly Lord Hartington and Lawley might at one time be seen, their sleeves rolled up, busily washing their pocket-handkerchiefs, and not far off Colonel Leslie energetically at work with a huge pole beating up a heap of mud to a proper temper for the construction of a new chimney to Major Fitzhugh's tent. The day following had been fixed on by our English friends for their departure, but as we had good reason to expect Stuart's immediate return, they yielded to our persuasions and consented to await his arrival, accepting meanwhile an invitation to General Jenkins of South Carolina, where we had an excellent dinner, and enjoyed a very pleasant evening listening to the music of one of the regimental bands, considered the best in the whole army. On returning at a late hour to our headquarters we found to our great delight that Stuart had come back from his raid, which had proved most successful, and resulted in the capture of numerous prisoners and a large amount of booty. Accordingly the General was in buoyant spirits, and gave us a most entertaining account of the entire expedition.

He had as usual operated far in the rear of the Yankees, had damaged their communications, and contrived, more-over, to throw a great part of the army and the generals sent in pursuit of him into a state of utter confusion by intercept-ing their telegraphic messages, and answering them himself in a manner that scattered his eager pursuers in opposite directions all over the country. General Stuart was always accompanied by his own telegraph operator, who had no difficulty in connecting his portable instrument at any point of the wires, and could thus read off and reply to the messages *in transitu*. One of these, on the occasion in question, was addressed to the Quartermaster-General, who had just sent off to the Federal army a large number of mules, all of which had fallen into the hands of Stuart. Accordingly, the following message was despatched to this official:—

"I am much satisfied with the transport of mules lately sent, which I have taken possession of, and ask you to send me soon a new supply.

"J.E.B. STUART."

The excitement and consternation this produced in the Northern capital may be imagined. But besides these blood-less devices there had been a good deal of hard fighting in the course of this expedition, and we had to mourn, among others, the loss of the gallant Captain Bullock, whose name has already occurred in these Memoirs. While being carried with a severe wound from the field by one of his friends, a second shot struck him and ended his life. The time had now come when the departure of our friends could no longer be delayed, and they took leave of us the following morning, the carriage I had purchased coming into requisition to drive them over (which I did with my own hands) to the station at Hamilton's Crossing.

CHAPTER XIX

LIFE IN CAMP DURING JANUARY AND FEBRUARY — AN
ENGLISH VISITOR — RIDE TO A WEDDING — A NEW ENGLISH
VISITOR — A FORTNIGHT AT CULPEPPER COURT-HOUSE —
FIGHT AT KELLEY'S FORD — PELHAM'S DEATH AND FUNERAL
HONOURS IN RICHMOND — BREAKING-UP OF WINTER
QUARTERS.

WITH the New Year set in a continuance of bad weather.
The cold increased, snow and damp alternated in rapid
succession, and our poor animals continued exposed to the
severest hardships. As for my own plight, I had returned to
my large tent, where I managed by a variety of ingenious
shifts, the offspring of hard necessity, to surround myself with
not a few practical comforts. A planked floor was laid down,
and over it was spread the rough resemblance of a carpet in
the shape of a large square of old canvass; a packing-case
which had served for the despatch of saddlery from the
ordnance department did duty very efficiently for a bedstead;
and with an empty whisky-cask, which, by sawing down on
one side to within a foot of the floor, stuffing the bottom with
blankets, and leaving only so much of the upper portion as
would comfortably support the back, became a capital easy-
chair, my assemblage of "sticks" was by no means contempt-
ible. With the inward man, however, matters began to assume

a very unsatisfactory condition. While the Christmas provision could be still eked out, we got on well enough, though at the cost of many an alarm sounded by the vigilant Bob, and many a hurried night-chase given to the Texan marauders to preserve the turkeys, while any yet survived, to our own use. But when the last of these interesting animals had in due turn adorned the mess-table, the dearth of food which thereafter ensued and continued was most painfully felt by officers and men. The almost invariable message with which our negroes returned from the commissary was, "Nothing to be had;" and when by an extraordinary chance they were enabled to bring back some sort of supplies, these consisted of beef so tough or bacon so rancid that only the sharpest pangs of hunger could induce a human being to tackle it as food. By using bullets cut into small pieces as a substitute for shot, I managed to bring down with my gun a number of small birds, such as blackbirds, robins, and sparrows, and so to purvey a certain modicum of fresh animal food, but so limited that there was never enough to satisfy the whole company; and often would four or five small birds appear at our long mess-table, to be divided among twelve hungry men, for any one of whom they would have been but a scanty meal. On one occasion a windfall came to us from the Lower Rappahannock (called the Tappahannock), in the shape of a waggon-load of oysters. These we fed on with great relish for a few days; but, being destitute of salt, pepper, or butter, or any condiment that might replace them, they soon palled, and a delicacy which would have been prized, under other circumstances, beyond all expression, became so nauseous that the very sight of an oyster turned us sick.

It was a tantalising fact, in the midst of our famine, to know that a flock of sheep existed in the neighbourhood, the property of an old planter, who, however, obstinately refused to part with one of them except at the most exorbitant price.

No entreaties in the world could induce the obdurate old gentleman to abate his demands; and the consequence was, that he ultimately suffered for his greed in the manner we are about to relate. Day after day these sheep would be found straying about our camp, attracted by the fodder of our horses, which was not a little diminished by their felonious nibblings. We had the greatest trouble to prevent these depredations; and, moreover, the sight to our hungry eyes of fat loins enriched at our expense, but on which we were prohibited to feed, added insult to injury. After sending several warnings to the old flockmaster, our couriers hit upon a cunning device, which should at once rid them of a nuisance and procure them delicious mutton. Deep trenches were dug wherever the sheep were in the habit of trespassing, ostensibly for the protection of our provender; and these, being covered with pine branches and straw, became so many pitfalls into which the poor animals tumbled, rolling over and over, and seldom escaping without such injuries as necessitated their immediate slaughter. The accident was then notified, not without bitter complaints, to the proprietor, who, having himself no use for the entire carcass, would make the best of the matter by selling us the greater part of the meat; and this mode of purveying mutton lasted till the old planter was persuaded to take better care of his flock.

In spite of deficient food, scanty supply of blankets, and extreme scarcity of shoe-leather, in the midst of the most trying weather, the good spirits of the army were unabated. Joyous sounds of song and laughter broke forth continuously from amidst the camps, and the bands of all the different regiments played merrily every evening. A theatre even was erected, where the performances of negro minstrels and other entertainments afforded immense delight to officers and men, and attracted all the young ladies of the neighbourhood. About the middle of the month some interruption to the usual monotonous routine of our camp was made by the visit of Colonel Bramston, of the battalion of Grenadier Guards stationed in Canada, with whom I, with great pleasure, shared the accommodation of my tent. The shortness of his furlough, however, deprived us of his presence a few days after his arrival. Just at this time a pressing invitation came to the General and myself from our friends at Dundee, in Hanover County, where Dr P.'s eldest daughter was to be married to Dr Fontaine, one of our comrades then acting as surgeon to Fitz Lee's brigade. That we could accept it seemed impossible; for on the very same day a review of William Lee's command was ordered to take place near Moss-Neck, Jackson's headquarters, and the distance thence to our friend's house was not less than five-and-forty miles. Nevertheless, to leave still a chance open, and hoping I might persuade Stuart to undertake the ride, I sent a courier with a relay of horses to Bowling-Green, a village about half-way between Moss-Neck and the spot we were to reach. It seemed as if the review would never be over; hour after hour flitted by, till at last it was a quarter to three by the time all was over, when Stuart rode over to me, and called out with a laugh, "Well, Von! how about the wedding? Shall we go?" Without hesitation I declared myself ready, only observing that as the wedding ceremony was appointed at seven o'clock we should have some difficulty in being present. "Oh, that's nothing." rejoined the General—"let's be off." And away we started at the rate of ten miles an hour. Bowling-Green was reached in capital time, where we mounted our relays; and before the clock struck the appointed hour of seven we rode through the gate of the hospitable Dundee.

A joyful and most demonstrative reception awaited us, for our arrival had been given up; and though our high riding-bootings covered with mud, and splashed uniforms, presented a contrast to the elegant dresses of the ladies and the correct costumes of the gentlemen, the favour with which we were regarded was none the less marked. Stuart was in his element, and the gayest of the gay. When the ceremony was over we amused ourselves with music, songs, and *tableaux vivants*. In one of the latter I had the honour of performing a prominent part in conjunction with a very pretty young lady, Miss Antoinette P., with whom it was my pleasing office to form a group imitating the coat of arms of the State of Virginia, bearing the motto, *Sic semper tyrannis,* which the soldiers translated, "Take your foot off my neck," from the action of the principal figure in the group in question, representing Liberty, who, with a lance in her right hand, is standing over the conquered and prostrate tyrant, and apparently trampling on him with her heel. To play the part of the poor tyrant who is suffering this ill-treatment, as it was my lot to do, would, I confess, under ordinary circumstances, offer but little gratification even to the most humbly disposed; but when the avenging goddess of Liberty is beautiful, and spurns you with a foot of such small proportions as in this case, the position of the conquered party is one of comparative triumph and felicity. Our performance gave as much satisfaction to the spectators as it certainly did to myself; and as for the General, his enthusiasm appeared excessive, for he insisted on having the *tableau* repeated several times; but it turned out that this was pure benevolence towards me, for he rallied me afterwards, saying he was sure I wanted to be *sic semper.* At last daylight streaming through the jalousies gave the signal for our party to break up, and seek the rest of which I myself felt in extreme want.

Doleful in my ears was the sound of Stuart's voice ordering our horses, and welcome was the rain which soon after poured down in torrents and caused Stuart's iron will to give way and yield to the urgent solicitations of our host to remain through the day, which, gloomy as it continued outside, did not damp the gaiety with which within doors the hours were wiled away till deep in the night, when we took leave of the company, and just as they were retiring comfortably to rest, set off on our long ride through the dark, chill, rainy morning. About half-way home we were met by a courier with a message informing us that the enemy had been making serious demonstrations on the river between Fredericksburg and Port Royal; so, urging our steeds to a quicker pace, we made all haste to gain headquarters, and it was still quite early in the morning when, having reached our destination, we found that the heavy rain had conveniently impeded the movements and altered the intention of the Yankees, among whom all again was quiet.

Towards the end of the month we received the visit of another Englishman, Captain Bushby, who turned out a warm admirer of Confederate principles, and a stanch sympathiser with the cause; and though he made but a short stay with us, ere he left he had become a general favourite at headquarters. Captain Bushby had just run the blockade into Charleston, after an exciting chase by the Federal cruisers, and could only spare a few days to look at our army and make acquaintance with its most conspicuous leaders, for several of whom he had brought very acceptable presents. To General Lee he presented an English saddle of the best make, to General Stuart a breech-loading carbine, while for Jackson he had provided himself with an india-rubber bed. For the presentation of this last article I escorted him to old Stonewall's headquarters; and on the ride an occasion befell me of astonishing my English friend and myself not a little, by a wonderful shot with my revolver, bringing down, as we galloped along, a turkey buzzard flying high overhead. I must confess I was vain enough to assume the air of treating the extraordinary success of this shot as a matter quite of course, whereas it was much more the result of accident than good shooting. Jackson received us with all his usual affability, and was much pleased with the present, promising to use it regularly. During the conversation which ensued, Captain Bushby asked the General for his autograph—a request which was at once granted; but in the act of writing, a blot fell on the paper, which was immediately thrown on the floor as useless. Bushby, however, picked it up and carefully treasured it in his pocket; and Jackson, noticing this action, said, with a modest smile, "Oh Captain, if you value my simple signature so much, I will give you a number of them with the greatest pleasure," and thereupon filled a large sheet with his sign-manual and presented it to him.

The condition of our horses continued to grow worse and worse, especially in Hampton's brigade, on which was imposed the fatiguing duty of picketing nearly forty miles of the Rappahannock, with very few opportunities of procuring provisions. In consequence of this state of things, I was ordered, in the commencement of February, by Stuart to proceed in that direction on a tour of inspection. It was a mournful sight to see more than half the horses of this splendid command totally unfit for duty, dead and dying animals lying about the camps in all directions. One regiment had lost thirty-one horses in less than a week. According to the recommendation of my report, Fitz Lee's brigade, which for months had been having a comparatively good time, was at once ordered to relieve Hampton's command; and Stuart wishing personally to hold a final inspection of the two brigades, Pelham, Lieutenant Price, and myself, were on the 17th ordered to proceed to Culpepper, where the General and the rest of his Staff would join us next day. We set off in the midst of a snow-storm, which increased in violence every hour. The snow ere long lay a foot deep, and the track of the road was soon so completely obliterated, that we stood in danger in the midst of the vast wilderness and forest tract, which in that part of the country extends for many miles, of being lost altogether. At last, however, just as night was falling, we reached the house of a free negro, situated about ten miles from our ultimate destination. Both ourselves and our horses were now about equally near exhaustion, and further progress being out of the question, we determined to seek shelter in this abode until the morning. But the hospitality we had reckoned on was not granted so readily as we had anticipated. After gaining, through the open door, a glimpse of a comfortable interior lit up by the blaze of a huge wood-fire, whose friendly warmth seemed almost at that distance to reach our shivering limbs, what was our dismay at being suddenly shut out from this paradise, and having the door slammed in our faces, with the remark on the part of the black-faced proprietor of the mansion, that he would have "nothing to do with no stragglers."

Our disappointment was utter, for the position we were thus left in was, in fact, desperate, and for some minutes we stood wrapt in disconsolate silence. At last Pelham broke out: "This won't do at all; we can't possibly go on: to remain out of doors in this terrible weather is certain destruction; and as we are under the obligation of preserving our lives as long as possible, for the sake of our cause and our country, I am going to fool this stupid old nigger, and play a trick off on him, which I think quite pardonable under the circumstances." Having by repeated loud knocks induced the inhospitable negro to reopen the door, he addressed him thus: "Mr Madden" (this was the man's name), "you don't know what a good friend of yours I am, or what you are doing when you are about to treat us in this way. That gentleman there" (pointing to me) "is the great General Lee himself; the other one is the French ambassador just arrived from Washington" (this alluded to Price, who, being lately from Europe, and much better equipped than the rest, had rather a foreign appearance); and I am a staff-officer of the General's, who is quite mad at being kept waiting outside so long after riding all this way on purpose to see you. In fact, if you let him stay any longer here in the cold, I'm afraid he'll shell your house as soon as his artillery comes up." The old negro was so perfectly staggered by this long harangue, which was uttered with a perfectly serious countenance, that he immediately invited us in, with all manner of excuses for his mistake. Our horses were soon sheltered in an empty stable, and such a feed of corn was laid before them as they had not had for a long time, while we dried our garments before the blazing wood-fire, our present sense of comfort being enhanced by anticipations of the future raised by the savoury odours which reached us from the kitchen, where Mr Madden was superintending in person the preparation of a repast suited to the distinguished rank of his guests. Pelham was delighted at the success of his diplomatic ruse, and went on hoaxing the old negro in the same strain, till nothing could persuade him that all he had been told was not quite true; and though in the morning we endeavoured to undeceive him, and paid him a liberal indemnity for the stratagem, he continued to inflate himself with a sense of his own importance at having been honoured with a visit from such distinguished guests.

We reached Hampton's headquarters, near Culpepper Court-house, before noon, where we met Stuart; and in the evening we all went by invitation to the village, where Fitz Lee's men had got up a negro-minstrel entertainment, and, with the assistance of Sweeney and Bob, succeeded in giving us a performance which would have rivalled any in London. Next day Stuart started for Richmond, accompanied by his Staff, leaving Pelham and myself, with some of our couriers, at Culpepper. We took up our quarters at the large Virginia Hotel, where we had the satisfaction of having our horses once more well stabled, and our own comfort cared for in every possible way by the stout landlady, who seemed bent on showing her gratitude for some service we had rendered her son, a private in Fitz Lee's brigade.

Culpepper Court-house is a pleasant village of several hundred inhabitants, and the main street, in which we were located, is lined with pretty villa-like residences. The street itself, however, was without pavement, and the constant snow and rain had soaked into the red clayey soil so completely that the mud was several feet deep, and the passage of any vehicle through it being out of the question, we were literally confined to our own side of the street. To overcome this inconvenience Pelham and I set to work to construct a sort of bridge, by resting planks on a number of blocks of stone, and by this means we were enabled to pay frequent visits to the house of our opposite neighbour, Mr S., where we were treated with great kindness, and our time passed pleasantly away. A constant visitor, like ourselves, at this house was Major Eales of Rosser's regiment, who, being just released from a Yankee prison, and still on parole, relished the gaiety of our society with peculiar zest. The fortune of war played sad havock with this happy trio. Poor Pelham expired not many weeks after in the very house where he had so pleasantly spent his time; and in a few months Eales was killed on the day before I myself received a wound which at the time was regarded as mortal.

Although we expected Stuart back in a few days, it was a fortnight before we heard from him, when we received a telegram ordering us back to headquarters at Fredericksburg. We felt very sad at leaving pleasant old Culpepper, and the hardships and monotony of our camp life fell on us the more heavily after an interval of comparative ease and abundance. The remnant of February and a part of March dragged slowly by, so dull and eventless that existence was scarcely tolerable, and we looked forward to the commencement of spring and the reopening of the campaign with intense longing. On the 15th of March Stuart left for Culpepper, where he had to appear as a witness at a court-martial; and Pelham, who was very anxious to see our lady friends there again, accompanied him—a pleasure which I was not allowed to share, as the General had placed me in charge over the pickets at the different fords up the Rappahannock, from Fredericksburg to the mouth of the Rapidan. On the morning of the 17th, which was one of those mild, hazy March days that betoken the approach of spring, we were suddenly stirred up, in the midst of our lazy, listless existence, by the sound of a cannonade which seemed to come from the direction of United States Ford on the Rappahannock, about ten miles above Fredericksburg. I was in my saddle in a moment, fancying that the enemy was attempting to force a passage at one of the points placed under my charge; but when I had galloped in hot haste up to the river, I found that the firing was much further off, and, as it seemed to me, towards the mouth of the Rapidan. This supposition proved to be correct, for when I reached my pickets I received a report that a heavy fight was going on in the direction of Culpepper Court-house, near Kelley's Ford, at least fifteen miles in a straight line higher up the river. The cannonade, which seemed growing louder and fiercer all through the morning, gradually slackened as the day advanced, and in the evening, when I returned to camp, was completely silenced.

The country bordering the Rappahannock is covered with dense forest, whence it has justly acquired the name of the Wilderness, and in many places it presents scenes of wild and romantic beauty. It is not traversed by regular roads, but a number of small bride-paths wind through the tangled undergrowth of laurels and brambles, which, interlacing with the vines and creepers that hang down from the larger trees, form thickets which no human being could penetrate. It was a beautiful calm evening, the silence of which was broken only by the song of the thrush or the monotonous tapping of the woodpecker—one of those evenings that seem made for a melancholy and sentimental mood; and, strange to say, by such a mood was I now completely overcome, my thoughts constantly reverting to my dear friend Pelham, with an obstinate foreboding that some dreadful fate must have befallen him.

A trifling incident occurred near headquarters which happened to amuse me, and sufficed to divert my thoughts from their melancholy course. On my way towards the river I had consulted a sturdy farmer as to a short cut, and now, on my return, I met him again; but as I had since our first meeting taken off my cloak and tied it to the saddle, the old fellow did not recognise me as his morning's acquaintance, and accosted me thus: "Have you met a fellow on the road in a big overcoat, and riding a horse something like yours? He asked me some questions, and talked very like a Dutchman. My notion is he's nothing more than a d—d Yankee spy." Whereupon I informed him that I was the identical person; but nothing could persuade him of this, for he now vowed I had no Dutch accent at all, in fact, complimented me on my excellent English pronunciation. So I left him to his obstinate conviction, and continued my route to the camp, which I reached shortly after dark.

Next morning, about an hour before daylight, I was roused from my slumbers by hearing some one riding up to my tent, and startled out of bed by the voice of one of the couriers Stuart had taken with him, who, with much agitation of manner, reported that the General had been engaged with Fitz Lee's brigade in a sanguinary battle against far superior numbers of the enemy, and had beaten them, but at the cost of many lives, and among them that of Pelham, the gallant chief of our horse-artillery. Poor Pelham! He had but just received his promotion to the rank of Lieutenant-Colonel, and now met his death in a comparatively small engagement, after passing safely through so many great battles. Being on a visit of pleasure, he had been taken unprepared, and, at the first sound of the cannon, hastened unarmed, on a horse borrowed from Sweeney, to the field of action. His batteries had not come up to answer the enemy's cannon, but his ardour would not allow him to wait for their arrival, and he rushed forward into the thickest of the fight, cheering on our men and animating them by his example. When one of our regiments advancing to charge was received with such a terrible fire by the enemy as to cause it to waver, Pelham galloped up to them, shouting, "Forward, boys! forward to victory and glory!" and at the same moment a fragment of a shell, which exploded close over his head, penetrated the back part of the skull, and stretched the young hero insensible on the ground. He was carried at once to Culpepper, where the young ladies of Mr S.'s family tended him with sisterly care; but he never again recovered his senses, and the same evening his noble spirit departed. This sad intelligence spread through the whole camp in a few minutes, and the impression of melancholy sorrow it produced on all is beyond description, so liked and admired had Pelham been, and so proud were we of his gallantry. One after the other, comrades entered my tent to hear the confirmation of the dreadful news, which everybody tried as long as possible not to credit. Couriers and negroes assembled outside, all seemingly paralysed by the sudden and cruel calamity; and when morning came, instead of the usual bustling activity and noisy gaiety, a deep and mournful silence reigned throughout the encampment. I was much touched by the behaviour of Pelham's negro servants, Willis and Newton, who, with tokens of the greatest distress, begged to be allowed at once to go and take charge of their master's body—a permission which I was, however, constrained to refuse.

Early in the morning I received a telegram from Stuart ordering me to proceed by the next train to Hanover Junction, there to receive Pelham's body and bring it to Richmond, and then to make all the arrangements necessary to have it conveyed to Alabama, his native State. I started at once and reached the Junction in time to receive the corpse, which, along with several others, was enclosed in a simple wooden case and under the charge of one of our artillerymen, who, with tears in his eyes, gave me the particulars of his gallant commander's death. I did not reach Richmond until late at night, and not finding the hearse, which I had telegraphed to be in readiness, at the station, was obliged to remove the body into the town in a common one-horse waggon. Immediately on arriving I went to Governor Letcher, an old and stanch friend of Stuart's and mine, who kindly afforded all the assistance in his power, and placed a room at my disposal in the Capitol, where the Confederate Congress held its sessions. The coffin was placed in it, covered with the large flag of the State of Virginia, and a guard of honour was placed over it. The next day I procured a handsome iron coffin, and with my own hands assisted in transferring the body to its new receptacle. I was overcome with grief as I touched the lifeless hand that had so often pressed mine in the grasp of friendship. His manly features even in death expressed that fortitude and pride which distinguished him. By special request I had a small glass window let into the coffin-lid just over the face, that his friends and admirers might take a last look at the young hero, and they came in troops, the majority being ladies, who brought garlands and magnificent bouquets to lay upon the coffin. Meantime I had communicated with several members of Congress from Alabama, friends of Pelham's father, and it had been decided that his remains should be conveyed to Alabama in charge of a young soldier, a connection of the family, who had just been released from one of the Richmond hospitals. The afternoon of the following day was appointed for the departure, and at five o'clock we carried the coffin to the station, the Richmond battalion of infantry doing the military honours, and a large number of dignitaries of the Confederate States, friends and comrades, following. Alabama paid as solemn a tribute of respect to her gallant son as he deserved to have shown him. As soon as the frontier of the State was reached, a guard of honour escorted the coffin, and at every station on the road ladies were waiting to adorn it with flowers.

General Stuart arrived in Richmond on the day following, still deeply affected by the loss of his young friend, and greatly grieved that he had not been able to attend the funeral ceremonies. Having obtained leave to remain in Richmond a few days, I saw many of my old friends again, and among them Lawley, through whom I made acquaintance with Prince Polignac, who was serving as a brigadier-general of infantry in the Western Army. On my return to headquarters another sad message came to us, announcing the death of Captain Redmond Burke, who was attached to our Staff. While with a scouting party on the Upper Potomac with two of his sons, he had been imprudent enough to remain during the night at a house close to the enemy's position at Shepherdstown. The Yankees, informed by treachery of his presence, sent a body of cavalry after him, who surrounded the house and summoned the inmates to surrender; but the brave trio sought to break through the compact circle, and in the attempt Burke himself was killed, one son was wounded, and the other taken prisoner. Not long afterwards we heard of the death of Lieutenant Turner, a promising young officer of our Staff, who had been despatched with certain instructions to the well-known guerilla chief Mosby, and had been severely wounded in a skirmish which took place the very day of his arrival. Having been left at a plantation within the enemy's lines, he was in a fair way of recovery, when a small party of Federal cavalry entered the house, tore him from his bed, and so ill-treated the poor fellow that his wounds reopened and he died shortly after. All these misfortunes did not fail to cast a gloom over our little military family; and it was an intense relief to us when, on the 9th of April, we received orders to march to Culpepper Court-house; and the ringing of the bugle sounding to horse and announcing the commencement of a new campaign, with all its wild excitement, raised our spirits once more to the highest pitch.

CHAPTER XX

THE SPRING CAMPAIGN OF 1863: CAMP NEAR CUL-
PEPPER — FIGHTS ON THE RAPPAHANNOCK — VISIT OF A
PRUSSIAN OFFICER — RIDES IN THE NEIGHBOURHOOD —
HOOKER'S ADVANCE AND FLANK MARCH — NIGHT-FIGHT
NEAR TOD'S TAVERN.

ON our arrival at Culpepper we found it greatly improved in aspect. True, the roads were still nearly
impassable; but the country round, under the influence of
frequent rains and the mild air of April, had clothed itself in
tender verdure, interspersed here and there with blooming
patches by the now blossoming peach orchards. Our headquarters were established not more than a quarter of a mile
from Culpepper, on a height thickly covered with pine and
cedar trees, skirted by the road leading to Orange Court-
house, and commanding a view of the village and the
surrounding country, picturesquely bordered in the distance
by the beautiful Blue Ridge Mountains. Only W. Lee's and
Fitz Lee's brigades were with us. The former picketed the
fords in the immediate vicinity of Culpepper, and the latter
was stationed higher up the river. Hampton's command had
been left behind for recruiting, most of its dismounted men
having been furloughed to their distant homes in Mississippi
and the Carolinas to supply themselves with fresh horses.

Our animals were now beginning to get into better condition, forage having become more abundant, and being valuably supplemented by the new grass and clover. Provisions for the men had also grown more plentiful, and our kind friends in the neighbourhood did their best to keep the mess-table of the General and his Staff copiously supplied.

In the mean time, after the battle of Fredericksburg, the supreme command had been transferred into the hands of General Hooker, an officer who had gained a high reputation by his gallantry—he was nicknamed by his men "Fighting Joe"—and the good management of his division, but who eventually proved himself to be utterly incapable of commanding a large army. Great credit, however, was due to him for having availed himself of the interval of inaction to improve his cavalry, which was now completely recruited, men and horses, and augmented by fresh brigades; while new order and discipline had been instilled into the entire force. A large part of the cavalry of the Army of the Potomac, as it was still called, had been concentrated on the Upper Rappahannock, and it was this fact which had caused our rapid departure from Fredericksburg. The restless activity of our neighbours on the other side of the river, their constant marching and countermarching, indicated that some serious enterprise was impending; and the renewal of the picket-firing created the daily expectation, after so long an interval of tranquillity, of a brush with our antagonists.

We had already, on the 13th, been brought into the saddle by a sudden alarm, but had found, on hastening to the front, that the gallantry and good firing of our pickets had foiled every effort of the Federals to effect a crossing over the Rappahannock. On the following morning, however, we were abruptly startled by a report that the Yankees had forced a passage at several points of the river, had driven our pickets back, and were advancing in large force upon Culpepper. All was hurry and confusion at headquarters on the receipt of this intelligence; tents were struck, horses saddled, waggons loaded and teams harnessed, for an immediate start—the General and his Staff galloping off to throw ourselves, with W. Lee's brigade, across the enemy's path. It was on the plain near Brandy Station—that battle-ground so often mentioned already—that we once more encountered the advancing foe, and before long the action developed along all our line. The enemy fought with great obstinacy, and at first we had to yield ground to them for some distance; but in the course of the afternoon we succeeded, by a general and united movement in advance, in driving them back across the river. The fighting was only kept up during the evening by an exchange of firing between the Yankee guns mounted on an old redoubt close to the opposite shore and our batteries on two hills, about a mile apart, in the space between which Generals Stuart and Lee, with their respective Staffs, had taken up their position, carelessly stretched on the ground, chatting and laughing and watching the effect of the shells crossing each other over their heads, as unconcerned as if there were no enemy within miles. I myself was posted a little to the right, narrowly observing, by the aid of the excellent glass I had captured from General Pope's baggage, the movements of the enemy, and wondering in my mind how it was a numerous group of officers so close under the Yankee cannons had thus long escaped their attention. Suddenly I saw the officer commanding the Federal battery mount the parapet, and, after scanning the knot of officers through his glass, assist with his own hands in pointing one of the guns upon them. In spite of my warning, which was received with mockery, the joyous assembly continued their seance till, a few seconds after, the shot was heard, and a shell fell plump in their midst, burying in the earth with itself one of General Lee's gauntlets, which lay on the ground only a few feet from the General himself, and bespattering all who were nearest to it with earth and mud. It was now my turn to laugh as I beheld my gallant comrades stampede right and left from the fatal spot, chasing their frightened horses, followed by a rapid, though happily less well-directed, succession of shots from the enemy's guns. With this little incident closed the fight for that day. A heavy shower now descended, lasting many hours, which, in the absence of the shelter of our tents, left unpitched in the hurry and excitement of the events of the day, caused us to spend a night of wretched discomfort.

General Stuart was led to believe that, the river being much swollen by the rain, the Yankees would leave us undisturbed; but at the very earliest gleam of day, this supposition was dispelled by the intelligence that the enemy, strongly reinforced, had succeeded again in forcing a passage to our side; and once more, wet through and shivering, we were summoned to the front. The conflict, as on so many previous occasions, commenced near Brandy Station; but, notwithstanding their vastly superior numbers, our adversaries did not make a very obstinate stand, probably owing to the rapid rising of the Rappahannock, which in a few hours more might be rendered impassable. Stuart, desirous on this very account to draw the enemy into a battle, vigorously pushed his troops forward after the retreating foe, but was unable to prevent the safe crossing of the entire cavalry force of the enemy, with the exception of their rear-guard, composed of two squadrons of the 3d Indiana regiment. These we brought to a stand a few hundred yards from a mill-creek which intersects the road at a distance of about half a mile from the river, and generally presents scarcely a foot's depth of water, but which was now swollen to a wide and rapid stream not to be crossed, even at the shallowest points, save with the greatest difficulty. As soon as the head of our column approached this spot, a number of dismounted sharpshooters, posted here to protect the Yankees' rear, opened a severe fire, killing and wounding several of our men. Stuart at once ordered a squadron of our 9th Virginia regiment, who were leading the advance, to charge. Having been refused the General's permission to join in the attack, I galloped, on my own account, about a hundred yards to the right of the road in the direction of the hostile sharpshooters, whose particular attention I at once engaged, a number of bullets flying round my head unpleasantly quick and near. Having got within about forty yards of their position, I shouted out to them to surrender; but in the fancied security offered by the broad foaming stream, which flowed between them and their assailants, they treated my summons with defiance, and answered it only by a brace of bullets, one of which nearly cut off a lock of my hair. Exasperated out of all patience at this, I spurred my horse and dashed with a tremendous leap into the middle of the creek, and for a moment its waters seemed to close over my head; but quickly surmounting the torrent, my brave horse gallantry swam to the opposite shore, and, by a strenuous effort of every sinew, succeeded in scrambling up the steep bank to the high ground above.

The boldness and rapidity of this feat seemed to perfectly paralyse the objects of my wrath—a corporal and a private of the 3d Indiana Cavalry, who, as I pounced upon them with uplifted sword, threw away their arms and begged for mercy on their knees. In the first excitement, I felt but little inclined to heed their prayers, seeing that but a few minutes before they had shot down one of our men, and had spent their last cartridge in the attempt to do the like for me; but the poor wretches were so terror-stricken, and begged so hard for their lives, that I was content to commute the penalty of death to treating them with just such a cold bath as I had had; and so I sent them through the water to the other side, where one of our couriers, who had hastened up to my assistance, took them in charge. In the mean time, the fight had ended in our favour. The enemy, after a short but severe combat, had broken in utter confusion, and had been chased by our men across the creek to the river, where a heavy fire from the opposite bank put an end to the pursuit. Some thirty prisoners and horses fell into our hands, and the enemy lost severely besides in killed and wounded—a good number of their men having been unhorsed in the hurried passage of the creek, and whelmed in the angry waves.

Stuart, who had witnessed the whole course of my little exploit, was much amused at the plight in which I returned, soaked through, and beplastered with mud. He had never, he said, expected to see me emerge after my plunge; and added, that as I climbed up the bank I looked like a terrapin crawling out of the mud. For some little time longer the firing was kept up by the artillery on both sides; but as the enemy soon entirely disappeared from the opposite side of the Rappahannock, we returned to our camping ground, pitched our tents, and established once more, in regular order, our cavalry headquarters.

As the continued rains rendered the crossing of the Rappahannock impracticable, an interval of tranquillity succeeded these few days of conflict and excitement. It speeded away, however, rapidly enough, amidst visits in the neighbourhood and pleasant horseback excursions in the company of our lady acquaintances. On the 21st I had an agreeable surprise in a visit from a fellow-countryman, Captain Scheibert, of the Prussian engineers. He had been sent on a mission by his Government to take note as an eyewitness of the operations of the war, and derive what profit he could from its experiences. I had already seen him at General R. E. Lee's headquarters, where he was a guest of the General's, for he had been several weeks with our army, and was now about, at my urgent prayer, to make a further stay with us. My tent and its comforts, sadly curtailed however by the results of the heavy rains, which on several occasions had completely deluged it, were gladly shared with my visitor. Just as at our old headquarters, near Fredericksburg, we had been annoyed by the aggressions of straying sheep, we now suffered from the daily irruptions upon our camp of pigs exploring and devouring everything that fell under their snouts. Not seldom, indeed, these intruders had the impudence to break into my tent in the middle of the night, having set their fancy on a pair of large cavalry boots of mine, which once or twice they succeeded in dragging off far into the woods, giving my negro Henry and myself infinite trouble before we could recover these precious parts of my accoutrement. Our evenings were mostly passed in the village, in the company of our lady acquaintances, whom Scheibert delighted by his excellent pianoforte-playing, to say nothing of the amusement they derived from his original practice with the idiom and pronunciation of the English language.

On the 28th, Stuart and the members of his Staff, including our visitor, dined by invitation under the roof of an old widow lady, a very particular friend of mine, who resided on a pretty little plantation close to Culpepper. Mrs S. was a poetess, and had exercised her talents to the glorification of Lee and Jackson, so that when, after dinner, she asked permission to read a new poem, we all naturally expected that it was now Stuart's turn. What was my astonishment, however, and embarrassment to find myself the theme of her eloquent and touching verses, wherein my praises were most flatteringly sounded! Blushing, and transfixed to my chair with stupefaction, as I heard the loud applause which greeted the conclusion of the piece, for a moment I was at a loss how to behave; then suddenly rousing myself, I advanced towards Mrs S., and in the fashion of the knights of old, I knelt on one knee, and with a kiss mutely impressed my thanks on the hand from which I received my poetical diploma of merit. "That won't do, Von," cried out Stuart, and, stepping forward, he printed a hearty kiss on the old lady's cheek—a liberty which she received with a very good grace, saying, "General, I have always known you to be a very gallant soldier, but from this moment I believe you to be the bravest of the brave." Music, dance, and merriment chased away the remaining hours of the day, and it was late in the night ere we reached our headquarters, and retired to rest, little divining how soon we should be roused up again.

It was about three in the morning when I was awakened by the General himself, who informed me he had just received intelligence that the enemy were approaching the river at several points with a strong force composed of infantry, cavalry, and artillery, and that we must hasten to the front without delay. The words were no sooner spoken than the bugle sounded to horse, and a few minutes after we galloped away from the camp, where all were busy with preparations for moving at a moment's notice. We reached the famous plateau near Brandy Station a little after daybreak, and found there W. Lee's brigade in line of battle, and two batteries of artillery in position. Fitz Lee's command arrived soon afterwards; and on this spot, so favourable for defence, Stuart decided to await the enemy's advance, making all preparations for a desperate resistance. A dense fog, which clung to the plain, precluded all observation of the hostile movements; but our pickets, which by this time had been forced back from the river and were receding towards us before vastly superior numbers, reported that a large body of troops of all arms had passed over to our side of the Rappahannock, and, to judge from the sounds which reached them, still more were crossing on several pontoon-bridges. In the midst of the anxious suspense in which the morning passed away a prisoner was brought in, who, misled by the fog, had ridden straight into our lines, and as he was led up to us by two of our men, he was vainly trying to make himself understood. Addressing this excited gentleman in French, I found that he was a Belgian artillery officer who, anxious to have the best opportunity possible of witnessing the operations in the field, had attached himself to the Staff of some Yankee General, temporarily adopting the Federal uniform. My new acquaintance very naturally declined to afford us any information as to the enemy's strength and their intentions; but, observing how small comparatively were our numbers, he said, with a shrug of his shoulders, "Gentlemen, I can only give you one piece of advice—that is, to try and make your escape as quickly as possible; if not, your capture by the large army in front of you is a certainty." I replied, laughing, "That we preferred to wait a little while yet, and that it was our habit always to fight before retreating." Our *brave Belge*, with great earnestness, claimed his neutral privileges, and exhibited a profound disinclination to be sent as a captive to Richmond; but, being taken in full Yankee uniform, no exception could be made in his case, and accordingly he was eventually sent, with other prisoners, to that objectionable locality, there to await his regular exchange.

Hour after hour passed away in this trying state of uncertainty, until at last, towards mid-day, the fog cleared away, and we were enabled to discover that our antagonists had for once completely deceived us. The advance in front had only been made by some cavalry to occupy our attention while the main body had marched in the direction of the Rapidan river. With his accustomed quickness, Stuart divined at once the intentions of the Federal commander, and, leaving one regiment behind to watch the movements of the hostile cavalry, we directed our march with all rapidity towards Stevensburg and Germana Ford on the Rapidan, trusting to be able to throw ourselves in the way of the enemy before he could reach the latter important point, where our engineers had just been completing a bridge. Unfortunately we were too late; and on reaching the intersection of the road, near the free negro Madden's house, previously mentioned, we found the greater part of the Federal troops had passed already, and could see, at a distance of not more than three hundred yards, the dense masses of their rear-guard marching steadily along. To give the Yankees an idea how close we were on their track, Stuart ordered the attack at once, and our dismounted sharpshooters, advancing through the undergrowth, opened fire simultaneously with our artillery, advantage being taken by the latter of several openings in the forest to throw a shower of shell and canister into their closely serried ranks. The confusion and consternation caused amongst them by this unexpected attack passes all description. In utter helpless stampede they pressed forward in double-quick, completely heedless of the efforts of their officers to make them stand and fight, and animated by the one sole object of escaping from the deadly fire, which again and again plunged into the hostile columns until the last man had disappeared. The road was covered with their dead and wounded, and sixty who had straggled off into the woods were taken prisoners.

We learned from these prisoners that the force consisted of three *corps d'armée*—the 5th, 11th, and 12th; that their destination was Germana Ford and Chancellorsville; and that their cavalry, under General Stoneman's command, was to march towards Culpepper Court-house. In accordance with this information General Stuart resolved to leave William Lee's brigade behind to impede as much as possible Stoneman's advance, and with Fitz Lee's command to fall again upon the enemy's flank. By the time we reached Racoon's Ford it was already dark, and after crossing the river we dismounted here for an hour to feed our horses. The night was wet and chilly, a fine sleet drizzling down incessantly;

and we felt cold, hungry, and uncomfortable, when, after a short rest, we rode on again through the darkness. We were marching along the plank-road, which, coming from Orange Court-house, strikes across that leading from Germana to Chancellorsville, at a small village called the Wilderness, when at that point the Federal army, already in motion, came in sight. The day being just breaking we attacked without delay; but found this time the Federals better prepared, several of their infantry regiments forming at once into line of battle, and their artillery most effectively answering the fire of our battery. After a short but severe contest we had to retire; but, striking into a road parallel with the enemy's line of march, we renewed the conflict, whenever a favourable opportunity seemed to present itself, until late in the evening, when General Stuart gave the order to turn off in the direction of Spotsylvania Court-house and go into bivouac about eight miles hence, at a place called Tod's Tavern.

We reached this point about nightfall, and here General Stuart decided to leave the regiment behind, and, accompanied only by myself, some members of the Staff, whom Captain Scheibert volunteered to join, and a few couriers, to ride across through the woods to General R. E. Lee's headquarters, which, as the crow flies, were about twelve miles distant. Knowing we should have to pass quite close to the enemy's lines, I endeavoured to persuade the General to take one of our squadrons along with him as an escort, but the General refused, believing the road to be quite clear; so, by way of precaution, I sent a courier on ahead to serve as a kind of advanced-guard. We had been riding for some time silently through the forest, whose darkness was only relieved by occasional glimpses of the new moon, when suddenly a pistol-shot was heard a few hundred yards ahead of us, and presently the courier hurried back to us, reporting, in the most excited manner, that he had been fired at by a Yankee cavalry picket stationed only a short distance from us in the road. Stuart, perfectly convinced that the courier was deceived, and had taken some of our own men for the enemy, requested me to ride ahead and investigate the matter.

Accompanied by Major Terril of our Staff, I pricked forward and soon discovered a body of thirty horsemen before us, who in their light-blue overcoats, just discernible by the feeble light of the moon, looked most decidedly like Federals. To make quite sure, however, we approached to within about fifty yards, and I then called out and asked them to what regiment they belonged. "You shall see that soon enough, you d—d rebels," was the answer, and at the same moment the whole party came full gallop towards us. Firing our revolvers at the charging foe, we quickly turned our horses' heads and rode as fast as our steeds would carry us to the rear, followed by our pursuers shouting and firing after us to their hearts' content. Resistance when so completely out-numbered would have been folly; and accordingly I had the pleasure of seeing our General, who had now lost all doubts as to the real character of these cavalrymen, for once run from the enemy. The Yankees soon slackened their pace, however, and at last gave up the chase altogether, when we halted, and General Stuart despatched Captain White of our Staff to Fitz Lee, with the order to send on one of his regiments as quickly as possible, and to follow slowly himself with the remainder of his brigade. After an anxious half-hour the regiment came up, and we had the satisfaction of turning the tables on our pursuers and driving them before us as rapidly as we had fled before them. The feeble light of the moon was now nearly extinguished by the clouds scudding rapidly across the sky. General Stuart and his Staff were trotting along at the head of the column, when, at the moment of emerging out of the dark forest, we suddenly discovered in the open field before us, and at a distance of not more than 160 yards, the long lines of several regiments of hostile cavalry, who received us with a severe fire, which, concentrated on the narrow road, in a few moments killed and wounded a large number of our men and horses, causing considerable confusion in our ranks, and speedily checking our onward movement. Fully conscious of our critical position, Stuart drew his sword, and, raising his clear ringing voice, gave the order to attack, taking the lead himself. For once our horsemen refused to follow their gallant commander; they wavered under the thick storm of bullets; soon all discipline ceased, and in a few minutes the greater part of this splendid regiment, which had distinguished itself in so many battle-fields, broke to the rear in utter confusion. In vain did the General, myself, and the other members of the Staff, do our utmost to restore order; we only succeeded in rallying about thirty men round us.

At this moment the enemy's bugle sounded the charge; and a few seconds after we brunted the shock of the attack, which broke upon us like a thunder-cloud, and bore our little band along with its vehement rush as driven by a mighty wave, sweeping us along with it into the darkness of the forest. And now ensued a wild, exciting chase, in which friend and foe, unable to recognise each other, mingled helter-skelter in one furious ride. I cannot describe the sensation that came over me, as, feeling assured that everything was now lost, I tightly grasped the hilt of my sword, resolved to sell my life as dearly as possible. Relying merely on the instinct of their horses, most of the men followed the straight road by which we had come, but I and a number of others turned off into a small by-road to the left. Here I discovered by the gleams of the moonlight, which now broke out more brightly, that those immediately round me were friends, but every effort to stop and rally them was in vain. "The Yankees are close behind; we must run for our lives," was all the answer I received to my appeals; and on went the hopeless stampede more furiously than before. A tremendous fence standing across our path, too high for a leap, and only to be pulled down at the risk of dismounting, seemed likely to bring our wild retreat to a stop; but by dint of rider pressing on rider, and horse plunging against horse, it at last yielded to the accumulated weight of the impetuous horsemen, and broke down with a loud crash, leaving the way open to the disorderly flight. Just as, at the end of a rapid ride of more than an hour through dense forest, I reached an open field, a rider, who had been close at my side for some time, startled me with the exclamation, "Von, is that you?" in tones which, to my intense delight and relief, I recognised to be Stuart's, who had followed the same route as myself.

We were soon joined by some other members of our Staff, all of whom had had wonderful escapes; and by our united efforts we at last succeeded in rallying some sixty of our men, whom we put in charge of one of their officers, with orders to wait for further instructions. Meanwhile we set off with the project of rejoining the rest of the brigade, which, in a dark night and through an unknown and forest-covered country, was a task of some difficulty. On our road we fell in with several of our former pursuers, who, being bewildered in the vast forest, now surrendered to us with little hesitation; two of these were captured by Stuart himself. At the end of an hour's tedious ride we came upon Fitz Lee's column trotting onward to the field of action, whither the 2d Virginia had already preceded them. On reaching the scene of our recent defeat, we found that our brave fellows of the 2d, led by their gallant colonel, Munford, had come up just in time to protect their flying comrades, and had thrown themselves with such ardour on the Federals as to break their lines and scatter them in every direction, many killed and wounded being left on the field, and some eighty prisoners and horses falling into our hands.

As all seemed now over, Stuart ordered the troops to march on to Spotsylvania Court-house, and there encamp, the 2d Virginia taking the lead, and the prisoners and remaining regiments following. We were quietly marching along with the advanced-guard, chatting over the incidents of the evening, when several shots suddenly sounded on our left, followed by brisk firing in our rear. Immediately cries of "The Yankees are on us!" "The Yankees are charging!" broke out from our column; sabres flew out of their scabbards, revolvers from their holsters, and everybody seemed on fire to oppose the enemy, without exactly knowing in what direction to look for him. The scene of confusion which ensued is not to be described; firearms exploded in all directions, bullets traversed the air from all quarters; and, for want of a visible foe, friend seemed likely to come into collision with friend. General Stuart and several others, including myself, did our utmost to quell the disorder, but our voices were drowned in the general hubbub. Suddenly a fresh cry of "Here are the Yankees; here they come," broke out from the men around me as they fired off their revolvers into the bushes to the right. Calling on them to follow, I spurred my horse forward in the same direction, when, at the same moment, I was met by a rider galloping towards me, who levelled a shot at me so close, the bullet passing through my hat, that I was completely blinded. Before I had quite recovered and could deliver my thrust, my adversary lost no time in firing his second shot, which entered the head of my brave bay, and stretched us both on the ground, myself under the horse. Luckily, however, I was able to disengage myself from the super-incumbent weight of the dying animal; and, jumping up to look after my assailant, found that, fortunately for me, he had disappeared, without waiting to take advantage of my prostrate condition.

Nevertheless my position was a ticklish one still; the firing continued in all directions round me, and our men were galloping about in wild excitement, some calling on me to save myself, as the woods were full of Federals. As I did not much fancy leaving my saddle and bridle a spoil to the enemy, I had managed to detach the precious articles from my dead steed, when one of our couriers rode up to me, leading a Yankee horse which he had caught for me as it was running about riderless. It was an odd-looking, stumpy-legged little pony; and when mounted on it, my legs dangling nearly to the ground, my large English hunting-saddle covering the pony's neck, and leaving his ears only sticking out, I must have presented a remarkable figure, especially as the little beast was in such a state of excitement, plunging and snorting wildly, that I had some trouble in keeping my seat. At last, with no little difficulty, I succeeded in finding Stuart again, who, in the midst of his ill-humour and dissatisfaction at the behaviour of his men, was unable to resist the ludicrous effect of my appearance. He now told me that discipline and order had at last been re-established, and that the whole rout had been caused by less than a hundred of the enemy's cavalry dispersed in the woods by the charge of the 2d Virginia, and who, in the darkness, had been taken for a much larger force. He added that our men had mistaken each other for enemies; and that two of our regiments, the 1st and 3d Virginia, under this mutual delusion, had charged through each other in a splendid attack before they discovered their error, which was fortunately attended with no worse consequences than a few sabre-cuts. All this was a lesson how dangerous night-attacks always are, and taught me that, whenever possible, they should be avoided.

Our regiments having been collected, and our prisoners

brought together again, we continued our march to Spotsylvania, which we reached without further interruption at
about two in the morning, and our brigade went into
bivouac. I here exchanged my pony for another of the
captured horses, and rode on, with the untiring Stuart, eight
miles further in the direction of Fredericksburg, to General
R. E. Lee's headquarters, where we arrived just at day-break,
and I was enabled to snatch an hour's rest and tranquillity
after all the excitement and fatigue of the night. Our acci-
dental encounter with the enemy turned out of the utmost
importance in its consequences, as the cavalry force with
which we came into collision was, in fact, the advanced-
guard of a much larger force sent by the Federals to destroy
our railway communications—an enterprise which, after this
partial defeat, they abandoned altogether. The main body of
the Federal army, numbering about 100,000 men, had in the
meanwhile centred in the neighbourhood of Chancellorsville,
the three corps coming from the Rapidan having united with
those which had crossed the Rappahannock at United States
and Banks Ford. A strong force still remained opposite
Fredericksburg, watched on our side by Early's division. The
bulk of our army confronted the enemy in line of battle,
almost perpendicularly to the Rappahannock—Anderson's
and M'Laws's divisions of Longstreet's corps forming the
right, Jackson's corps the left wing, our whole numbers
amounting to about 50,000 men.*

---

*General Longstreet himself, with Picket's and Hood's divisions, had some time
since been detailed to North Carolina, where he was operating against a Federal
army in the neighbourhood of Suffolk.

CHAPTER XXI

FIGHT NEAR THE FURNACE — NARROW ESCAPE OF JACK-
SON AND STUART — JACKSON'S FLANK MARCH — FIRST
BATTLE OF THE WILDERNESS, 2D MAY 1863.

AFTER doing a large amount of sleep in a very short time, we started again, considerably refreshed, for Spotsylvania Court-house, to join our cavalry there, and take up our position on Jackson's left. Towards eight o'clock, our entire army commenced a forward movement on the enemy, who had only a few isolated detachments posted in our immediate front. With these a few lively skirmishes occurred, as we encountered them in succession, and drove them gradually before us upon the main body of their troops. For many miles round the country was covered with dense forest, with only occasional patches of open space, so that we made but slow progress, and in many places our cavalry and artillery had to surmount considerable difficulties in their advance. At about four o'clock we reached a place called "The Furnace," from some productive iron-works formerly established there; and having received an intimation from our advanced-guard that a strong body of the enemy's infantry were occupying a position about half a mile further on, immediately across our road, drawn up in line of battle to oppose our advance, Stuart at once ordered the 1st regiment of cavalry to charge. So heavy a fire met our brave fellows, however, and they were so impeded by the nature of the ground, utterly unfit for cavalry operations, that they returned about as quickly as they had started, and we had to remain stationary, awaiting reinforcements from Jackson's infantry. A Georgia brigade soon came up, and, after a short but severe contest, we succeeded in driving the enemy back some distance, till they came under the protection of numerous batteries of their artillery, posted on a ridge of hills, and whose fire thundered down with such fearful effect as to check all further progress. Just at this moment Jackson galloped up, and begged Stuart to ride forward with him in order to reconnoitre the enemy's lines, and find out a point from which the enemy's artillery might be enfiladed.

A small bridle-path branching forth from the main road to the right conducted to a height about half a mile distant; and as this seemed a favourable point for their object, both Generals, accompanied by their Staffs, made for it, followed by six pieces of our horse-artillery. On reaching the spot, so dense was the undergrowth, it was found impossible to find enough clear space to bring more than one gun at a time into position; the others closed up immediately behind, and the whole body of us completely blocked up the narrow road. Scarcely had the smoke of our first shot cleared away when a couple of masked batteries suddenly opened upon us at short range, and enveloped us in a complete storm of shell and canister, which, concentrated on so narrow a space, did fearful execution among our party, men and horses falling right and left, the animals kicking and plunging wildly, and everybody eager to disentangle himself from the confusion and get out of harm's way. Jackson, as soon as he had found out his mistake, ordered the guns to retire; but the confined space so protracted the operation of turning, that the enemy's cannon had full time to continue its havoc to a most fearful extent, covering the road with dead and wounded.

That Jackson and Stuart with their officers escaped was nothing short of miraculous, the only exception being Major Channing Price of our Staff, who was struck a few paces from me by a piece of shell. Poor fellow! imagining that, as no bone was broken, the wound was not dangerous, he remained at his post till he fainted in his saddle from the loss of blood, and had to be carried to a plantation about a mile in our rear. The firing now gradually slackened, and soon ceased altogether as darkness came on. As there was nothing more to be done for the present on our side, and the enemy showed no intention of continuing the fight, Jackson gave orders for the troops to fall back a short distance and go into bivouac. The position of our encampment being quite close to the house whither our wounded comrade had been conveyed, General Stuart accompanied us thither to look after his comforts and nurse him during the night. Sad was the intelligence that awaited us; poor Price was dying. The fragment of shell had severed a principal artery, and, the bleeding not having been stopped in time, he was rapidly and hopelessly sinking. It was a cruel spectacle to see the gallant young fellow stretched on his deathbed surrounded by his sorrowing friends, just able to recognise them and answer the pressure of their hands as a last farewell. His own brother, who had joined us but a few months before, leant over him to the last, watching in silent agony the pitiless progress of death. About midnight our dear friend breathed his last, and General Stuart advised us to seek some rest against the work of the ensuing day, but no sleep could I find. My heart full of grief, and my thoughts busy with memories of the departed and of his family at Richmond, who had become dear friends of mine, I wandered about all through that mild night of May, until the sounding bugle and the rolling drums roused me from my reveries, to summon me to new scenes of death and destruction.

All was bustle and activity as I galloped along the lines, on the morning of the 2d, to obtain, according to Stuart's orders, the latest instructions for our cavalry from General Lee, who was located at a distance of some miles to our right. Anderson's and M'Laws's sharpshooters were advancing, and already exchanging shots with the enemy's skirmishers—the line of battle of these two divisions having been partially extended over the space previously occupied by Jackson's corps, that they might cover its movements. This splendid corps, meanwhile, was marching in close columns in a direction which set us all wondering what could be the intentions of old Stonewall; but as we beheld him riding along, heading the troops himself, we should as soon have thought of questioning the sagacity of our admired chief, as of hesitating to follow him blindly wherever he should lead. The orders to the cavalry were to report to Jackson, and to form his advanced-guard; and in that capacity we marched silently along through the forest, taking a small by-road, which brought us several times so near the enemy's lines that the stroke of axes, mingled with the hum of voices from their camps, was distinctly audible.

Thus commenced the famous flank march which, more than any other operation of the war, proved the brilliant strategical talents of General Lee, and the consummate ability of his lieutenant. About two o'clock a body of Federal cavalry came in sight, making, however, but slight show of resistance, and falling back slowly before us. By about four o'clock we had completed our movement without encountering any material obstacle, and reached a patch of wood in rear of the enemy's right wing, formed by the 11th corps, Howard's, which was encamped in a large open field not more than half a mile distant. Halting here, the cavalry threw

forward a body of skirmishers to occupy the enemy's attention, while the divisions of Jackson's corps, A. P. Hill's,
Colston's, and Rodes's, numbering in all about 28,000 men,
moved into line of battle as fast as they arrived. Ordered to
reconnoitre the position of the Federals, I rode cautiously
forward through the forest, and reached a point whence I
obtained a capital view of the greater part of their troops,
whose attitude betokened how totally remote was any suspicion that a numerous host was so near at hand.

It was evident that the whole movement we had thus so
successfully executed was regarded as merely an unimportant
cavalry raid, for only a few squadrons were drawn up in line
to oppose us, and a battery of four guns was placed in a
position to command the plank-road from Germana, over
which we had been marching for the last two hours. The
main body of the troops were listlessly reposing, while some
regiments were looking on, drawn up on dress parade;
artillery horses were quietly grazing at some distance from
their guns, and the whole scene presented a picture of the
most perfect heedlessness and *nonchalance,* compatible only
with utter unconsciousness of impending danger. While com-
placently gazing on this extraordinary spectacle, somewhat
touched myself apparently with the spell of listless incaution
in which our antagonists were locked, I was startled by the
sound of closely approaching footsteps, and turning in their
direction beheld a patrol of six or eight of the enemy's
infantry just breaking through the bushes, and gazing at me
with most unmistakable astonishment. I had no time to lose
here, that was quite certain; so, quickly tugging my horse's
head round in the direction of my line of retreat, and digging
my spurs into his sides, I dashed off from before the
bewildered Yankees, and was out of sight ere they had time to
take steady aim, the bullets that came whizzing after me
flying far wide of the mark.

On my return to the spot where I had left Stuart, I found him, with Jackson and the officers of their respective Staffs, stretched out along the grass beneath a gigantic oak, and tranquilly discussing their plans for the impending battle, which both seemed confidently to regard as likely to end in a great and important victory for our arms. Towards five o'clock Jackson's adjutant, Major Pendleton, galloped up to us and reported that the line of battle was formed, and all was in readiness for immediate attack. Accordingly the order was at once given for the whole corps to advance. All hastened forthwith to their appointed posts—General Stuart and his Staff joining the cavalry, which was to operate on the left of our infantry. Scarcely had we got up to our men when the Confederate yell, which always preceded a charge, burst forth along our lines, and Jackson's veterans, who had been with difficulty held back till that moment, bounded forward towards the astounded and perfectly paralysed enemy, while the thunder of our horse-artillery, on whom devolved the honour of opening the ball, reached us from the other extremity of the line. The more hotly we sought to hasten to the front, the more obstinately did we get entangled in the undergrowth, while our infantry moved on so rapidly that the Federals were already completely routed by the time we had got thoroughly quit of the forest.

It was a strange spectacle that now greeted us. The whole of the 11th corps had broken at the first shock of the attack; entire regiments had thrown down their arms, which were lying in regular lines on the ground, as if for inspection; suppers just prepared had been abandoned; tents, baggage, waggons, cannons, half-slaughtered oxen, covered the foreground in chaotic confusion, while in the background a host of many thousand Yankees were discerned scampering for their lives as fast as their limbs could carry them, closely followed by our men, who were taking prisoners by the hundreds, and scarcely firing a shot. The broken nature of the ground was against all cavalry operations, and though we pushed forward with all our will, it was with difficulty we could keep up with Jackson's "Foot-cavalry," as this famous infantry was often called. Meanwhile a large part of the Federal army, roused by the firing and the alarming reports from the rear, hastened to the field of action, and exerted themselves in vain to arrest the disgraceful rout of their comrades of the 11th corps. Numerous batteries having now joined the conflict, a terrific cannonade roared along the lines, and the fury of the battle was soon at its full height. Towards dark a sudden pause ensued in the conflict, occasioned by Jackson giving orders for his lines to re-form for the continuation of the combat, the rapid and prolonged pursuit of the enemy having thrown them into considerable disorder. Old Stonewall being thoroughly impressed with the conviction that in a few hours the enemy's whole forces would be defeated, and that their principal line of retreat would be in the direction of Ely's Ford, Stuart was ordered to proceed at once towards that point with a portion of his cavalry, in order to barricade the road, and as much as possible impede the retrograde movement of the enemy.

In this operation we were to be joined by a North Carolina infantry regiment, which was already on its way towards the river. Leaving the greater part of the brigade behind us under Fitz Lee's command, we took only the 1st Virginia Cavalry with us, and, trotting rapidly along a small by-path, overtook the infantry about two miles from the ford. Riding with Stuart a little ahead of our men, I suddenly discovered, on reaching the summit of a slight rise in the road, a large encampment in the valley to our left, not more than a quarter of a mile from where we stood, and further still, on the opposite side of the river, more camp-fires were visible, indicating the presence of a large body of troops. Calling a halt, the General and I rode cautiously forward to reconnoitre the enemy a little more closely, and we managed to approach near enough to hear distinctly the voices and distinguish the figures of the men sitting round their fires, or strolling through the camp. The unexpected presence of so large a body of the enemy immediately in our path entirely disconcerted our previous arrangements. Nevertheless Stuart determined on giving them a slight surprise and disturbing their comfort by a few volleys from our infantry. Just as the regiment, mustering about a thousand, had formed into line according to orders, and was prepared to advance on the enemy, two officers of General A. P. Hill's Staff rode up in great haste and excitement, and communicated something in a low tone to General Stuart, by which he seemed greatly startled and affected. "Take command of that regiment, and act on your own responsibility," were his whispered injunctions to me, as he immediately rode off, followed by the other officers and the cavalry at their topmost speed.

The thunder of the cannon, which for the last hour had increased in loudness, announced that Jackson had recommended the battle, but as to the course or actual position of affairs I had not an iota of information; and my anxiety being moreover increased by the suddenness of Stuart's departure on some unknown emergency, I felt rather awkwardly situated. Here was I in the darkness of the night, in an unknown and thickly-wooded country, some six miles from our main army, and opposite to a far superior force, whom I was expected to attack with troops whom I had never before commanded, and to whom I was scarcely known. I felt, however, that there was no alternative but blind obedience, so I advanced with the regiment to within about fifty yards of the enemy's encampment, and gave the command to fire. A hail of bullets rattled through the forest, and as volley after volley was fired, the confusion and dismay occasioned in the camp was indescribable. Soldiers and officers could be plainly seen by the light of the fires rushing helplessly about, horses were galloping wildly in all directions, and the sound of bugles and drums mingled with the cries of the wounded and flying, who sought in the distant woods a shelter against the murderous fire of their unseen enemy. The troops whom we thus dispersed and put to flight consisted, as I was afterwards informed, of the greater part of Averil's cavalry division; and a great number of the men of this command were so panic-stricken, that they did not consider themselves safe until they had reached the opposite shore of the Rapidan, when they straggled off for miles all through Culpepper County.

Our firing had been kept up for about half an hour, and had by this time stirred up alarm in the camps on the other side of the river, the troops of which were marching on us from various directions. Accordingly, I gave orders to my North Carolinians to retire, leaving the task of bringing his command back to the colonel, while, anxious to rejoin Stuart as soon as possible, I galloped on ahead through the dark forest, whose solemn silence was only broken by the melancholy cry of hosts of whip-poor-wills. The firing had now ceased altogether, and all fighting seemed to have been entirely given up, which greatly increased my misgivings. After a tedious ride for nearly an hour over the field of battle still covered with hundreds of wounded, groaning in their agony, I at last discovered Stuart seated under a solitary plum-tree, busily writing despatches by the dim light of a lantern. From General Stuart I now received the first information of the heavy calamity which had befallen us by the wounding of Jackson. After having instructed his men to fire at everything approaching from the direction of the enemy, in his eagerness to reconnoitre the position of the Federals, and entirely forgetting his own orders, he had been riding with his staff-officers outside our pickets, when on their return, being mistaken for the enemy, the little party were received by a South Carolina regiment with a volley which killed or wounded nearly every man of them, and laid low our beloved Stonewall himself. The Federals advancing at the same time, a severe skirmish ensued, in the course of which one of the bearers of the litter on which the General was being carried was killed, and Jackson fell heavily to the ground, receiving soon afterwards a second wound. For a few minutes, in fact, the General was in the hands of the enemy; but his men, becoming aware of his perilous position, rushed forward, and speedily driving back the advancing foe, carried their wounded commander to the rear.

A. P. Hill, the next in rank, having, soon after this, been likewise disabled, Stuart had been sent for to take the command of Jackson's corps; but meantime the golden opportunity had slipped by, the enemy had been strongly reinforced, and the renewal of the battle was necessarily postponed until the following morning. Stuart's position was one of undoubted difficulty, his knowledge of the position of the troops being, from the suddenness with which he was called to assume the chief command, naturally imperfect, and most of Jackson's Staff were disabled, or were in attendance on their wounded chief. Of his own Staff, only myself and one or two others happened to be present, but we pledged ourselves to exert all our energies, and strain every nerve in aid of our General, and in the discharge of our duty. General Stuart informed me that the attack was to be renewed at the earliest dawn of day; and as that hour was now rapidly approaching, I discarded all idea of sleep, and sat up the rest of the night with poor Lieutenant Hullingham of our Staff, who had been wounded in the shoulder late in the evening, and was suffering intense pain.

CHAPTER XXII

THE BATTLE OF CHANCELLORSVILLE AND CONSEQUENT
EVENTS, MAY 3 TO 6.

THE dawn of this memorable Sunday—destined, as by a
strange series of coincidences had been so many others,
to be a day of fighting instead of rest and prayer—was just
streaking the sky, when I was sent by Stuart to order the
skirmishers to advance; our three divisions, numbering still
about 28,000 men, having in the mean time formed in line of
battle *en échelon* across the Germana plank-road—A. P.
Hill's in the first line, Colston's in the second, and Rodes's in
the third. The bulk of the artillery and cavalry were placed in
reserve, the nature of the ground at the commencement of the
engagement not admitting the employment of more than a
certain number of light batteries acting in concert with the
infantry. General Lee, with Anderson's and M'Laws's divisions, pressed on the enemy from the Fredericksburg side,
and was engaged in quite a distinct battle until towards the
end of the conflict, when his extreme left joined our right, and
the whole of our army operated in one united movement. The
enemy, fully three times our number, occupied a piece of
wood extending about two miles from our immediate front
towards the plateau and open fields round Chancellorsville, a
village consisting of only a few houses. The Federals had

made good use of their time, having thrown up in the wood during the night three successive lines of breastworks, constructed of strong timber, and on the plateau itself, occupied by their reserves, had erected a regular line of redoubts, mounted by their numerous artillery, forty pieces of which were playing on the narrow plank-road. This plateau of Chancellorsville rises abruptly about three hundred yards from the skirts of the forest, and is bordered by a creek with swampy borders, forming a strong natural work of defence. Notwithstanding the fearful odds arrayed against us, the many disadvantages under which we were labouring, and the fatigues of the last few days, during which scarcely any rations had been given out, our men were in excellent spirits, and confident of success. The sharpshooters advanced rapidly through the dense undergrowth, and were soon engaged in a lively skirmish with the tirailleurs of the enemy, whom they speedily drove to the first line of their intrenchments, where a well-directed fire checked the pursuers.

All our divisions now moving forward, the battle soon became general, and the musketry sounded in one continued roll along the lines. Nearly a hundred hostile guns opening fire at the same time, the forest seemed alive with shot, shell, and bullets, and the plank-road, upon which, as was before mentioned, the fire of forty pieces was concentrated, was soon enveloped in a cloud of smoke from the bursting of shells and the explosion of caissons. This road being our principal line of communication, and crowded therefore with ambulances, ammunition-trains, and artillery, the loss of life soon became fearful, and dead and dying men and animals were strewing every part of it. How General Stuart, and those few staff-officers with him who had to gallop to and fro so frequently through this *feu infernal*, escaped unhurt, seems to me quite miraculous. Several of our couriers were wounded; one had a leg torn from his body by a cannon-ball while I was in the act of giving him some directions, and died soon afterwards. General Stuart had a horse killed under him in the first half-hour of the fight, and my own was twice wounded, first in the back by a musket-ball, and next in the chest by a piece of shell, from the effects of which it died the following morning, though it was fortunately able to carry me through the day. Stuart was all activity, and wherever the danger was greatest there was he to be found, urging the men forward, and animating them by the force of his example. The shower of missiles that hissed through the air passed round him unheeded; and in the midst of the hottest fire I heard him, to an old melody, hum the words, "Old Joe Hooker get out of the Wilderness."

After a raging conflict, protracted for several hours, during which the tide of battle ebbed and flowed on either side, we succeeded in taking the advanced works, and driving the enemy upon their third line of intrenchments, of a still stronger character than those before it. This partial success was only gained with a sad sacrifice of life, while countless numbers were seen limping and crawling to the rear. The woods had caught fire in several places from the explosion of shells—the flames spreading principally, however, over a space of several acres in extent where the ground was thickly covered with dry leaves; and here the conflagration progressed with the rapidity of a prairie-fire, and a large number of Confederate and Federal wounded thickly scattered in the vicinity, and too badly hurt to crawl out of the way, met a terrible death. The heartrending cries of the poor victims, as the flames advanced, entreating to be rescued from their impending fate—entreaties which it was impossible to heed in the crisis of the battle, and amidst duties on which the lives of many others depended—seem still in my ears. Among the heart-sickening scenes of this terrible conflict which are still vivid in my memory, is one no lapse of time can ever efface, and in contemplating which I scarcely could check the tears from starting to my eyes. Riding to the front, I was hailed by a young soldier, whose boyish looks and merry songs on the march had frequently attracted my attention and excited my interest, and who was now leaning against a tree, the life-blood streaming down his side from a mortal wound, and his face white with the pallor of approaching death. "Major," said the poor lad, "I am dying, and I shall never see my regiment again; but I ask you to tell my comrades that the Yankees have killed but not conquered me." When I passed the place again half an hour afterwards I found him a corpse. Such was the universal spirit of our men, and in this lay the secret of many of our wonderful achievements.

The enemy had in the meanwhile been strongly reinforced, and now poured forth from their third line of intrenchments a fire so terrible upon our advancing troops that the first two divisions staggered, and, after several unsuccessful efforts to press onward, fell back in considerable confusion. In vain was it that our officers used every effort to bring them forward once more; in vain even was it that Stuart, snatching the battle-flag of one of our brigades from the hands of the colour-bearer and waving it over his head, called on them as he rode forward to follow him. Nothing could induce them again to face that tempest of bullets, and that devastating hurricane of grape and canister vomited at close range from more than sixty pieces of artillery, and the advantages so dearly gained seemed about to be lost. At this critical moment, we suddenly heard the yell of Rodes's division behind us, and saw these gallant troops, led by their heroic general, charge over the front lines, and fall upon the enemy with such impetus that in a few minutes their works were taken, and they were driven in rapid flight from the woods to their redoubts on the hills of Chancellorsville.

A slight pause now intervened in the conflict, both sides,

after the terrible work of the last few hours, being equally willing to draw breath awhile; and this gave us a opportunity to re-form our lines and close up our decimated ranks. The contest, meanwhile, was sustained by the artillery alone, which kept up a heavy cannonade; and the nature of the ground being now more favourable, most of our batteries had been brought into action, while from a hill on our extreme right, which had only been abandoned by the enemy after the charge of Rodes's division, twenty 12-pounder Napoleons played with a well-directed flank-fire upon the enemy's works, producing a terrible effect upon their dense masses. About half-past ten we had news from General Lee, informing us that, having been pressing steadily forward the entire morning, he had now, with Anderson's and M'Laws's divisions, reached our right wing. I was at once despatched by Stuart to the Commander-in-Chief to report the state of affairs, and obtain his orders for further proceedings. I found him with our twenty-gun battery, looking as calm and dignified as ever, and perfectly regardless of the shells bursting round him, and the solid shot ploughing up the ground in all directions. General Lee expressed himself much satisfied with our operations, and intrusted me with orders for Stuart, directing a general attack with his whole force, which was to be supported by a charge of Anderson's division on the left flank of the enemy. With renewed courage and confidence our three divisions now moved forward upon the enemy's strong position on the hills, encountering, as we emerged from the forest into the open opposite the plateau of Chancellorsville, such a storm of canister and bullets, that for a while it seemed an impossibility to take the heights in the face of it. Suddenly we heard to our right, piercing the roar and tumult of the battle, the yell of Anderson's men, whom we presently beheld hurled forward in a brilliant charge, sweeping everything before them. Short work was now made of the Federals, who, in a few minutes, were driven from their redoubts, which they abandoned in disorderly flight, leaving behind them cannons, small-arms, tents, and baggage in large quantities, besides a host of prisoners, of whom we took 360 in one redoubt.

A more magnificent spectacle can hardly be imagined than that which greeted me when I reached the crest of the plateau, and beheld on this side the long lines of our swiftly advancing troops stretching as far as the eye could reach, their red flags fluttering in the breeze, and their arms glittering in the morning sun; and farther on, dense and huddled masses of the Federals flying in utter rout towards the United States Ford, whilst high over our heads flew the shells which our artillery were dropping amidst the crowd of the retreating foe. The Chancellorsville House had caught fire, and was now enveloped in flames, so that it was with difficulty that we could save some portion of the Federal wounded lying there, to the number of several hundreds, the majority of whom perished. In this building General Hooker had fixed his headquarters, and hence he had directed the battle, until a shell, striking the roof of the porch within which he stood, brought down such an overwhelming heap of plaster and stones upon his head, that he was taken up from the ground insensible, and for more than an hour was unable to attend to his duties. The flight and pursuit took the direction of United States Ford, as far as about a mile beyond Chancellorsville, where another strong line of intrenchments offered their protection to the fugitives, and heavy reserves of fresh troops opposed our further advance.

Eight hours of severe fighting had now considerably exhausted our troops, and General Lee, having sent me off at about 11 o'clock A.M. to recall the advanced division, ordered the whole army to halt and rest for the present. The next few hours passed away in comparative quietude, interrupted only at intervals by cannonading, or the more brisk firing of the skirmishers, and it soon became evident that the battle would not be renewed that day. Our men had in the mean time occupied themselves throwing up a line of intrenchments along the plank-road, as a protection against a sudden rush of the enemy, and were now some of them engaged in tending the wounded and burying our dead, while others were busying themselves cooking the rations left behind them in abundance by the Federals. I was myself suffering severely from hunger, having eaten little or nothing for several days, and coming upon an apparently well-stored haversack fastened on the back of one of the disfigured corpses on the field, I was held back by no morbid loathings from helping myself to its contents, and enjoyed a hearty meal off the dead Yankee's provisions—a thing which not many months before would have seemed to me impossible. Even my negro Henry was affected with more squeamishness, for I soon afterwards met him, after he had been collecting a heap of plunder, which so loaded my poor mule Kitt as to leave only her legs visible, standing wistfully beside a fine pair of boots upon a dead Yankee's feet, and eyeing them, with his finger in his mouth, and a most melancholy expression of regret and longing on this black visage. Knowing how much the fellow was really in want of such articles, I advised him to possess himself of them before some one else was beforehand with him, when he whined out, "Oh! I like so much to have them boots, but I can't; I'se afraid de ghost of dis 'ere Yankee come in de night and take dem dar boots back agin." And nothing could persuade this generally enterprising darkey from despoiling the dead, although he would have had little hesitation in cutting a living man's throat for the sake of the same alluring prize.

In the course of the afternoon a heavy cannonade came booming over to us from Frederisckburg, and early in the evening it was reported to General Lee that, after a sanguinary conflict, our troops, yielding to far superior numbers, had been driven from the heights opposite that town, and the hostile forces were pressing forward in the direction of Chancellorsville. This startling intelligence, rendering our position now a very precarious one, was received by our Command-in-Chief with a quietude, and an absence of all emotion, which I could not but intensely admire. Referring, with the utmost calmness, to Sedgwick's advance, he quietly made his dispositions, ordering M'Laws's division to march to the support of Early, who had been retreating to Salem Church—a place about five miles from Fredericksburg. By this firm and tranquil demeanour did General Lee inspire confidence and sanguine hope of success in all around him. Notwithstanding our extreme fatigue, the whole of the latter part of the evening we were busy carrying water to the wounded, hundreds of whom still lay in the field, it being impossible to convey so large a number to the hospitals before night. Nor did we cease our merciful task till after darkness had set in, when we returned to the centre of the plateau, where in the mean time Stuart had temporarily established his headquarters. Here we found General Lee and Stuart seated by a small bivouac-fire discussing the day's events, and speculating on the chances of a continuation of the battle; and here, too, I found my Prussian friend, Captain Scheibert, greatly elated over an adventure he had met with in the early part of the day, his original way of recounting which greatly amused us all.

He had been riding my black horse, for which he had a particular affection; and in the hope of procuring provender for it, which it much needed—perhaps, too, actuated by like intentions on his own account—he determined, after the actual fighting was over, to make an excursion to some of the neighbouring houses. Neither knowing anything of the adjacent country, nor of the relative positions of the armies, he started off straight in the direction of the enemy; and coming up to a small plantation, where he made sure he should find all he wanted, he encountered six Yankees, armed with muskets, coming out of the house towards him. Scheibert, well aware that the worst thing he could do would be to turn tail, with admirable presence of mind drew his sword; and, flourishing it wildly over his head, rode up to the astonished Yankee, crying out, in broken English, "Surrender, you scoundrels! all my cavalry is right behind me." The bewildered soldiers at once dropped their arms, and the gallant Prussian marched the whole six triumphantly back to General Lee, by whom he was highly complimented for his coolness and pluck. A rapid succession of despatches and reports reached our Commander-in-Chief during the night, which he had considerable difficulty in deciphering by the flickering light of the bivouac-fire. Like Longfellow's Ajax, his prayer was for light "throughout that long and dreary night." It so chanced that, during our advance on Chancellorsville, I had discovered, among other luxuries, a box of excellent candles, which now lay a little outside our lines, and quite close to the enemy's skirmishers. To attempt the adventure with the hope of bringing the much-desired relief to the eyes of our beloved commander, was more than I could resist, so I set forward on foot towards the spot, crawling cautiously through the bushes, and, favoured by the darkness, succeeded in finding the box, and providing myself with a sufficient provision of candles, without attracting the attention of the enemy's videttes. On reaching the temporary headquarters, and presenting my prize to General Lee, he eyed me with his calm penetrating glance, and said, "Major, I am much obliged to you; but I know where you got these candles, and you acted wrongly in exposing your life for a simple act of courtesy." I willingly submitted to the rebuke, only too happy to have been able personally to oblige one whom we all so much admired, and for whom not one of us but would gladly have risked his life.

During the night we were allowed but little sleep, frequent alarms calling us into the saddle; moreover, the place which Stuart had selected for our repose, because it was close to the centre of our lines, being also exactly in range of the hostile artillery, which opened whenever the skirmishing grew louder, we were several times roused from our slumbers by shells plunging all around us, one of which actually burst in the top of a cherry-tree under which I reposed, covering me with a litter of torn and scattered branches. Not more than 150 yards from us, in and around a large barn, were collected more than 300 Federal wounded, and the tenement which sheltered them being ever and anon struck by the cannon-balls, the pitiful cries of the poor fellows, many of whom were finally despatched, while others received fresh wounds, added to the horrors and confusion of this dreadful night. The morning of the 4th was fraught, in like manner, with excitement and disquiet; at times the skirmishing and the cannonade which followed it grew so warm as to lead, until about ten o'clock, to the expectation of an advance of the Federal army. About noon, however, everything sank into tranquillity again, and we were enabled to continue our ministrations towards the wounded, and to bury our dead. All the Federal dead, however, as well as the innumerable carcasses of animals, still encumbered the ground, and the effuvium was already growing unpleasant. But I will not attempt to go into the horrors of this battle-field; they surpassed all that I had ever seen before, the fearful effect of the artillery firing going beyond all that had occurred on any previous occasion. In the course of the afternoon we received cheerful news of the proceedings of M'Laws and Early, who, attacking the enemy simultaneously, had succeeded in forcing them back upon Fredericksburg, retaking the heights, and finally, by a spirited attack, driving the whole of Sedgwick's corps to the other side of the river. Several ammunition and provision trains, besides prisoners, had fallen into our hands, and, but for the extreme caution of our generals, the whole of this portion of the hostile forces might have been annihilated.

The night of this day passed over much in the same way as its predecessor, and was followed by a misty, sultry morning; and this kind of weather promoting the process of putrefaction, the air was poisoned with emanations from the dead to such an extent as to be almost insupportable. There being, moreover, danger of the men's health being affected, all that could be spared from the front were employed burying the hundreds of disfigured corpses. The enemy being very quiet all the morning, Stuart, suspecting a retrograde movement of their army, ordered our skirmishers to advance, who discovered soon enough, however, that the Federals were still in large force in our front, and posted behind works of a formidable character. Accordingly, after a severe skirmish, accompanied by a heavy cannonade, lasting more than an hour, our men were withdrawn to their original position. The afternoon brought a sudden change in the weather; the temperature fell considerably for the season of the year, and heavy rain, with violent winds, continued all the evening and a great part of the night. Meanwhile General Lee had determined to assault the enemy in their strong position. M'Laws's and Anderson's divisions had already approached United States Ford on the 5th, by a circuitous march, thus menacing the left flank and line of retreat of the Federal army; and at earliest dawn on the 6th Jackson's corps received orders to advance, Rodes's division taking the lead. My own instructions from General Stuart having been to move forward with the skirmishers and reconnoitre the enemy's position as closely as possible, I cautiously made my way through the woods, expecting at every instant to hear the skirmishers open fire, followed by the thunder of the artillery; but finding all quiet, I continued to advance until I reached the formidable intrenchments thrown up by the Federals, extending several miles, which I found they had entirely abandoned, leaving behind in them a large quantity of ammunition and stores of provisions, which they had not taken time to destroy. Just as I was entering the fortifications, General Rodes rode up, saying, "I am sure the enemy is in full retreat, and is probably by this time on the other side of the river." Both of us being equally eager to discover what had really become of the great Federal army, we galloped off entirely by ourselves along the muddy road, leaving everybody behind.

General Hooker had done wonders amidst the difficulties of this wild entangled forest. Works of great strength and extent had been constructed at nearly every quarter of a mile's distance; roads had been cut and cleared through the dense undergrowth, along which telegraph wires were laid to the principal headquarters of the army; and wherever branch-roads turned off to the different corps, divisions, and brigades, large signs were conspicuously erected to guard against mistakes or confusion. Notwithstanding these wise precautions, however, considerable numbers of the Yankee soldiers became mazed amidst these extensive woods, and we continually encountered them along our route, sometimes in squads of six or eight. These poor devils, all bespattered with mud, and soaked to their skins by the drenching rain, not recognising us as enemies, our grey uniforms being concealed beneath large india-rubber cloaks, innocently accosted us to inquire the way towards their regiments, and on discovering our real character, surrendered with alacrity, laying down their arms, and marching off rapidly to the rear at our request, as submissively as though they had been our own men. General Rodes and I in this way captured, merely our two selves, more than sixty of these stragglers, who, had they been tempted to act at all pluckily, might easily either have killed or made prisoners of us both. We had not far to ride in order to discover that the hostile army had entirely disappeared from our side of the Rappahannock; and as we approached the river, we could just catch sight of their rearguard climbing the hills on the opposite shore, where several batteries of artillery were placed in position, while a number of riflemen were posted along the banks of the stream. With these our sharpshooters, on coming up, became engaged in a slight skirmish, and we were favoured with several shots from the hostile batteries; but soon even these parting tokens of farewell from Hooker's great army were discontinued, and, vanishing entirely, it ceased to give forth any sign.

Seeing his army greatly demoralised by a succession of defeats, and all his plans and combinations frustrated, General Hooker had already on the previous day determined to withdraw his troops to the other side of the Rappahannock, the waters of which were rapidly rising, and threatened to carry away the pontoon-bridges, and render retreat impossible. The retrograde movement was commenced at about dusk on the 5th, and was conducted with considerable order; the bridges had been covered with layers of twigs and small branches, in order to deaden the rumbling sound of the artillery and trains passing over them, while the heavy fall of rain during the evening, followed up by bursts of thunderstorm in the night, completely masked the sounds of the retreating hosts, whose movements, exactly as at Fredericksburg under similar circumstances, entirely escaped in vigilance of our pickets. As Hooker was retracing his course back towards his old position near Falmouth, so did our troops commence at about noon their march towards their old camping-ground near Fredericksburg. A. P. Hill, having now entirely recovered from his slight wound, assumed the command of Jackson's corps; and as his men marched past us they spontaneously raised an enthusiastic cheer for General Stuart, thus testifying their admiration of the gallant chief who had led them so splendidly against the enemy, and directed them to the achievement of a brilliant victory, and one for which, in my opinion, Stuart never gained sufficient credit from his superiors. Thus ended the battle of Chancellorsville, and the short but decisive spring campaign. The losses of the Federal army amounted to at least 20,000 men, of whom nearly 8000 were made prisoners. There were captured, besides, thirty pieces of artillery, large quantities of ammunition, and more than 30,000 stand of small-arms. The loss on our side was severe, amounting to nearly 10,000 men in prisoners, killed, and wounded—our beloved and ever-famous Stonewall being among the latter, a fact which filled every soldier's heart with grief. It was not at that time at all anticipated that Jackson's wounds would end fatally; and several days after the unfortunate incident, I heard from the mouth of the surgeon who attended him, that the General was doing very well, and that from the state of his health at that time there was every prospect of his speedy recovery.

General Hooker, after all his disasters, had the audacity to speak of his operations as successful; and, in order to blind the eyes of the North to the true state of affairs, he ended his campaign by issuing to his soldiers an order congratulating them on their achievements and success.

CHAPTER XXIII

WHILST the bulk of our army was marching in the
direction of Fredericksburg, General Stuart and his
Staff started with Fitz Lee's brigade towards Spotsylvania
Court-house, where we arrived late in the evening, and our
regiment went into bivouac. Quite close to the camp was Mr
F.'s plantation; here, during the winter, I had been a frequent
visitor, and in consideration of the hardships and fatigues we
had already undergone, General Stuart acceded to my friend's
invitation to make his house our headquarters for the night.
Accordingly the supper-hour found us all assembled round
Mr F.'s hospitable and well-furnished board, the honours of
which were done by the pretty young ladies of the family; and
under these advantageous circumstances we once more relished the comforts of life with a zest which only soldiers feel
after the privations of a rough campaign. It seemed that I had
but just lain down to sleep when I heard Stuart's voice in the
morning calling me up to ride with him to General Lee's,

whose headquarters were fixed in the old spot near Fredericksburg. Here we first heard of Stoneman's raid in the direction of Richmond. Leaving one of his brigades to occupy William Lee's command, the General, with a body of several thousand cavalry, had crossed the Rapidan, struck the Richmond-Gordonsville Railway at Louisa Court-house, and, pushing to within four miles of the Confederate capital, had taken a multitude of negroes and horses, capturing, besides, a number of trains, and several hundreds of our wounded soldiers on their way to the hospitals. Both our lines of railway communication having been damaged, and the telegraph wires cut, it was not till unfortunately late that we received this disastrous news. In the hope there might yet be a chance of cutting off the retreat of the Federal raiders, our Commander-in-Chief ordered Stuart to set out at once in pursuit of them; and a few hours later we were making our way through the woods with Fitz Lee's brigade in the direction of Gordonsville. After marching all night, we learned at daybreak that the whole Federal raiding force, turning from Richmond towards the White House, had crossed the Pamunkey river, and was now entirely beyond our reach. This, of course, completely altered the plans of our General; and as we were then not far from Orange Court-house, where our trains had been ordered to assemble, and we were sure to find supplies both for man and beast, thither, after a short rest, it was determined to march. None more than myself welcomed the order to halt, for the only charger I had now left was completely broken down, and my servant Henry, leading a Yankee horse I had captured after Chancellorsville, was still far off. Badly off as I was in this particular, I was delighted to hear of a magnificent horse for sale at a plantation in Louisa County; and permission having been readily granted me by General Stuart, I set off thither, accompanied by one of our couriers as a guide, and a few hours later the command continued its march towards Orange. On reaching my destination, I found the animal far exceeded all my expectations. He was a tall thoroughbred bay, of beautiful form and action, and the price demanded being comparatively cheap—namely, a thousand dollars—I at once concluded the bargain; and after spending the rest of the day and the night beneath Mr T.'s hospitable roof, I rode off towards Orange just as the first cheerful beams of the morning sun were darting through the fresh green masses of the gigantic chestnuts and beeches which hemmed round the plantation, happy in the consciousness that the fine animal curvetting under me with such elastic steps was my own. As, *en route*, I had to pass by the little village of Verdiersville, where, it will be remembered, I had such a narrow escape in August '62, I stopped to pay my respects to the kind lady who had so courageously assisted me in my retreat. I had never failed to do so whenever chance brought me to the neighbourhood, and always found myself received with the most cordial welcome. On this occasion, however, I was not destined to meet the same kind of reception; for, instead of the cheerful greeting to which I had been accustomed, the old lady, as soon as she caught sight of me, turned suddenly pale, and, with a loud shriek, fled into the house. Puzzled beyond measure at so extraordinary a proceeding, I pressed for an explanation, when a Richmond paper was handed to me and my attention directed to a paragraph commencing, "Among those who fell at the battle of Chancellorsville we regret to report the death of Major von Borcke," &c. Here followed a flattering estimate of my personal qualities, and a minute account of my death. My amiable friend was so firmly impressed with the fact of my demise, that when I accosted her she believed it was my ghost; and even during our subsequent interview I found some difficulty in persuading her of my identity. The rumour of my having been killed spread over the whole country, and was accepted as true by every part of our army where I had not been seen since the battle, and the regret expressed at my loss, and manifest pleasure exhibited by both soldiers and citizens to know me still among them, administered not a little to my self-esteem. Beside the many letters of condolence and offers received by Stuart on my account, greatly to his amusement, a request was despatched by Governor Letcher to General Lee to have my body forwarded, and claiming the privilege of having it interred with all the honours of the State of Virginia. To this demand, General Lee sent the following characteristic reply: "Can't spare it: it's in pursuit of Stoneman."

Our headquarters were established on one of the hills forming a semicircle round one side of the beautiful little valley in which the pleasant village of Orange Court-house is situated, and we overlooked the town, as well as a great part of the rich country around it, clad in the fresh bright verdure of May. The weather was perfect; provisions of every sort were abundant, and men and beasts were rapidly recovering from the fatigues and privations of the late rough campaign. Orange enjoys an enviable renown for the beauty of its women; and in the female society which it afforded we took every opportunity our duties permitted to pass a few agreeable hours, which were sometimes devoted to dancing and sometimes to horseback excursions. A cloud soon came over our happiness, however, in the sad news of the death of our beloved Stonewall Jackson, who expired on the 9th, partially from his wounds, but more directly from pneumonia, the result of a severe cold which he caught on the night when he was struck, and which the treatment he insisted on adopting rendered thus fatal.* Few men have ever been more

---

*The immediate cause of Jackson's death is not generally known. I received the particulars of it from Dr M'Guire, who attended the General, and who told me

regretted—few more respected by foe, no less than friend, than was Stonewall Jackson; and his soldiers grieved over his death as though they had been bereft of a father. To me it was a sad blow to lose at once a kind and dear friend and a leader for whom I felt the heartiest admiration. Brought so frequently into contact with this great soldier in the field of battle or in camp, where he often shared his blankets with me when I had come to him late at night, bringing in my reports, or applying for orders, I had every opportunity of estimating, both in its grandeur and in its familiar traits, his noble and generous character. Jackson had certain whimsical peculiarities which exhibited themselves in his manner and in his dress, but most of the stories current at the time, turning upon his eccentricities, were entire fabrications. He was a sincerely pious man, but without a taint of Puritanism, and enjoyed the pleasure of life and a harmless joke as much as anybody. His conversation was lively and fascinating, and he would often chime in with us in our merry talk and laughter round the camp-fires. For General Lee his admiration and affection were alike unbounded; and, in the native modesty of his character, he as persistently undervalued his own services. Concerning these he would often say, "All the credit of my successes belongs to General Lee; they were his plans on which I acted, and I only executed his orders." But General Lee knew full well how to appreciate the great military qualities of his lieutenant, and the value of his assistance; and when the news reached him of the hero's death, he exclaimed, "It would have been better for the country if I had fallen rather than Stonewall Jackson." The

---

that, against his urgent dissuasion, he had insisted on treating his cold by the application of wet blankets, which so aggravated its severity that, weakened as was his system by loss of blood and the shock of amputation, this imprudence became fatal.

sad intelligence was officially communicated to his mourning army by the Commander-in-Chief in the following order, dated the 11th:—

"The daring will and energy of this great and good soldier, by a decree of an all-wise Providence, are now lost to us; but while we mourn his death, we feel that his spirit lives, and will inspire the whole army with his indomitable courage and unshaken confidence in God, as our hope and our strength. Let his name be a watchword for his corps, who have followed him to victory in so many fields. Let officers and soldiers imitate his invincible determination to do everything in the defence of our beloved country.

"R. E. Lee."

According to his wish, Jackson's remains were buried at Lexington, Virginia, where in his simple grave he now sleeps, while his memory lives fresh in the hearts of all who knew him, and both hemispheres regard him as the greatest of those who fell for their principles in this gigantic civil war.

The remaining weeks of the beautiful month of May passed away in quiet, so far as regards any interruption on the part of the enemy; but were actively employed in preparations for the summer campaign, and in reorganising our whole army, the ranks of which were rapidly filled by the return of the absentees, and strengthened by the arrival of numerous reinforcements—Longstreet having been recalled with his two divisions from North Carolina, and several brigades joined to these from Beauregard's army. The army of Northern Virginia was now divided into three equal and distinct corps, each numbering about 20,000 men. Longstreet commanded the 1st corps, consisting of Hood's, M'Laws's, and Picket's divisions; Ewell the 2d, consisting of Early's, Rodes's, and Johnson's divisions, formerly under Jackson's command, and now committed to this general in accordance with a request made by Stonewall on his deathbed, in his solicitude for the welfare of his veterans. The 3d corps was placed under the command of A. P. Hill, and was formed of Anderson's, Pender's, and Heth's divisions. The cavalry, which had also been strengthened by several new brigades from the South, was formed into a separate corps of three divisions, commanded by Hampton, Fitz Lee, and William Lee. About the 18th of May, General Lee, who had continued to confront the enemy at Fredericksburg, began gradually to shift the position of his troops towards Gordonsville and Orange. The cavalry had to give place to the infantry, and on the 20th we received orders to march to Culpepper Courthouse, where we established our headquarters, close to the old camping ground, stationing our divisions nearer the river, which was again closely picketed. Our tents were pitched in a beautiful spot, overshadowed by magnificent hickory and tulip-poplar trees, and surrounded by broad clover fields, where our horses were richly pastured, and through which the pretty little river "Mountain Run" rolled its silver waters between picturesque banks, and afforded us the chance of a magnificent cool bath, and plenty of sport with the rod and line. Our cavalry were in the highest spirits, and were kept in constant and salutary activity by incessant drilling and other preparations for the impending campaign. Hundreds of men flocked in daily from their distant homes, bringing with them fresh horses. General Robertson had joined us with his splendid brigade from North Carolina, as also had General Jones, with his command from the valley of Virginia; and nearly all the men of Hampton's division had returned from South Carolina and Mississippi. Our horse-artillery, under command of Pelham's successor, Major Berkham, had been augmented by several batteries, and the old ones had been supplied with fresh horses, so that altogether we now possessed a more numerous and better equipped force then ever before.

We all looked with pride upon this magnificent body of troops; and as a review had been ordered for the 5th of June, all the commencement of the month we were busy preparing for that important event. Invitations having been sent out to the whole circle of our acquaintances far and near, the hotels of the town, and as many private houses as had any accommodation to spare, were got ready for the reception of our guests, many of whom, after all, we had to put under tents. Among those we expected on this occasion, was General Randolph, the former Secretary of War, a warm friend of Stuart's and mine, and to whom it will be remembered I was indebted for so much kindness on my first arrival in Richmond. Gladly eager to give him a proof of my esteem, and the sense I had of his kindness, I started off on the morning of the 4th for Gordonsville, to meet our friend on his road, and I had the pleasure of bringing him by special train into Culpepper with all honours, our battle-flag floating from the locomotive. Every train that afternoon brought in fresh crowds of our guests, and we all assembled at the station to receive them, and forward them to their destination by the ambulances and waggons we had got prepared for that purpose. In the evening there was a ball at the Town Hall, which went off pleasantly enough, although it was not, in the language of the reporter, "a gay and dazzling scene, illuminated by floods of light streaming from numerous chandeliers," for our supply of light was limited to a few tallow candles; and when the moon rose, we were glad to avail ourselves of her services by adjourning to the spacious verandah. As the morning of the 5th dawned bright and beautiful, we completed our preparations, and gave the last touch to our arms and equipments; and about eight o'clock General Stuart and his Staff mounted their horses and made for the plains of Brandy Station, which that day were for once to be the scene, not of a battle in all its sanguinary tumult, but of a military spectacle comparatively peaceful in character. Our little band presented a gay and gallant appearance as we rode forth to the sound of our bugles, all mounted on fine chargers, and clad in our best accoutrements, our plumes nodding, and our battle-flag waving in the breeze. I myself had on a uniform new from head to foot; and the horse on which I was mounted seemed to me in the very perfection of beauty as it danced with springing step upon the turf, its glossy coat shining like burnished gold in the morning sun. As our approach was heralded by the flourish of trumpets, many of the ladies in the village came forth to greet us from the porches and verandahs of the houses, and showered down flowers upon our path. But if the smiles and patriotic demonstrations of the daughters of old Virginia were pleasant and flattering to us as mortal men, not less grateful to our soldiers' hearts were the cheers of more than 12,000 horsemen, which rose in the air as we came upon the open plain near Brandy Station, where the whole cavalry corps awaited us, drawn out in a line a mile and a half long, at the extreme right of which twenty-four guns of our horse-artillery thundered forth a salute. About ten o'clock the marching past commenced. General Stuart had taken up his position on a slight eminence, whither many hundreds of spectators, mostly ladies, had gathered, in ambulances and on horseback, anxiously awaiting the approach of the troops. The corps passed first by squadrons, and at a walk, and the magnificent spectacle of so many thousand troopers splendidly mounted made the heart swell with pride, and impressed one with the conviction that nothing could resist the attack of such a body of troops. The review ended with a sham charge of the whole corps by regiments, the artillery advancing at the same time at a gallop, and opening a rapid fire upon an imaginary enemy. The day wound up with a ball; but as the night was fine we danced in the open air on a piece of turf near our headquarters, and by the light of enormous wood-fires, the ruddy glare of which upon the animated groups of our assembly gave to the whole scene a wild and romantic effect.

Our army having been all this while slowly approaching Culpepper, division after division, on the 7th we marched by order of General Lee, who was now among us, closer to the Rappahannock, taking up our headquarters on the heights near Brandy Station. Next day the cavalry corps had the honour of being reviewed by our Commander-in-Chief, but this time the spectators were no longer ladies, our fair visitors having departed, but the whole of Hood's division, amounting to about 10,000 men, who were present as lookers-on, at their own request. No sooner was the review over than a courier galloped up with the report that the enemy had made his appearance in strong force on the river. This called us at once to the front with several brigades, and for a time we were in momentary expectation of a serious engagement. After some demonstrations, however, at the different fords, which were promptly met by our pickets, the Yankees disappeared again, and our troops marched back to their camps. On my return to headquarters I found, to my intense disgust, that my negro servant Harry having, against orders, turned two of my horses and Kitt my mule loose, they had straggled off, and every effort to find them had till then failed. To lose my steeds thus, on the very eve of active operations, was a serious affair; horses were stolen daily, and among the thousands of animals assembled around us, it was a difficult matter to find them again. I was the more put out, as by bad luck I had been splendidly mounted, having, besides my new purchase, which was still left me, two fine chargers—a stout bay which I had from Major Berkham, the chief of our horse-artillery, in exchange for my captured Yankee horse, and my old black, which was now in fine condition. All the rest of the day was spent in further efforts to discover the stray animals, till at last I returned late at night, tired and out of humour, to the camp.

After a few hours' sleep I was awakened about day-break by the sound of several cannon-shots. In an instant I was on my legs, and stepping out of my tent I distinctly heard a brisk firing of small-arms in the direction of the river. An orderly shortly afterwards rode up, reporting that the enemy, under cover of the fog, had suddenly fallen upon our pickets, had crossed the river in strong force at several points, and pressed forward so rapidly that they had come upon Jones's brigade before the greater part of the men had had time to saddle their horses. It was fortunate that the sharpshooters of this command, seconded by a section of our horse-artillery, were enabled by a well-directed fire to impede the movements of the attacking foe, so as to give our regiments time to form, and by falling back some distance to take up a position further to the rear. It was evident, both to General Stuart and myself, that the intentions of the Federals in this movement were of a serious character, and that they were determined on making a further advance, although we differed in opinion as to the best way of opposing resistance to them. The General wished to march with his whole force against the enemy, and fight them wherever he might meet them. My proposal was to place the greater part of the corps and our 24 guns on the heights, and wait there till the designs of the Yankees, who were still hidden by the woods, and their numbers, should be more clearly disclosed, and then, by offering a feint with a few of our advanced brigades, to draw them towards us. As no favourable position for their artillery would be found in the plains, our guns would play with great effect on their dense ranks when they emerged into the open before us, and for once our horsemen would have a chance of showing their superiority over the hostile cavalry by a united charge of our whole force. But Stuart's ardour was impatient of delay; and being, besides, under the impression that to allow the enemy to proceed further would let them know too much of the position of our infantry, which it was our duty to cover, he resolved to move at once against the advancing foe, and gave me orders to ride to the front and rapidly reconnoitre the state of affairs, while he would follow as quickly as the troops could be brought into action. Major Berkham had hastily placed some of his batteries in position upon an eminence which I had just passed, and was reaching a patch of wood where Jones's men were engaged in a sharp skirmish with the Federals, when in overwhelming numbers they made a sudden dash upon the most advanced regiment of that brigade, which broke in utter confusion, carrying everything with them in their flight. A scene of disgraceful stampede ensued—single horsemen galloped off the field in all directions, waggons and ambulances which had been detained to carry off camp utensils rattled over the ground, while with loud shouts of victory a dense mass of Federal horsemen broke froth from the woods. At this critical moment Berkham opened a rapid fire, throwing such a shower of canister and grape at close range upon the pursuing host, that they recoiled and retired again into the forest, thus affording an opportunity of rallying and re-forming our demoralised troops. Just as the confusion was at its height, my eye alighted on my little mule Kitt, on which one of the waggoners was mounted, and was passing me at full speed. The temptation to recover this valuable piece of property was not to be withstood, even under the exciting circumstances of the occasion; and quickly overtaking the fellow, I ordered him to give up my property, but the fear of falling into the hands of the enemy so possessed the poor devil that he begged to be allowed to bring it back to me at headquarters. Thinking, however, it was only a just punishment on him to let him make good his escape by the aid of his own legs, I made him dismount, and sent Kitt to the rear by one of the couriers who accompanied me, where Henry greeted the return of his favourite with every mark of delight. All our brigades having now arrived from the more distant camps, our line of battle, nearly three miles in length, could be regularly formed; and along the woods which border the Rappahannock the multitudinous firing of our dismounted sharpshooters sounded like the rattle of musketry in a regular battle. We held our ground tolerably well for some time, but it soon became evident that the enemy were in far superior numbers and supported by infantry, large columns of which were reported by William Lee, who commanded on our extreme left, to be crossing the river. Towards this point I was sent by General Stuart to watch the movements of the enemy, with orders to send a report every quarter of an hour by one of the body of couriers whom I took with me. William Lee's brigade was placed on a ridge of hills, with its skirmishers on the river-bank and along a formidable stone fence running across an open field, over which the Federals advanced in strong numbers, but were again and again repulsed as soon as they came within range of our sharpshooters, who were well seconded by the accurate firing of one of our batteries on the heights. Buried in the deep grass, William Lee and I lay close to our guns watching the progress of the battle, when we were startled by a heavy cannonade in our rear, apparently in the direction of our headquarters at Brandy Station. Thither I hastened off at once, promising General Lee to send him information as soon as I had discovered the state of affairs. From some stragglers who galloped past me as I approached the station, I gathered, in a confused way, that the Federals were in our rear. To this report I gave little credit, but on emerging from the forest I found that they had only spoken the truth, for there a sight awaited me which made the blood run cold in my veins. The heights of Brandy and the spot where our headquarters had been were perfectly swarming with Yankees, while the men of one of our brigades were scattered wide over the plateau, chased in all directions by their enemies. Seeing one of our regiments still in line, but already swerving and on the point of breaking, I rode up to the Colonel, who seemed to have lost all presence of mind, and threatened to arrest him on the spot, and to prefer a charge of cowardice against him, if he did not at once lead his men on to the attack. This had the desired effect, and with a faint cheer the regiment galloped forward against the enemy; but two hostile regiments starting to meet us, the space we were charging over diminished with increasing rapidity, until at last, when only a hundred yards apart, our disheartened soldiers broke and fled in shameful confusion. Carried along for a moment by the torrent of fugitives, I perceived that we were hastening towards an opening in a fence which had been made to facilitate the movements of our artillery, and, soon outstripping the rest by the fleetness of my charger, I reached the gap, and placed myself in the centre, calling out to them that I would kill every man who tried to pass me, and knocking over with the flat of my sabre two of those who had ventured too near me. This had the effect of arresting the flight for a time, and I then managed to rally round me about a hundred of these same men whom, on this identical ground, I had, on a previous occasion, led to victory. "Men!" I shouted, "remember your previous deeds on these very fields; follow me—charge!" and, putting spurs into my charger's flanks, the noble animal bounded forth against the Federals, who were now close upon us, but whose lines, by the length of the pursuit, had become very loose. The very same men, however, who had fought so gallantly with me before had lost all self-confidence, and after following me a short distance, they turned again to flight, abruptly leaving me quite alone in the midst of the charging foe. A great hulking Yankee corporal, with some eight or ten men, immediately gave chase after me, calling on me to surrender, and discharging their carbines and revolvers in my direction. Not heeding this summons, I urged my horse to its highest speed; and now turning to the rear myself, and clearing the fence at a part where it was too high for them to follow, I soon left my pursuers far behind. I had not galloped many hundred yards further, however, when I overtook Captain White of our Staff, who had received a shot-wound in his neck, and was so weak as scarcely to be able to keep himself up in the saddle. Having to support my wounded comrade, whom I was determined to save, retarded my pace considerably, and several times the shouts and yells of the Yankees sounded so close at our horses' heels that I gave up all hope of escape. Suddenly, however, the Yankees gave up the pursuit, and I was enabled to draw bridle after a very exciting run. A courier happening to pass, I left Captain White in his charge, and hastened once more to the front, full of anxiety as to the final result of the conflict. To my great astonishment, as I rode on I could see nothing of the enemy; and, by the time I had reached the plateau of Brandy, I found the state of affairs had taken an entirely altered aspect. Instead of a menacing host of Federals, their dead and wounded thickly strewed the ground: one of their batteries, every horse of which had been killed, stood abandoned; and to the right, far away, a confused mass of fugitives were seen closely pursued by our men, over whose heads our artillery were throwing shell after shell on the retreating foe. I was not long in meeting with General Stuart, whom I found directing the operations from the highest part of the plateau. I was informed by him that the portion of Federal cavalry which had rendered our position so critical had consisted of two brigades, commanded by General Perry Windham, an Englishman in the Yankee service, who, by taking a circuitous route along an unguarded bridle-path, had succeeded in taking us in the rear, so causing all the confusion and panic which had very nearly decided the fate of the day. But just when the danger was at the highest and the stampede in full career—namely, at the very crisis I was unfortunate enough to witness—the Georgia regiment of Hampton's old brigade, under its commander, the gallant Colonel Young, and the 11th Virginia, under Colonel Lomax, had come up to the succour, and, throwing themselves with an impetuous charge on the temporary victors, had completely routed and driven them to flight, many killed and wounded, as well as prisoners, besides a battery, being left behind. General Windham himself was shot through the leg during the short *mêlée,* and had a narrow escape from capture; and several colonels and other officers were among the dead. The flight of the Federals had been so sudden and headlong that it gave rise to a number of odd incidents, among which may be recalled an accident which befell one of their buglers, who, in the blindness of his hurry, rode straight up against an old ice-house, breaking through the wooden partition, and tumbling headlong, horse and all, into the deep hole within. The horse was killed on the spot, but the rider escaped miraculously, and was hauled up with ropes amidst shouts of laughter from the by-standers at so ridiculous an adventure of battle.

The greater part of our corps was now placed along the ridge, in exactly the position I had recommended in the morning, whilst further on, in the plains below, were arrayed in line of battle many thousand Federal cavalry, supported by two of their divisions of infantry, whose glittering bayonets could be easily discerned as they deployed from the distant woods. Meanwhile our Commander-in-Chief had arrived at the scene of action, and a division of our infantry had come up to our support, which was still in the woods about a quarter of a mile to the rear, but quite in readiness to act when necessary. The time was now about four in the afternoon, and the fire, which in our immediate front had gradually slackened to a desultory skirmishing of the dismounted sharpshooters, but supported by a regular cannonade, grew hotter and hotter on the left, where William Lee, who had given up his original position soon after I left him, was slowly falling back before the enemy, turning and giving battle whenever too closely pressed by his pursuers. This splendid command could just be seen emerging from the woods on our left, where Jones's brigade was drawn up to support it, when Stuart, thinking the time had come for an aggressive movement, sent me off to order the two brigades to move forward in a united charge upon the pursuing enemy. Feeling that prompt action was necessary, I rode down the hillside with incautious speed, and my horse, broken down by the excessive exertions of the day, stumbled and rolled heavily over with me. Stuart, believing that horse and rider were struck down by a cannon-ball, ordered some couriers to my assistance, and was just sending off some one else with the orders I was charged with, when the animal regained its legs, and, vaulting quickly into the saddle, I started off again faster than before. About fifty yards further, coming upon very broken ground, my horse fell again, so contusing my leg that I fancied at first it was broken; but as the eyes of many hundreds of my comrades were on me I proudly fought against the agony I suffered, and, with difficulty remounting, I continued my ride, and in a few minutes was, without further accident, at the point of destination. Lee's and Jones's men received the order to charge with loud cheers—the former moving forward to the attack in such magnificent style that an enthusiastic shout of applause rose along our lines on the heights, whence the conflict could be plainly witnessed. The enemy received us with a shower of bullets. General William Lee fell wounded in the thigh. Colonel Williams was shot dead at the head of his regiment, and many other officers fell killed and wounded. But nothing could arrest the impetuous charge of the gallant Virginians; and in a few minutes the Federal lines were broken and driven in disorderly flight towards the river, where the fire of several reserve batteries, posted on the opposite shore, put a stop to the pursuit. This success on our left decided the fate of the day. About dusk, the main body of the Federal cavalry, seeing their right flank now entirely exposed, commenced a retreat under protection of their infantry, and by nightfall the whole of the hostile force had once more recrossed the Rappahannock. Thus ended the greatest cavalry battle ever fought on the American continent, about 12,000 men being engaged on our side, and about 15,000 on that of the Federals, besides the infantry support; and the combat lasted from daybreak till nightfall. The loss of our opponents was very severe in dead and wounded, and a great number of officers fell, among whom was a brigadier-general, several colonels, besides many other of subordinate rank. About 400 privates and 40 officers were captured, and a battery of four guns already mentioned. The victory was a dearly-bought one on our side, and numbers of those who but a few days before had gaily attended the review, were now stretched cold and lifeless on the same ground. Among those whose death we mourned, was the gallant Colonel Hampton of the 2d South Carolina, brother of General Hampton, and Colonel Williams of the 2d North Carolina; General William Lee, Colonel Butler, and many other officers of rank, were among the wounded. Our Staff had suffered very severely: Captain White wounded, Lieutenant Goldsborough taken prisoner, and the gallant Captain Farley killed. Poor Farley! after innumerable escapes from the perils into which his brilliant gallantry led him, his fate had overtaken him at last, and he died as heroically as he had lived. While riding towards the enemy, side by side with Colonel Butler, a shell which passed clean through their horses, killed both these, shattered at the same time one of Butler's legs below the knee, and carried off one of Farley's close up to the body. When the surgeon arrived he naturally wished to attend first to the Captain as the more dangerously wounded, but this the brave young fellow positively refused, saying that Colonel Butler's life was more valuable to the country than his own, and he felt he should soon die. Two hours afterwards he was a corpse. We passed the night at a farmhouse close to the battle-field; but in spite of the fatigues of the day I could find no rest, and passed the best part of the night bathing my injured leg, which was very swollen and painful, with cold water.

I did not allow this, however, to prevent my accompanying General Stuart on the following morning on a ride towards the river and over the plains, which presented all the appearance of a regular battle-field. Principally was this the case in the immediate neighbourhood of our old headquarters, where the ground was thickly strewn with carcasses, on which hundreds of turkey buzzards had been gorging themselves, and were lying about in numbers. In one spot, a few acres broad, where the cavalry had charged close up to a fence held by our skirmishers, I counted as many as thirty dead horses struck down by the bullets of our sharpshooters. On our return to headquarters, which in the mean time had been transferred to the shade of an oak grove a mile further to the rear, and close to a fine plantation possessed by a Mr Bradford, my negro Henry met me with an air of triumphant exultation, having with untiring energy, backed by cunning adroitness, succeeded in recovering one of my two missing horses—the stout bay. The illegitimate appropriator of the poor beast had frightfully disfigured it to avoid detection; its beautiful mane and tail were hacked short, but the sharp eyes of the negro had not be baffled by this villanous trick. I had been the subject of General Stuart's raillery *apropos* of my lost horses, but ere long I was enabled to turn the laugh against him, for two of his best horses went astray and were lost in the same way, nor were they recovered for months after. Large numbers of the enemy being still on the other side of the river and displaying considerable activity, we expected that the late unsuccessful reconnaissance in force would be shortly renewed, and on the 13th we were even called to our saddles by an alarm. It proved a groundless one, however; and the following days passed without further active demonstration on the part of the Federals.

CHAPTER XXIV

COMMENCEMENT OF THE SUMMER CAMPAIGN — FORWARD
MOVEMENT OF THE ARMY OF VIRGINIA — CAVALRY FIGHTS
IN LOUDON AND FAUQUIER COUNTIES — THE CAVALRY
FIGHT NEAR MIDDLEBURG, 19TH OF JUNE — I AM SEVERELY
WOUNDED — STAY AT UPPERVILLE, AND RETREAT FROM
THERE TO MR B.'S PLANTATION — THE LAST EIGHTEEN
MONTHS OF MY STAY IN THE CONFEDERACY — DEPARTURE
FOR RICHMOND, AND SOJOURN AT THE CAPITAL AND IN
THE VICINITY — WINTER 1863-64 — STUART'S DEATH —
DEPARTURE FOR ENGLAND.

GENERAL Lee had by this completed his preparations for
an advance into the enemy's country, whither the theatre
of war was now to be transferred; and, whilst a comparatively small body of troops still maintained a show in front of
the Federals at Fredericksburg, the bulk of our army was
being concentrated in the vicinity of Culpepper, apparently
without any suspicion of the fact on the part of the enemy's
commander-in-chief. The first object General Lee sought to
compass, was to clear the valley of Virginia of its hostile
occupants and to capture the town of Winchester. Ewell with
his troops had already started in that direction some days
before, and on the 15th the rest of our infantry began to
move forward. Stuart was ordered to cover the movements of

our army and protect its flank by marching on the Fauquier side of the Blue Ridge Mountains; and accordingly the morning of the 16th found us betimes *en route*, and in high glee at the thought of once more invading Yankeedom. Having crossed the Hazel and Rappahannock rivers, we marched on in the same line we had followed in our retreat of November '62, and at noon halted for an hour to feed our horses at the little town of Orleans, where General Stuart and his Staff made a point of visiting our old friend Mrs M., by whom we were received with her usual kindness and hospitality. Our march thence lay through the rich and beautiful county of Fauquier, which as yet showed but little signs of suffering from the war, and at dark we reached the Piedmont Station of the Baltimore-Ohio Railway, where we bivouacked. Next morning as soon as it was light the famous guerilla chief Major Mosby, who had selected this part of the country for the scene of his extraordinary achievements, made his appearance in camp, reporting that the enemy's cavalry, which till recently had fronted us near Culpepper, was rapidly following a line of march parallel to our own, although as yet only small detachments were occupying the neigbouring county of Loudon. Our march was continued accordingly towards the village of Upperville, where our cavalry separated into several commands, with instructions to move by different roads towards the Potomac. Stuart, taking with him Robertson's and Fitz Lee's commands, the latter of which turned off towards Aldie, proceeded in the direction of Middleburg, which place he and his Staff, galloping ahead of the troops, reached late in the afternoon. We were received in this pleasant little town with marked demonstrations of joy; and as my friends here had heard from Richmond the news of my death, but not its contradiction, I underwent another ovation at my quasi-resurrection. While paying one of the many visits I had to make to give bodily assurance of my presence in the world of the living, and relating my adventures to a circle of pretty young ladies, the streets suddenly resounded with the cry of "The Yankees are coming!" raised by a party of horsemen who galloped through the town in frantic excitement, having formed part of one of our pickets, on whom the enemy, not supposed to be so near, had rather suddenly fallen. I had just time to rush out of the house and mount my horse when the enemy's cavalry poured into the town from various directions. I soon joined General Stuart, however, and the remainder of his Staff, who were riding off as fast as their steeds could carry them in the direction of our advancing troops, which we soon reached; and General Stuart gave orders that General Robertson should move his regiments at a trot upon Middleburg, and drive the enemy from the town without delay. As I had a better knowledge of the country than Robertson I was ordered to accompany the General, who was an old friend, and gladly consulted me as to the best mode of attack. It was already dark by the time we came up with our advanced pickets, about half a mile from Middleburg, and we found them supported by their reserve, under the command of Captain Woolridge of the 4th Virginia, engaged in a lively skirmish with the hostile sharpshooters. We were informed by this brave officer that the Federals held the town in considerable force, and had erected a barricade at its entrance, which he begged as a favour to be allowed to storm. This was of course granted; and with a cheer forward went the gallant little band, driving the tirailleurs rapidly before them, and taking the barricade after a short but sanguinary struggle. At the same moment our sabres rattled from their scabbards, and the main body of the brigade dashed forward to the charge at a thundering gallop along the broad turnpike road and down the main street, while two of our squadrons went round outside the village to protect us from a flank attack. As I had felt rather ashamed at having been forced to run from the enemy under the very eyes of my fair friends, and was naturally anxious to afford them a spectacle of a totally different character, I assumed my place of honour, leading the charge with General Robertson, and to my intense satisfaction plunged into the enemy's ranks opposite the precise spot whence I had commenced my flight, and whence, regardless of danger, the ladies now looked on and watched the progress of the combat. It lasted but a few seconds, for the enemy, unable to withstand the shock of our charge, broke and fled in utter confusion—a part of the fugitives taking the straight road along the main street, and the other turning off by the shorter route out of the town to the right. Leaving General Robertson to pursue the former with one of his regiments, I took upon myself the responsibility of following the latter with several squadrons, anticipating that the Federal reserves were in this direction. My supposition proved only too correct, for they were soon at hand to rescue their comrades, and in a few minutes we were engaged in a severe conflict. Bullets whizzed from either side—men and horses fell dead and wounded amidst unavoidable confusion through the extreme darkness of the night, and for a time it seemed doubtful whether I should be able to hold my ground against numbers so far superior. Fortunately General Robertson, hearing the firing, soon came up with his regiment, and, taking now the offensive, we charged the Federals with our united force in front, while the squadron we had sent round the village to the right took them in flank, the effect of which was to force our antagonists into a rapid retreat, in the course of which we took several officers and 75 privates prisoners. On our return to Middleburg the General an I remained another hour with our lady friends, who, with their accustomed devotedness, were busy nursing the wounded, large numbers of whom were collected in several of the residences. It was late in the night by the time we reached Mr Rector's plantation, about two miles to the rear, when our troops encamped. This spot is situated on a formidable hill, and being the crossing point of several of the principal roads, was a point of considerable strategical importance.

Early the following morning a report was received from Fitz Lee announcing an encounter with a strong body of Federal cavalry near Aldie, which had ended in the repulse of the enemy and the capture of 60 prisoners, among whom was a colonel and several other inferior officers. Our own loss had been heavy in killed and wounded, and among the former I lost my poor friend Major Eales of the 5th Virginia, who was struck by several bullets while leading his men to the charge. We got news also from William Lee's troops, commanded by Chamblis, who had come quite suddenly and unexpectedly on the cavalry we had driven from Middlesburg, killing and wounding a great number and taking 140 prisoners. The glorious accounts had meantime reached us of the capture of Winchester and Martinsburg by Ewell, with more then 4000 prisoners, 30 pieces of artillery, and innumerable stores of ammunition and provisions, rendering the opening of the campaign as favourable to its prospects as possible. As the prisoners taken during the last few days amounted to several hundreds, I was sent to Upperville, whither they had been despatched, to superintend their transfer by detachments to Winchester—a duty in which I was occupied the greater part of the day, until toward evening the sound of a brisk cannonade recalled me back to the front. There I found that the Federals had advanced in strong force on Middleburg, had driven back our troops, and were once more in possession of the town, and that all our efforts to retake it had been vain—the cause of these failures being attributed to General Stuart's hesitation to direct the fire of our artillery on the village, fearing to inflict too much damage on the patriotic little place. The fighting was kept up till' midnight, when, finding the enemy showed no intention of pushing their advantage any further for the present, our troops, with the exception of a strong cordon of pickets, were withdrawn towards Rector's cross-roads, where we all encamped.

The morning of the 19th dawned with all the bright beauty of the month of June, but the rising of the sun was also the signal for the recommencement of hostilities, and before we had had time to breakfast, a rapid succession of cannon-shots summoned us to the front. The enemy in strong force were advancing upon a patch of wood about a mile from Middleburg, which was held by our troops, consisting of Robertson's and William Lee's commands; the dismounted sharpshooters on both sides were exchanging a lively fire, and the shells from a number of hostile batteries were bursting with a sharp crack in the tree-tops. General Stuart took up his position on a hill about half a mile to the rear, commanding a good view of the plain in front, and over the fields to the right and left. Our Chief of Artillery being engaged in another direction, I received orders to place our batteries in position; and the nature of the ground allowed this to be done so favourably that the cross-fire of our guns at a later period saved us from serious disaster. I then rode forward to the extreme front, and, carefully reconnoitring the position of the enemy, I found that their force was far superior to our own, and that they were overlapping us on either wing. General Stuart gave me so little credit for the accuracy of my report that he was for some time convinced that he could hold his ground with ease, and even entertained the intention of sending off the greater part of William Lee's troops towards Aldie. Through my earnest remonstrances this was deferred, however, and I was again despatched to the front to see if I had not overrated the forces of the enemy. What I saw only too thoroughly confirmed my first observations; and I reported to General Stuart that in my opinion he would be forced to retreat, even if he kept the whole of his force together. But again he refused credit to the result of my observations, and said laughingly, "You're mistaken for once, Von; I shall be in Middleburg in less than an hour," — requesting me at the same time to write out a permit for Longstreet's Commissary, Major N., who wished to visit his friends in the town, to go there unmolested. I was just writing the document, and remarking to the Major that I was afraid he would not be able to make use of it, when suddenly the firing increased in heaviness, and we saw our men hastening from the woods in considerable confusion, followed by a dark mass of Federals in close pursuit. "Ride as quickly as you can, and rally those men; I will follow you immediately with all the troops I can gather," were Stuart's hasty instructions to me as he suddenly, though rather late, became convinced that I had all along been right. Just as I reached our breaking lines, the 9th Virginia, which had been in reserve, dashed forward in a magnificent charge; the batteries I had previously posted opened a well-directed cross-fire on the Federal horsemen; the flying regiments responded to my call, and turned upon their pursuers, whom we drove rapidly back into the woods, killing and wounding a large number, and taking many prisoners, until a severe fusillade from the enemy's sharpshooters, posted on the outskirts of the wood, protected their retreat. I had just succeeded in re-forming our own men, about 200 yards from the woods, when Stuart came up, and, riding along the lines of his troops, who always felt relieved by his appearance in the moment of extreme danger, was received by them with enthusiastic cheers. He now ordered the regiments to withdraw by squadrons to a better position—a movement which was executed under cover of a spirited fire from our batteries. The General and his Staff being the last to remain on the spot, we soon became a target for the Federal sharpshooters, who, by the cheering, had become well aware that Stuart was in that small group of officers. Being dressed in the same fashion as the General—a short jacket and grey hat, with waving ostrich plume, and mounted on my handsome new charger—I was mistaken for him, and my tall figure soon engaged their particular attention, for the bullets came humming round me like a swarm of bees. A ball had just stripped the gold-lace from my trousers, and I was saying to the General, riding a few steps before me on my left—"General, those Yankees are giving it rather hotly to me on your account,"—when I suddenly felt a severe dull blow, as though somebody had struck me with his fist on my neck, fiery sparks glittered before my eyes, and a tremendous weight seemed to be dragging me from my horse. After a few moments of insensibility, I opened my eyes again, to find myself lying on the ground, my charger beside me, and a number of officers and men pressing round and endeavouring to raise me. My left arm hung stiff and lifeless, and the blood was spouting from a large wound on the side of my neck, and streaming from my mouth at every breath. Unable to speak, I motioned to my comrades to leave me, and save themselves from the hail of bullets the enemy were concentrating on them, two of the soldiers about me having already fallen lifeless. At the same moment, I saw the Yankees charging towards us from the woods; and, certain that a few minutes more would leave me a prisoner in their hands, the hateful thought inspired me with the courage to summon all my strength and energy, and, managing to regain my legs, with the assistance of Captain Blackford and Lieutenant Robertson of our Staff, I mounted my horse, and rode off from the field, supported by these two officers, whose devoted friendship could not have been proved by a more signal act of self-sacrifice. After a painful ride of more than a mile, coming across an ambulance, my comrades placed me in it, gave orders to the driver to carry me further to the rear, and then galloped off in another direction in search of our surgeon, Dr Eliason. Meanwhile the Federals were rapidly advancing, and numbers of their shells burst so near the ambulance that the driver was seized with fright, and, believing that anyhow I was nearly dead, drove off at a gallop over the rocky road, regardless of my agonised groans, every movement of the vehicle causing a fresh effusion of blood from my wound. At last I could stand it no longer, and, crawling up to him, I put my cocked pistol to his head, and made him understand that I should blow out his brains if he continued his cowardly flight. This proved effectual, and, driving along at a moderate pace, we were overtaken by Dr Eliason, who at once examined my wound, and found that the ball had entered the lower part of my neck, cut through a portion of the windpipe, and, taking a downward course, had lodged somewhere in my right lung, and that my left arm was entirely paralysed by the same shot. A shadow passed over the Doctor's face as he examined me, for he had a liking for me; and reading in my eyes that I wished to have his undisguised opinion, he said, "My dear fellow, your wound is mortal, and I can't expect you to live till the morning," offering at the same time to execute my last wishes. This was sad enough intelligence for me; but the very positiveness of the opinion aroused within me the spirit of resistance, and I resolved to struggle against death with all the energy I possessed. In this determined mood I was enabled to attend to some matters of duty, and to give orders on a piece of paper for our ordnance-waggons, which we met on the road. I was conveyed to Dr Eliason's house, where a bed was put up for me in the parlour, and I was attended by the ladies of the family, who nursed me as though I had been a son of the house, whilst the Doctor's blind child was sobbing by my bedside. A dose of opium procured me a kind of half slumber or trance, during which, though unable to move, I could see and hear everything that was going on about me. One after the other all my comrades dropped in during the afternoon, and seeing my face and neck swollen and disfigured by an accumulation of air, while my features were deadly pale, I could see by their expression that they believed me dead already, and could hear the Doctor answer the repeated question, "Is he alive yet?" with "Yes, but he will not live over the night." At last Stuart himself came, and, bending over me, he kissed my forehead, and I felt two tears drop upon my cheek as I heard him say, "Poor fellow, your fate is a sad one, and it was for me that you received this mortal wound." I would have given anything to have had the power of grasping my friend's hand, and pronouncing a few words of thankfulness for his heartfelt sympathy; and when, in later times, I stood by his own deathbed, these friendly words came vividly before my recollection. I passed the night in a calm sleep, and the following morning found me, to the astonishment and delight of the Doctor and my comrades, not only alive, but wonderfully refreshed and strengthened by my long sleep. The whole of the day I was much excited by the sound of a heavy cannonade, and received frequent information through a courier who was detached to me as to the progress of a severe fight, in which the Yankees, supported by infantry, were pressing Stuart slowly back towards Upperville. The next night I again passed favourably, and on the forenoon of the 21st I had the extreme gratification of seeing General Stuart again, who told me how much he had missed me during the action, of which he gave me a minute account. He told me, at the same time, it was quite possible that during the day he might be forced to fall back beyond Upperville, in which case I should be informed in time by one of his officers, and an ambulance would be in readiness to carry me out of reach of the enemy.

In the early part of the forenoon the fighting re-commenced, the thunder of the cannon and the rattle of musketry sounded closer and closer, wounded men and stragglers began to pass through the village, and I became more and more nervous and excited. As hour after hour passed while I awaited full dressed the arrival of Stuart's promised conveyance and message, I repeatedly sent my courier out into the street, but the report was always, "Nothing heard of the General yet." The battle seemed raging in the immediate vicinity, and the shells bursting right over the village, when, to my great joy, my Prussian friend Captain Scheibert entered my room. At the first news of my misfortune, he had hastened from the distant headquarters of our army, bringing along with him General Longstreet's private ambulance, which the latter had placed at my disposal, sending me at the same time many kind messages urging me to start at once. This I declined to do, however, as I was anxious to hear from General Stuart, for whose safety I entertained apprehensions. At last Captain Clarke, temporarily attached to our Staff, galloped in and informed me that General Stuart, wishing to avoid my being moved unnecessarily, and hoping to be able to hold his ground for a day longer, had delayed his message as long as possible; but the Federal cavalry, strongly supported by infantry, having suddenly attacked with overwhelming numbers, he had been forced to a precipitate retreat, which rendered it necessary that I should be moved away without an instant's delay. It was certainly a moment of no small excitement, when, after a cordial leave-taking with my kind host, I was carried by my friends to the ambulance, in the midst of shells bursting in the streets and crashing through the house-tops, fugitives rushing wildly by, wounded men crawling out of the way, riderless horses galloping distract-edly about, whilst close at hand were heard the triumphant shouts of the pursuing foe. As my condition would not admit of my being conveyed so far as the infantry reserves, which were eight miles away in the direction of the Shenandoah, it was decided that I should be carried to Mr B.'s plantation, not more than two miles off, which, being only accessible by a small road, it was hoped the enemy would not visit. Turning to the left after leaving Upperville, we had, on our way thither, to pass for a short distance along the main road, whence I could see a great part of the battle-field and our men everywhere in rapid retreat; the Federals, in hot pursuit, being not more than 500 yards from us, and their bullets frequently whizzing round our ears. The ambulance-driver did his best to get out of the way, while Scheibert and my servant Henry, who was leading my horses, in trying to keep up with us, presented a scene in which over-anxiety assumed a comical aspect. The Captain with the flat of his sword was thrashing the mule Kitt, who was kicking and plunging in an obstinate mood, while Henry in front was dragging her forward, and answering the Captain's intimations, that he was doing more harm than good, with a grin of obtuse satisfaction. At last Mr B.'s plantation was reached without accident, and we found the proprietor waiting for us at the gate. He was very willing to receive me into his house, but instead, to avoid discovery, that my ambulance and escort should leave as quickly as possible, and, while I was being carried into the mansion by two old negroes, I saw them just plunging amidst the dense foliage of the neighbouring woods. A room was prepared for me on the ground-floor; and so utterly exhausted was I, it was almost in a fainting condition that I fell upon the bed. Scarcely, however, had I been half an hour there, when I was awakened by the trampling of horses and the rattling of sabre scabbards, and an old servant entered, telling me in a whisper that the Yankees had come, and were surrounding the house. This alarming intelligence darted like an electric shock through my frame; and knowing that to be captured in my shattered state would be certain death, I resolved, with desperate energy, not to die without resistence. I reached down my arms with a painful effort, and placing my unsheathed sword, and revolver ready cocked, on the bed, prepared to shoot down the first of the enemy's troopers who should enter. Fully convinced that my last hour was come, I lay waiting to see the Yankees come in every moment; but although I could hear them talking, and see them passing to and fro on the verandah, through the jalousies of the window, close to which my bed was placed, I was astonished to find they did not make their appearance. After about half an hour of the most thrilling anxiety, all seemed to have become suddenly quiet again; and my kind-hearted host made his appearance, with the news that the Federals had gone for the present, but were still in the neighbourhood, and had stationed a picket on a hill a few hundred yards off. He added that the hostile soldiers, whose hearts he had won by a liberal supply of every kind of refreshment, had mentioned that they had been searching every house in Upperville and the vicinity for the prominent Confederate (supposed for some time to be Stuart himself), who had fallen severely wounded, but that to all appearance he had died, and his body had been buried by the rebels previous to their retreat.* The rest of the evening passed rapidly away, nor were we again disturbed by the Federal soldiers, one or two only coming on separate occasions to fetch milk or other eatables. Next morning I was greatly surprised at the appearance of my servant Henry, who, in his anxiety about my fate, had crossed over from the opposite side of the Shenandoah, where he had left my horses in safety,

---

*The same story was published afterwards in the Northern papers. "The big Prussian rebel, who was Stuart's right arm," they said, "had been killed at last, and his body buried at Upperville."

and, hiding the mule in the woods about a mile off, had managed to steal unobserved through the Federal lines. I was quite touched at the fidelity of my negro, who sat all day at my bedside, anxiously watching every breath I drew. Later in the evening, to my great astonishment and delight, I received a visit from Dr Eliason, who informed us that the enemy was retreating, Stuart having retaken Upperville, and being in pursuit of the Federals in the direction of Middleburg. The Doctor was satisfied with my progress towards recovery, and told me if I reached the ninth day he believed my wound would get quite well. The following day my friends from all parts of the army called in large numbers, among them Generals Stuart, Hampton, and Robertson; and I was delighted to have recovered my voice sufficiently to thank them for all their kindness and friendship. General Longstreet sent his three doctors, with all of whom I was intimate, and they brought me a message from him, stating that he was sorry he could not come himself, but that he would have advanced a whole division to get me out of the enemy's hands had they not retreated. Our army had in the mean time continued steadily advancing through the valley; and on the 25th all our troops left the vicinity of Upperville to march onward to the Potomac, leaving me behind, sad that I was no longer able to share in their fatigues, their dangers, and their glory.

Henceforward my strength improved very rapidly; the outer wound had nearly closed; from only being able to swallow a little cream I could now take more substantial food, and was allowed to sit up an hour or two in the verandah to enjoy the cool aromatic breeze travelling hither from the beautiful Blue Ridge Mountains. Every kindness was shown me by Mr B. and his family, and I received many kind messages from the ladies of the neighbourhood, who sent me nosegays every day; so that I should have felt perfectly happy had not my mind been troubled with the thought of being away from my comrades, and had not, moreover, the frequency of the Federal scouting parties crossing the Potomac rendered it dangerous that I should remain, my presence having become much more widely known in the vicinity. After postponing my departure several times I at last took leave of my kind hosts, and started off in an ambulance which General Robertson had placed at my disposal, accompanied by a courier who had been detached to me, and by Henry with my horses. The journey to Culpepper was a tedious one, and the jolting of the ambulance along the rough roads was so painful that I had to ride on horseback the greater part of the way. I arrived, however, without accident, except, indeed, the upsetting of my vehicle in the swollen waters of the Hazel river, through which I lost all my traps, with the exception of my arms and a little bag in which I kept my diary, and which I saved by jumping into the foaming stream at the imminent peril of my life. Leaving Henry with my horses behind me at Culpepper, I went in a hand-car to Orange, and thence by rail to Richmond, where I met with a kind and cordial reception under the hospitable roof of Mr P., which for some time was to become my home. With the heat of the month of June my sufferings commenced, and were greatly aggravated by the conflicting rumours which reached me from Lee's army after the battle of Gettysburg. I could scarcely draw my breath, and coughed continually night and day, bringing up quantities of blood with small fragments of the shattered rings of my windpipe, and pieces of clothing which the bullet had carried along with it. I was frequently attacked with fits of suffocation, which sometimes came upon me while walking in the street, and were so violent that I had to be carried home in a state of insensibility resembling death. At last my doctor, who had but little hope of my recovery, recommended me to try the effects of country air; and having received pressing invitations from my friends at Dundee, in Hanover County, I went there towards the end of August. The very day after my arrival, my attacks, accompanied by severe fever, became so violent that I was prostrated on a sick-bed for two long months, every day of which my kind friends expected would be my last. The natural strength of my constitution, however, carried me through all these trials; and about the middle of October I was allowed to leave my room, but reduced to a skeleton, having lost ninety pounds in weight, and so weak I had to be carried about in a chair. On the first day I left my bed I was startled by the report that a body of Federals was approaching the house; and, dreading the danger of capture more than the consequences of exposure, I insisted, against the earnest entreaties of my friends, on immediate departure. A fatiguing ride in a buggy over eighteen miles of rough road to Richmond produced, as was anticipated, a relapse, and I was again laid prostrate for nearly two months, during which I received the kindest attentions from the inhabitants of Richmond, principally Mr and Mrs P. and their family, at whose house I was staying, and who nursed and tended me as though I had been their own son. I had frequent tidings from General Stuart and my comrades, and received from them letters full of friendship and affection. In one of these the general said:—"My dear Von, my camp seems dull and deserted to me since you left. On the battle-field I do not know how to do without you, and I feel as if my right arm had been taken away from me." My chief had, even before I was wounded, tried to have me promoted to a Brigadier-Generalship, to which rank he considered me entitled, in consideration of my services and the facility with which on several occasions I had shown I could handle large bodies of troops. These recommendations for promotion were approved by General Lee, and desired, I am proud to say, by all the officers and men of the cavalry crops; but the repeated applications made by my General with this object were as often rejected by the officials at Richmond, who hesitated, as it seemed, to promote a foreigner too rapidly. Great satisfaction, however, was afforded me by the public acknowledgment of my insignificant services, which took place during the month of January 1864, in the form of a joint resolution of thanks by both Houses of the Confederate Congress. Lafayette was the last foreigner to whom this honour was accorded in America, and out of courtesy the resolution was couched in the same words as had been used on that occasion, and which were as follows:—

"Whereas Major Heros Von Borcke of Prussia, Adjutant and Inspector-General of the Cavalry Corps of the Army of Northern Virginia, having left his own country to assist in securing the independence of ours, and by his personal gallantry on the field having won the admiration of his comrades, as well as of his Commanding General, all of whom deeply sympathise with him in his present sufferings from wounds received in battle, therefore—Resolved by the Congress of the Confederate States of America, that the thanks of Congress are due, and the same hereby tendered to Major Heros Von Borcke for his self-sacrificing devotion to our Confederacy, and for his distinguished services in support of our cause. Resolved, That a copy of these resolutions be transmitted to Major Von Borcke by the President of the Confederate States."

This document I received with a very flattering autograph letter from the President, which was followed by hundreds of congratulatory epistles from my comrades in the army, and from friends in all parts of the country. My health was progressing but slowly, although I daily gained strength, and I was gradually recovering the use of my left arm, the revivification of which, however, was attended with severe nervous pain. The winter in Richmond passed gaily away amidst a succession of balls, dinner-parties, and private theatricals; and being in my invalid state an object of sympathy, I had the luxury of being much petted by fair residents and visitors of the capital. I had frequently the pleasure of seeing Stuart during the winter months, and once or twice visited him in his camp near Culpepper, where I was received on all hands, from the General down to the last courier, with so much tender attention that I was deeply touched, and felt it hard to tear myself from the gallant fellows to whom I was attached by so many ties of past association. As my health grew stronger I tried repeatedly, after the opening of the spring campaign, to take the field again, but each time I was severely punished for my imprudence by being thrown upon a sick-bed for weeks, and I had to confine my ambition to the discharge of office duty in Richmond, while General Lee was fighting the grand battles of the Wilderness and Spotsylvania, and Stuart was adding to his fame by new victories.

On the morning of the 11th May 1864, Richmond was thrown once more into a state of excitement by the rapid advance against it of the Federal cavalry under General Sheridan, who had managed to march round our lines. Several brigades of infantry hastened from the south side of the James river to the defence of the city; the militia was called out, and all expected that the outer lines of fortifications would every moment become the scene of a serious combat. Everything continued quiet, however, in that direction until about eleven o'clock, when a sudden cannonade sounded in the rear of the enemy—the indefatigable Stuart having followed in their track, and with the small force, which was all he had been able, owing to the rapid marching, to take with him, being now enabled to cut off the Federal line of retreat. The sound of our light guns, which I recognised so well, did not fail to rouse me into a state of excitement; and as an old war-horse prances and curvets at the shrill ringing of the trumpet, I felt the blood pour like electric fire through my veins, and rushed about in feverish uneasiness. I fancied I heard my sword rattling in its scabbard to summon me to the scene of conflict by my General's side; but, as I was separated from my own chargers, I tried to borrow a horse for the occasion from one of my many friends. All my endeavours to this effect, however, were vain; everybody had already hastened to the front, and, unable to bear the suspense any longer, I impressed by force one of the horses from the first Government team I came across, and, throwing my saddle on its back, hurried off to the scene of action. The animal I had laid hold of was a miserable little pony, but I managed to spur him forward at a tolerably swift pace; and rapidly passing our double line of intrenchments, I soon reached our last infantry pickets, where I endeavoured to ascertain the exact position of our own troops and of the enemy. As the hostile force lay immediately between ours, it was not easy to get this information; but a road was pointed out to me with such assurance that it would take me to General Stuart without bringing me into collision with the Yankees, that I galloped along it with very little precaution, and had just crossed over a bridge, when, from the woods on the right and left, a scattered band of Federal cavalry bore down upon me with loud shouts, firing their revolvers at me, and demanding my surrender. I immediately turned my pony's head round, and galloped off to the rear with all the speed I could, and an exciting chase now ensued for several miles, till it was put a stop to by the fire of our pickets, whom I reached completely exhausted, and thoroughly surprised at my narrow escape. It was sufficiently evident, by the sound of the firing, that Stuart was hardly pressed, and I hastened at once to General Bragg, commanding our infantry, which, from a succession of reinforcements, was now of considerable strength, begging him at once to advance several

brigades to the assistance of Stuart. The cautiousness characteristic of that general, however, induced him to resist my
appeals, and finding further effort useless, I slowly retraced
my steps to Richmond. The rapid run and the excitement of
my pursuit had proved too much for my strength, and I had
scarcely reached the outskirts of the town when, as I approached a friend's house, the blood began to stream from
my mouth, and I was carried, half fainting, to my temporary
domicile at Mr. P.'s, where I was immediately put to bed.
After a long and refreshing sleep, I was awakened suddenly
about daybreak by the voice of Dr Brewer, Stuart's brother-
in-law, who informed me that my General had been wounded
severely, and carried during the night to his place, where he
was anxious to see me. Forgetting my own condition at these
sad tidings, I dressed myself in a few minutes and hastened to
the bedside of my dear friend, whom I found in a small room
of the Doctor's house, surrounded by most of the members of
his Staff. He received me with a smile, saying, "I'm glad
you've come, my dear Von; you see they've got me at last, but
don't feel uneasy. I don't think I'm so badly wounded as you
were, and I hope I shall get over it as you did." He then
recounted to me all the incidents of the combat, and the
manner in which he had been wounded. Hoping every hour
to hear of General Bragg's attack, which in all probability
would have resulted in the annihilation of the whole force of
the enemy, he had successfully resisted their efforts to break
through his lines, and for more than six hours had fought
with eleven hundred men against eight thousand. At about
four o'clock, the Federals succeeded by a general charge in
breaking and driving back one of our regiments which
General Stuart was rallying in an open field. When continuing their advance the enemy were met by the 1st Virginia and
driven back again in confusion. Seeing near him some of the
dismounted Federal cavalry, who were running off on the

opposite side of a high fence, Stuart rode up to them calling on them to surrender, and firing at them as they continued their flight. He had just discharged the last barrel of his revolver when the hindmost of the fugitives, coming close up to the fence, fired his revolver at him, the ball taking effect in the lower part of the stomach and traversing the whole body. Stuart, finding himself severely wounded, and the enemy at the same time renewing their attack, turned his charger quickly round and galloped half a mile further to the rear, where he was taken from his horse nearly insensible from loss of blood, and sent in an ambulance to Richmond. During the early part of the morning the General felt comparatively easy, and the physician entertained great hope that the wound might not prove fatal. Towards noon, however, a change took place for the worse, and our fears began to be greatly excited. About this time President Davis visited the prostrate hero; taking his hand, the President said, "General, how do you feel?" He replied, "Easy, but willing to die if God and my country think I have fulfilled my destiny and done my duty." As evening approached mortification set in, and no hopes could any longer be entertained. He became delirious, and his mind wandered over the battle-fields where he had fought, then to his wife and children, and again to the front. Mrs Stuart was absent with her children in the country, and several messages had been despatched informing her of her husband's state, and urging her instant return to Richmond; and in the intervals of relief from pain and delirium, the General frequently inquired if she had not yet come, beginning now to doubt the possibility of his recovery. About five o'clock the General asked Dr Brewer, his brother-in-law, how long he thought it possible he could live, and whether he could survive through the night; and being told that death was rapidly approaching, he nodded, and said, "I am resigned, if it be God's will; but I should like to see my wife. But

God's will be done." He then made his last dispositions, and took leave of us all, I being the last. I had been sitting on his bed, holding his hand in mine, and handing him the ice, which he ate in great abundance, and which was applied to his burning hot wounds to cool them. Drawing me towards him, and grasping my hand firmly, he said, "My dear Von, I am sinking fast now, but before I die I want you to know that I never loved a man as much as yourself. I pray your life may be long and happy; look after my family after I'm gone, and be the same true friend to my wife and children that you have been to me." These were the last connected words he spoke; during the next few hours the paroxysms of pain became more frequent and violent, until at about seven o'clock death relieved the suffering hero from his agonies. Poor Mrs Stuart arrived an hour after the General's death. Of all the messages sent to her, my telegram alone had reached; but the operator hearing, after I had left the office, that Stuart was getting better, altered the words "the General is dangerously wounded," and substituted "slightly wounded." The poor lady arrived at Dr Brewer's house, unaware of her husband's death; and when, on asking if she could see the General, and receiving an affirmative answer, she rushed up-stairs, expecting to find him alive, it was only in the most cruel manner, by the spectacle of her husband's cold pale brow, that she learned the terrible misfortune which had befallen her and her children. I myself mourned my chief as deeply as if I had lost a beloved brother; and so many of my friends being soon after called away, I really felt possessed with a longing that I might die myself. On the evening of the 13th, in the midst of the roaring of the enemy's cannon, which reached us from Drewry's Bluff, we carried Stuart's remains to the beautiful cemetery at Hollywood, near Richmond, where he lies in a simple grave by the side of his beloved little daughter Flora. Of a calm summer evening I frequently rode out to this quiet spot, sitting for hours on my leader's grave, recalling his excellent qualities, and musing over the many glorious battles through which we had fought side by side.

General Lee announced the death of General Stuart in the following order:—

"HEADQUARTERS OF THE ARMY OF NORTHERN VIRGINIA,
May 20, 1864.

"The Commanding General announces to the army with heartfelt sorrow the death of Major-General J. E. B. Stuart, late Commander of the cavalry corps of the Army of Northern Virginia. Among the gallant soldiers who have fallen in this war, General Stuart was second to none in valour, in zeal, in unflinching devotion to his country. His achievements form a conspicuous part of the history of this army, with which his name and services will be for ever associated. To military capacity of a high order, and all the noble virtues of the soldier, he added the brighter graces of a pure life, sustained by the Christian's faith and hope. The mysterious hand of an all-wise God has removed him from the scene of usefulness and fame. His grateful countrymen will mourn his loss and cherish his memory. To his comrades in arms he left the proud recollection of his deeds, and the inspiring influence of his example.

"R. E. LEE, GENERAL."

My grief at the death of Stuart, and the excitement of the last few days, had a very injurious effect on my health for months afterwards, and again I had to resign the hope of once more taking the field. During the month of June, General Randolph wrote to General Lee in the name of several prominent citizens by whom, as well as by himself, it was considered a measure of safety for the capital, requesting that I might be put in command of a brigade of cavalry, to be stationed near Richmond. This application was strongly seconded by General Hampton, Stuart's worthy successor, and by General Lee himself, but it was rejected at the War-Office, on the score of my health, and an infantry officer was afterwards put in command of the same troops. Under these circumstances, instead of doing service in the field I had to spend the summer and autumn in light duties, inspections, &c., filling up the rest of my time with visits to friends in the mountains of Virginia, where my poor suffering lungs had the benefit of the cool aromatic breezes. As winter approached, a proposal already mooted several times—namely, that of sending me abroad on Government duty, but which, till then, I had always refused, hoping soon to be able to go into active campaigning—was renewed. There being very little chance of active service during the cold weather, and General Hampton, General Lee, and President Davis, urging me to go on a mission for the Government to England, I at last yielded to their wishes, hoping to be back for the spring campaign. My commanding officer had in the mean time urgently requested that my rank should be raised to that of Colonel, and the day before my departure I had the gratification of receiving my promotion from the hands of the President. After a tedious journey of four days and four nights, I reached Wilmington on Christmas-day; and while the heavy guns were roaring at the first bombardment of Fort Fisher, I ran the blockade in the late Confederate war-steamer Tala-hassee, arriving in England, after a circuitous route by the West India Islands, in the month of February 1865. There I was saved the grief of being an eyewitness of the rapid collapse of the Confederacy, and the downfall of a just and noble cause.

Lee's glorious army is no longer in existence: the brave men who formed it have, after innumerable sufferings and privations, bowed to the enemy's power and numbers, and dispersed to follow peaceful pursuits. But those who have survived the fearful struggle for independence, can look back upon a series of battles and victories unequalled in history; and every one of us will for ever speak with pride of the time when he was a soldier of the army of Northern Virginia. I myself am still an invalid. The ball which I carry in my lungs gives me frequent suffering, and has broken my once so robust health; but as every renewal of my pains reminds me of the past, they are alleviated and almost effaced by the pleasure with which I revert to the time when I fought side by side with those brave men; and I shall ever rejoice that I drew my sword for the gallant people of the late Confederacy.

THE END.

ABOUT THE AUTHOR

In the spring of 1862, twenty-six year old Lieutenant Heros von Borcke of the Second Brandenburg Dragoons set sail on a Confederate blockade runner bound for South Carolina. After narrowly escaping capture in Charleston Harbor, he made his way to Richmond, where he joined the staff of Confederate cavalry commander J.E.B. Stuart and quickly earned an officer's commission.

He participated in the battles of Seven Pines, the Seven Days, Fredericksburg, Chancellorsville and Brandy Station before being wounded in a skirmish near Middleburg, Virginia, at the beginning of the Gettysburg Campaign.

Prevented by his wounds from continuing in active service, he was promoted to the rank of lieutenant-colonel and sent by the Confederate Congress on a diplomatic mission to England. When the war ended in April 1865 he remained abroad. Back in his native Prussia, he later served with distinction in the Franco-Prussian War.

Heros von Borcke returned to his beloved Virginia only once, in 1884, where his former comrades organized a banquet in his honor. He died in 1895.